The COMPLETE INFIDEL'S GUIDE to IRAN

The

COMPLETE
INFIDEL'S GUIDE

to

IRAN

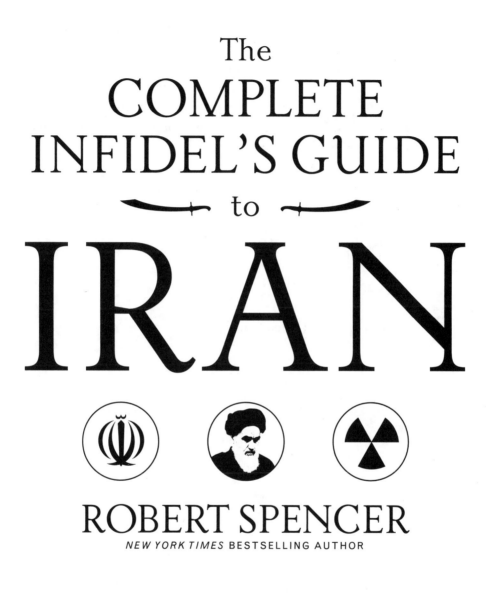

ROBERT SPENCER

NEW YORK TIMES BESTSELLING AUTHOR

REGNERY
PUBLISHING
A Division of Salem Media Group

Regnery® is a registered trademark of Salem Communications Holding Corporation

Cataloging-in-Publication data on file with the Library of Congress

ISBN 978-1-62157-516-0

Published in the United States by
Regnery Publishing
A Division of Salem Media Group
300 New Jersey Ave NW
Washington, DC 20001
www.Regnery.com

Manufactured in the United States of America

10 9 8 7 6 5 4 3 2 1

Books are available in quantity for promotional or premium use. For information on discounts and terms, please visit our website: www.Regnery.com.

Distributed to the trade by
Perseus Distribution
250 West 57th Street
New York, NY 10107

This book is dedicated to all those Iranians, inside and outside Iran,
who know that Iran deserves better than the Islamic Republic

CONTENTS

A Note on Transliteration

No system of transliteration for Persian or Arabic words and names is entirely satisfactory; nor is a single system agreed upon for either alphabet. Many Persian words and names are alternatively rendered with a *gh* or a *q*, for example, Mossadegh or Mossadeq; I have chosen one form or the other not systematically but generally by which form is more common in English.

AN IRAN TIMELINE

From great world empire to leader of
worldwide Islamic revolution

Soon after 1000 BC

By this time Persians, Medes, and
Parthians, all descendants of "Aryan"
tribes of Indo-European origin who have
migrated to the Iranian plateau in the
previous millennium are settled in the
area that will become Iran.

Late seventh century BC

Iran is first unified under the rule of the
Medes.

Circa 553–549 BC

Cyrus the Great throws off the rule of the
Medes and establishes the first Persian
Empire, the Achaemenid Empire. Over
the next decade he conquers both the
Lydian kingdom of Croesus in Asia Minor
and the Neo-Babylonian Empire (his son
Cambyses will conquer Egypt). Cyrus's
rule over the peoples he has conquered is
a model of enlightened respect for their
institutions; in 538 BC he allows the Jews
to return from the Babylonian exile and
rebuild the Temple in Jerusalem.

499–449 BC

The Persian Wars between the
Achaemenid Empire and the Greek city-
states.

331 BC

Alexander the Great defeats Darius III
at the Battle of Gaugamela and conquers
Persia.

224 BC

Arsaces I breaks away from the Seleucid
Empire of Alexander's successors and
founds the Parthian Empire, which will
last for nearly five hundred years and
become Rome's great rival on the world
stage.

224 AD

The Sassanid (Neo-Persian) Empire
succeeds the Parthian Empire.

260

Roman Emperor Valerian is captured by
Persian Emperor Shashur I.

283 and 298

The Romans sack Ctesiphon, the Persian
capital.

309–379

Reign of Shapur II, who fights against
Arab tribes and builds a wall to protect
the Persian Empire against their
incursions.

628

Byzantine Roman Emperor Heraclius
wins a decisive but Pyrrhic victory over
the Persians, as his success leaves
Roman forces spread too thin to defend
the Empire's new larger borders.

631

According to Islamic tradition, Muhammad raids Tabuk in northern Arabia—nominally within the Byzantine Empire—and finds it undefended. Before his death the next year, the prophet of Islam is said to have foretold the destruction of both Persian and Byzantine Empires.

633–651

The Arabs invade and conquer Persia; they will ultimately succeed in imposing Islam on the Persians (and nearly eradicating Zoroastrianism, the religion of Persia from the time of the Achaeminid Empire).

661

Death of Ali, the fourth successor to Muhammad, whose supporters (the Shiat Ali, or party of Ali) will become the first Shi'ite Muslims. Ali is revered by the Shi'ites as the first Imam.

874

The eleventh Imam dies and, according to Shi'ite belief, is succeeded by his five-year-old son, who soon goes into "occultation." Shi'ites believe that the Twelfth Imam is still alive but hidden on the earth, and that he will reappear in the end times.

10th–12th centuries

Persia is ruled by Turks.

1219

The Mongols lay waste to Persia.

1232

Birth of Safi od-Din of Arabil, the founder of the Safavid religious order, a Sufi Muslim group that will eventually convert from Sunni Islam to Twelver Shi'ism, making that minority strain of Islam a force for rallying resistance to the Persians' foreign rulers.

1453

Ottoman Turkish sultan Mehmet the Conqueror takes Constantinople, bringing a final end to the Roman Empire. As the successor to the Byzantines, the Ottoman Caliphate will regularly clash with the Persian Empire, shortly to be revived under the Safavid dynasty.

1508

Ismail I becomes the first Safavid shah to rule over a united Persia; he will impose Shi'ism on the Persians.

1629

Death of Shah Abbas I, after whose victorious reign (Abbas had defeated the Ottomans and driven Portuguese adventurers out of the Persian Gulf) Persia goes into decline again.

1722

Peter the Great invades Persian territory. Two years later the Russians and the Ottomans conclude a treaty to divide Persia between them. The Persians will struggle to resist Russian hegemony for the next 150 years.

1870

The Great Persian Famine; as many as 2 million die.

1872

Baron Paul Julius de Reuter concludes a sweeping agreement that would give him control of Iran's customs revenue and its banks, a railway concession, and the right to tap Iranian natural resources—inaugurating an era of British and European exploitation of Iran.

1906

Shah Muzaffareddin approves the first Iranian constitution; the first Majlis, or Iranian parliament, is convened soon afterward.

1908

Oil is first struck in Persia.

1914–1918

The "Persian Campaign" of World War I: Britain and Russia fight the Ottoman Empire on ostensibly neutral Persian territory.

1925

Former military officer Reza Khan, the British-backed prime minister of Persia, deposes the last shah of the Qajar dynasty and establishes a new dynasty he calls Pahlavi, or "heroic."

1935

Reza Khan decrees that henceforth Persia will be known by its ancient name Iran—a word closely related to "Aryan" and possibly signaling his sympathy with the racial theories of Hitler, who is much admired by Iranians. The same year, government troops suppress an uprising at a shrine in Mashhad. Both religious resistance to the Pahlavis' attempts to modernize, Westernize, and secularize Persia, on the one hand, and intermittently violent repression of that resistance by the Pahlavis, on the other, will continue for more than four decades.

1941

Britain and Russia invade Iran to secure its oil for the Allies; they depose Reza Shah and replace him with his son Mohammed Reza Pahlavi.

1951

Mohammed Mossadegh, vowing to end British exploitation of Iran's oil, becomes prime minister.

1953

Mossadegh is removed from office in a coup masterminded by the British MI6 spy service and the CIA.

1957

The establishment of SAVAK, the shah's notorious secret police.

1962

Ali Shariati, a radical Shi'ite writer and activist living in self-imposed exile in Paris, arranges for Jalal Al-e Ahmad's *Gharbzadegi* (*Weststruckness*)—indicting Iranian society for falling prey to the "plague" of Western culture—to be published clandestinely in Iran.

1963

The Shah announces the White Revolution, to include land reform, a literacy campaign, and new political rights for women. Ayatollah Ruhollah Khomeini fulminates against the reforms and the Shah in numerous public appearances, and is arrested and released.

1964

Khomeini is sent into exile.

1971

Marxist Iranian People's Fedai Guerrillas attack a police outpost, commencing political violence that will continue until the success of the Islamic Revolution. The Shah hosts a lavish, champagne-fueled celebration of the 2,500th anniversary of the Persian Empire at a cost of more than $16 million.

1976

The election of Jimmy Carter, who announces that the defense of human rights worldwide will be a focus of his presidency.

1978

"Black Friday" and "The Day Tehran Burned." In September, the Shah imposes martial law and bans demonstrations; police shoot into a crowd of protesters defying the ban and kill fifty-eight people. Two months later, rioters egged on by the mullahs attack movie theaters, the British Embassy, government buildings, and police installations.

1979

The Islamic Revolution is triumphant: The Shah and his family leave Iran, and the Ayatollah Khomeini returns, to the acclaim of the Iranian people, millions of whom throng the airport to welcome him. A referendum on the establishment of an Islamic Republic passes overwhelmingly. Members of the "Muslim Student Followers of the Imam's Line" take over the American Embassy and make hostages of American diplomats.

1980

Saddam Hussein attacks Iran, beginning the eight-year Iran-Iraq War.

1981

After 444 days in captivity, the American hostages are freed on Ronald Reagan 's inauguration day.

1983

In two separate attacks, suicide bombers linked to Iran attack the U.S. embassy and barracks where Marines are stationed in Beirut, killing more than 350 people.

1984

William Buckley, the CIA station chief in Beirut, is kidnapped by Hizballah, the Iran's client Shia terror group in Lebanon.

1985

Buckley is killed after more than a year of captivity and torture.

1986

The Iran-Contra scandal: the Reagan administration's sale of arms to Iran—in an effort to win the freedom of Americans kidnapped by Iranian clients in Lebanon— and its use of proceeds from the arms deal to support the Nicaraguan Contras becomes public.

1988

The long and bloody Iran-Iraq War ends in a stalemate.

1996

Bombing of the Khobar Towers, housing members of the U.S. Airforce in Saudi Arabia; nineteen are killed. In 2006, U.S. District Judge Royce C. Lamberth will find that the Islamic Republic bankrolled the bombing.

1998

Over two hundred people are killed when truck bombs hit the U.S. Embassies in Kenya and Tanzania. National security experts will testify in federal district court that the bombings were facilitated by an alliance between al-Qaeda on the one hand and Iran and Iran's client terror organization Hizballah on the other, and that the Islamic Republic and Hizballah had trained al-Qaeda members to bomb large buildings.

2001

The September 11 attacks on the United States. Iranian Ministry of Intelligence and Security agent Abolghasem Mesbahi—according to his later testimony in U.S. district court after he defects from Iran—is briefed during the summer on a secret operation entitled *Shaitan dar Atash* ("Satan in Flames"), which will involve flying hijacked passenger jets into the World Trade Center, Pentagon, and White House. In the months leading up to the attacks, at least eight of the hijackers travel repeatedly to Iran and meet with Iranian agents there, but their passports are left unstamped by Iranian border guards so that they will be able to enter the United States undetected.

2003

The International Atomic Energy Agency announces that Iran has been secretly enriching uranium.

2006

The United Nations imposes sanctions on Iran over its nuclear program.

2008

Presidential candidate Barack Obama sends former U.S. ambassador William G. Miller to assure the Iranians that an Obama administration will be friendly toward them.

2009

The Green Revolution in Iran: election fraud sparks massive protests, which are brutally repressed by the government. Obama and members of his administration, who have already begun to court Iran for a nuclear deal, offer only tepid words in support of the protesters.

2010

The Obama-era CIA takes extraordinary steps to dissuade witnesses from testifying in the *Havlish, et al. v. bin Laden, et al.* case about Iran's role in planning the 9/11 attacks.

2011

In his final ruling in *Havlish*, U.S. District Judge George B. Daniels finds Iran and Hizballah liable for damages to be paid to relatives of the victims of the September 11, 2001, jihad attacks, as both the Islamic Republic and its Lebanese proxy Hizballah actively aided al-Qaeda in planning and executing those attacks.

2012

Canada closes Iran's embassy in Ottawa and recalls its own diplomats from Tehran in protest of subversive activities by Iranians in Canada, directed from the Embassy.

2015

The United States, Russia, China, the UK, and the EU conclude a deal with Iran over its nuclear program. Within months, Iran announces ballistic missile tests.

2016

The U.S. indicts seven Iranian hackers linked to the government of the Islamic Republic for cyber attacks on U.S. banks and a dam in New York state.

INTRODUCTION

This is not a travelogue, although some impressions of life inside the Islamic Republic are included. This is not a history, although there is here a broad outline of Persian history. This is not an introduction to Shi'ite Islam, although Iran's history since 1501 cannot be told without a general understanding of what Shi'ite Islam is all about, and so that, too, is included here.

The title of this book succinctly indicates what it is: *The Complete Infidel's Guide to Iran* explains why, of all the adversaries of America and rogue states in the world, Iran is the most lethal—and yet it is simultaneously the least well understood, even as it shares a place in the global rogue's gallery with the Islamic State (ISIS or, as Barack Obama insists on calling it, ISIL) and the murderous comic-opera personality cult of North Korea.

The Islamic Republic of Iran is simultaneously the modern exponent of one of the oldest and greatest civilizations on the planet, with a glorious history that stretches back five thousand years, and a closed, suspicious, authoritarian, paranoid, confrontational regime whose leaders (and people) regularly chant "Death to America."

In *The Complete Infidel's Guide to Iran*, I will explain how Iran came to be both of those things, tracing its history, geostrategic importance, religious development, and above all, its modern-day political adventurism, from the Iranian Revolution and the transformation of modern Iranian society to Iran's funding of jihad terror groups that are warring against Israel, including both Shi'ite Hizballah and Sunni Hamas, to its development of nuclear energy and nuclear weapons, including the full and appalling story of the Obama-Kerry deal that gives a green light to Iran's most sinister global aspirations.

I'll illuminate the Islamic doctrines that form the foundation of Iran's fanatical hatred of the United States and Israel and the funding of some of our most bloodthirsty enemies; the bold and brazen strategy Shi'ite Iran is implementing to try to vault to a position of leadership of the entire Islamic world, Sunni as well as Shi'ite, and to attain nothing less (as fantastic as it sounds) than global hegemony; and the astonishing apocalyptic fantasies that lead the Iranian mullahs to believe that they can press ahead with an avowedly genocidal nuclear program that could result in a war that would cause the deaths of tens of millions of Iranians.

It's imperative that American lawmakers drop their politically correct fantasies and deal with the Iranian threat realistically—before it's too late. This book is an attempt to provide information that will inspire Americans to prod our self-serving and self-deluded political class into doing just that.

Chapter One

"THE ULTIMATE SCREWING"
THE IRAN NUCLEAR DEAL

Barack Obama had triumphed.

Over six years after winning the Nobel Peace Prize, the president had accomplished something that he clearly believed would be the foundation of lasting peace: he had brought the Islamic Republic of Iran to the negotiating table and won its acceptance of an agreement that would prevent it, once and for all, from developing nuclear weapons. The United States, Russia, China, the United Kingdom, and the European Union concluded the agreement with the Islamic Republic in Vienna on July 14, 2015.

"We have stopped the spread of nuclear weapons in this region"

Flush with victory as he announced the conclusion of the deal, Obama proclaimed that Iran's "every pathway to a nuclear weapon" had been blocked.[1] "We have stopped the spread of nuclear weapons in this region."[2]

1

In his hour of victory, Obama couldn't resist taking a swipe at the naysayers—both those who had said that the U.S. couldn't negotiate with the Islamic Republic, and those who had said it shouldn't. "This deal," he declared, "demonstrates that American diplomacy can bring about real and meaningful change, change that makes our country and the world safer and more secure." The United States, he said, had "negotiated from a position of strength and principle."

The president warned Congress that rejecting the deal could have severe consequences: "Put simply, no deal means the chance of more war in the Middle East."[3] To calm the fears of doubters, he insisted that the deal was "not built on trust. It is built on verification."[4]

"We are . . . taping the whole deal, 24–7 for 20 years"

Obama's Secretary of State, John Kerry, who had negotiated much of the deal personally, agreed: the deal was foolproof. "We have a 20-year televised insight into their centrifuge production," he told the *Atlantic*'s Jeffrey Goldberg. "In other words, we are watching their centrifuge production with live television, taping the whole deal, 24–7 for 20 years. But even more important, and much more penetrating, much more conclusive, we have 25 years during which all uranium production—from mine to mill to yellowcake to gas to waste—is tracked and traced. The intelligence community will tell you it is not possible for them to have a complete, covert, separate fuel cycle. You can't do the whole cycle; you can't do the mining and milling covertly."[5]

Kerry explained, "Now, in a civil nuclear program, all facilities are declared and all facilities are inspectionable [sic]. So every facility maintains 24–7 visibility. You can't crank up—see, the comprehensive safeguards agreement provides for a range of IAEA inspections, including verifying the location, the identity, the quantity, and composition of all nuclear materials subject to the safeguards, and the design of the facility and so forth."

Thus, Kerry asserted, it would be "physically impossible" for Iran to develop a nuclear bomb without its being detected by the international community. "And therefore, when you add the Additional Protocol with 25 years of uranium tracking, we're more than confident that this is something unusual that doesn't exist in any other agreement in the world. They will not be able to get a bomb."[6]

"They will not be able to get a bomb"—verifiably. Peace in our time.

"America is the very epitome of arrogance"

But the spirit of peace was not exactly reigning in Tehran.

Two days before the deal was concluded, Iran's state-run Fars News Agency announced the release of "Missile Strike," a cellphone game in which players fired nuclear missiles into the Israeli city of Haifa. Mehdi Atash Jaam, the game's project manager, explained, "The anti-Zionist game displays Iran's missile power and the Zelzal, Zolfaqar and Sejjil missiles [Iranian domestic missiles] are used by the players in the game's first stage. In this game, users break into the Zionist regime's air defense and target Israel."[7]

The Joint Comprehensive Plan of Action (JCPOA) with Iran had just been concluded when the Islamic Republic's Supreme Leader, Ayatollah Ali Khamenei, reaffirmed his nation's hostility toward the U.S.: "Even after this deal our policy towards the arrogant U.S. will not change. We don't have any negotiations or deal with the U.S. on different issues in the world or the region."[8]

Five days before the nuclear deal was finalized, Khamenei's office posted a photograph on his official website of the Supreme Leader walking across an Israeli flag painted on the pavement. The photo caption read: "The Zionist Regime is Condemned to Vanish. The Zionist regime is a regime with

WHAT A DEAL!

"Our policy will not change with regards to the arrogant US government."

—Iran's Supreme Leader Sayyed Ali Hossaini Khamenei after the conclusion of the nuclear deal[9]

very shaky pillars. The Zionist regime is doomed. The Zionist regime is an imposed regime and was created with intimidation. Nothing created with intimidation can last long and this one will not last long either."[10]

Two days later, Khamenei said in a speech, "According to Qur'anic principles, fighting against arrogance and global imperialism is never-ending and today, America is the very epitome of arrogance."[11]

And just four days after the JCPOA agreement was signed, Khamenei praised the Iranian people for screaming "Death to America" and "Death to Israel" at nationwide rallies on Al-Quds Day, an annual observance in Iran during which the nation reaffirms its commitment to the Palestinian jihad against Israel.

Al-Quds Day in 2015 fell on July 10, four days before the agreement was finalized. Referring to the observances in a speech on July 18, Khamenei stated that "the slogans of the people of Iran…indicated what directions they're heading for."

In what directions were the Iranians heading? "You heard 'Death to Israel', 'Death to the US.' You could hear it. The whole nation was shaken by these slogans. It wasn't only confined to Tehran. The whole of the nation, you could hear, that was covered by this great movement. So we ask Almighty God to accept these prayers by the people of Iran."[12]

"If war breaks out, it will be the aggressive, cruel American that loses"

In the same speech, Khamenei declared that the nuclear deal would not change Iran's hostile stance toward the U.S., or its support for enemies of U.S. allies in the region: "The Islamic Republic of Iran will not give up support of its friends in the region—the oppressed people of Palestine, of

Yemen, the Syrian and Iraqi governments, the oppressed people of Bahrain and sincere resistance fighters in Lebanon and Palestine."[13] Khamenei claimed, "Plainly we don't want war. But if war breaks out, it will be the aggressive, cruel American that loses."[14]

As he said all this, the appreciative crowd enthusiastically chanted "Death to America" and "Death to Israel."[15] In another address that same day, less than a week after the nuclear deal was concluded, Khamenei blamed "big powers"—that is, America and America's allies—for the disunity of Muslims worldwide: "If the Islamic Ummah were united and relied on their own commonalities, they would certainly be a unique power in the international political scene but big powers have imposed such divisions on the Islamic Ummah to pursue their own interests and safeguard the Zionist regime."[16]

U.S. "forced to accept and stand the spinning of thousands of centrifuges"

Khamenei was jubilant regarding the nuclear agreement: "This is the outcome of the Iranian nation's resistance and bravery and the creativity of dear Iranian scientists." He said that the U.S. and its allies had been "forced to accept and stand the spinning of thousands of centrifuges and continuation of research and development in Iran, and it has no meaning but the Iranian nation's might."[19]

Khamenei was contemptuous about the possibility of working with the U.S. to bring peace and stability to the Middle East: "Our policies and those

WILL THE REAL TERRORISTS PLEASE STAND UP?

. . .

"The Americans dub the Lebanese resistance as terrorist and regard Iran as a supporter of terrorism because of its support for the Lebanese Hezbollah, while the Americans, themselves, are real terrorists who have created Daesh [the Islamic State] and support the wicked Zionists."[17]

—Supreme Leader Khamenei (who also excoriated the U.S. for supporting the "Zionist, terrorist and infanticidal" Israelis) on July 18, 2015, four days after the nuclear deal[18]

WHAT A DEAL!

"We won't allow American political, economic or cultural influence in Iran."

—Supreme leader Khamenei, the month after the deal [22]

of the US in the region are 180 degree different, so how could it be possible to enter dialogue and negotiations with them?"[20]

This defiant and hostile speech left Secretary of State Kerry nonplussed and unsettled: "I don't know how to interpret it at this point in time, except to take it at face value, that that's his policy." Still he held out hope: "But I do know that often comments are made publicly and things can evolve that are different. If it is the policy, it's very disturbing, it's very troubling."[21]

But by then the deal was done, and was not going to be undone. A month later, Khamenei was still just as confrontational, crowing, "They thought this deal—and it is not clear if it will be passed in Iran or in America—will open up Iran to their influence. We blocked this path and will definitely block it in the future."[23]

"Benjamin Netanyahu is ready to kill himself"

Before the deal was even concluded, Israeli Prime Minister Benjamin Netanyahu expressed forebodings about it: "This deal, as it appears to be emerging, bears out all of our fears, and even more than that.... talks continue as usual and go on, on a deal that from everything that we hear paves Iran's way to the bomb."[24]

The Iranians showed no interest in allaying his fears. All through the summer of 2015, in the aftermath of the conclusion of the agreement, the Iranian government seemed determined to emphasize that the nuclear deal did not mean peace with the United States. On Friday, July 20, 2015, just two days after Khamenei's bellicose remarks, Iran's state-run media essentially declared victory outright, releasing photos of Ayatollah Mohammad

Ali Movahedi Kermani—whom Khamenei had chosen to lead Friday prayers in Tehran—at a podium emblazoned in Persian, "We will trample upon America," and in English, "We Defeat the United States."[25]

With the declarations of victory came new threats. On July 25, Khamenei tweeted an image of Barack Obama in silhouette, holding a pistol to his own temple. The image was accompanied by a graphic that quoted Khamenei's July 18 speech: "We welcome no war, nor do we initiate any war, but if any war happens, the one who will emerge the loser will be the aggressive and criminal U.S."[26]

That same day, Iranian Foreign Minister Mohammed Javad Zarif responded with contempt to Kerry's suggestion that if the Iranians did not abide by the agreement, the U.S. could resort to military action: "Unfortunately the US Secretary of State once again talked about the rotten rope of 'the ability of the US for using military force.'" Zarif decried the "uselessness of such empty threats against the nation of Iran and the resistance of the nation of Iran." Such threats, he said, belonged "to the last century," and what's more, even the Americans "have repeatedly admitted that these threats have no effect on the will of the people of Iran and that it will change the situation to their disadvantage."[27]

Two days later, still less than two weeks after the agreement was signed, Zarif crowed that "Benjamin Netanyahu is ready to kill himself if it helps to stop this nuclear agreement because this agreement puts the Zionist regime in an irrecoverable danger. The abominable Zionist Regime has never been so isolated among its allies."[28]

Ominously, Zarif also asserted that Iran's "violating the arms and missiles embargo" of the United Nations "does not violate the nuclear agreement."[29]

And within three months, Iran would announce that it had test-fired a precision-guided ballistic missile with a range that would allow it to reach Israel—all the while insisting that the tests were not prohibited under the terms of the nuclear deal.[30] In the months between the signing of the agreement and the ballistic missile tests, the Iranians continued to crow about their victory over the Great Satan at the negotiating table. After a spate of ballistic missile tests on March 8, 2016, Iranian Brigadier General Amir Ali Hajizadeh referred on Iranian television to "our main enemies, the Americans."[31] The next day, Iran test-fired two ballistic missiles on which "Israel must be wiped out" was written in Hebrew.[32]

In September of 2015, foreign ministry spokeswoman Marzieh Afkham boasted that the U.S. had been "forced into negotiating" with Iran because of the "failure of the U.S. policy of sanctions and threats."[34] Iranian President Hassan Rouhani dubbed the deal "evident victory," after the name in Islamic tradition of Muhammad's raids on the caravans of the pagan Arabs of Mecca. The deal, said Rouhani, was "the greatest diplomatic victory in Islamic history."[35] Not just Iranian history, but Islamic history.

WHAT A DEAL!

"The U.S. president, fruitlessly, tries to claim the results of the nuclear negotiations, but the truth is…the U.S. had no alternative but giving up its excessive demands."

—Iranian foreign ministry spokeswoman Marzieh Afkham, heaping contempt on President Obama's attempts to spin the deal as victory[33]

"Symbolic of the desire of our two peoples never to go to war with one another again"

Even before the deal was concluded, the comparison had already been circulating for months: the Iran nuke deal was another Munich, another exercise in appeasement of a bloodthirsty tyrant, and Barack Obama was another Neville Chamberlain.

Republican Presidential candidate Ted Cruz declared, "The deal being negotiated today is reminiscent of Munich in 1938. And when the administration comes back to America and promises peace in our time, we shouldn't believe them now any more than we should have believed them then."[36] John Bolton, former U.S. Ambassador to the United Nations, agreed: "The deal is an American Munich. Barack Obama is trying to appease the mullahs in Tehran by making one concession after another."[37] Conservative actor and pundit Ben Stein went even further, predicting that the Iran deal would "make Neville Chamberlain's Munich Pact with Hitler seem trivial by comparison."[38]

Just like the Munich Pact, the Iran nuclear deal promised peace in our time. The Joint Comprehensive Plan of Action between the Western powers and Iran claimed to "ensure that Iran's nuclear programme will be exclusively peaceful," and asserted that the "full implementation" of the agreement would "positively contribute to regional and international peace and security." Iran, it said, "reaffirms that under no circumstances will Iran ever seek, develop or acquire any nuclear weapons."[39]

The resonance between this and British Prime Minister Chamberlain's words at London's Heston Aerodrome on September 30, 1938, after meeting with Adolf Hitler in Munich and agreeing to the dismemberment of Czechoslovakia at the demand of the Third Reich was obvious:

> The settlement of the Czechoslovakian problem, which has now been achieved is, in my view, only the prelude to a larger settlement in which all Europe may find peace. This morning I had another talk with the German Chancellor, Herr Hitler, and here is the paper which bears his name upon it as well as mine. Some of you, perhaps, have already heard what it contains but I would just like to read it to you: "We, the German Führer and Chancellor and the British Prime Minister have had a further meeting today and are agreed in recognizing that the question of Anglo-German relations is of the first importance for the two countries and for Europe. We regard the agreement signed last night and the Anglo-German Naval Agreement as symbolic of the desire of our two peoples never to go to war with one another again."[40]

But despite the similarities—the rashly premature assertion of success, the naïve trust in an obviously hostile negotiating partner—the mainstream media was quick to dismiss the Munich comparison. The *Christian Science Monitor* published a piece entitled, "Is the Iran nuclear deal like Munich 1938? Not really," huffing that "such comparisons not only make little historical sense, they also demonstrate how minor the Iranian 'threat' is compared to Nazi Germany."[41] The *Los Angeles Times* mused wryly that the Right always indulged in this sort of hysteria: "a review of American diplomatic history shows that no agreement with a rival, no matter how wise or necessary, can be considered complete until it has endured allusions to Munich and Chamberlain. It may as well be in the Constitution as a step in the treaty ratification process."[42]

Atlantic correspondent James Fallows ticked off some differences: "The Germany of 1938 was much richer and more powerful than the Iran of today. Germany was rapidly expansionist; Iran, despite its terrorist work through proxies, has not been. The Nazi leaders had engulfed the world in war less than a decade after taking power. Iran's leaders, oppressive and destructive, have not shown similar suicidal recklessness. European Jews of 1938 were stateless, unarmed, and vulnerable. Modern Israel is a powerful, nuclear-armed force."[43] Fallows did not explain how Iran's financial and material support for Hizballah in Lebanon could be reconciled with his judgment that the Islamic Republic "has not been" "rapidly expansionist" or how its aid for Hamas's terror attacks in Israel and oft-repeated genocidal boasts that soon the "Zionist regime" would vanish from the earth didn't make Jews "vulnerable."

Fallows also did not address the aggressive and bellicose rhetoric coming out of Iran as the deal was concluded. Nor did he discuss one key difference between Obama and Chamberlain: Chamberlain made a disastrous and unprecedented mistake. It was only in the wake of Munich that "appeasement" became a byword. Obama had Chamberlain's example before him, warning him of the dangers of appeasing a bloodthirsty tyrant. Yet he charged ahead anyway.

Neville Chamberlain benefits from the comparison.

"This will be the ultimate screwing"

Despite all the bellicosity coming out of Iran as the nuclear agreement was finalized, John Kerry insisted in a lengthy August 2015 interview that the side that needed to show a good faith commitment to peace was not Iran, but the United States. He argued urgently that the deal should be approved by Congress, because if it wasn't it would prove to Khamenei that he had been right about the Americans all along, that we were untrustworthy. According to Kerry, the Ayatollah was extremely reluctant to make a deal with the Americans and had had to be cajoled by the purportedly moderate Rouhani: "The ayatollah approached this entire exercise extremely charily. He gave a kind of dismissive OK to Rouhani and company to go do this, in the sense that he didn't want to be blamed if this didn't work. It was all Rouhani's risk. He was playing the IRGC [Islamic Revolutionary Guards Corps], and this and that. And so it was clear to me from my many conversations with Zarif and from the entire dynamic how fragile that journey was with him. The ayatollah constantly believed that we are untrustworthy, that you can't negotiate with us, that we will screw them."

For Kerry, the Ayatollah's suspicion of America was a major reason the U.S. had to follow through and approve and hold to the deal—otherwise, Khamenei would lose faith in the U.S. entirely: "This will be the ultimate screwing. We cut a deal, we stand up, it's announced, five other countries believe in it—six other countries, because Iran signs off, and we're the seventh—but you know, China, Russia, France, Germany, Britain, all sign off. Now the United States Congress will prove the ayatollah's suspicion, and there's no way he's ever coming back. He will not come back to negotiate. Out of dignity, out of a suspicion that you can't trust America. America is not going to negotiate in good faith. It didn't negotiate in good faith now, would be his point."[44]

Kerry didn't seem to have any concern about whether the Ayatollah's men had negotiated with *us* in good faith—it was only American trustworthiness that was in question.

"Remarkably naive and incredibly reckless"

Iranian good faith, in fact, was taken for granted to such an extent that the assumption of it was built into the agreement itself. On July 30, 2015, Iran's Deputy Foreign Minister, Abbas Araghchi, pointed out, "American and Canadian inspectors cannot be sent to Iran. It is mentioned in the deal that inspectors should be from countries that have diplomatic relations with Islamic republic of Iran." International Atomic Energy Agency (IAEA) inspectors, he added, would not be given access to "sensitive and military documents."[45]

In an interview with Al Jazeera the following day, Ali Akbar Velayati, a senior advisor to Khamenei, further broadened these restrictions to apply to other signatories to the deal as well: "Regardless of how the P5+1 countries interpret the nuclear agreement, their entry into our military sites is absolutely forbidden."[46]

Yet just days later, John Kerry secured the Gulf States' approval of the deal by assuring them that Iranian nuclear sites would be subject to close inspection. After meeting with Kerry, Qatar's Foreign Minister Khalid al-Attiyah declared that the Secretary of State "let us know that there is going to be live oversight over Iran not to gain or to get any nuclear weapons. This is reassuring to the region."[47]

How could there be any effective "live oversight" of Iran's nuclear sites if "entry into [Iran's] military sites is absolutely forbidden" to any country whose inspectors would bring a critical eye to the process? On August 19, 2015, the Associated Press dropped a bombshell. Confirming rumors that had circulated since the agreement was signed, it reported that a secret side deal between the International Atomic Energy Agency (IAEA) and Iran allowed the Iranians to conduct *their own* inspections of *their own* sites:

> Iran, in an unusual arrangement, will be allowed to use its own experts to inspect a site it allegedly used to develop nuclear arms under a secret agreement with the U.N. agency that normally carries out such work, according to a document seen by The Associated Press. The revelation is sure to roil American and Israeli critics of the main Iran deal signed by the U.S., Iran and five world powers in July. Those critics have complained that the deal is built on trust of the Iranians, a claim the U.S. has denied. The investigation of the Parchin nuclear site by the International Atomic Energy Agency is linked to a broader probe of allegations that Iran has worked on atomic weapons. That investigation is part of the overarching nuclear deal. The Parchin deal is a separate, side agreement worked out between the IAEA and Iran. The United States and the five other world powers that signed the Iran nuclear deal were not party to this agreement but were briefed on it by the IAEA and endorsed it as part of the larger package. Without divulging its contents, the Obama administration has described the document as nothing more than a routine technical arrangement between Iran and the U.N.'s International Atomic Energy Agency on the particulars of inspecting the site.[48]

AP observed, rather mildly, that this side agreement "diverges from normal inspection procedures between the IAEA and a member country by essentially ceding the agency's investigative authority to Iran. It allows Tehran to employ its own experts and equipment in the search for evidence for activities that it has consistently denied—trying to develop nuclear weapons." Such an accommodation was unprecedented: "Olli Heinonen, who was in charge of the Iran probe as deputy IAEA director general from 2005 to 2010, said he can think of no instance where a country being probed was allowed to do its own investigation."[49]

The predictable firestorm ensued. Senate Foreign Relations Committee chairman Bob Corker of Tennessee declared, "This type of unorthodox agreement has never been done before by the IAEA and speaks to the great lengths our negotiators took to accommodate the ayatollah despite repeated assurances from the administration that this deal is not based on trust." Republican senator John Cornyn of Texas said, "This revelation only reinforces the deep-seated concerns the American people have about the agreement."[51]

House Foreign Affairs Committee Chairman Ed Royce said flatly, "International inspections should be done by international inspectors. Period."[52] A dry-eyed House Speaker John Boehner added, "President Obama boasts his deal includes 'unprecedented verification.' He claims it's not built on trust. But the administration's briefings on these side deals have been totally insufficient—and it still isn't clear whether anyone at the White House has seen the final documents."[53]

The left-wing media responded with a firestorm of its own: leftist "media watchdog" Media Matters crowed, "Conservative Media Run With Flawed AP Report To Claim Iran Will Conduct Inspections On Its Own Facilities."[54] Media Matters asserted that "on August 20," that is, a day after AP dropped its bombshell, "the Arms Control Association's Tariq Rauf clarified that the inspections at Iran's Parchin military basewould [sic] determine past activity and that the IAEA would have 'managed access' to the site."[55] In other words, the IAEA would allow Iran to conduct

> ## YA THINK?
>
> . . .
>
> "Trusting Iran to inspect its own nuclear site and report to the U.N. in an open and transparent way is remarkably naive and incredibly reckless."
>
> —Senator John Cornyn[50]

its own inspections relating only to past nuclear activity, not to the possibility of the present-day development of nuclear weapons. Already a month before the AP story broke, the Arms Control Association had issued a statement saying: "Congressional critics of the JCPOA [Joint Comprehensive Plan of Action] are misinterpreting information received in briefings about the process for IAEA inspections at sensitive sites. Under managed access procedures that may be employed the IAEA, the inspected party may take environmental swipe samples at a particular site in the presence of the IAEA inspectors using swabs and containment bags provided by the IAEA to prevent cross contamination. According to former IAEA officials, this is an established procedure."[56]

On the evening of the day the AP story appeared, however, NBC News confirmed that report's central claim and disputed the counterclaim that Iran's self-inspections would relate only to past activity. "Iran," NBC reported, "will inspect itself at its most sensitive known military complex to clear up suspicions of past military activity, NBC News has confirmed." Then it invoked "two senior U.S. officials" denying the Arms Control Association's claim that the permission for self-inspections related only to "past military activity. " The same officials flatly contradicted the claim that "UN inspectors, including IAEA Director Yukiya Amano, would be on site to supervise the Iranians at every step of the way." On the contrary, NBC reported, "a senator who opposes the deal and attended classified briefings on the IAEA's role at the Parchin complex southeast of Tehran" told NBC News that it was "categorically untrue that IAEA inspectors will be inside the Parchin facility while soil samples are being taken." The senator declined to be named.[57]

The following day, IAEA Director Amano disputed the story, saying "I am disturbed by statements suggesting that the IAEA has given responsibility for nuclear inspections to Iran. Such statements misrepresent the way in which we will undertake this important verification work."[58]

But Amano refused to reveal the terms of the side agreement. Thus even in disputing the self-inspection claim, he didn't actually deny it. "The separate arrangements under the Road-map agreed between the IAEA and Iran in July," Amano said, "are confidential and I have a legal obligation not to make them public—the same obligation I have for hundreds of such arrangements made with other IAEA Member States. However, I can state that the arrangements are technically sound and consistent with our long-established practices. They do not compromise our safeguards standards in any way."[59]

The Obama White House issued a statement assuring the world that all was well: "As we've said before, including in classified briefings for both chambers of Congress, we're confident in the [IAEA's] technical plans for investigating the possible military dimensions of Iran's former program—issues that in some cases date back more than a decade. Just as importantly, the IAEA is comfortable with arrangements which are unique to the agency's investigation of Iran's historical activities."[60] Significantly, this statement didn't deny the self-inspection claim.

Despite the lack of substance in these denials, however, AP deleted its original report and eight days later issued this correction: "In a story Aug. 19 about an arrangement over alleged past nuclear weapons work between Iran and the International Atomic Energy Agency, The Associated Press erroneously referred to Parchin as a 'nuclear site.['] In fact, it's a military site where some believe nuclear work occurred."

The correction didn't touch upon the central claim of the original story—that Iran would conduct its own nuclear inspections. The "corrected version" read, "An unusual secret agreement with a U.N. agency will allow Iran to use its own experts to inspect a site allegedly used to develop nuclear arms, according to a document seen by The Associated Press. The revelation is sure to roil critics who argue the deal is built on trust of the Iranians. The investigation of the Parchin military site by the U.N. International Atomic

Energy Agency is linked to a broader probe of nuclear weapons allegations."[61]

The claim that Iran would conduct self-inspections remained, unretracted and uncorrected. The correction centered upon the Parchin site, "allegedly used to develop nuclear arms." Nuclear researcher Cheryl Rofer explained, "What is the purpose of sampling at Parchin? The IAEA is looking for residues of experiments that are alleged to have been done to develop a design for a nuclear weapon. They were most likely carried out before 2003, when U.S. intelligence estimates find that Iranian nuclear weapons work ended, although the IAEA has expressed concern that experiments may have been carried out after 2003."[62]

In other words, the inspections at Parchin are not only going to be conducted by the Iranians themselves. They're also going to be limited to looking for evidence of past nuclear weapons development. Might Iran be conducting nuclear testing or development at Parchin now? An IAEA report issued in November 2011 noted that "the Agency has serious concerns regarding possible military dimensions to Iran's nuclear programme. After assessing carefully and critically the extensive information available to it, the Agency finds the information to be, overall, credible. The information indicates that Iran has carried out activities relevant to the development of a nuclear explosive device. The information also indicates that prior to the end of 2003, these activities took place under a structured programme, and that some activities may still be ongoing."[63]

Might these ongoing nuclear weapons activities be taking place at Parchin? There was nothing definitive to rule out that possibility—and it was at Parchin that Iran would be able to provide its own soil samples to the IAEA. What's more, in February 2016, satellite photos confirmed that construction had been going on at Parchin at a furious rate during the period in which the nuclear agreement was being negotiated, perhaps to conceal work on nuclear weapons.[64]

Rofer had no way of knowing that while writing six months before that discovery, of course, but she had ample reason to be suspicious of the Iranians, given their bellicose rhetoric at the very least. Yet she waved away concerns about Iran's self-inspection by noting that "other countries have given up nuclear weapons programs without full disclosure, and they have kept to their nonproliferation obligations. South Africa, Brazil, Argentina, Sweden, and Switzerland all had nuclear weapons programs at one time and have given them up."[65]

Rofer seemed to have missed a key point: South Africa, Brazil, Argentina, Sweden, and Switzerland never held mass rallies in which their citizens chanted "Death to America" and "Death to Israel." Iran clearly has a motivation for continuing its nuclear weapons program that these other countries never shared.

As August drew to a close, the story about Iran's self-inspections receded from the headlines—roundly denounced but never actually denied or effectively refuted.

"Can you imagine giving a drug dealer 24 days' notice before you inspect the premises?"

Beyond the self-inspection problem, there is a great deal more wrong with the Iran deal.

1. The expiration dates. While the Joint Comprehensive Plan of Action (JCPOA) does include real restrictions on Iran's nuclear activities, these are all slated to expire within a period of years. The agreement anticipates the "conclusion of consideration of the Iran nuclear issue by the UN Security Council 10 years after the Adoption Day"—that is, the July 14, 2015, adoption of the agreement itself.[66] It contains stipulations such as this: "There will be no additional heavy water reactors or accumulation of heavy water in Iran for 15 years."[67] What about after that? The agreement doesn't say.

"Iran," says the agreement, "will allow the IAEA to monitor the implementation of the voluntary measures for their respective durations, as well as to implement transparency measures, as set out in this JCPOA and its Annexes. These measures include: a long-term IAEA presence in Iran; IAEA monitoring of uranium ore concentrate produced by Iran from all uranium ore concentrate plants for 25 years; containment and surveillance of centrifuge rotors and bellows for 20 years; use of IAEA approved and certified modern technologies including on-line enrichment measurement and electronic seals; and a reliable mechanism to ensure speedy resolution of IAEA access concerns for 15 years..." Another provision: "Iran will not conduct any uranium enrichment or any uranium enrichment related R&D [research and development] and will have no nuclear material at the Fordow Fuel Enrichment Plant (FFEP) for 15 years."

Such stipulations are peppered throughout the agreement, raising the inevitable question: What about after that? The Joint Comprehensive Plan of Action is silent on that key point.

Perhaps the JCPOA's framers were working from the assumption that politics in Iran works much like the election cycle in a Western country, and that in fifteen, twenty, or twenty-five years, the Iranian regime would be substantially different in character from what it is now. Regime change can never be ruled out, but given the fact that the Ayatollahs have been in power in Iran since 1979, this would be an unrealistic assumption. And yet the Obama team appeared to be banking on the idea that by the time the restrictions expired, the Iranian regime would not be as bellicose and genocide-minded as it is now—or perhaps they really believe the Iranians' protestations that even now they have no interest in possessing nuclear weapons.

2. The delay in inspections. The day after the conclusion of the Joint Comprehensive Plan of Action, Israeli Prime Minister Benjamin Netanyahu pointed out, "I think Iran has two paths to the bomb: One if they keep the deal, the other if they cheat on the deal." They can get the bomb even if they keep the deal because the JCPOA contains the provision that Iran can delay requested IAEA inspections for up to twenty-four days. "Can you imagine," Netanyahu asked, "giving a drug dealer 24 days' notice before you inspect the premises? That's a lot of time to flush a lot of meth down the toilet."[68]

As preposterous as this delay sounds, Netanyahu was right. The JCPOA states:

> If the absence of undeclared nuclear materials and activities or activities inconsistent with the JCPOA cannot be verified after the implementation of the alternative arrangements agreed by Iran and the IAEA, or if the two sides are unable to reach satisfactory arrangements to verify the absence of undeclared nuclear materials and activities or activities inconsistent with the JCPOA at the specified locations within 14 days of the IAEA's original request for access, Iran, in consultation with the members of the Joint Commission, would resolve the IAEA's concerns through necessary means agreed between Iran and the IAEA. In the absence of an agreement, the members of the Joint Commission, by consensus or by a vote of 5 or more of its 8 members, would advise on the necessary means to resolve the IAEA's concerns. The process of consultation with, and any action by, the members of the Joint Commission would not exceed 7 days, and Iran would implement the necessary means within 3 additional days.[69]

That amounted to exactly the twenty-four-day period to which Netanyahu was referring: if the IAEA feared that Iran was not complying with the agreement, first Iran would have fourteen days to "reach satisfactory arrangements" with the IAEA; then, if they couldn't come to an agreement by that point, the Joint Commission would "advise on the necessary means to resolve the IAEA's concerns," presumably including recommending inspection of Iranian nuclear sites, within another seven days, with their recommendations to be implemented within another three days.

This long delay, of course, amounts to no effective right to inspect Iranian nuclear sites at all. It renders John Kerry's confident assurance that "every facility" will be subjected to "24-7 visibility"[70] hollow.

3. The removal of sanctions. Even before the deal, it was questionable how effective the economic sanctions that the U.S. and UN had placed upon Iran really were: in March 2015, Thomas Erdbrink, the Tehran bureau chief of the *New York Times*, a longtime resident of Iran, remarked, "As the politicians are talking for months to end the sanctions, my shopkeeper tells me he has more foreign products for sale than ever."[71]

Nonetheless, the JCPOA is quite definite about removing all economic sanctions on Iran. "This JCPOA will produce the comprehensive lifting of all UN Security Council sanctions as well as multilateral and national sanctions related to Iran's nuclear programme, including steps on access in areas of trade, technology, finance and energy."[72]

This included the removal of sanctions that had originally been intended to be removed only when Iran definitively gave up its nuclear program; now the Islamic Republic was being given sanctions relief and allowed to continue its nuclear program, only with certain restrictions that would all eventually expire anyway.

American officials insisted that if Iran didn't comply with the agreement, it allowed for the "snapback"—the reapplication—of the sanctions. Barack Obama claimed, "If Iran violates the deal, all of these sanctions will snap back into place. So there is a very clear incentive for Iran to follow through and there are very real consequences for a violation." John Kerry was no less adamant: "I want to underscore: If Iran fails in a material way to live up to these commitments, then the United States, the E.U., and even the U.N. sanctions that initially brought Iran to the table can and will snap right back into place. We have a specific provision in this agreement called 'snap-back' for the return of those sanctions in the event of noncompliance."[73]

The JCPOA itself, however, is ambiguous on this point, seeming to state that the sanctions, once removed, cannot be put back:

> The EU will refrain from re-introducing or re-imposing the sanctions that it has terminated implementing under this JCPOA, without prejudice to the dispute resolution process provided for under this JCPOA. There will be no new nuclear-related UN Security Council sanctions and no new EU nuclear-related sanctions or restrictive measures. The United States will make best efforts in good faith to sustain this JCPOA and to prevent interference with the realisation of the full benefit by Iran of the sanctions lifting specified in Annex II. The U.S. Administration, acting consistent with the respective roles of the President and the Congress, will refrain from re-introducing or re-imposing the sanctions specified in Annex II that it has ceased applying under this JCPOA, without prejudice to the dispute resolution process provided for under this JCPOA. The U.S. Administration, acting consistent with the respective roles of the President and the Congress, will refrain from imposing new nuclear-related sanctions.[74]

And any new sanctions would be a justification for Iran to pull out of the agreement—something that is also stated in the JCPOA itself: "Iran has stated that it will treat such a re-introduction or re-imposition of the sanctions specified in Annex II, or such an imposition of new nuclear-related sanctions, as grounds to cease performing its commitments under this JCPOA in whole or in part."[75]

4. The lack of any consequences for breaking the agreement. The 159-page Joint Comprehensive Plan of Action goes into tremendous detail about the Iranian nuclear program and how it is to be temporarily restricted in various ways. It also expatiates at length on exactly which sanctions are to be removed. But it is conspicuously lacking in specifying penalties for Iran's not holding to the agreement.

The only specific penalty for Iranian non-compliance in the entire JCPOA is one that stands in tension with other statements in the agreement about how the sanctions will not be restored once they have been removed. The JCPOA stipulates that if a country privy to the agreement finds Iran in noncompliance, then once "the complaining participant" has made "good-faith efforts" to "exhaust the dispute resolution process," the UN Security Council will "vote on a resolution to continue the sanctions lifting."[76] That is, it could halt the lifting of sanctions, and reimpose them.

If Iran were found to be in non-compliance, the old sanctions could be re-imposed, "unless the UN Security Council decides otherwise"—a very large loophole, considering the significant number of political and economic reasons for Security Council members to avoid the re-imposition of the sanctions.[77] If Iran's friends and allies can muster the votes, it can keep the sanctions specified in old Security Council resolutions from being re-imposed.

And even if the sanctions were ever re-imposed, they "would not apply with retroactive effect to contracts signed between any party and Iran or Iranian individuals and entities prior to the date of application, provided that the activities contemplated under and execution of such contracts are consistent with this JCPOA and the previous and current UN Security Council resolutions."[78] In other words, if Iran is found to be violating the terms of the deal and the old sanctions are reapplied, they won't apply to deals Iran made before it was found in noncompliance.

These terms are almost absurdly easy on Iran. In the unlikely very worst case scenario for the Iranians, they may possibly find themselves in *just as bad a position as they were before the JCPOA*. What exactly is the rest of the world getting out of this agreement?

"Iran will have some additional resources for its military and for some of the activities in the region that are a threat to us and a threat to our allies"

The difficulty or outright impossibility of re-imposing the sanctions, and the exemption of new deals from any such reapplied sanctions, amounted to an invitation to the nations of the world to strike while the iron was hot and conclude business deals with Iran posthaste. It also rendered meaningless the only leverage that the U.S. and our allies had in the agreement.

Michael Oren, former Israeli Ambassador to the United States, pointed out, "These [sanctions] cannot be 'snapped back' if Iran were to violate the deal, as its defenders contend, but reinstated only after a lengthy international process that excludes all the contracts signed by Iran before it were to cheat. As such, the deal serves as an incentive for foreign companies to sign a great number of short- and medium-term contracts with Iran. The windfall is estimated to reach $700 billion, according to Israeli government sources."[79]

The removal of the sanctions could be the most damaging aspect of the JCPOA. The day after the agreement was concluded, Obama acknowledged that the sanctions relief would give Iran a considerable amount of money that it could use to increase its funding of Hamas, Hizballah, and other jihad terror groups, but he insisted this was unimportant: "Do I think it's a game-changer for them? No.... The truth is, that Iran has always found a way to fund these efforts. And whatever benefit Iran may claim from sanctions relief pales in comparison to the danger it could pose with a nuclear weapon."[80]

But it was hard not to see this money as a game changer, especially with Iran standing to gain as much as a staggering $700 billion. Yet in a major address defending the nuclear deal, Obama insisted that he was no Pollyanna: "We have no illusions about the Iranian government or the significance of the Revolutionary Guard and the Quds Force. Iran supports terrorist organizations like Hezbollah. It supports proxy groups that threaten our interests and the interests of our allies, including proxy groups who killed our troops in Iraq." But again he downplayed the threat: "Contrary to the alarmists who claim Iran is on the brink of taking over the Middle East, or even the world, Iran will remain a regional power with its own set of challenges."[82]

Maybe so, but the billions in sanctions relief could go a long way to helping Iran overcome those challenges. In September 2015, buoyed by the lifting of sanctions as specified in the Joint Comprehensive Plan of Action, Iran significantly increased its funding of both Hamas and Hizballah.[83] In January 2016, after the IAEA certified that Iran was in compliance with the nuclear deal and Iran released five Americans it had imprisoned (as part of a prisoner swap that involved the U.S. dropping a $10 million claim against an Iranian engineer accused of violating the now-dead sanctions), the U.S. released $400 million in Iranian funds that had been frozen since 1981, and added $1.3 billion in interest.[84]

In February 2016, after a spate of Palestinian stabbings of Israeli civilians, Mohammad Fathali, the Iranian ambassador to Lebanon, announced, "Continuing Iran's support for the oppressed Palestinian people, Iran announces the provision of financial aid to families of Palestinian martyrs who were

> **WHAT A DEAL!**
>
> "Do we think that with the sanctions coming down, that Iran will have some additional resources for its military and for some of the activities in the region that are a threat to us and a threat to our allies? I think that is a likelihood, that they've got some additional resources."
> —President Barack Obama[81]

killed in the 'Jerusalem intifada.'" Iran would award $7,000 to the families of Palestinians killed while trying to murder Israelis, and $30,000 to those whose homes were destroyed by the Israelis because of their jihad terror activity.[85]

Apparently aware of how bad it looked to be turning over billions of dollars to a state sponsor of terror, in March 2016 Colin Kahl, Vice President Joe Biden's National Security Advisor, claimed that $100 billion in unfrozen assets that had already been released to Iran according to the terms of the nuke deal were "being used for domestic investment, to the dismay of [Quds Force chief] Qassem Soleimani."[86] Kahl's claim was flatly false, and apparently fabricated in order to try to save some face over the increasingly obvious disaster that was the nuclear deal. In reality, the Iranians were spending their newfound wealth on weaponry: flush with JCPOA cash, they had been in discussions with the Chinese about buying Chinese jet fighters; shopped for materiel in Russia; and supplied the Islamic Revolutionary Guards Corps with drones.[87]

"It would be contrary to their faith to obtain a nuclear weapon"

Why has the United States agreed to all these disastrous provisions? Possibly because our president and secretary of state are convinced that the Iranians don't even want a nuclear bomb. "The Ayatollah has issued a fatwa," John Kerry claimed in August 2015, at the height of the national debate over the agreement, "declaring no one should ever possess a nuclear weapon in Iran. We said, let's take the fatwa and codify it into the agreement."[88]

This celebrated anti-nuke fatwa had long been a staple of the Obama administration's case for believing the Iranians would abide by an agreement limiting their capacity to build nuclear weapons. Obama himself said in September 2013: "I do believe that there is a basis for a resolution" of the nuclear disputes with Iran, because "Iran's Supreme Leader has issued a fatwa against the development of nuclear weapons."[89]

At a joint press conference with German Chancellor Angela Merkel in February 2015, Obama showed that his faith had not wavered: "We are presenting to them in a unified fashion, the P5+1 supported by a coalition of countries around the world are presenting to them a deal that allows them to have peaceful nuclear power but gives us the absolute assurance that is verifiable that they are not pursuing a nuclear weapon. And if in fact what they claim is true, which is they have no aspiration to get a nuclear weapon, that in fact, according to their Supreme Leader, it would be contrary to their faith to obtain a nuclear weapon, if that is true, there should be the possibility of getting a deal. They should be able to get to yes."[90] The P5+1 countries were China, France, Russia, the United Kingdom, the U.S., and Germany.

Back in April 2012, then-Secretary of State Hillary Clinton showed herself to be a believer in the fatwa as well: "The other interesting development which you may have followed was the repetition by the Supreme Leader Ayatollah Khamenei that they would—that he had issued a fatwa against nuclear weapons, against weapons of mass destruction.... And if it is indeed a statement of principle, of values, then it is a starting point for being operationalized, which means that it serves as the entryway into a negotiation as to how you demonstrate that it is indeed a sincere, authentic statement of conviction. So we will test that as well."[91]

American policymakers were not the only believers. Turkey's Foreign Minister Ahmet Davutoglu declared in April 2012 that there was no chance that "Khamenei's fatwa forbidding the possession and use of nuclear weapons might be disobeyed in Iran."[92]

Hooshang Amirahmadi, the president of the American Iranian Council (AIC), praised Obama for his trust in the fatwa as he applauded the beginning of the negotiations between the U.S. and Iran: "Fortunately, President

Obama has decided to tentatively trust the Supreme Leader on his words that '[the] nuclear bomb is forbidden in Islam.'"[93]

Khamenei had indeed spoken out against nuclear weapons. In February 2012 he said that possessing a nuclear bomb "constitutes a major sin."[94] The Supreme Leader explained, "There is no doubt that the decision makers in the countries opposing us know well that Iran is not after nuclear weapons because the Islamic Republic, logically, religiously and theoretically, considers the possession of nuclear weapons a grave sin and believes the proliferation of such weapons is senseless, destructive and dangerous."[95]

At an August 2012 summit of the Non-Aligned Movement, Khamenei reiterated, "Our motto is nuclear energy for all and nuclear weapons for none."[96] Former Iranian President Mahmoud Ahmadinejad referred to the fatwa in a speech that same year: "Based on Islamic teachings and the clear fatwa of the supreme leader, the production and use of weapons of mass destruction is haram (forbidden) and have no place in the Islamic Republic of Iran's defense doctrine."[97]

Iranian Foreign Minister Ali Akbar Salehi wrote in April 2012, "We have strongly marked our opposition to weapons of mass destruction on many occasions. Almost seven years ago, Iranian Supreme Leader Ayatollah Ali Khamenei made a binding commitment. He issued a religious edict—a fatwa—forbidding the production, stockpiling and use of nuclear weapons."[98] The head of the Iranian judiciary, Ayatollah Sadeq Amoli Larijani, declared, "The fatwa that the Supreme Leader has issued is the best guarantee that Iran will never seek to produce nuclear weapons."[99] In 2013, former Iranian Foreign Ministry Spokesman Ramin Mehman-Parast said, "There is nothing more important in defining the framework for our nuclear activities than the Leader's fatwa."[100]

The only problem with all this was that the fatwa everyone kept referring to didn't exist.

Given the importance and prominence that it has taken on in the international debate over Iran's nuclear program and the nuclear deal, it is extremely curious that no one in the Obama administration seems to have seen the actual fatwa—or to be troubled by its absence. There is no such fatwa among official published collections of Khamenei's fatwas, and its text is not available anywhere.

In April 2012 researchers from the Middle East Media Research Institute (MEMRI) attempted to locate the fatwa and instead discovered that "no such fatwa ever existed or was ever issued or published, and that media reports about it are nothing more than a propaganda ruse on the part of the Iranian regime apparatuses—in an attempt to deceive top U.S. administration officials and the others mentioned above."[101]

MEMRI concluded that "Iranian regime officials' presentation of statements on nuclear weapons attributed to Supreme Leader Ali Khamenei as a fatwa, or religious edict, when no such fatwa existed or was issued by him, is a propaganda effort to propose to the West a religiously valid substitute for concrete guarantees of inspectors' access to Iran's nuclear facilities. Since the West does not consider mere statements, by Khamenei or by other regime officials, to be credible, the Iranian regime has put forth a fraudulent fatwa that the West would be more inclined to trust."[102]

Mehdi Khalaji, a senior fellow at the Washington Institute for Near East Policy, in a detailed analysis of the purported fatwa and Iran's stance toward nuclear weapons, claimed that "no written texts exist for the Supreme Leader's fatwas, though Shiite juridical tradition grants equal weight to an oral and written legal opinions."[103] In reality, however, there is an entire website devoted to Khamenei's fatwas—and the supposed fatwa condemning nuclear weapons is not among them.[104] MEMRI noted that "an exhaustive search of the various official websites of Iranian Supreme Leader Ali Khamenei turned up no such fatwa, either on his fatwa website or on his personal website."[105]

University of Michigan professor Juan Cole took issue with MEMRI, claiming that ten years before the nuclear deal was concluded, in August 2005, the state-controlled Islamic Republic News Agency (IRNA) had published an article stating, "The Leader of the Islamic Republic of Iran, Ayatollah Ali Khamenei has issued the Fatwa that the production, stockpiling and use of nuclear weapons are forbidden under Islam and that the Islamic Republic of Iran shall never acquire these weapons."[106]

IRNA did not publish the actual text of this fatwa, however, and the August 2005 article announcing it has disappeared from its website. But that did not deter Cole, who insisted, "That this old posting has gone into the deep web and isn't at the IRNA site is irrelevant. The fatwa was announced by IRNA and has been repeatedly reaffirmed by Khamenei."[107] Yet the absence of a published text, especially when so many other fatwas from Khamenei are readily available, renders Cole's optimism suspect. IRNA simply asserted that the fatwa existed, as have Ali Akbar Salehi, Ayatollah Larijani, and other Iranian officials—along with John Kerry, Barack Obama, and Hillary Clinton. But IRNA's word doesn't carry any more weight than theirs. The existence of the fatwa is almost universally taken for granted. So why can no one produce its text or any documentary evidence that there ever was any such thing?

Also casting doubt on Cole's claims is the fact that he has a vested interest in defending the Iranian regime: Juan Cole is a board member of the National Iranian American Council (NIAC), which has been established in court as a lobbying group for the Islamic Republic.[108] According to political analyst Michael Rubin, "Jamal Abdi, NIAC's policy director, now appears to push aside any pretense that NIAC is something other than Iran's lobby. Speaking at the forthcoming 'Expose AIPAC' conference, Abdi is featured on the 'Training: Constituent Lobbying for Iran' panel."[109]

Iranian freedom activist Hassan Daioleslam "documented over a two-year period that NIAC is a front group lobbying on behalf of the Iranian regime."[110] NIAC had to pay him nearly $200,000 in legal fees after they sued him for defamation over his accusation that they were a front group for the mullahs, and lost.[111]

On March 15, 2012, Khamenei had the perfect opportunity to declare nuclear weapons un-Islamic. This question was asked of the Supreme Leader on Facebook: "Your Excellency has announced a ban on the use of nuclear weapons, and considering that nuclear weapons are a requirement for deterrence and that the aim of obtaining them is to intimidate the enemies in order to prevent them from acting aggressively, and in light of what is written in Surat Al-Anfal, Verse 60...is it also forbidden to obtain nuclear weapons, as per your ruling that their use is prohibited?"[112] Surat Al-Anfal, Verse 60 is chapter 8, verse 60, of the Qur'an: "Against them make ready your strength to the utmost of your power, including steeds of war, to strike terror into the enemies of Allah and your enemies..." The implication of the question was that it might be permissible to use nuclear weapons to "strike terror into the enemies of Allah."

Khamenei replied, "Your letter has no jurisprudential aspect. When it has a jurisprudent position, then it will be possible to answer it. Summary: No answer was given."[113]

This was an extraordinarily curious answer. If Khamenei had already issued a fatwa saying that the use of nuclear weapons was forbidden—"almost seven years ago," as Ali Akbar Salehi would assert in April 2012, just the next month,[114] why didn't the Ayatollah refer to it in answering this question? If he was firmly opposed to the use of nuclear weapons, even without having issued a formal fatwa, why not say so in this connection instead of declining to answer the question at all?

Meanwhile, Obama was betting the future of the free world on the existence of this fatwa, and making disastrous concessions to Iran on the basis of it. In an interview defending the deal, Secretary of State Kerry said: "An Iran without a nuclear weapon is better to deal with than Iran with a nuclear

JUST WHOSE FATWA IS IT, ANYWAY?

Iranian political analyst Amir Taheri wrote in September 2015 that the principal source for the existence of the fatwa was none other than—Barack Obama: "Those who refer to the fatwa, including some mullahs, always credit Obama as the source of their information."[115]

weapon, and they have decided that they—the ayatollah has decided they're not going to have one anyway."[116]

If Kerry actually believed that, why did he enter into negotiations at all—dismantling the sanctions that had been designed to prevent Iran from developing nuclear weapons? Why did he give up America's only leverage over Iran in exchange for a promise not to do something that he believed the Iranians weren't going to do in the first place? Even as the Obama administration wagered the future of the free world on the existence of this shadowy fatwa that no one had actually seen, Obama's secretary of state acknowledged that the Islamic Revolutionary Guards Corps "still wants" a nuclear weapon "and they are opposed to this agreement."[117] Kerry had placed himself in the peculiar position of believing that there was a fatwa, but that the shock troops of Iran's Islamic Revolution, the IRGC, did not consider themselves to be bound by it.

It is likely that the Iranian talk of the fatwa was *taqiyya*, a religiously sanctioned tactic of deception that is a central element of Shi'ite Muslims' dealings with their adversaries.[118] This is especially likely in light of the fact that the very existence of the Iranian nuclear program was only discovered in 2002.[119] If the nuclear program was wholly dedicated to peaceful purposes, why the secrecy? And as soon as the program was revealed, the

Iranians started trying to reassure the West that it was nothing to worry about. Hence the fatwa that wasn't.

"The changes we seek would require substantial rewriting of the text"

The initial indications were that no one in Iran considered himself bound by the agreement that the U.S. had won at such enormous costs in lost leverage, new funding opened up to terrorists, and tortured mental gymnastics. Khamenei himself displayed distaste for the deal. After having crowed in mid-

TAQIYYA WATCH

"The Iranian nation has never been seeking an atomic weapon and never will be."
—Supreme Leader Khamenei[120]

July that the agreement was "the outcome of the Iranian nation's resistance and bravery and the creativity of dear Iranian scientists" and boasting that the U.S. had been "forced to accept and stand the spinning of thousands of centrifuges and continuation of research and development in Iran," the Supreme Leader did not explicitly express approval of the deal, and several weeks later struck a decidedly different tone.[121] Hossein Shariatmadari, spokesman for Khamenei and editor of the newspaper *Kayhan*, criticized the agreement as threatening "the sacred system of the Islamic Republic of Iran," and said that its implementation would be "disastrous" for Iran.

Shariatmadari noted that Khamenei had said in July, "Whether this text is approved or disapproved, no one will be allowed to harm the main principles of the Islamic system." Shariatmadari explained, "Using the phrase 'whether this text is approved or disapproved' shows his lack of trust in the text of the deal. If His Excellency had a positive view, he would have not insisted on the need for the text to be scrutinized through legal channels.... It leaves no doubt that His Excellency is not satisfied with the text."[122]

Despite the Supreme Leader's misgivings, however, and to the delight of Barack Obama and the international media, on October 13, 2015, news reports announced that the Iranian Parliament (Majlis) had approved the Joint Comprehensive Plan of Action by a 161–59 vote, with thirteen abstentions.[123] Five days later, Barack Obama sent an order to the secretaries of State, Treasury, Commerce and Energy: "I hereby direct you to take all necessary steps to give effect to the US commitments with respect to sanctions described" in the nuclear deal—in other words, to prepare to remove the sanctions.[124]

Secretary of State Kerry reassured doubters, "These waivers will not take effect until Implementation Day, after Iran has completed all necessary nuclear steps, as verified by the International Atomic Energy Agency."[126] Implementation Day was set for December 15, 2015.

But Obama was so confident that Iran would arrive at Implementation Day in full compliance with the agreement that he announced on Adoption Day, October 18, 2015, "Today marks an important milestone toward preventing Iran from obtaining a nuclear weapon and ensuring its nuclear program is exclusively peaceful going forward."[127]

There was just one catch. On October 11, two days before the vote in the Iranian Parliament, Iran analyst Amir Taheri had pointed out a largely unnoticed fact—one that, had it been acknowledged, would have put a considerable damper on Obama's Adoption Day good cheer: "The Iranians have signed nothing and have no plans for doing so. The so-called Joint Comprehensive Plan of Action (JCPOA) has not even been discussed at the Islamic Republic's Council of Ministers. Nor has the Tehran government bothered to even provide an official Persian translation of the 159-page text."[128]

OSTRICH ALERT

"Iran will now begin taking all of the necessary steps outlined in the [deal] to restrain its nuclear program and ensure that it is exclusively peaceful going forward."[125]

—Secretary of State John Kerry

In that case, what was the Majlis voting on? According to Taheri, the Iranian parliament was "examining an unofficial text and is due to express its views at an unspecified date in a document 'running into more than 1,000 pages,' according to Mohsen Zakani, who heads the 'examining committee.'"[129] Zakani said, ominously: "The changes we seek would require substantial rewriting of the text."[130]

Thus when the parliament approved of the nuclear deal on October 13, it wasn't actually approving of the Joint Comprehensive Plan of Action at all. Instead, it was approving a revised version of the deal—one that had been drawn up in Iran with no participation from the United States or any of the other powers that had been part of the negotiations of the JCPOA.[131] This revised version included nine points approved by the Majlis. Point Six, according to Taheri, "forbids inspection of any military site and interviewing any officer, key elements of Obama's Nuke deal."[132]

The Majlis-approved version of the deal also stipulated that Iran would hold its negotiating partners to strict compliance with what they had promised: "The government will monitor any non-performance by the other party [to the agreement] in the matter of failing to lift the sanctions, or restoring the canceled sanctions, or imposing sanctions for any another reason...."[133]

The Middle East Media Research Institute (MEMRI) noted that several provisions of what the Majlis approved actually contradicted stipulations of the JCPOA, particularly provisions of the agreement that allowed for the much-vaunted "snapback" of sanctions if Iran is found to be not complying with the deal. MEMRI concluded, "It follows that the Majlis decision constitutes ratification of a nonexistent document. It was not a ratification of the JCPOA as it stands, but rather of additional demands made by Iran after the JCPOA was agreed upon on July 14, 2015 in Vienna.... Therefore the Majlis' approval is meaningless."[134]

Heedless of or indifferent to this fact, numerous countries began acting as if the agreement had been fully ratified and implemented and it was time to welcome Iran back into the peaceful and harmonious family of nations. Britain removed a long-standing ban on twenty-two Iranian banks. Germany and India sharply increased trade with Iran. Sticking close to the issue at hand, China signed agreements to aid Iran in constructing more nuclear reactors. Russia sold Iran anti-aircraft missile systems.[135]

Rouhani crowed, "The structures of sanctions built over decades is crumbling."[136] All this meant $400 million a month for the Islamic Republic, and a great deal more was on its way.[137] The huge amount of money involved in the sanctions relief, and the desperate state of the Iranian economy, led Khamenei to drop his objections and accept the JCPOA as it had been negotiated in January 2016.[138]

"Iran continues to act as a nuclear weapons outlaw"

But just two months earlier, on November 29, 2015, Admiral Ali Shamkhani, secretary of Iran's Supreme National Security Council (SNSC), which oversees the nuclear deal, warned that Iran would not implement the deal or consider itself bound by it unless all investigations of its past attempts to develop a nuclear weapon were ended. "Without the closure of the file regarding past issues," he declared, "there is no possibility of implementing the JCPOA. The P5+1 must choose between the JCPOA and leaving open the so-called PMD file." Iranian deputy foreign minister Abbas Araghchi echoed Shamkhani's intransigence on this point.[139]

A report published just days later by the watchdog group United Against Nuclear Iran (UANI), which is headed by Mark D. Wallace, former U.S. Ambassador to the United Nations, and former Democratic senator Joseph Lieberman of Connecticut, pointed out that a new IAEA report showed that contrary to all its denials Iran had tried to develop a nuclear bomb—and could be continuing to do so: "The IAEA report is disturbing as it reveals that Iran continues to act as a nuclear weapons outlaw. It exposes that, at minimum, Iran continued nuclear weapons development through 2009. Notably, the IAEA could not describe the extent of Iran's nuclear weapons program after 2009 because Iran failed to answer basic questions and provide requested information.... Iran's intractable refusal to offer transparency regarding its illegal nuclear weapons program is the latest wakeup call regarding the dangerous nature of the Iranian regime."[140]

Amir Taheri concluded, "The Obama deal may end up as the biggest diplomatic scam in recent history."[141] Indeed: it was an already toothless agreement, unilaterally revised by Iran so as to be even more toothless, and then finally agreed to by the Islamic Republic, while Iranian officials continued to issue threats of destruction against Israel and the United States. For a deal that was supposed to be the harbinger of peace in our time, blocking Iran's "every pathway to a nuclear weapon" and demonstrating that "American diplomacy can bring about real and meaningful change," in President Obama's words, it certainly seemed to augur nothing but war.

But no one in the Obama administration seemed particularly concerned. On January 16, 2016, the IAEA certified that Iran was in compliance with the nuclear deal, and the Islamic Republic immediately reaped the rewards. European Union foreign policy official Federica Mogherini declared. "This historic deal is both strong and fair, and it meets the requirements of all," adding that it would "improve regional and international peace, security and stability."[142] Accordingly, she said, "The multinational economic and financial sanctions related to Iran's nuclear program are lifted."[143] Obama signed executive orders lifting the sanctions.[144]

Two days later, MSNBC's Joe Scarborough asked Kerry, "What would you say to our allies in Israel and across the Middle East to let them know that this is actually in their best interest, as well as Iran's best interest in the long run?"[145]

Kerry replied, "Well, they are safer today. The world is safer today. Before we had this agreement, Iran had a completely invisible, unaccountable, unverified nuclear program. They had 19,000 centrifuges. They had enough nuclear material to make 10 to 12 bombs and they were hurtling towards a program that was going to create inevitability of confrontation. Today, that is not true. That is entirely reversed. Not only do we now have verification that is unprecedented, but they have rolled back their program, sent their nuclear material out of the country, destroyed their plutonium reactor, ceased any enrichment activities at their hidden Fordow facility and allowed 130 additional inspectors from the IAEA to come into the country to verify this going forward. So we have gone from a two-month breakout period, Joe, to over-years breakout period now. So they are absolutely safer."[146]

He might have said that the nuclear deal was "symbolic of the desire of our two peoples never to go to war with one another again."

Symbolic, on the other hand, of Iran's determination to remain hostile to the United States, as well as to wring more concessions out of the compliant Obama administration, was the Islamic Republic's March 2016 claim that the U.S. was not holding up its side of the Iran deal, and threat to walk away from the whole thing.[147]

The Islamic Republic Returns to Vienna

The choice of Vienna as the site for the nuclear negotiations was piquant. The last time the Islamic Republic had a significant presence in Vienna was on July 13, 1989, when assassins from the Islamic Republic posing as negotiators murdered the leader of the Kurdistan Democratic Party of Iran, Abdol-Rahman Ghassemlou. The head of the "negotiating team," Mohammad Ja'fari Sahraroudi, was rewarded for the operation with a promotion to leadership of the Quds Force intelligence unit. Coordinating such operations at the time was Iran's Supreme National Security Council, which was headed up in 1989 by Hassan Rouhani, the supposedly "moderate" president of Iran during the negotiations for the nuclear agreement.[148]

A KINDER AND GENTLER IRAN

Clearly the Islamic Republic had become kinder and gentler since 1989, in keeping with Rouhani's widespread reputation as a moderate: unlike in 1989, in 2015, the Iranian delegation didn't pull out guns and shoot John Kerry and the other negotiators.

"This is the Treaty of Hudaybiyya . . . and it will be followed by a 'conquest of Mecca'"

On November 24, 2013, in Geneva, Iran and the U.S. and its allies had concluded a preliminary agreement on Iran's nuclear program that paved the way for the JCPOA. Several weeks later, Iranian political analyst Mohammad Sadeq Al-Hosseini gave a revealing interview that should have given the Western powers pause about going ahead with a nuclear deal with Iran—but didn't.

"Obama," said Hosseini, "had to make a great retreat. He was forced to accept a handshake from President Rouhani, whom he considered a kind of Gorbachev or Sadat, so that the day would not come when he would be forced to kiss the hands of Hassan Nasrallah and Imam Khamenei, so that they would hold their fire in the great war that was prepared to annihilate Israel."[149] Clearly al-Hosseini knew Rouhani wasn't really a Gorbachev or Sadat—that is, a reformer or a peacemaker.

Nor was Hosseini himself: "It has been revealed that our missiles can now very easily reach Tel Aviv. We have weapons that can make Israel go blind."[150]

Hosseini was contemptuous of the notion that the Geneva deal represented a new friendship between the U.S. and Iran: "There is no honeymoon. We are engaged in a fierce war with the Americans on all levels.

This is the Treaty of Hudaybiyya in Geneva, and it will be followed by a 'conquest of Mecca.'"[151] This was most ominous: Muhammad, the prophet of Islam, concluded the Treaty of Hudaybiyya with the pagan Arabs of Mecca at terms disadvantageous to the Muslims, but only to give them time to gather strength. When the Muslim forces were much stronger several years later, he broke the agreement, marched on Mecca, and conquered it.

Hosseini boasted openly about Iran's long-term plan: "The Geneva agreement was achieved due to three things. The first was our strategic patience. Iran has maintained strategic patience for a very long time—10 or 11 years. We have been patient, preparing for the day that comes after those 10 years. We were preparing a large quantity of enriched uranium, so that when it is reduced.... The [Iranians] have raised the level of uranium enrichment far beyond the level they really needed, so that when the level would be lowered, they would emerge victorious."[152]

"When you conduct political negotiations with Iran," said Hosseini, "you lose even when you think you have won."[153] That certainly seemed to be the case a year and a half later, when the nuclear deal was done.

Hosseini had been a political advisor to Moham-

THE AYATOLLAH'S SPIT LIST

"Popular opinion more and more blames the Muslim religion itself for that violence, suggesting that there is something inherent in Islam itself that's responsible for this kind of violence. That equation needs to be challenged, both in the name of truth and in the name of what's best in us as Christians."
—Roman Catholic priest Ronald Rolheiser, writing in the *Tidings*, the official newspaper of the Archdiocese of Los Angeles[154]

"Islam is a religion that prevents men from waging war? I spit upon those foolish souls who make such a claim."
—the Ayatollah Khomeini[155]

mad Khatami, the president of Iran from 1997 to 2005—who was widely respected in the West as a moderate.

"We have our compadres"

The deception was by no means on the Iranian side alone; the Obama administration was doing its fair share of misleading people as well. But the Obama team was not deceiving the Iranians; in selling the Iran deal, it was deceiving the American people. In May 2016, the *New York Times* published an effusive profile of the little-known figure it dubbed "Obama's foreign-policy guru," Ben Rhodes.[156] "Rhodes strategized and ran the successful Iran-deal messaging campaign," according to *Times* reporter David Samuels, whose profile of Rhodes was more revealing than it was intended to be: it showed that Obama, Rhodes, and other administration officials deliberately misled the public about the Iran deal.[157]

Rhodes's assistant Ned Price explained to Samuels how the Obama administration would "shape the news" by reaching out to friendly reporters and columnists: "We have our compadres, I will reach out to a couple people…I'll say, 'Hey, look, some people are spinning this narrative that this is a sign of American weakness,' but—" Samuels, himself a friendly reporter, finished his thought: "In fact it's a sign of strength!" Price went on: "And I'll give them some color, and the next thing I know, lots of these guys are in the dot-com publishing space, and have huge Twitter followings, and they'll be putting this message out on their own."[158]

Nowhere was the media more thoroughly manipulated into presenting weakness as strength than with the Iran nuclear deal. Samuels reveals that "the way in which most Americans have heard the story of the Iran deal presented—that the Obama administration began seriously engaging with Iranian officials in 2013 in order to take advantage of a new political reality in Iran, which came about because of elections that brought moderates to power in that country—was largely manufactured for the purpose for selling the deal. Even where the particulars of that story are true, the implications that readers and viewers are encouraged to take away from those particulars are often misleading or false."[159]

The chief false and misleading aspect of Obama's presentation of the deal to the American public was his claim that he was dealing with moderate elements of Iran's Islamic regime—that, according to Samuels, was a "narrative that Rhodes shaped."[160] Rhodes propagated the falsehood that Iranian President Hassan Rouhani, elected in 2013, was a "moderate" who was struggling against "hard-liners" within the regime. Samuels describes this as "actively misleading," and notes that "the idea that there was a new reality in Iran was politically useful to the Obama administration. By obtaining broad public currency for the thought that there was a significant split in the regime, and that the administration was reaching out to moderate-minded Iranians who wanted peaceful relations with their neighbors and with America, Obama was able to evade what might have otherwise been a divisive but clarifying debate over the actual policy choices that his administration was making."[161]

Samuels heard from no less an authority than former CIA director Leon Panetta that this was all a lie: "I ask him about a crucial component of the administration's public narrative on Iran: whether it was ever a salient feature of the C.I.A.'s analysis when he ran the agency that the Iranian regime was meaningfully divided between 'hard-line' and 'moderate' camps."[162]

Panetta responded: "No. There was not much question that the Quds Force and the supreme leader ran that country with a strong arm, and there was not much question that this kind of opposing view could somehow gain any traction."[163]

The entire Obama case for the Iran deal was based on a lie. Mohammad Sadeq Al-Hosseini, who invoked the deceptive Treaty of Hudaybiyya to describe the Iranians' perspective on the nuclear negotiations with the Americans, would have been impressed.

Chapter Two

"WE WELCOME WAR WITH THE US"
IRAN'S AMBITION TO CONQUER THE WORLD FOR ISLAM

•

On July 28, 2015, two weeks after the JCPOA was finalized, Secretary of State John Kerry appeared before the House Foreign Affairs Committee, where Republican representative Ted Poe of Texas asked him, "It is the policy of the ayatollah—if you can answer for him—that Iran wants to destroy the United States? Is that still their policy, as far as you know?"[1]

Kerry replied, "I don't believe they've said that. I think they've said 'Death to America' in their chants, but I have not seen this specific."[2]

Poe wasn't buying it: "Well, I kind of take that to mean that they want us dead. That would seem like that would be their policy. He said that. That— you don't think that's their policy? I'm not mincing words. Do you think it's their policy to destroy us?"[3]

To that, Kerry responded, "I think they have a policy of opposition to us and of great enmity, but I have no specific knowledge of a plan by Iran to actually destroy us. I do know that the rhetoric is uh, is beyond objectionable. I know that we, you know, are deeply concerned with Iran's behavior in the region, deeply concerned with their past activities. Which is why President Obama felt—"[4]

When Poe interrupted, Kerry interrupted him in turn, saying "If they did want to destroy us, they've got a much better shot of doing it if they had a nuclear weapon."[5]

Aware of how bad Iran's frequent public chanting of "Death to America" made his Iran deal look, Kerry asked the Iranians to stop it. He recounted before the Council on Foreign Relations, "I also told them that their chants of Death to America and so forth are neither helpful, and they're pretty stupid."[6]

The Iranians, however, not only rejected Kerry's request but are ramping up the genocidal rhetoric. On November 2, 2015, a commanding majority of the Majlis, 192 of its 290 members, agreed to this statement: "The martyr-nurturing nation of Iran is not at all prepared to abandon the slogan of 'Death to America' under the pretext of a nuclear agreement."[7]

The assembled parliamentarians also added their support to the assertion that "Death to America," which continued to be chanted at every Friday prayer in Iranian mosques as well as at anti-American protests, had "turned into the symbol of the Islamic Republic and all struggling nations."[8]

Chanting "Death to America" is the "symbol of the Islamic Republic." A communal desire to destroy the United States and commit mass murder of its citizens is the Islamic Republic of Iran's very identity.

"Iran's Islamic Revolution, as part of the new world order, has shaken the foundations of the order imposed by the West"

Speaking about the nuclear deal in July 2015, Israeli Prime Minister Benjamin Netanyahu warned the United States, "We think this is not only a threat to us. We think this is a threat to you as well. Iran has killed more

Americans than anyone other than al Qaeda. They're going to get hundreds of billions of dollars to fuel their terror and military machine." He added, "Iran is different. It's a zealot country. It's killed a lot of Americans. It's killing everybody in sight in the Middle East."[10]

Even as the Islamic State was horrifying the world with its barbarism, Netanyahu saw Iran as the greater threat: "Iran's growing aggression is several times more dangerous than that of IS, which is dangerous enough. And this aggression, which aims to reach every corner of the world, has the ultimate true aim of taking over the world."[11]

That assertion met with widespread derision. The anti-Israel paleocon writer Justin Raimondo quipped: "For a country that's on the way to world conquest, Iran should surely be spending more on the military: their $10 billion defense budget is relatively minuscule."[12] Juan Cole, the American academic and member of the advisory board of NIAC, the Islamic Republic's lobbying group in Washington, ridiculed Netanyahu's claim, calling it "silliness."[13]

TAQIYYA WATCH

Iran's President Hassan Rouhani, true to his worldwide reputation as a "moderate," tried to soften the impact of the ubiquitous "Death to America" chants: "This slogan that is chanted is not a slogan against the American people. Our people respect the American people. But...the policies of the United States have been against the national interests of Iranian people (so) it's understandable that people will demonstrate sensitivity to this issue."[9]

Yet Netanyahu's assertion was not as overstated as Cole and others wanted Americans to believe. Echoing the Israeli prime minister's claim that Iran had global ambitions was Ali Wambold, whose understanding of the aspirations and goals of the Islamic Republic was well founded: "I can claim some understanding of Iran.... My family ruled the country as Shahs of the Qajar Dynasty between 1785 and 1925, and again under a democratically-elected prime minister, Mohammad Mossadegh, between 1951 and 1953. I witnessed Ayatollah Khomeini consolidate his

THEIR MONEY IS AS GREEN AS ANYONE ELSE'S

Despite the Islamic Republic's relentless hostility toward the United States, and clear evidence establishing the National Iranian American Council (NIAC) as a front group for the mullahs, in February 2016 presidential candidate Hillary Clinton attended a fundraiser that was hosted by, among others, NIAC board member Lily Sarafan, along with Noosheen Hashemi, a member of Ploughshares, another Iranian advocacy group.[14] Did their money buy influence over the Democratic Party front runner? Neither side was saying.

power in the summer of 1979."[15] (The Qajars did not return to rule Iran during Mossadegh's tenure as Prime Minister; he was referring to his family's role in the ruling group at that time, while Mohammed Reza Pahlavi reigned as the Shah of the Pahlavi dynasty.)

Wambold pointed out that the Constitution of the Islamic Republic "proclaims 'the ideological mission of jihad,' which it defines as 'extending the sovereignty of God's law throughout the world,' through Iran's Army and the Islamic Revolutionary Guards Corps." Thus, he said, "to treat with the Islamic Republic over the particulars of its weaponry while failing to address the very purpose of its bellicosity is delusional. The so-called Joint Comprehensive Plan of Action does nothing to change the fact that, in plain Farsi, Iran is committed to world conquest by Islam, with its clerics as warlords. Those to be conquered include America (the 'Great Satan'), Israel (the 'Little Satan') and the Sunni-led Gulf States."[16]

Back in July 2005, then–Iranian President Mahmoud Ahmadinejad had said essentially the same thing: "The message of the Revolution is global, and is not restricted to a specific place or time. Have no doubt…Allah willing, Islam will conquer what? It will conquer all the mountain tops of the world."[17]

Was this just a pious hope for the success of Islamic proselytizing? Hardly, given Ahmadinejad's reference to the Islamic Revolution, the violent movement that had brought the Islamic Republic of Iran into being in 1979. Khamenei declared in November 2015 that Iran's foreign policy was "based on Islam and stems from the aspirations and goals of the Revolution."[18] No less an authority than the Ayatollah Khomeini had said from the beginning that the goals of that Revolution were global: "We shall export our revolution to the whole world. Until the cry 'There is no god but Allah' resounds over the whole world, there will be struggle."[19] And the Iranian politician Mohsen Rezaei once told a cheering Iranian crowd: "We will build a force that will demolish the enemies of Islam, continue the path of our great prophet Muhammad, and raise the flag of Islam in all corners of the world."[20]

A neon sign in Tehran's Mehrabad International Airport reads, in English, "In future Islam will destroy Satanic sovereignty of the West."[21] Iran's commitment to world conquest in the name of Islam—and to the defeat of America in particular—precludes lasting peace with the United States.

According to IRGC deputy commander Hossein Salami on February 1, 2014, Israel and the U.S. can be defeated—if only Muslim unity can be achieved: "This region is ideologically united by similar faiths and common goals. If these goals can be merged, and the Muslim peoples are ideologically, strategically, and politically united, then Western, and particularly American, political breathing space will be restricted. Even the Zionist regime, which is America's political, military, economic, and security bridgehead, will have no air to breathe."[22] Salami also issued this threat: "Whoever seeks to talk to our nation in intimidating language—we will not be deterred by geographic borders from endangering their interests. Wherever they may be—we will be there as well. We will not confine the conflict to any border. We announce this loud and clear."[23]

Apparently even the lack of unity in the Muslim world is the fault of America and Israel. A month after the conclusion of the nuclear agreement,

MY WAY OR THE HIGHWAY

"There are only two things that would end enmity between us and the US. Either the US president and EU leaders should convert to Islam and imitate the Supreme Leader, or Iran should abandon Islam and the Islamic revolution. If they are not going to turn Muslim, we are not going to abandon Islam or the revolution either. But I do not know why some people believe that some day we will make peace with the US and start relations with them."

—Iran's Brigadier General Qolamhossein Qeib-parvar of the
Islamic Revolutionary Guard Corps (IRGC)[24]

Supreme Leader Khamenei accused the United States and Israel of trying to prevent Muslim unity from being achieved. They were conspiring, he said, "against the [Qur'an] and not Shiism and Iran, because they know that the [Qur'an] and Islam are the center of awakening nations." The "Death to America" and "Death to Israel" chants were popular among Iranians, he said, because they "realized that their real stubborn enemy is the world arrogance of Zionism."[25] Khamenei claimed that "the world bullies are fully, seriously seeking to stir violence and discord under the name of Islam and are trying to disrepute the religion of Islam, foment internal fights among Islamic nations and even among the people of one nation to weaken the Muslim Ummah [the worldwide Islamic community]." Speaking to Iranian officials in charge of the Hajj, the annual pilgrimage to Mecca, Khamenei offered to strike back against these attempts to divide Muslims by "transferring the Iranian nation's experience about unity and recognition of the enemy to other nations in the Hajj season," which, he said, "can defuse these plots."[26]

The next month, he wrote, "In these days, the evil policy of America in this region is causing war and bloodshed, destruction, displacement, poverty, backwardness, and religious and sectarian division.... The plots of the global tyranny [the U.S.] in this matter must be identified, and ways to resolve [this matter] must be considered. The nations must demand this of their governments, and the governments must be true to their responsibilities..."[27]

Other Iranian officials have also expressed the notion that their nation is uniquely equipped to bring about the unity among Muslims that will be needed in order to fight America's "global tyranny"— despite the fact that Iran adheres to the minority Shi'ite sect of Islam, to which only ten to fifteen percent of Muslims worldwide belong. That idea follows from the Iranians' vision of their revolution as the vanguard of a world-conquering Islamic jihad. Back in June 2011, the chief of staff of Iran's Armed Forces, Major General Hassan Firouzabadi, expatiated on what it means that Iran's foreign policy stems from these jihadist aspirations: "According to the Supreme Leader," he said, "the Islamic Revolution has given us the culture of jihad as a gift and now jihadists should grant it to other nations."[29]

This "gift" would mean the destruction of the existing world political order and its replacement with a new, Islamic one. In a Friday sermon in September 2014, senior Iranian cleric Hujjat al-Islam Sayyed Mohammad Sa'idi declared that Iran's Islamic Revolution heralded a "new world order": "Iran's Islamic Revolution, as part of the new world order, has shaken the foundations of the order imposed by the West on Muslim nations. This success is due to the efforts and guidance of the late Imam Khomeini and those of Ayatollah Khamenei."

WHAT A DEAL!

On September 23, 2015, two months after the JCPOA was finalized, Supreme Leader Khamenei published an article entitled "The Idols Will Be Shattered," illustrated with a drawing of the Statue of Liberty shattered in pieces. In it he declared, "The idol of the soul, the idol of pride, [and] the idol of sexual lust; the idol of tyranny and subservience; the idol of global tyranny [that is, the U.S.]; the idol of sloth and irresponsibility; and the other idols that shame the precious human soul—a plan that will spring forth from the depths of the heart will shatter them."[28]

According to Iran's state-run Ahlul Bayt News Agency, "the Qom Friday Prayer leader stressed that the custodians of the old order, with slogans such as freedom, democracy and human rights has attracted some people but that for a long time, Westerners and Americans have based their slogans on deceptive rhetoric. They seek to dominate the intellectual and moral values of the world. However, they have suffered a disadvantage because their slogans have faded and people have found them to be false.[30]

Freedom, democracy, and human rights were on their way out. Islam was coming in to replace them, courtesy of the Islamic Republic of Iran.

"The military option that the westerners speak of constantly is ridiculous"

And some Iranian officials seemed determined that human rights and these other Western aspirations would be forced from the scene in a bloody confrontation with the United States. They actively looked forward to war to with America—and were utterly unfazed by the rather hollow threats of military action that were meant to be the ultimate guarantee of Iran's compliance with the nuclear deal.

In July 2015, after having made so many disastrous concessions and claimed, counterfactually, that "Iran has proved that it is willing to change its priorities and its strategy," Barack Obama asserted that if Iran did not abide by its commitments, the U.S. could still strike the Iranians militarily: "We have sent a clear message to the Iranians—though we closed the deal, we still have not closed account. I hope that solutions will be reached diplomatically, but if necessary, there is also a military option."[31]

The Iranians were more than ready for that eventuality. In January 2014, the Chief Commander of the Islamic Revolution Guards Corps, Major General Mohammad Ali Jafari, had boasted that "Islam's leaders have long ago prepared us for a great and decisive confrontation.... The sun of America's imperialist civilization is nearing its setting." He claimed that "the US will never understand the Islamic Republic of Iran's offensive scope." Offensive, not defensive.[32]

Iranian officials have repeatedly sneered at the threat of military action by the U.S. In May 2015, Islamic Revolutionary Guards Corps commander Major General Mohammad Ali Jafari boasted, "Today, the Islamic Republic of Iran's pride and might has made the world's biggest materialistic and military powers kneel down before the Islamic Republic's might. The military option that the westerners speak of constantly is ridiculous and they know that if the military option could have produced any result, they would have already used it many times, and today they have shifted their focus to other types of threats."[33]

The following month, Islamic Revolutionary Guard Corps Brigadier General Mohammad Ali Asoudi taunted the American president for his weakness: "We should thank Obama for refreshing us by referring to his 'options on the table', including the military one; we just relax and laugh at such ridiculous words."[34]

In any case, a military confrontation with America would just be the next phase of the endless war with the U.S. that the Iranians consider themselves to be involved in already. As Supreme Leader Khamenei declared in June 2014, "Battle and jihad are endless because evil and its front continue to exist…. This battle will only end when the society can get rid of the oppressors' front with America at the head of it, which has expanded its claws on human mind, body and thought…. This requires a difficult and lengthy struggle and need for great strides."[35]

"We welcome war with the US"

On February 11, 2014, Revolution Day, the thirty-fifth anniversary of the Islamic Revolution, Khamenei praised the 1979 seizure of the U.S. Embassy in Tehran as "an even greater revolution than the first one," that is, than the ouster of the Shah and beginning of the Islamic Republic. Defense Minister

Hossein Dehghan said, "The Defense Ministry is working to ensure that the Iranian people are armed and ready to confront any enemy threat. Yesterday's successful test of Iranian-made ballistic missiles was also a crushing response to the nonsense of the American officials who frequently threaten Iran. It is a clear answer to their military option. The Defense Ministry and the Iranian nation are always ready, and Iran will welcome it if the Americans again put themselves to the test and face the consequences. The Americans will again be defeated, just as they were in the Iran-Iraq war. If they implement their nonsense, the Iranian nation will hand them a crushing defeat."[36]

This saber-rattling was a common refrain among Iranian officials. Chief of Staff Hassan Firouzabadi boasted, "Iran is prepared for the decisive war against the U.S. and the Zionist regime.... Iran has been making plans, conducting maneuvers, and preparing its forces for this battle for years now."[37]

Islamic Revolutionary Guards Corps Navy Commander Rear Admiral Ali Fadavi said that he was confident of victory against the United States because the Iranians would be fighting for Allah and Islam: "The Americans can spot swift boats, sea mines, and anti-ship missiles but they cannot grasp axioms such as... 'God, the Islamic Revolution, and the Supreme Leader.' On the chest of the IRGC is the [Qur'an] verse that clearly says that the use of measures against the infidels and the enemies must be promoted. The Americans notice only some of our capabilities; only on the battlefield will they fully internalize the bulk of our capabilities. The Americans will know [Iran's true power] when their warships, with over 5,000 aboard, sink during a confrontation with Iran, and when they have to search the depths of the sea for their bodies."[38]

Such threats weren't limited to Revolution Day. In a Friday sermon on February 21, 2014, Ayatollah Ahmad Jannati, the head of Iran's influential twelve-member Council of Guardians, preached, "The Imam Khomeini said that the U.S. is the Great Satan, and we expect the officials" of the Iranian government "to recognize the enemy. The U.S. is the Great Satan, yesterday and today.... While the enemy carries out ugly actions and says evil things, the Iranian nation has shown fervor and, with its enthusiastic turnout [for the February 11 Revolution Day celebrations a week and a half before], made it known that will not tolerate humiliation."[39]

Jannati thundered, "The first option on our table is 'Death to America.' The entire people's slogan is 'Death to America'.... Another option on our table is the defense of Palestine; other messages from the Iranian people to their officials are not to fear the enemy and not to fear death." The Americans, he added, "already want us to capitulate on the nuclear issue—but on what basis are they interfering in Iran's affairs? If we let them, the Americans will destroy Islam and the Revolution, because they have no honor and no humanity.... See how they left the helpless people of Iraq. They carry out massacres in Palestine, and support takfiris who slaughter people."[40] (*Takfir* is the practice of declaring a Muslim who is considered to hold a heretical form of Islam to be a non-believer. Shi'ites often refer to Sunni jihadis as *takfiris*, because the Sunnis do not regard Shi'ites as true Muslims.)

In May 2014, senior Iranian commander Massoud Jazayeri warned that if the U.S. attacked Iran, the results would be not only "the annihilation of the Israeli regime" but war in the U.S. itself. The Americans, Jazayeri said, "know that aggression against the Islamic Republic of Iran would mean annihilation of Tel Aviv and spread of war into the United States."[41]

In an interview the same month, Rear Admiral Fadavi said, "Today the Americans and the entire world know that one of our operational goals is destroying US Navy Forces."[42] One specific target would be aircraft carriers, since they "provide US airpower in combat; therefore it is natural that we want to sink them...destroying, annihilating, and sinking US boats has and will be in our plans."[43] According to the American Enterprise Institute's Iran Tracker, "Fadavi claimed that IRGC speed boats can travel at a top speed of 40 knots, while US vessels are stuck at 31 knots. He added that Iran planned to increase its boats' speed to 80 knots, which he said was three times the speed of US destroyers."[44] Then in September 2014, Fadavi asserted that Iran already had hegemony in the Persian Gulf: "The US is obedient and passive in the Persian Gulf and we impose our sovereignty right in the Persian Gulf very powerfully.... We observe confrontations and, as a matter of fact, debates between Iran and the foreign vessels in the Persian Gulf and the Strait of Hormuz on a daily basis and they always comply."[45]

In February 2015, the Islamic Revolutionary Guards Corps conducted a drill dubbed "Great Prophet 9," in which Iranian forces destroyed a replica of an American aircraft carrier. IRGC commander Jafari said that the drill was intended to be a "message of (Iran's) might" to "extraterritorial powers."[46] Iranian TV coverage of the drill focused on a banner that read, "If the Americans are ready to be buried at the bottom of the waters of the Persian Gulf—so be it," a quotation from the father of the Islamic Republic, the Ayatollah Khomeini.[47]

During this drill the IRGC tested what it called a "new strategic weapon" that it said would be an important part of the coming war with the United States. Said Admiral Fadavi, "The new weapon will have a very decisive role in adding our naval power in confronting threats, particular by the Great Satan, the United States."[48] He refused to describe the weapon further.

In May 2015, the IRGC's Salami said that Iran wanted war with the United States: "We have prepared ourselves for the most dangerous scenarios and this is no big deal and is simple to digest for US; we welcome war with the US as we do believe that it will be the scene for our success to display the real potentials of our power."[49]

"It cannot even attack Iranian facilities without the White House being destroyed in under 10 minutes"

On June 17, 2015, the Iranian newspaper *Kayhan*, which is controlled by Khamenei, published an extraordinary editorial. It began routinely enough, expatiating upon the glories of Ramadan, the Muslim month of fasting and rededication of the believer to Allah. It hailed Ali, the founding figure of Shi'ite Islam, as the one who "destroys the gates of Khaybar to annihilate the foundations of idolatry."[50] According to Islamic tradition, at the Khaybar oasis in Arabia, the Islamic prophet Muhammad carried out a surprise attack against the Jews who lived there, massacring many and exiling the survivors. Lauding some Iranians who had been killed in the Iran-Iraq war, the editorial said that "they knew that war is war, and that dying in the path of God is one kind of victory. They convey to us that it is better to die, even with bound hands, than to be humiliated, and that it is inconceivable for us to submit to Satan."[51] This was a hint that the Iranian leadership was preparing to defy the United States—the "Great Satan"—even to the point of provoking an attack that they knew would rain destruction down upon Iran.

But the editorial promised the ultimate victory to Iran, proclaiming: "Iran is now in the era of Badr and Khaybar."[52] At Badr, according to Islamic tradition, the Muslims won a decisive victory over a vastly larger and better-armed force of the pagan Quraysh, the Arabs of Mecca. The Qur'an attributes this victory to divine intervention: "And already had Allah given you victory at Badr while you were few in number. Then fear Allah; perhaps you will be grateful. When you said to the believers, 'Is it not sufficient for you that your Lord should reinforce you with three thousand angels sent down?' Yes, if you remain patient and conscious of Allah and the enemy come upon you in rage, your Lord will reinforce you with five thousand angels having marks" (3:123–125).

An Iranian victory over the United States today would likewise be a matter of faith: "Let us have faith that America is incapable of any misstep, and that it cannot even attack Iranian facilities without the White House being destroyed in under 10 minutes."[53]

How could the White House be destroyed in under ten minutes by Iran unless Iran had nuclear weapons?

"Let us have faith that the old 'village leader' has fallen onto his deathbed, and that even in his youth, he never made the mistake, and that he, like Israel, remains mired in quicksand."[54] The "old 'village leader'" was the U.S., and the mistake it had never made was launching a military attack against Iran. "Let us have faith that Britain is a wily fox, and that its laughter is deceptive. Let us have faith in the Koran that says that the enemies are not men of their word, and that God has not permitted the infidels to gain supremacy over the believers."[55]

Addressing the martyrs of the Iran-Iraq War, the editorial proclaimed the imminent redemption of the world, and of Islam itself, from the baneful influence of the U.S. and Israel:

> Brothers, your jihad is blessed, and your lot is Paradise. You, who sat with God during the month of God's Prophet and the month of God, will understand us and honor us—not by means of bread but by means of the redemption of the world that is mired in deception, and by means of redeeming Islam, which is entangled by the Jews' deception and by the trickery of the American "Great Satan" and old fox [Britain].... Our hands are not closed before Satan, but are full, and we believe that just as the hands of God never remained closed, the straight path [that is, Islam] will also never reach a dead end.[56]

"We will chase them even to the Gulf of Mexico"

IRGC deputy commander Salami amplified these threats in September 2015, saying of U.S. forces that "we monitor their acts day and night and will take every opportunity to set fire to all their economic and political interests if they do a wrong deed." If the U.S. and Israel move against Iran, he said, the Iranians will "cut off enemies' hands and fingers [and] will then send its dust to the air.... Today the US knows that the slightest move against the Islamic Iran will ruin its house of dream."[57]

Regarding the claim by Obama administration officials that "all military options are still on the table," Salami sneered: "The Americans have always resorted to bullying because they lack diplomatic skills."[58]

The lieutenant commander of the Islamic Revolution Guards Corps, Navy General Alireza Tangsiri, sounded an even more bellicose note in October 2015, issuing this warning to the United States: "I declare now that if the enemy wants to spark a war against Iran, we will chase them even to the Gulf of Mexico and we will do it." This war would involve jihad-martyrdom suicide attacks: the Americans, Tangsiri said, "have tested us once and if necessary, there are people who will blow up themselves with ammunitions to destroy the US warships."[59]

Brigadier General Amir Ali Hajizadeh, the Commander of the IRGC's Aerospace Force, claimed that American military bases in the Middle East could all be reached by Iranian missiles: "Some of the threats by the US are aimed at appeasing the Zionists, while others are for the purpose of domestic consumption, but what is important is that they are aware of and acknowledge our capabilities and deterrence power; we do not feel any need to increase the range of our missiles and targets are fully within the range of our missiles."[60]

Iran backed up these threats with harassment of U.S. ships in the Persian Gulf. In September 2015, a Pentagon official admitted laconically that "U.S.

Naval forces are routinely approached by Iranian warships and aircraft as they operate in the region, with the majority of all interaction by the Iranians conducted in a safe and professional manner." The majority! "This happens," the official added, "on a near daily basis." He explained, "The Iranians' primary purpose for approaching U.S. forces is for ISR [Intelligence, Surveillance, and Reconnaissance] so these interactions are almost always characterized by the presence of Iranian photographers capturing photos and video. During these interactions we, too, capture imagery for the record. Safe, professional, and routine interactions are of no concern, and we are fully confident in the ability of U.S. Naval forces to defend themselves. We also publicly acknowledge those interactions with the Iranians which we consider to be unsafe."[61]

In light of Iran's aggressive rhetoric, the official's bland assurance that "we also publicly acknowledge those interactions with the Iranians which we consider to be unsafe" made him sound like a pious schoolmarm dealing with Al Capone.

In January 2016, just as the IAEA was about to certify Iran's compliance with the nuclear deal, paving the way for the lifting of U.S. and European Union sanctions, Iran seized two U.S. Navy boats and briefly held ten American sailors hostage. U.S. officials struggled to put the best possible spin on the events. Obama White House spokesman Josh Earnest said the hostage-taking illustrated why the nuclear deal was so urgently needed: "We continue to be concerned about this situation. That precisely is why the president made preventing Iran from obtaining a nuclear weapon a top national security priority, and we're making progress in actually accomplishing that goal."[62]

After the sailors were released, Vice President Joe Biden dismissed the entire episode as a routine incident involving mechanical difficulties. Denying that the U.S. had apologized to Iran over the incident, as had been widely rumored, Biden said, "When you have a problem with the boat, (do) you apologize the boat had a problem? No. And there was no looking for any apology. This was just standard nautical practice." In fact the American sailors were blindfolded, made to kneel at gunpoint, and interrogated for hours."[63]

Defense Secretary Ash Carter sounded a similar note, thanking Secretary of State John Kerry "for his diplomatic engagement with Iran to secure our sailors' swift return. Around the world, the U.S. Navy routinely provides assistance to foreign sailors in distress, and we appreciate the timely way in which this situation was resolved."[65]

Kerry expressed gratitude toward the Iranians: "All indications suggest or tell us that our sailors were well taken care of, provided with blankets and food and assisted with their return to the fleet earlier today."[66] He ascribed the Iranians' swift release of the sailors to communications channels that had been opened during the nuclear negotiations: "I think we can all imagine how a similar situation might have played out three or four years ago, and in fact it is clear that today this kind of issue was able to be peacefully resolved and officially resolved, and that is a testament to the critical role that diplomacy plays in keeping our country safe, secure and strong."[67] Kerry thanked the Iranians for their "cooperation and quick response."

That was that; it was another triumph of diplomacy: "These are situations which, as everybody here knows, have the ability, if not properly guided, to get out of control."[68]

Iranian officials were equally pleased with the incident, which they described very differently.

Deputy commander of Iran's Islamic Revolutionary Guard Corps Hossein Salami boasted that "since the end of the Second World War, no country has been

OSTRICH ALERT

"The Iranians picked up both boats—as we have picked up Iranian boats that needed to be rescued.... [The Iranians] realized [the American sailors] were there in distress and said they would release them, and released them—like ordinary nations would do."

—Vice President Joe Biden[64]

able to arrest American military personnel"—until the Iranians captured these ten sailors. He crowed that the "American sailors started crying after arrest, but the kindness of our Guard made them feel calm."[69]

"I saw the weakness, cowardice, and fear of American soldiers myself. Despite having all of the weapons and equipment, they surrendered themselves with the first action of the guardians of Islam," IRGC commander Ahmad Dolabi exulted. "American forces receive the best training and have the most advanced weapons in the world. But they did not have the power to confront the Guard due to weakness of faith and belief."[70]

The head of Iran's armed forces, Major General Hassan Firouzabadi, declared, "This incident in the Persian Gulf, which probably will not be the American forces' last mistake in the region, should be a lesson to trouble-makers in the U.S. Congress."[71]

It looked like a cage match between Darth Vader and Mister Rogers. The contrast between the bellicose Iranian statements and the Americans' attempts to sweep the whole incident under the rug couldn't have been more stark. Kerry did acknowledge that when he saw the footage that the Iranians released of the sailors kneeling at gunpoint, his first thought was not con-ciliatory: "I was very angry. I was very, very frustrated and angry that that was released. I raised it immediately with the Iranians. It was not put out by the Ministry of Foreign Affairs or the government directly, it was put out I think by the military over there, the (Revolutionary Guard), who is opposed to what we are doing."[72]

But Kerry didn't produce any evidence that the Iranian government was opposed to what the military was doing. Nor did he explain how the military could have attained such independence of action in what is, by all accounts, an authoritarian regime. And on January 24, 2016, Iran's political leadership joined in the taunting of the U.S. over the incident, with Supreme Leader Khamenei tweeting photos of the American sailors kneeling and with their hands behind their heads, along with pictures of himself congratulating the

Islamic Revolutionary Guards Corps forces who had seized the Navy boats. He included also some of his words to the IRGC men: "What you did was very great, interesting and timely and it was in fact God's deed that took Americans to our waters so that through your timely job they raised their hands over their heads and were arrested."[73] That didn't sound as if the Iranian government was opposed in the slightest degree to what the military was doing.

The Iranian government gave those who seized the Navy boats the Fath (Victory) medal, an honor bestowed on war heroes.[74] During celebrations of the thirty-seventh anniversary of the Islamic Revolution on February 11, 2016, actors playing the captured sailors were paraded in chains through the streets of Tehran. To portray the Americans, the Iranians chose fat young men, one of them who repeatedly dabbed at his eyes with a handkerchief, and a young woman (or possibly a young man made to appear as a woman) wearing heavy makeup—thereby sending the signal that the U.S. was flabby, weak, immoral, and ripe for the taking.[75] The following month, the Islamic Republic announced its intention to build a statue commemorating their capture of the sailors.[76]

During those celebrations, General Yahya Rahim Safavi, advisor to Iranian Supreme Leader Ali Khamenei, reiterated Iran's unremitting hostility to the United States: "America is the Iranian nation's No. 1 enemy. America's hands are drenched in the blood of the martyrs of the Iranian, Iraqi, Syrian, and Palestinian nations. Some try to depict the enemy as a friend, and are unaware of the deceptions and plots of the arrogance [i.e. the U.S.] against the Iranian nation, as well as the plans of the enemies."[77]

He boasted that "the Islamic Revolution brought about the collapse of this bipolar regime of world power [i.e. of the U.S. and the Soviet Union]. Now, the world's power centers are splitting, and, with God's help, Islam's might will be revealed in this century. The liberal-democratic Western culture, and the Western capitalist economy, do not promote humanity's salvation from poverty, injustice, and warmongering."[78] The solution? Islam:

> The [Islamic] Revolution has championed a message of salvation to the nations of the world, by inspiring an atmosphere of hope and enthusiasm among them. [This message] has crossed geographic [borders] and taught the Islamic nations—Palestine, Iraq, and Yemen—the path of hostility towards the arrogance [i.e. the U.S.], of demanding justice, and of attaining liberty and independence.[79]

Safavi accused the U.S. and Israel of creating the jihad terror threat: "Over the past 50 years, America, the Zionist regime, and some of those that depend on America such as the Al-Saud and Turkish regimes, have dispatched tens of thousands of takfiri terrorist soldiers and launched proxy wars."[80] ("Takfiris" are those who declare that other Muslims are not Muslim and can lawfully be killed; it is a favorite term for Sunni jihadis among Shi'ites.) They did this, he claimed, in order to ensure "peace and security for the Zionist regime as well as the destruction of the infrastructures of the Islamic nations, with the aim of turning them into burned-out, backwards countries."[81] However, things were looking up: "The Iran-Russia-Syria-Hizbullah Lebanon coalition is on the verge of victory. America must know that Iran is determining the fate of the region in favor of the Islamic resistance. Iran has become the strongest country in western Asia."[82]

"Iran's role in Iraq is very destructive"

All this was not just incendiary rhetoric. A remarkable Jerusalem Center for Public Affairs report published in March 2015 laid bare the full extent of Iran's global adventurism, showing that it had been going on for years. In line with its self-image as a rival of the U.S. that will eventually supplant it in global influence, Iran has been waging war by various means against the United States since the beginning of the Islamic Republic. By 2007, according to a report of the Institute for the Study of War, Iran was actively aiding the enemies of the U.S. forces in Iraq: "Iran, and its Lebanese proxy Hezbollah, have been actively involved in supporting Shia militias and encouraging sectarian violence in Iraq since the invasion of 2003— and Iranian planning and preparation for that effort began as early as 2002."[83]

In September 2007, General David Petraeus, at that time the commander of Multinational Force Iraq, said, "When we captured the leaders of these so-called special groups...and the deputy commander of a Lebanese Hezbollah department that was created to support their efforts in Iraq, we've learned a great deal about how Iran has, in fact, supported these elements and how those elements have carried out violent acts against our forces, Iraqi forces and innocent civilians." Petraeus concluded, "So Iran's role in Iraq is very destructive."[84]

The U.S. ambassador to Iraq, Ryan C. Crocker, acknowledged that "Iran's role" in Iraq was "harmful." He explained, "They are supporting radical militias. They are supplying the explosively formed projectiles that target our troops as well as Iraqis. And they are playing a destabilizing role."[85] But Crocker remained optimistic, saying that he had had several productive meetings with the Iranian ambassador to Iraq. In a statement quite similar to many that American officials would make at the time of the nuclear deal that was still several years down the road, Crocker said, "We've laid out very clearly what our concerns are and said that what they need to do is align practice on the ground with their stated policy of support for a stable, democratic Iraq. I think you see a collision in Iran between their long-term strategic interests and their narrow tactical desires."[86]

Unfortunately, Iran's "narrow tactical desires" continued to win out—or perhaps their "long-term strategic interests" were not quite what Crocker thought they were, given the Iranians' commitment to world conquest in the name of Islam. So effective was the Iranian proxy war against the United States in Iraq that in August 2010, James F. Jeffrey, the new American ambassador to Iraq, said, "Up to a quarter of the American casualties and some of the more horrific

PROXY WAR IN IRAQ

• • •

"Iran has consistently supplied weapons, its own advisors, and Lebanese Hezbollah advisors to multiple resistance groups in Iraq, both Sunni and Shia, and has supported these groups as they have targeted Sunni Arabs, Coalition forces, Iraqi Security Forces, and the Iraqi Government itself. Their influence runs from Kurdistan to Basrah, and Coalition sources report that by August 2007, Iranian-backed insurgents accounted for roughly half the attacks on Coalition forces...."

—the Jerusalem Center for Public Affairs[88]

incidents in which Americans were kidnapped...can be traced without doubt to these Iranian groups."[87]

"Iran's Qods Force provided training to the Taliban in Afghanistan on small unit tactics, small arms, explosives, and indirect fire weapons"

Supplying their fellow Shi'ites in Iraq with training and weaponry in their jihad against the Americans was not all that surprising. But Iran has waged proxy war against the United States in Afghanistan as well. In April 2007, American forces in Afghanistan discovered that supplies of Iran-made weapons had been delivered to the Taliban—a discovery that, according to one State Department official, "sent shock waves through the system."[89] In January 2008, William Wood, the American ambassador to Afghanistan declared, "There is no question that elements of insurgency have received weapons from Iran."[90] Tayeb Jawad, the American-backed Afghan regime's ambassador to the United States, remarked, "Iran has become a more and more hostile power."[91]

And since the early days of the Islamic Republic, Iran has not hesitated to take its war into the United States itself.

"In Islamic religious terms, taking a life is sometimes sanctioned and even highly praised, and I thought that event was just such a time"

Not long after the Islamic Republic was founded, one of its operatives struck against one of its enemies right in the heart of the Great Satan itself.

David Belfield was an American who had converted to Islam and taken the name Dawud Salahuddin. He was, by his own account, an angry young man: "I was primed for violence, and I thought about cratering the White House a quarter century before Al Qaeda did. It would be accurate to say that my biggest aspiration was to bring America to its knees, but I didn't know how."[93]

He found a way: working for the Islamic Republic. On July 22, 1980, he had a job as a security guard at the Iranian Interest Section of the Algerian Embassy in Washington, D.C., which handled Iranian affairs in Washington after the severing of diplomatic relations between the U.S. and Iran as a result of the hostage crisis. That day, Salahuddin disguised himself as a postal worker and went to the Maryland home of Ali Akbar Tabatabai, who had served as a press attaché at the Iranian Embassy in Washington under the Shah's government and was now an outspoken dissident who had founded the Iran Freedom Foundation, an organization that opposed the Islamic regime.

... AND IN AFGHANISTAN

"Iran's Qods Force provided training to the Taliban in Afghanistan on small unit tactics, small arms, explosives, and indirect fire weapons. Since at least 2006, Iran has arranged arms shipments to select Taliban members, including small arms and associated ammunition, rocket-propelled grenades, mortar rounds, 107mm rockets, and plastic explosives."

—U.S. State Department's 2009 *Country Reports on Terrorism*[92]

Salahuddin shot Tabatabai dead in what the police report termed a "political assassination" provoked by the fact that Tabatabai had been "founder of an organization whose goal was the overthrow of the present regime in Iran."[94]

Salahuddin later said that he had been recruited to murder Tabatabai by "someone in Washington...passing along instructions" from Tehran, and been paid $5,000. He had wanted to kill Henry Kissinger and Kermit Roosevelt, the CIA operative who helped the Shah regain power in Iran in 1953, but the Iranians insisted on Tabatabai instead. Montgomery County,

Maryland, prosecutor Douglas Gansler commented in 2002, "The Iranians came here to recruit homegrown terrorists, and they found one in Salahuddin." Salahuddin also recounted that he was encouraged at the time to do everything he could to aid the Khomeini regime by his friend and mentor Said Ramadan, son of the founder of the Muslim Brotherhood, Hasan al-Banna, and father of the renowned Islamic "reformer" Tariq Ramadan.[95]

Salahuddin, who fled to Iran after the assassination and has lived there since, openly admits that he killed Tabatabai and shows no remorse: "I shot him. It was an act of war. In Islamic religious terms, taking a life is sometimes sanctioned and even highly praised, and I thought that event was just such a time." The Iranians tried to get him to find other times as well: Salahuddin has said that agents of the Islamic Republic tried to convince him to hijack planes, but he refused: "There is something about being trapped inside of something that I would not give in to."[96]

That would be left to al-Qaeda.[97] But the Iranians may have made use of Salahuddin's unorthodox talents at least one more time: on March 9, 2007, Salahuddin met with FBI and CIA agent Robert Levinson on the Iranian resort island of Kish shortly before Levinson vanished. Salahuddin, however, has vehemently denied any involvement in Levinson's disappearance.[98] Levinson was not part of a prisoner exchange that followed the lifting of sanctions on Iran in January 2016; he remains in Iranian custody.

"He's like a colonel, the guy. . . . He's got the government behind him"

Dawud Salahuddin is not the only killer the Iranians have employed inside the United States. Manssor Arbabsiar was a used car salesman in Corpus Christi, Texas, with dual Iranian and American citizenship. He was a well-known figure in the community for a quarter of a century. Corpus Christi locals knew him as "Jack"; his close friends, on the other hand, called him "Scarface," after he got in a knife fight over a woman back when he was a hot-blooded young man.

He seemed to have calmed down, to the extent that when he was arrested in September 2011 for trying to hire hit men to murder the Saudi ambassador to the United States, his longtime friend Mitchell Hamauei was "very shocked to see what happened, you know. That's out of character for him and he's a businessman. Maybe he thought it was a joke. I don't know. I just don't know what's going on in his mind."[99]

It was no joke. Apparently "Scarface" had remained hot-blooded, but was channeling his passions in a different direction. He had tried to hire what he thought were assassins from a Mexican drug cartel to kill the ambassador in exchange for $1.5 million. The plot revolved around bombing a restaurant; when Arbabsiar was told that this would result in many more dead than just the Saudi ambassador, he replied, "No problem. No big deal."[100]

Arbabsiar was not acting alone. His accused accomplice in the assassination plot was Gholam Shakuri, a member of the Quds Force, a special unit of the Iranian Islamic Revolutionary Guard Corps. Attorney General Eric Holder explained that the plot was "directed and approved by elements of the Iranian government and, specifically, senior members of the Quds Force.... High-up officials in those agencies, which is an integral part of the Iranian government, were responsible for this plot."[101]

"Scarface" ultimately pleaded guilty and was sentenced to twenty-five years in prison, while Iranian officials continued to deny that they had any involvement in the plot.[102]

But there is considerable evidence that they did. When he was arrested in September 2011, Arbabsiar had a travel itinerary indicating that after paying the hit men he had planned to fly from Mexico to Tehran. He agreed to waive his Miranda rights and explain the plot, which he said was conceived and directed by the Quds Force, which had recruited him.[103]

Arbabsiar said that Shakuri had given him money and instructed him to refer to the plot to kill the ambassador as "the Chevrolet." Accordingly, in a phone call that was recorded by law enforcement officials, he said to Shakuri: "I wanted to tell you, the Chevrolet is ready, it's ready, uh, to be done. I should continue, right?"[104]

Shakuri responded, "Yes, yes, yes...yes, buy all of it."[105]

Other conversations in which Arbabsiar and Shakuri discussed the plot were recorded. The car dealer also met with Shakuri in Tehran and told his contacts in Mexico, who turned out to be law enforcement agents, that the individual bankrolling the operation was "like a colonel, the guy." He explained, "This is politics, OK.... It's not like, eh, personal.... He's got the government behind him.... He's not paying from his pocket."[106]

Scarface Jack Arbabsiar was a better car dealer than he was international terrorist, but the plot revealed the audacity of the Iranian government and their utter disregard for the consequences of defying the United States: in plotting to murder the ambassador of a hated rival state in a crowded place on American soil, the Iranians showed that they were ruthless, completely unafraid of the United States intelligence and law enforcement apparatus, and heedless of any diplomatic difficulties that might ensue. The mullahs confirmed, in other words, that the Islamic Republic of Iran operates as comfortably in the shadowy world of international terrorism as in the venerable corridors of the United Nations.

The Islamic Republic of Iran, in other words, is the very definition of a rogue state.

Iran's clandestine activities in the U.S. continued after Arbabsiar's arrest. In January 2014, a dual citizen of the U.S. and Iran named Mozaffar Khazaee was arrested as he was on his way out of the United States with sensitive information about two U.S. Air Force planes that he had picked up while at work as an engineer at the American defense contractor Pratt & Whitney.[107]

It turned out that Khazaee had already emailed some of the technical details to contacts inside Iran, telling them that the information was "very controlled...I am taking big risk."[108]

Khazaee protested his innocence, insisting, "I never sold anything to anybody."

U.S. District Judge Vanessa Bryant was unconvinced, and sentenced Khazaee to eight years in prison. "He not only minimizes his criminal conduct," she explained, "but genuinely fails to understand the significance of his actions, and that is especially troubling."[110] The significance of giving Iran detailed information about the engines of American military planes was unmistakable to anyone who cared about the national security of the United States.

TAQIYYA WATCH

"Had I known that making a Powerpoint presentation to an Iranian university in my attempt to get a job was breaking the law, I never would have taken the documents at all."

—Mozaffar Khazaee, after he was caught trying to take classified information about U.S. Air Force planes to Iran[109]

"I required the Holy Qur'an as unique reference of my trial and the judgement of all matter of people's life"

Other operatives with ties to Iran plotted blood and mayhem in the United States. On September 23, 2015, two Muslims in Canada, Raed Jaser and Chiheb Esseghaier, were sentenced to life imprisonment for their roles in a jihad terror plot to derail a passenger train that travels between New York City and Ontario.[111]

Throughout the trial proceedings, Esseghaier remained defiant, insisting that only the Qur'an, not a Canadian court, could judge him and shouting Qur'an verses at the jury.[112] He wrote a statement to the jury explaining, "I required the Holy Qur'an as unique reference of my trial and the judgement of all matter of people's life."[113]

According to Canadian officials, this bloodthirsty and unrepentant fanatic had gone to Iran within two years of beginning to plan the jihad plot, to which his trip was related. Royal Canadian Mounted Police Assistant Commissioner James Malizia said that Esseghaier and Jaser had been given "support from al Qaeda elements located in Iran." These elements, he said, also gave them "direction and guidance."[114] According to American officials involved with the case, al-Qaeda operated out of the Iranian town of Zahedan, near the Iranian borders with Afghanistan and Pakistan, passing men and money through Iran.[115]

Canadian officials said that they had no indication that the Iranian government itself was involved with the plot of Esseghaier and Jaser.[116] But the al-Qaeda cell in Zahedan operated with the apparent full knowledge and consent of the Iranian regime. The Iranians had briefly detained its leader, Yasin al Suri (also known as Ezedin Abdel Aziz Khalil), but released him despite knowing what he was doing.

A U.S. State Department official explained, "As head al Qaeda facilitator in Iran, al Suri is responsible for overseeing al Qaeda efforts to transfer experienced operatives and leaders from Pakistan to Syria, organizing and maintaining routes by which new recruits can travel to Syria via Turkey and assisting in the movement of al Qaeda external operatives to the West."[117] A Treasury Department official added, "He's an al Qaeda operative, Al Nusrah is an al Qaeda affiliate, and we know he's moving money and extremists into Syria for al Qaeda elements there, so I think you can draw that conclusion."[118]

According to the *Long War Journal*, "Al Suri operates under an agreement that was struck between the Iranian regime and al Qaeda years ago. He first began working inside Iran in 2005."[119]

On February 6, 2012, the Treasury Department designated Iran's principal intelligence organization, the Iranian Ministry of Intelligence and

Security (MOIS), a supporter of terrorism. The main reasons for this designation, explained Under Secretary for Terrorism and Financial Intelligence David S. Cohen, were Iran's mistreatment of its own people and its support of the al-Assad regime in Syria: "Today we have designated the MOIS for abusing the basic human rights of Iranian citizens and exporting its vicious practices to support the Syrian regime's abhorrent crackdown on its own population."[121]

But Cohen also said, "In addition, we are designating the MOIS for its support to terrorist groups, including al Qa'ida, al Qa'ida in Iraq, Hizballah and HAMAS, again exposing the extent of Iran's sponsorship of terrorism as a matter of Iranian state policy."[122] The Treasury Department statement asserted that "MOIS has facilitated the movement of al Qa'ida operatives in Iran and provided them with documents, identification cards, and passports. MOIS also provided money and weapons to al Qa'ida in Iraq (AQI), a terrorist group designated under E.O. 13224, and negotiated prisoner releases of AQI operatives."[123]

The Iranian support for al-Qaeda is extremely curious, especially since the Iranian mullahs are actively backing Bashar al-Assad's regime in Syria in its struggle against al-Qaeda and the Islamic State (which itself is an offshoot of al-Qaeda). It may be that Iran sees the precariousness of al-Assad's position and is hedging its bets against his eventual fall, hoping that those who topple his

NOT THAT THIS HAS ANYTHING TO DO WITH ISLAM

"I encourage you to retreat from the charge that has been affected to you as a first step of your sincere repentance to God."[120]

—Chiheb Esseghaier, exhorting jury members to exonerate him and convert to Islam regime will be beholden to Iran and not turn their wrath against it, despite the Sunni Islamic State's contempt and hatred for "rafidite dogs"—a Sunni term of opprobrium for Shi'ites. Or it may simply be that Iran's often-declared hatred for the U.S. has manifested itself in a willingness to aid America's enemies even if they are also fighting against friends of Iran. As the old saying goes, "My brother against my brother, but both of us against our cousin."

"Our hostility to the Great Satan is absolute"

In addition to its involvement in these plots, Iran has also acted in the United States through its Lebanese Shi'ite proxy, Hizballah. Hizballah leader Hassan Nasrallah shares his Iranian masters' hatred for the U.S., as he made abundantly clear in 2002: "Let the entire world hear me. Our hostility to the Great Satan [America] is absolute.... Regardless of how the world has changed after 11 September, 'Death to America' will remain our reverberating and powerful slogan: 'Death to America.'"[124]

That same year, Salim Boughader Mucharrafille, a Mexican national of Lebanese descent, was sentenced by a Mexican court to sixty years in prison for smuggling people into the United States, including Hizballah operatives.[125] Then on November 19, 2003, a Lebanese Muslim named Mahmoud Youssef Kourani, who lived in Dearborn, Michigan, was indicted for conspiring to "knowingly provide material support and resources" to Hizballah. The indictment identified Kourani as a "member, fighter, recruiter and fund raiser for Hizballah." Kourani was, it said, "a dedicated member of Hizballah who received specialized training in radical Shiite fundamentalism, weaponry, spy craft, and counterintelligence in Lebanon and Iran."[126]

Investigators found audiotapes in Kourani's Dearborn home containing statements such as "You alone are the sun of my lands, Nasrallah! Nasrallah! ... your voice is nothing less than my jihad." Hassan Nasrallah is the head of Hizballah. "We offer to you Hizballah, a pledge of loyalty," said another tape. "Rise for Jihad! ... I offer you, Hizballah, my blood in my hand."[127] Kourani had entered the United States illegally on February 4, 2001, by crossing the Mexican border hidden in the trunk of a car.[128]

Kourani was not singular. In September 2007, Texas Homeland Security Director Steve McCraw gave a speech to the North Texas Crime Commission in which he revealed that Hizballah operatives, as well as jihadis from Hamas and al-Qaeda, had been arrested crossing the Mexican border into Texas.[129] Hizballah operatives who made it into the U.S. were patient. According to Thomas Fuentes, the FBI's special agent in charge of the International Operations, "they want to maintain a low profile by engaging in criminal activity [but] not direct attacks.... They've not been enthusiastic about doing it on US soil because of the attention and reaction that would occur."[130]

However low profile they tried to be, some Hizballah operatives inside the United States could not keep their activities concealed. In July 2007, the Treasury Department shut down the Goodwill Charitable Organization (GCO) of Dearborn, Michigan, for funneling money to Hizballah. It called the GCO "a Hezbollah front organization that reports directly to the leadership of the Martyrs Foundation in Lebanon" and explained that "Hezbollah recruited GCO leaders and had maintained close contact with GCO representatives in the United States."[131]

According to the Treasury Department, Hizballah operative Qasem Aliq had been in "frequent contact" with the GCO, which regularly sent him money. The GCO gave "financial support to Hezbollah directly and through the Martyrs Foundation in Lebanon. Hezbollah's leaders in Lebanon have instructed Hezbollah members in the United States to send their contributions to GCO and to contact the GCO for the purpose of contributing to the Martyrs Foundation. Since its founding, GCO has sent a significant amount of money to the Martyrs Foundation in Lebanon."[132]

"Satan in Flames"

But by far the most significant manifestation of Iran's war against the United States is its little-noted role in the 9/11 attacks—a subject of desperate U.S. coverup attempts.[133]

On December 22, 2011, U.S. District Judge George B. Daniels ruled in *Havlish, et al. v. bin Laden, et al.*, that Iran and Hizballah were liable for damages to be paid to relatives of the victims of the September 11, 2001, jihad attacks in New York and Washington, as both the Islamic Republic and its Lebanese proxy had actively aided al-Qaeda in planning and executing those attacks.[134]

Daniels found that Iran and Hizballah had cooperated and collaborated with al-Qaeda before 9/11 and continued to do so after the attacks.

Before 9/11, Iran and Hizballah were implicated in efforts to train al-Qaeda members to blow up large buildings—resulting in the bombings of the Khobar Towers in Saudi Arabia in 1996, the bombings of the U.S. embassies in Kenya and Tanzania in 1998, and the attack on the USS *Cole* in 2000.[135]

Shortly after the *Cole* attack, the 9/11 jihad plot began to come together—and Iran was involved. Former MOIS operative Abolghasem Mesbahi, a defector from Iran, testified that during the summer of 2001, he received messages from Iranian government officials regarding a plan for unconventional warfare against the U.S., entitled *Shaitan dar Atash* ("Satan in Flames").[136]

"Satan in Flames" was the elaborate plot to hijack passenger jets packed full of people and crash them into American landmarks: the World Trade Center, which jihadis took to be the center of American commerce; the Pentagon, the center of America's military apparatus; and the White House.[137]

A classified National Security Agency analysis referred to in the 9/11 Commission report reveals that eight to ten of the 9/11 hijackers traveled to

Iran repeatedly in late 2000 and early 2001. The 9/11 Commission called for a U.S. government investigation into Iran's role in 9/11, but none was ever undertaken. So Kenneth R. Timmerman of the Foundation for Democracy in Iran was, in his words, "engaged by the *Havlish* attorneys in 2004 to carry out the investigation the 9/11 Commission report called on the U.S. government to handle."[138]

Timmerman noted that during the 9/11 hijackers' trips to Iran they were "accompanied by 'senior Hezbollah operatives' who were in fact agents of the Iranian regime."[139] Iranian border agents did not stamp their passports, so that their having been inside the Islamic Republic would not arouse suspicion against them when they entered the United States.[140]

The CIA, embarrassed by its failure to recognize the import of these trips, tried to suppress this revelation.[141] But Timmerman contends that even the available evidence is explosive enough, revealing that the Islamic Republic of Iran, in his words:

- helped design the 9/11 plot;
- provided intelligence support to identify and train the operatives who carried it out;
- allowed the future hijackers to evade U.S. and Pakistani surveillance on key trips to Afghanistan where they received the final order of mission from Osama bin Laden, by escorting them through Iranian borders without passport stamps;
- evacuated hundreds of top al Qaeda operatives from Afghanistan to Iran after 9/11 just as U.S. forces launched their offensive;
- provided safe haven and continued financial support to al Qaeda cadres for years after 9/11;

- allowed al Qaeda to use Iran as an operational base for additional terror attacks, in particular the May 2003 bombings in Riyadh, Saudi Arabia.[142]

In an affidavit, Timmerman provided extensive evidence that "the Government of Iran, through the IRGC, was knowingly engaged in financial transactions with al Qaeda long prior to 9/11, and took steps to keep those ties secret."[143] He noted that "A number of lower level Guantanamo Bay detainees describe facilities provided to them as al Qaeda members by Iran."[144] According to Timmerman, "the 9/11 Commission discovered evidence of Iran's material support for the al Qaeda 9/11 hijackers just one week before the Commission sent its final report to the printer in July 2004. The evidence came in the form of 75 highly classified U.S. intelligence documents, which were reviewed by Commission staff on a Sunday morning in a secure facility at the National Security Agency. These documents detailed assistance the Iranian government and its Lebanese proxy, Hizballah, provided to al Qaeda before the September 11, 2001, attacks."[145]

The Ayatollah Khamenei knew about the plot. During the summer of 2001, he instructed Iranian agents to be careful to conceal their tracks and told them to communicate only with al-Qaeda's second in command, Ayman al-Zawahiri, and Imad Mughniyeh of Hizballah.[146]

Mughniyeh was Iran's key player in the 9/11 "Satan in Flames" plot. During the *Havlish* trial, former CIA agents Clare M. Lopez and Bruce D. Tefft submitted an affidavit based on the Timmerman team's depositions of former Iranian intelligence officers turned defectors and other witnesses. It stated that "Imad Mughniyah, the most notable and notorious world terrorist of his time, an agent of Iran and a senior operative of Hizballah, facilitated the international travel of certain 9/11 hijackers to and from Iran, Lebanon, Saudi Arabia, and Afghanistan, and perhaps various other locations for the purpose of executing the events of September 11, 2001. This support enabled two vital aspects of the September 11, 2001 plot to succeed: (1) the continued training of the hijackers in Afghanistan and Iran after securing their United States visas in Saudi Arabia, and (2) entry into the United States."[147]

Judge Daniels determined that Iran, Hizballah, the Islamic Revolutionary Guard Corps, the Iranian Ministry of Intelligence and Security, and other Iranian government departments, as well as the Ayatollah Khamenei himself and former Iranian president Ali Akbar Hashemi Rafsanjani were all directly implicated in Iranian efforts to aid al-Qaeda in its 9/11 plot.[148] He awarded the plaintiffs in the *Havlish* case $394,277,884 for economic damages, as well as $94,000,000 for pain and suffering, $874,000,000 for mental anguish and grief, and $4,686,235,921 in punitive damages, along with $532,338,640.43 in pre-judgment interest, for a total of $6,580,842,445.43.[149]

The *Havlish* plaintiffs were unlikely to receive a check for that amount from the Islamic Republic of Iran neatly signed by the Ayatollah Khamenei. In March 2014, however, as part of the *Havlish* judgment, the court awarded ownership of a $500 million office tower in midtown Manhattan—one that had been owned by Iranian companies—to a court-appointed receiver, giving the *Havlish* plaintiffs a chance of receiving some compensation.[150]

While this award could never recompense these families for the loss of life and the years of trauma that they had suffered as a result of the Islamic Republic's war against the United States, it nonetheless stood as a small but tangible acknowledgment of Iran's role in the 9/11 attacks.

Clearly, Iran is at war with the United States, and over a period of many years has conducted that war on numerous unconventional fronts, while threatening conventional attacks if its agenda is thwarted in any way. For the Islamic Republic this war is very real, a principal focus of its energy and expenditures. But it appears that only one side is fighting. That fact was underscored in March 2016, when it came to light that Iranian hackers who were accused of being tied to the Islamic Republic had attempted to hack into the operating system of the Bowman Avenue Dam north of New York City, as well as into the systems of the banking conglomerates Bank of America, JP Morgan Chase, Citibank, and HSBC, along with the New York Stock Exchange. Said Attorney General Loretta Lynch, "These attacks were relentless, they were systematic, and they were widespread."[152] Such attacks, if they had been successful, could have caused catastrophic damage to New York City and the American economy.

In response, the Obama administration indicted the accused (none of which it had in custody), but announced no measures whatsoever against the Iranian government.[153]

"Barack Hussein Obama is the son of a Shiite father. . . . Some people call him the Iranian lobby in America."

Why has Barack Obama been so solicitous of Iran? Many have speculated that he sees the Iran deal as the cornerstone of his legacy, which he continues to hope will be peace for the Middle East and the world—even as the

IT'S NOT THE CRIME, IT'S THE COVERUP

The Obama-era CIA went to great pains to try to ensure that information about Iran's role in 9/11 did not come out in the *Havlish* case. In August 2010, a CIA official pressured a *Havlish* witness to withdraw his testimony in exchange for a new identity, new passport, and new job. In December of that year, another CIA operative approached a different *Havlish* witness, showed him documents stolen from the case, and took him to a U.S. embassy where he was subjected to five hours of interrogation and finally offered cash if he recanted his testimony. Says Timmerman, "After I reported those attempts at witness tampering to a Congressional oversight committee, they ceased."[151]

Islamic world is engulfed in flames and the Islamic State threatens to bring that fire to Europe and the U.S.

Others believe Obama has darker motives. On March 25, 2015, Syrian writer Muhydin Lazikani asserted that Obama's favorable posture toward Iran stemmed from his family background: "There is one thing we must not forget. I am not peddling some theory, and I am not being racist. But Barack Hussein Obama is the son of a Shiite Kenyan father." Lazikani wrote under the false impression that the young Barack "spent much of his childhood in Mombasa, south Kenya," a Shiite area and that "[a]ll the childhood memories of the man who rules the White House are Shiite memories." Thus the American president is "anxious for Iran to emerge victorious, and for Syria and all the countries of the Arab Gulf to be shattered."[154]

On April 10, Iranian opposition leader and Sunni Muslim Abu Muntasir Al-Baloushi, speaking from London, echoed the same rumors, extrapolating upon them to suggest the self-contradictory idea that Obama's support of Iran and of Shi'ite Islam in general was a legacy from his father, but also part of a larger plot to destroy Islam:

> Barack Hussein Obama is the son of a Shiite father. There is no doubt that he is Iran's lifesaver. Some people call him the Iranian lobby in America. He suffers from a peculiar complex. He believes that "wherever we go, the Sunnis are fighting us." So what is the historical solution? Shiite expansion is ready. So he imposed this Shiite expansion on Iraq, Syria, Iran, and Afghanistan. Any wise enemy of Islam realizes that Shiite expansion is the best method to destroy Islam from within. Even America did not do what the Shiites have done in Iraq. Even the Zionist Jews did not do such things to the Palestinians. The Americans believe that they can fight the Sunnis—they call it terrorism. But this is not what they care about. They want to destroy the entire ideology. Shiite expansion is the

THE AYATOLLAH'S SPIT LIST

"Want to stop Islamic terrorism? Be nicer to Muslims."
—behavioral science researcher Sarah Lyons-Padilla[157]

"Islam is a religion that prevents men from waging war? I spit upon those foolish souls who make such a claim."
—the Ayatollah Khomeini[158]

best method to achieve this, and the Shiites are ready, because they have an ideology to that effect, they have the scholars, they have got it all. So America has used them. If I were in America's place, I would use them too.[155]

Obama has publicly identified his father as a man who was "born a Muslim but became an atheist."[156] Neither he nor anyone else other than Sunni conspiracy theorists has ever identified him as Shi'ite. Nonetheless, it is easy to understand why these conspiracy theories arose: Obama's solicitude toward Iran, despite and even in the midst of its unremitting hostility to the United States, was by any rational standard completely inexplicable.

Barack Obama's greatest triumph as president threatened the safety and security of the entire world.

Chapter Three

"WHEREVER A MOVEMENT IS ISLAMIC, POPULIST, AND ANTI-AMERICAN, WE SUPPORT IT"

IRAN'S MIDDLE EAST ADVENTURISM

While American and Iranian representatives were still negotiating the nuclear deal in March 2015, Israeli Prime Minister Netanyahu noted that as the negotiations were going on in Lausanne, "Iran's proxies in Yemen are conquering large swaths of land in an effort to overtake the Bab al-Mandab straits, so that they can change the balance of power in shipping oil."[1] He declared, "After the Beirut-Damascus-Baghdad axis, Iran is maneuvering from the south to take over the entire Middle East. The Iran-Lausanne-Yemen axis is dangerous for mankind and must be stopped."[2]

Did you know?

- Iran funds client states and terror groups throughout the Middle East
- The Lebanese terror group Hizballah was formed at a meeting with the Ayatollah Khomeini
- Hizballah tortured kidnapped CIA station chief William Buckley for more than a year

In Beirut, Iranian client Hizballah wielded significant influence; in Damascus, Iranian client Bashar al-Assad clung to power against the Sunni jihadist onslaught, and in Baghdad, a weak American-installed Shi'ite government was essentially a client of Iran. Now, Netanyahu was saying, Iran was making a move in Yemen and using the nuclear deal to expand its power and influence even farther—with the same goal of taking over "the entire Middle East."

This claim about Iran's ambitions wasn't new—or exclusive to Netanyahu. As far back as 2004, King Abdullah II of Jordan was warning that Iran was trying to establish a "Shi'ite crescent" across the Middle East stretching from Iran through Iraq to Syria and Lebanon.[3] Not everyone was convinced, of course. Juan Cole, advisory board member of the National Iranian America Council, which we have seen is a lobbying group for the Islamic Republic, disputed the idea of "wide-ranging Iranian Shiite incursion into the Middle East" and dismissed Netanyahu's warning as a "paranoid claim."[4]

"We are the sons of the *umma*—the Party of God, the vanguard of which was made victorious by God in Iran"

Unfortunately for Cole, however, there was considerable evidence that Iran was indeed attempting to assert hegemony in a "Shi'ite crescent." Once Israel is destroyed, Khamenei declared in the summer of 2015, "the West's hegemony and threats will be discredited," and "the hegemony of Iran will be promoted."[5] Iran had been working for years to promote that hegemony through a series of allies, clients, and proxies across the Middle East.

The assembly of the "Shi'ite crescent" began in Lebanon. Chief among Iran's Middle East proxies is the Lebanese Shi'ite jihad terror group Hizballah ("Party of Allah"), which rose to prominence during the Lebanese civil war of the early 1980s. Hizballah was an Iranian client from its inception.[6] The terror group began at a meeting in Tehran between the Ayatollah Khomeini and a delegation of Lebanese Shi'ites, including Hassan Nasrallah, who would become Hizballah's leader. At this meeting, Khomeini gave his approval to the creation of Hizballah as a competitor to the dominant Lebanese Shi'ite group, the Amal Movement, whose leader, Musa Sadr, opposed the idea of clerical rule that was the guiding principle of the Islamic Republic. Khomeini gave Shiekholislam Seyyed Ali Khamenei, who would later succeed him as Iran's Supreme Leader, the task of supervising the establishment of Hizballah. According to Nasrallah, Iran "offered Lebanon everything in its power: money, training, and advice."[7]

In a February 1985 "Open Letter," Hizballah associated itself with Iran's Islamic Revolution: "We are the sons of the *umma* (Muslim community)— the Party of God (Hizb Allah) the vanguard of which was made victorious by God in Iran. There the vanguard succeeded to lay down the bases of a Muslim state which plays a central role in the world."[8] The letter maintained that Hizballah's political program was simply an outgrowth of its commitment to Islam.

When the Palestine Liberation Organization (PLO) was attacking Israel from southern Lebanon in 1982, the Israelis entered southern Lebanon in order to root out the PLO forces. In the summer of that year, Khomeini sent 1,500 members of the Iranian Islamic Revolutionary Guards Corps to Lebanon to recruit and train Hizballah members.[10] Given Iran's intense hatred for the United States and the Iranian derivation

NOT THAT THIS HAS ANYTHING TO DO WITH ISLAM

"As for our culture, it is based on the Holy Koran, the Sunna and the legal rulings of the *faqih* [an Islamic jurist; in this case, Khomeini] who is our source of imitation (*marja'al-taqlid*). Our culture is crystal clear. It is not complicated and is accessible to all."

—from the 1985 letter aligning Hizballah with Iran[9]

of the group, it is not surprising that Hizballah became internationally notorious for the October 23, 1983, bombing of military barracks in Beirut, in which 241 American servicemen (including 220 Marines) and fifty-eight French military personnel were murdered.

Hizballah and Iran have always denied involvement in that bombing, but there is considerable evidence to the contrary—not least the fact that the truck carrying the over twenty-one thousand pounds of TNT that were exploded at the barracks was driven by an Iranian national, Ismail Ascari. On May 30, 2003, U.S. District Court Judge Royce Lamberth found Iran and Hizballah responsible for the bombing, which he called "the most deadly state-sponsored terrorist attack made against United States citizens before September 11, 2001."[11]

The Lebanese terror group also won notoriety for its jihad suicide bombing at the U.S. Embassy in Beirut on April 18, 1983, which killed sixty-three people, including seventeen Americans. As he did in the barracks case, Lamberth found that the Embassy bombing had been carried out by Hizballah and financed by Iranian officials.

"They had done more than ruin his body. His eyes made it clear his mind had been played with. It was horrific, mediaeval and barbarous."

Hizballah continued its actions against the United States by kidnapping the CIA station chief in Lebanon, William Buckley, on March 16, 1984. Buckley's captors subsequently delivered several videos to American embassies showcasing how they were torturing him. After viewing the first, CIA director William Casey said: "I was close to tears. It was the most obscene thing I had ever witnessed. Bill was barely recognisable as the man I had known for years. They had done more than ruin his body. His eyes made it clear his mind had been played with. It was horrific, mediaeval and barbarous."[12]

The second video, according to British author Gordon Thomas, "revealed Buckley continued to be horrifically treated.... His voice was fuzzy and he appeared often unable to shape words. His hands shook and his legs beat a tattoo on the floor as he mumbled pathetic pleas to be exchanged under a guarantee the United States would remove 'all of its influences' from Lebanon and would persuade Israel to do the same."[13]

Thomas recounted that "on Friday, October 26, 1984, two hundred and twenty-four days since Buckley was kidnapped, a third video arrived at the CIA. The tape was even more harrowing than its predecessors. Buckley was close to a gibbering wretch. His words were often incoherent; he slobbered and drooled and, most unnerving of all, he would suddenly scream in terror, his eyes rolling helplessly and his body shaking. From time to time he held up documents, which had been in his burn-bag, to the camera. Then he delivered a pathetic defence of his captor's right to self-determination in Lebanon. No one knows for certain when William Buckley did die. The likeliest date is sometime during the night of June 3, 1985, the 444th day of his captivity."[14]

"We see in Israel the vanguard of the United States in our Islamic world"

Although it made its name feared and loathed by targeting Americans, Hizballah's chief mission is to be the Lebanese extension of the Islamic Republic's fanatical hatred for Israel, pressing Israel from the north while Hamas, a Sunni client of Iran, presses the Jewish State from the south.

Hizballah's founder, Hassan Nasrallah, has made it clear that his determination to destroy Israel is part of a larger hatred. Hizballah's 1985 "Open Letter" contained a section entitled "The Necessity for the Destruction of Israel," which explained the Hizballah terrorists' hatred for Israel as a component of their hatred for the United States: "We see in Israel the vanguard of the United States in our Islamic world." The letter declared that Hizballah's jihad against Israel would end "only when this entity is obliterated. We recognize no treaty with it, no cease fire, and no peace agreements, whether separate or consolidated."[15]

In accord with this maximalist imperative, Hizballah went after Israel's occupying force in southern Lebanon, which had entered the country in order to prevent jihad attacks in Israel being mounted from that area. It harassed the Israelis to such an extent that, after Israel had suffered well over a thousand casualties, the Israelis pulled out in 2000, after eighteen years of occupation.

Hizballah trumpeted this withdrawal as "the first Arab victory in the history of Arab-Israeli conflict."[16] Speaking during the Hizballah-Israel conflict in the summer of 2006, Lebanon's President Emile Lahoud, a Maronite Christian, declared, "It wasn't the army that freed the occupied south of the country, rather it was the resistance which achieved that. Without this resistance Lebanon would still be occupied today." The "resistance" force that he had in mind was, of course, Hizballah.[17]

This "victory" made Nasrallah a hero of the jihad against Israel, and swelled Hizballah's membership to over a hundred thousand. Nasrallah took to the role with gusto, encouraging jihad suicide bombings of Israeli targets. In June 2002, he lauded suicide attacks for "creating a deterrence and equalizing fear" and intimated that more were coming: "We are trying to find a way for this weapon to become more developed, effective, and capable, leading the resistance movement in Palestine to a new and exceptional phase. This weapon is today the most powerful weapon the Palestinian people...could ever have."[18]

After Hizballah raiders killed seven Israeli soldiers and abducted two more, Israel began bombing southern Lebanon on July 12, 2006, and ground troops entered a week later. Israeli Prime Minister Ehud Olmert emphasized that Hizballah was acting in conjunction with the Lebanese government: "I want to make clear that the event this morning is not a terror act, but an act of a sovereign state that attacked Israel without reason. The government of Lebanon, of which Hezbollah is a part, is trying to shake the stability of the region."[19]

Lebanese Prime Minister Fouad Siniora, however, disclaimed any responsibility, saying that Lebanon had no foreknowledge of Hizballah's attack on the Israeli forces. Frederick Jones, a spokesman for the U.S.'s National Security Council, linked the attack not to Lebanon, but to Syria and Iran, Hizballah's mentor and chief supporter: "We also hold Syria and Iran, which directly support Hizbullah, responsible for this attack and the ensuing violence."[20]

Iran's President Mahmoud Ahmadinejad took the opportunity of the Israeli incursion into Lebanon to sound a theme that would become a staple of Iranian government rhetoric in the coming years: "In the near future," he said, "we will witness the rapid collapse of the Zionist regime."[21] Despite this bravado, the Iranian president's regime betrayed considerable anxiety about the possibility that the Israelis would strike Iran's client Syria. Ahmadinejad warned, "If the Zionist regime commits another stupid move and attacks Syria, this will be considered like attacking the whole Islamic world and this regime will receive a very fierce response."[22] Foreign Ministry spokesman Hamid Reza Asefi added, "We hope the Zionist regime does not make the mistake of attacking Syria, because extending the front would definitely make the Zionist regime face unimaginable losses. Iran is standing by the Syrian people. We have offered and will offer Syria and Lebanon spiritual and humanitarian support."[23]

Hizballah was so closely identified with Iran that Lebanese Druze leader Walid Jumblatt said four days after the conflict began that Hizballah's war in Lebanon was just a proxy for Iran's conflict with Israel: "The war is no longer that of Lebanon. It is an Iranian war."[24]

Iranian officials certainly behaved as if that were the case. Khamenei called Israel "satanic and cancerous" and said that Hizballah's conflict with it was part of a larger war. Referring to Israel, he said: "This regime is an infectious tumour for the entire Islamic world." Noting that President George W. Bush had called upon Hizballah to disarm, Khamenei declared: "This will never happen."[25]

As thousands of demonstrators marched against Israel in Tehran's Palestine Square soon after Israeli forces entered Lebanon, Majlis Speaker Gholam Ali Haddad Adel belied the Iranian government's claim that it was not involved in the conflict, warning Israel: "The towns you have built in northern Palestine [that is, Israel] are within the range of the brave Lebanese children. No part of Israel will be safe." Then, addressing the United States government, he issued another threat: "Either cut your support for Israel, or don't expect peace and compromise with the world." The enthusiastic Iranian crowd chanted, "Death to Israel!"[26]

Islamic Revolutionary Guard Corps soldiers were killed while fighting against the Israelis alongside Hizballah.[27]

Iranian president Ahmadinejad also hinted at a larger conflict, saying that by moving against Hizballah, Israel had "pushed the button of its own destruction." He added ominously: "Britain and the United States are accomplices of the Zionist regime in its crimes in Lebanon and Palestine," and warned that unless Israel withdrew and apologized, "the people of the region" would "respond." "Arrogant powers," said Ahmadinejad, "have set up a base for themselves to threaten and plunder nations in the region. But today, the occupier regime [Israel]—whose philosophy is based on threats, massacre and invasion—has reached its finishing line." Billboards featuring Hizballah leader Nasrallah and the claim that Muslims had a duty to "wipe out" Israel went up in Tehran.[28]

Hossein Safiadeen, Hizballah's representative in Iran, boasted: "We are going to make Israel not safe for Israelis. There will be no place they are safe."[29]

Recognizing that the increased belligerence could be a harbinger of Hizballah strikes inside the U.S., the FBI stepped up its scrutiny of the group and its supporters in America.[30]

President Mahmoud Ahmadinejad saw the Israeli incursion into Lebanon as a historic turning point: "In my opinion, Lebanon is the scene of an historic test, which will determine the future of humanity. Everyone must be put to the test. Everyone. It is inconceivable for anyone who calls himself a Muslim and who heads an Islamic state to maintain relations under the table with the regime that occupied Jerusalem. He cannot take pleasure in the [Israeli] killing of Muslims yet present himself as a Muslim. This is inconceivable, and must be exposed. Allah willing, it will. You will see."[31]

Ahmadinejad claimed that "England was the founder of this sinister regime. It is an accomplice to all its crimes. America, which supports it now, is an accomplice to all its crimes. They are the ones who started this fire. They are the ones who support [Israel], and encourage it to strike at the people in such a manner."[32]

In leveling such charges, Ahmadinejad was indicating that Hizballah's war against Israel was not just Iran's proxy war against the Jewish State, but a part of its war against the United States and the entire Western world. Iran behaved accordingly: in mid-August 2006, just before the conflict ended, Zalmay Khalilzad, the U.S. ambassador to Iraq, charged that Iran was pressuring Shi'ite groups in Iraq to attack American forces there in retaliation for Israel's incursion into Lebanon.

"Iran," said Khalilzad, "is seeking to put more pressure, encourage more pressure on the coalition from the forces that they are allied with here, and the same is maybe true of Hezbollah.... The concern that we have is that Iran and Hezbollah would use those contacts that they have with groups and the situation here, use those to cause more difficulties or cause difficulties for the coalition." He said that if the United Nations adopted a resolution against Iran, "Iran could respond to it by further pressing its supporters or people that it has ties with, or people that it controls, to increase the pressure on the coalition, not only in Iraq but elsewhere as well."[33]

The Israeli operation ended on August 14, 2006, when a United Nations–imposed ceasefire took effect. The result of the conflict was inconclusive: Ehud Olmert declared that Israel had eliminated Hizballah's "state within a state" in southern Lebanon, but Hassan Nasrallah proclaimed that Hizballah had won a "strategic, historic victory" over Israel.[34] He recounted that Bashar al-Assad had told him with some relief that if Israel had destroyed Hizballah, "the battle would have dragged to Syria."[35] But it did not, at least at that point—and Iran's war against Israel and the United States continued.

An uneasy peace between Israel and Hizballah prevailed after the 2006 conflict, punctuated by violence that did not escalate into all-out military action. But this was not a peace that could be taken by anyone as a permanent cessation of hostilities. The war threatened to flare up again in the summer of 2015, when the Saudi newspaper *Okaz* reported that Hizballah was trying to recruit Muslims to carry out jihad terror attacks inside Israel and in the West Bank. "Among those Hezbollah members involved in the operation," said *Okaz*, "is Kayis Ubayid, who was behind the kidnapping of [Israeli] Col. (res.) Elahanan Tenebaum in 2000."[36]

These efforts bore immediate fruit, as bombings and shootings south of Jerusalem in August 2015 were attributed to Hizballah's influence. "We estimate," said a Palestinian source, "that there are a number of youths who were drawn into joining Hezbollah's ranks and are now operating in the West Bank, because of economic hardship or the deterioration in the security situation."[37] Or perhaps because they believe that the jihad against Israel is a religious duty.

"We don't know how many people there are," the source added, "but there is no doubt that the phenomenon is gaining momentum among former Al Aksa Brigade youths that have been approached by Hezbollah to work in exchange for economic support. The matter is a personal choice of these youth, who have chosen to take action against Israeli targets."[38]

This effort may have originated in Tehran. In January 2015, Iranian Defense Minister Hussein Dehghan had declared that Israel would "not escape revenge" for killing Islamic Revolutionary Guards General Muhammad Allah-Dadi and jihad leader Jihad Mughniyeh in an airstrike that month. "Tehran," vowed Dehghan, would "continue to strengthen the axis of resistance in order to deal with the Zionist entity."[39] The "axis of resistance," consisted of Hizballah and the Sunni jihad groups in the West Bank and Gaza.

Hizballah leader Nasrallah continued to demonstrate his subservience to Tehran. In October 2015, as claims that the Israelis were planning to destroy the Al Aqsa Mosque in Jerusalem swept across the Muslim world, the government-controlled Iranian newspaper *Kayhan* announced, "Palestine is thirsty for a third Intifada," or uprising against Israel. "It is the duty of every Muslim to help start it as soon as possible."[40] Just a week later Nasrallah, echoing the Iranian government line, also called for a new intifada: "The renewed Intifada is the only way to free Palestinians from the occupation and to save Al-Aqsa—it is incumbent on everyone to help them." The Hizballah leader, as bloodthirsty as ever, praised the recent spate of stabbings of Israeli civilians: "Today there are generations who believe in resistance, in the holy places and Al-Aqsa, which is why they are ready to fight with knives those who barricade themselves in tanks or arm themselves with rifles." He said that those "carrying knives and rocks" were "the strongest army who instills in us the belief that the horizon is open and there will be no future for Israel."

The only acceptable outcome would be the destruction of Israel: "We will continue in the path of Jihad against Israel. We will continue to battle the Zionist project in the region and we will continue to fight alongside the Palestinians. There will be no future for the Zionist entity in the presence of the axis of the resistance."[41]

The following month, as Palestinian Muslims continued to target Israeli civilians with stabbing and hit-and-run attacks, Nasrallah praised this "new Palestinian Intifada" and called for more bloodshed. "What is going on now in Palestine," he said, "reflects a lofty and sublime Jihad spirit." And he called upon Muslims to support this new uprising, for the enemy was powerful: "Despite the fact the 'Greater Israel' scheme has been frustrated, the Zionist entity is still powerful and threatens all the region's peoples."[42]

"Iran can do anything it wants in Lebanon"

Meanwhile, Iran's client terror group has amassed enormous power in Lebanon—to the extent that in February 2016 Hanin Ghaddar declared on the Lebanese news website NOW that "Iran won Lebanon": "Hezbollah's chief Hassan Nasrallah declared his victory in Lebanon in his last speech and he's right. Hezbollah won Lebanon and no one seems to care." Iran's domination of the country, she suggested, was demonstrated by Hizballah's decisive influence on Lebanese electoral politics and the recent release of notorious Shi'ite terrorist Michel Samaha. Now, Ghaddar argued, "Iran can do anything it wants in Lebanon without any political opposition or challenges."

And the terror group's hegemony there only frees up Iranian resources, which in any case are burgeoning thanks to the nuclear deal, for initiatives in other parts of its Shi'ite crescent across the Middle East: "And now Iran can focus to win what it needs in Syria, while everyone is busy making business deals with the 'new Iran.'"[43]

Hizballah has gained so much political power in Lebanon that Imad Salamey, Associate Professor of Political Science and International Affairs at the Lebanese American University, referred to the "the Iranian-Syrian occupation of Lebanon."[44] That's a major step toward the regional domination Iran has been seeking in its Shi'ite crescent across the Middle East.

"Hezbollah is operating like a major drug cartel"

Despite Hizballah's recent acquisition of even greater influence over Lebanese politics and its focus on destroying Israel, it still finds time to target the United States—through Mexico, where it has teamed with drug cartels along the U.S. border. This partnership is mutually beneficial: Hizballah gets massive amounts of cash to finance its jihad operations, and the drug cartels receive extensive training in ways to strike terror into the hearts of their enemies. That is one principal reason why the Mexican drug cartels have recently adopted what had up until now been two trademarks of jihad groups: kidnapping and beheading.

WHAT A DEAL!

"Lebanon, on the other hand, is going to pay a very high price for all these deals and compromises, more so as Iran, Russia and the Assad regime are scoring more gains in Syria."

—Hanin Ghaddar[45]

The two came together in the horrific fate of one Mexican family. On October 11, 2012, a young man, Francisco Quiñónez Nava, was kidnapped; his captors demanded 300,000 pesos ($17,765) for his safe return. The money was not delivered, and Francisco Quiñónez Nava was never seen again. His father, Francisco Quiñónez Ramírez, was the mayor of the Mexican town of Ahuacuotzingo from 2009 to 2012; on June 28, 2014, he was shot dead at the entrance to the town. His widow, Aide Nava Gonzalez, decided to run for mayor of Ahuacuotzingo herself, but on March 10, 2015, she was kidnapped at a campaign event.[46] The next day, her headless body was discovered by the side of a road, along with a note that read: "This is what will happen to anyone who does not fall in line, f***ing turncoats."[47]

A local criminal gang, Los Rojos, signed the note, but it is virtually certain that behind them stood the shadowy presence of Hizballah, from which the gang learned to kidnap and behead its enemies.[48]

Meanwhile, Hizballah was getting rich in the drug trade. Marine General John Kelly, commander of the U.S. Southern Command, said in October 2014, "We know that some of the money that comes out of the United States is laundered into the coffers of Hezbollah."[49] And deputy commander Lieutenant General Kenneth E. Tovo told the Congressional Committee on Homeland Security and Governmental Affairs in March 2015 that Hizballah, "which has long viewed the region [that is, Mexico and Central and South America] as a potential attack venue against Israeli or other Western targets, has supporters and sympathizers in Lebanese diaspora communities in Latin America, some of whom are involved in lucrative illicit activities like money laundering and trafficking in counterfeit goods and drugs. I think it is fair to say that there is a good amount of profit that Lebanese Hezbollah makes off of illegal trafficking."[50]

Tovo warned that the jihadis could also make use of the smuggling routes by which illegal immigrants enter the U.S. from Mexico: "The relative ease with which human smugglers moved tens of thousands of people to our nation's doorstep also serves as another warning sign: these smuggling routes are a potential vulnerability to our homeland. As I stated last year, terrorist organizations could seek to leverage those same smuggling routes to move operatives with intent to cause grave harm to our citizens or even bring weapons of mass destruction into the United States."[51]

Tovo was right. In late 2012, Mexico was home to around four thousand Muslims—officially. But American intelligence officials estimated that there were around two hundred thousand illegal immigrants there from Syria and Lebanon, including many agents of Iran, Hizballah, and al-Qaeda. The drug cartels, making use of a sophisticated network of tunnels, had no problem transporting these people across the border into the United States.[52]

The partnership between Hizballah and the drug cartels was extraordinarily lucrative. In December 2011, a Lebanese drug lord Ayman "Junior" Joumaa was charged with drug trafficking and money laundering. He was accused of sending ninety thousand tons of cocaine into the United States and laundering over $250 million in drug money he had gotten in Mexico in dealings with the notorious drug cartel known as Los Zetas.[53]

Joumaa's organization was global. According to the indictment, his "coordination of money laundering activities occurred in the United States, Lebanon, Benin, Panama, Colombia, the Democratic Republic of Congo and elsewhere." Joumaa "typically picked up between $2 [million] and $4 million at a time in Mexico City."[54] He laundered a good deal of the money through a legitimate used car business.[55] Whether Joumaa ever employed Scarface Jack Arbabsiar is unknown, but when Arbabsiar was looking for hit men to murder the Saudi Ambassador, he met with men he thought were members of Los Zetas.[56]

U.S. Attorney Neil MacBride emphasized that Joumaa was a major player: "Money fuels the drug trade, and Mr. Joumaa is alleged to be at the center of it all. Working with those producing the vast majority of the world's cocaine to get their drugs safely into the hands of Mexican cartels, and then moving hundreds of millions in proceeds all around the world so the money can't be traced back to them in Colombia."[57]

After Joumaa was charged in December 2011, he continued money laundering, only through different venues. He had previously worked through the Lebanese Canadian Bank, but David S. Cohen, the Treasury Department's Under Secretary for Terrorism and Financial Intelligence, noted that "following Treasury's action against the Lebanese Canadian Bank, the Joumaa narcotics network turned to Rmeiti Exchange and Halawi Exchange to handle its money-laundering needs."[58]

Rmeiti Exchange and Halawi Exchange were money exchange organizations in Lebanon. In April 2013, the U.S. government blacklisted both for laundering tens of millions of dollars in drug profits for Hizballah. Derek Maltz, a special agent for the Drug Enforcement Administration, explained, "Hezbollah is operating like a major drug cartel. These proceeds are funding

NOT THAT THIS HAS ANYTHING TO DO WITH ISLAM

Ayman Joumaa lived a luxurious life with all this money, but he also had a social conscience of sorts, or at least the jihadi version of one: U.S. officials charged that Joumaa passed on a good deal of money to Hizballah.[59] He had established contact with a member of Hizballah's "1,800 Unit," which coordinates attacks against Israel. That 1,800 Unit member worked for a director of Hizballah's drug dealing organization.[60]

violence against Americans." According to U.S. officials, Haitham Rmeiti of Rmeiti Exchange was "a key facilitator for wiring money and transferring Hezbollah funds."[61]

While American officials worked hard to stop all this activity, the appetite for drugs in the U.S. and elsewhere was just too large. By tapping into it, Hizballah was ensuring that its activities would be lavishly bankrolled for years to come.

"Damascus was transformed into the transit center for transportation of weapons to Iran"

A shakier ally for the Iranians was another of Hizballah's principal longtime supporters, Bashar al-Assad in Syria. As the "Arab Spring" uprisings toppled Middle Eastern strongman after strongman—Zine El Abidine Ben Ali in Tunisia, Hosni Mubarak in Egypt, Ali Abdullah Saleh in Yemen, and Muammar Gaddafi in Libya—al-Assad's position grew increasingly precarious, until by August 2015 his government controlled only 17 percent of Syria's territory.[62] The Islamic Republic stuck by its embattled ally, but the end of the al-Assad regime, which had ruled Syria since 1970, seemed only a matter of time.

Bashar al-Assad's father, Hafez al-Assad, had first concluded the alliance with Iran in a rage over his longtime ally Egypt's peace treaty with Israel in 1979. Feeling hemmed in by Egypt on one side and Saddam Hussein's Iraq on the other, and seeing the possibility of an accord with Iran based on a shared hostility to Israel, al-Assad sent the Ayatollah Khomeini a pledge of cooperation, accompanied by a handsome gold-illuminated Qur'an.[63] The latter gift was perhaps designed to emphasize, however subtly, that the Alawite al-Assad was a Muslim, too, and thus deserving of Khomeini's support. Al-Assad's Alawite sect comprised only about twelve percent of Syria's population; Shi'ite Iran's backing could help al-Assad keep Syria's Sunni majority—and the Sunni leaders of Egypt, Iraq and other nearby Arab states—at bay.

Khomeini graciously accepted the gift, and thus began the alliance that continues to this day. Al-Assad was as useful to the Iranians as they were to him: during the Iran-Iraq War that lasted from 1980 to 1988, al-Assad's Syria stood with Iran alone among the states of the Arab League, thus preventing the formation of a unified Arab front against Iraq.[64] Iran gave Syria free oil, and Syria enabled the Iranians to circumvent the U.S. arms embargo. Mohsen Rafiqdust, Minister of the Islamic Revolutionary Guards Corps during the 1980s, recalled that during Iran's war with Iraq, "Damascus was transformed into the transit center for transportation of weapons to Iran."[65]

"Wherever a movement is Islamic, populist, and anti-American, we support it"

Syria's relationship with Iran has from the beginning been understood by both parties as an alliance against the U.S. and Israel. Iran's geopolitical ambitions for the region, as well as its religious vision for the entire world, give its alliance with Syria key strategic importance.

In June 2011, the Ayatollah Khamenei noted the growing unrest against Bashar al-Assad in Syria and declared, "In Syria, the hand of America and Israel is evident."[66] That made it all the more important for Iran to keep al-Assad in power. One Muslim cleric thought Syria was even more important to Iran: "If we lose Syria, we cannot keep Tehran."[67]

AN ALLIANCE WORTH ITS WEIGHT IN GOLD

• • •

"Syria is the golden ring of resistance against Israel, and if it weren't for Syria's active government the country would become like Qatar or Kuwait. Iran is not prepared to lose this golden counterweight."

—Ali Akbar Velayati, former Foreign Minister of Iran and a senior foreign affairs advisor to Khamenei[68]

The Syria-Iran alliance was sealed when Israeli forces entered Lebanon in 1982 and Hafez al-Assad agreed to the presence of Islamic Revolutionary Guards Corps forces in Lebanon to train Hizballah.[69] Al-Assad managed to maintain relatively good relationships with Syria's neighboring Arab states as well as with Iran, but his son Bashar, who took over after Hafez al-Assad's death in 2000, was less adroit: Syria moved steadily closer to Iran. On June 15, 2006, Syrian Defense Minister Hassan Turkmani and Iranian Defense Minister Mustafa Mohammad Najjar signed an agreement for military cooperation between the two countries and the formation of a joint Supreme Defense Commission against what they called their "common threats": Israel and the United States.[70]

At a joint news conference in Tehran, Turkmani said, "Our cooperation is based on a strategic pact and unity against common threats. We can have a common front against Israel's threats. Our cooperation with the Iranians against Israeli threats is nothing secret and we regularly consult about this with our friends."[71] Najjar added: "US threats are a kind of psychological operation. It is not new. With unity among the region's nations, these threats will not prevail."[72] He said that Iran "considers Syria's security its own security, and we consider our defense capabilities to be those of Syria."[73] He also announced that "Iran is ready to sign a non-aggression pact with regional countries"—not including Israel, of course.[74]

Bashar al-Assad himself went to Tehran in February 2007 and met with President Ahmadinejad, who boasted that the difficulties that the U.S. was facing with Iraq, along with Hizballah's supposed defeat of Israel in

2006, were "clear signs of the growing weakness of the United States and Zionism."[75]

In May 2013, when Israeli airstrikes hit Hizballah targets in Syria, Iran's Defense Minister Ahmad Vahidi emphasized that the Iran-Syria alliance was real and issued new threats: "The inhumane measures and adventures of the Zionist regime in the region will surge anti-Zionist waves and shorten the life of this fake regime.... [Israel's] attack in Syria, which occurred with a green light from the U.S., pulled the curtain back on the relationship between the mercenary terrorists and their supporters and the Zionist regime."[76]

Vahidi took the opportunity to position Iran as the coordinator of a unified response against Israel from Muslim countries. Iran, he said, "condemns the Zionist regime attack and recommends the regional countries to wisely stand against such aggressions."[77]

The commander of Iran's regular Army ground forces, General Ahmad Reza Pourdastan, offered to train the Syrians against Israel: "As a Muslim nation, we back Syria, and if there is need for training we will provide them with the training. But we won't have any active involvement in the operations."[78] Those words would eventually ring hollow, as Iranian forces got more and more enmeshed in Syria.

Iran and its proxies reiterated their backing for al-Assad as the Arab Spring uprisings spread to Syria and threatened the al-Assad regime. As usual, they blamed Israel.

On April 30, 2013, Hizballah's Nasrallah addressed the anti-Assad rebels, making it clear that he considered them puppets of the U.S. and Israel: "You will not be able to take Damascus by force and you will not be able to topple the regime militarily. This is a long battle. Syria has real friends in the region and in the world who will not allow Syria to fall into the hands of America or Israel."[79] He warned of armed intervention: "What do you imagine would happen in the future if things deteriorate in a way that requires the intervention of the forces of resistance in this battle?"[81] Major General Qassem Suleimani, the leader of Iran's Quds Force, said that the Iranians would do whatever it took to keep al-Assad in power: "We're not like the Americans. We don't abandon our friends.'"[82]

Iran's Islamic Revolutionary Guards Corps and other forces sent personnel to Syria to aid al-Assad militarily.[83] In July 2013, Iraqi Foreign Minister Hoshyar Zebari complained about this aid: "We reject and condemn the transfer of weapons through our airspace, and we will inform the Iranian side of that formally. But we do not have the ability to stop it."[84] Iran was not disposed to allow its military aid to al-Assad to be stopped by the Iraqis or anyone else.

IT'S ALWAYS THE JEWS

"Current events in Syria are designed by the foreign enemies and mark the second version of the sedition which took place in 2009 in Iran. The enemy is targeting the security and safety of Syria…[The protestors] are foreign mercenaries, who get their message from the enemy and the Zionists."[80]

—Ahmad Mousavi, Iran's former ambassador to Syria

"Death to America, death to Israel, curse the Jews, victory to Islam"

In June 2011 the Ayatollah Khamenei declared, "Wherever a movement is Islamic, populist, and anti-American, we support it."[85] That would include the Shi'ite Houthi rebels in Yemen. On September 21, 2014, Iran-backed Houthi forces, whose motto was "Death to America, death to Israel, curse the Jews, victory to Islam," captured much of the Yemeni capital, Sanaa, including some government offices.[86] Yemeni President Abdrabbah Mansour Hadi's government agreed to a deal with the Houthis, granting them the right to choose the next prime minister.[87]

Peace did not ensue. A week later, al-Qaeda forces that opposed Hadi but didn't want to see Yemen fall to the Shi'ites and Iran carried out a jihad suicide attack at a hospital that the Houthis were using as a base of operations, killing fifteen people and injuring fifty.[88] The Shi'ites got revenge the next month when they attacked the home of a Sunni politician, setting off a melee in which twelve people were killed.[89]

Then on January 20, 2015, Houthi forces stormed the presidential palace in Sanaa. Yemeni Information Minister Nadia Sakkaf announced, "The President has no control."[90] The rebel leader, Abdul Malik al-Houthi, took to the airwaves of his Beirut-based Houthi network to complain, "We are the victims of corruption and false promises. The government did not respect the peace and partnership deal from September. We are trying to bring some legitimacy to the government."[91] He declared that the "Yemeni people have two options—to move against the foreign agendas, or stand against them firmly since they seek to spread chaos in Yemen. This is why we moved with the Yemeni people though many powers inside and outside Yemen are angered. But the Yemeni people are with us and understand our goals."[92]

Al-Houthi didn't say anything about "foreign agendas" emanating from Tehran. The Houthi victories were made possible only by Iranian cash, weapons, and training, although Iranian officials denied this. A Reuters report quoted an unnamed senior Yemeni official who maintained, "Before the entrance into Sanaa, Iran started sending weapons here and gave a lot of support with money via visits abroad."[93] Another added that "weapons are still coming in by sea and there's money coming in through transfers."[94] Reuters also quoted an unnamed "Western source familiar with Yemen" who noted that "it's been happening for over a year. We've seen Houthis going out to Iran and Lebanon for military training. We think there is cash, some of which is channeled via Hezbollah and sacks of cash arriving at the airport. The numbers of those going for training are enough for us to worry about."[95]

An Iranian official, also unnamed, would acknowledge only that there were a "few hundred" members of the Quds Force in Yemen to train the Houthis. "Everything," he said, "is about the balance of power in the region.

Iran wants a powerful Shi'ite presence in the region that is why it has got involved in Yemen as well."[96] Salah al-Sammad, a Hadi advisor and also a Houthi, said that Iran's aid to the Houthis was all part of Iran's plan in "confronting the American project."[97]

With Houthis surrounding his home in late January, Hadi resigned. On February 6, the Houthis announced that they were dissolving the Yemeni parliament and taking over the government.[98] In a show of belligerence worthy of their Iranian masters, the Houthis seized U.S. Embassy vehicles at Sanaa's airport and wouldn't allow departing U.S. Marines to take their weapons with them.[99] Ever disinclined to acknowledge the reality of a world once again on the brink of war, the Western media went into damage control mode.

The Houthis' victory was not complete. On February 21, Hadi, having escaped from Sanaa and made his way to Aden, retracted his resignation and vowed defiance.[100] Yemen dissolved into a chaos of jihad attacks by the Houthis and the Sunni jihadists opposing them. On March 20, 2015, Sunnis murdered 142 people and wounded 351 in a series of attacks upon Shi'ite mosques in Sanaa.[101] The Islamic State (ISIS) claimed credit for the bombings.[102] Inside the Houthi Al-Hashoush Mosque, the worshippers were chanting: "Death to America. Death to Israel. Curse upon the Jews. Victory to Islam. Allah Akbar. Death to America. Death to Israel. Curse upon the Jews. Victory to—" At that point the bomb went off.[103]

Three days after those bombings, U.S. special forces left Yemen. Lieutenant Colonel Rick Francona, a CNN analyst, observed that the Saudis were feeling encircled by the Shi'ite crescent: "They believe now that Iran is in control in Beirut, in Damascus, in Baghdad and now on their southern border in Yemen. So the Saudis are beginning to feel a little threatened here and are hoping the Yemen situation doesn't spiral out of control."[104] Al-Houthi, for his part, professed not to understand why the neighboring Sunni states wouldn't welcome the Houthis' rise to power in Yemen: it was "very strange," he said, that the Sunni states would condemn the Houthis and not the United States, "the umbrella of tyranny in the world."[107]

The Saudis, unmoved, began bombing raids against a Houthi-controlled air base, military bases, and anti-aircraft installations on March 26. An outraged al-Houthi took to the airwaves to thunder that "Yemenis won't accept such humiliation" from the "stupid" and "evil" Saudis, and boast that Yemen would be "the tomb" of the Sunni invaders.[108] The Saudi Ministry of Islamic Affairs, meanwhile, ordered imams to devote their Friday sermons to denouncing the Houthis as "enemies of Islam" and to explaining that the Gulf States had a responsibility to save Yemen from "Houthi aggression and oppression."[109]

Sunni Yemenis situated the conflict with the Houthis in the context of the age-old struggle against the Shi'ites. Al-Qaeda–controlled mosques in the Yemeni city of Mukalla blared a call for "jihad against Shiites" from their loudspeakers.[110] Sunni mosques in Aden likewise broadcast a call to arms: "Allahu akbar! Rise for jihad!"[111] In late April 2015, the Islamic State declared that it had established a branch of its caliphate in Yemen and boasted that it had come to the country to "cut the throats of all Houthis." An Islamic State commander addressed the Houthis: "We have come to Yemen, with men hungry for your blood to avenge the Sunnis and take back the land they have occupied."[112]

The Houthis appeared anxious to escalate the conflict in a different way, taking four American hostages.[113]

In mid-June, the Islamic State set off five bombs in Shi'ite mosques right at the time of sundown prayers and at the home of a Houthi leader, killing thirty-one

OSTRICH ALERT

Rod Nordland of the *New York Times* claimed that the Houthis were "trying desperately" to be friends with the United States, and had merely seized the Embassy vehicles for "safekeeping."[105] When the Houthis screamed "death to America," Nordland insisted, they did not "mean it literally."[106]

people and injuring dozens more. In a statement, the Islamic State explained that the attacks were "revenge for Muslims against the Rafidi Houthis."[114] "Rafidi" is a pejorative Sunni term for Shi'ites.

Around the same time, UN-sponsored peace talks in Geneva between the warring Yemeni factions failed when Sunnis stormed a Houthi press conference, throwing shoes (a terrible insult among Arabs) at Houthi leader Hamza Al-Houthi and other Houthi officials. The Sunnis called the Shi'ites "criminals" and "dogs," and claimed that they were "killing the children of south Yemen."[115] The Houthis and the Sunnis then began brawling before the Sunnis were escorted out of the press conference.[116]

That episode epitomized the tinderbox aspect of the conflict in Yemen: it could at any point erupt into a full-scale international jihad between Sunnis and Shi'ites. Iran's attempt to expand its Shi'ite crescent to the Arabian Peninsula and gain hegemony in the entire Middle East, all in service of its proxy war against the Americans and Israel, threatened at any moment to spark a regional, and possibly even a global war.

"Hamas is funded by Iran"

In their ambition to lead the Islamic world, however, the Iranians knew they needed Sunni support, and they angled for it by using the one issue that most closely united all Muslims: hatred for Israel.

As far back as the late 1980s, Iran provided the Sunni Palestinian terror group Hamas with ten percent of its total budget. Between 1993 and 2006, Hamas received around $30 million from Iran each year.[117] After 2006, this amount sharply increased, so that in January 2010, Palestinian Authority President Mahmoud Abbas claimed that Hamas had received $250 million from Iran in 2009 alone, and may have received twice that much: "As far as I know," said Abbas, "Hamas receives $250 million. [Maybe] every six months, [maybe] every year. Hamas is funded by Iran. It claims it is financed by donations, but the donations are nothing like what it receives from Iran.

It doesn't amount to one fourth, one fifth, or even one percent of what [Hamas] gets from Iran."[118] And the Iranians didn't send just money.

The Arab Spring uprising against al-Assad threatened the Iran-Hamas alliance, as Iran backed its client al-Assad while Hamas sided with the Sunni jihad groups trying to unseat him. In November 2012, however, shared hatred for Israel brought the two back together again: Hamas and another Sunni jihad group, Islamic Jihad, bombarded the Jewish state with Iranian-made Fajr-3 and Fajr-5 missiles, and Israel finally retaliated with action against Gaza. Ziad al-Nakhla, the deputy leader of Islamic Jihad, gave credit where credit was due: "The arms of the resistance, including those of Hamas, are Iranian, from the bullet to the missile."[119] He added hysterically that "if it wasn't for these arms, the Israeli Army's weapons would have run over the bodies of our children," and praised Iran for its "great sacrifices" in sending this materiel to Gaza.[120]

Majlis speaker Ali Larijani wasn't shy about taking credit: "We proudly say we support the Palestinians, military and financially. The Zionist regime needs to realize that Palestinian military power comes from Iranian military power."[121] In a nod to Iran's larger ambitions, Larijani added, "We may have inflation, unemployment and other economic issues in our country. But we are changing the region, and this will be a big achievement."[122]

Mohammad Ali Jafari, the supreme commander of the Islamic Revolutionary Guards Corps, declared that missile technology had been "transferred to the resistance, and an unlimited number of these missiles is being built."[123]

Iran kept shipping rockets to Gaza. In March 2014, the Israelis intercepted one of these shipments; Britain's Ambassador to the United Nations, Mark Lyall Grant, noted, "This is not the first time that we have seen reports of potential arms transfers to Gaza involving Iran."[124] After Israel destroyed numerous Hamas weapons-smuggling tunnels reaching from Gaza into Israel during its Gaza incursion of summer 2014, the Iranians sent Hamas millions of dollars to finance their rebuilding.[125] In April 2015 it came to light that the Islamic Revolutionary Guards Corps had funneled tens of millions of dollars to Hamas over the previous several months, on the direct orders of Quds Force commander Major General Qassem Suleimani.[126]

But despite all this military aid the tensions between Iran and Hamas over Syria increased. In late July 2015, Moussa Abu Marzouk, a top Hamas official, announced that "the relations between Hamas and Iran are not advancing in a direction in which the organization (Hamas) is interested and aren't improving to the degree the organization wants in order to help the Palestinian issue."[127] In other words, the Iranians had turned off the cash spigot: "All assistance has stopped—both civilian aid to the Gaza Strip and military assistance to Hamas." Marzouk lamented that Iranian money had "greatly helped the resistance in Palestine; without this assistance it will be hard for us to cope."[128]

The next month, however, Iranian Foreign Ministry Spokeswoman Marzieh Afkham denied reports that Iran had cut off Hamas: "Iran's support for all resistance groups continues similar to the past."[129] Iran's Foreign Minister Mohammed Javad Zarif said that Iran would "continue providing weapons to support the Middle Eastern countries fighting terrorism," which presumably included Hamas and Hizballah fighting against the "terrorist" Israelis, although Zarif said this in the context of Iran's opposition to the Islamic State.[130] "Without Iran and the weapons it provided to the countries fighting terrorism," he asserted, "the capital cities of the Middle East would have been occupied by" the Islamic State.[131] Late in 2015, under orders from Quds Force commander Qasem Soleimani, the Islamic Revolutionary Guards Corps sent tens of millions of dollars to Hamas.[132]

At that same time, however, Hamas Deputy Foreign Minister Ghazi Hamad termed the relationship between Hamas and Iran "no good at all," adding, "Our problems with Iran are well known."[133] The real state of affairs became abundantly clear in January 2016, when Hamas rejected an Iranian offer to resume financial aid in exchange for Hamas's support against the

Saudis after the Saudi execution of Shi'ite cleric Nimr al-Nimr. A Hamas official explained, "The equation is clear: as a liberation movement, we need the support of everyone," but he emphasized that Hamas would "never join an alliance against the Sunni world."[135]

With its support for Hamas and other Sunni jihad groups in Gaza, which could be reestablished with a lessening of Sunni-Shi'ite tensions, and its aid for Hizballah, the Houthis in Yemen, the Alawite al-Assad in Syria, and the Shi'ite regime in Baghdad, Iran had made real progress toward dominating a Shi'ite crescent that stretched across the Middle East. "We have no need of America," said Khamenei's advisor Ali Akbar Velayati in October 2015. "Iran is the region's big power in its own right."[136] It was not an empty boast.

WHAT A DEAL!

"We will supply arms to anyone and anywhere necessary and will import weapons from anywhere we want and we have clarified this during the negotiations [over Iran's nuclear weapons program]."
—Iran's Foreign Minister Abbas Araghchi[134]

The primary obstacle to Iran's regional hegemony in the middle of the 2010s was not the United States, but the upstart Sunni caliphate, the Islamic State, that occupied much of Iraq and Syria and threatened Iran's client regimes in both Baghdad and Damascus. As the Islamic State issued detailed and repeated calls for violence against non-Muslims inside the United States and other infidel powers, those powers were caught on the horns of a dilemma: if they destroyed the Islamic State utterly, the region's chief beneficiary would be Iran.

Even after the nuclear deal, no one outside of Tehran wanted to see that.

"Iran has had its tentacles in Spain for quite some time"

According to the State Department, "while its main effort focused on supporting goals in the Middle East, particularly in Syria, Iran and its prox-

"A SINGLE APPARATUS JOINED TOGETHER"

The U.S. named Iran a State Sponsor of Terrorism in 1984, and since then the Islamic Republic has done nothing to show that it doesn't deserve the label. Some of the terror groups that Iran has supported include

- **Hizballah.** Iranian General Amir Ali Hajizadeh, the head of the Islamic Revolutionary Guard Corps' Aerospace Force, has said "the IRGC and Hizballah are a single apparatus jointed together."[137]
- **Hamas.** Iran has supplied this Sunni group with money and weapons for years, but recently the relationship has become tense as Sunni-Shia tensions have increased.
- **Palestine Islamic Jihad (PIJ),** which after Hamas is the second largest jihad group in Gaza, responsible for numerous murders of Israeli civilians. This relationship also became strained when the Saudis and other Sunnis moved against the Shi'ite Houthis in Yemen in May 2015; Iran pulled PIJ's funding, sending it to the brink of financial ruin.[138]
- **Popular Front for the Liberation of Palestine-General Command (PFLP-GC),** a group that started out as Marxist but has no trouble accepting the largesse of the Iranian mullahs.[139]
- **Kata'ib Hizballah,** a Shi'ite militia group in Iraq that, according to the U.S. State Department, has "committed serious human rights abuses against primarily Sunni civilians."[140]

ies also continued subtle efforts at growing influence elsewhere including in Africa, Asia, and, to a lesser extent, Latin America."[141]

An indication of at least one form that those "subtle efforts" took came in January 2016, when Spanish authorities began investigating allegations that Iran had given five million euros to a left-wing populist party, Podemos.[142] The Islamic Republic had come to power with the support of leftists in Iran, and had no trouble collaborating with the hard Left, perhaps because both the Marxists and the mullahs desired to establish an earthly utopia enforced by a reign of terror. In Spain, the trade-off was that Podemos got five million euros, and the Iranians got a foothold in Spain's politics and economy.

Joseph Humire, executive director of Center for a Secure Free Society (SFS), commented, "Iran has had its tentacles in Spain for quite some time. Iran has been busy building its legitimacy through its dedicated, state-owned Spanish broadcast network Hispan TV, and Iglesias from Podemos was Iran's mouthpiece for Spain through his show on that network."[143] Pablo Iglesias was the secretary general of Podemos.

"The northern region of Argentina, the eastern region of Paraguay and even Brazil are large terrains, and they have an organized training and recruitment camp for terrorists"

Less subtle were Iran's actions through its proxy Hizballah in South America. The group established a significant presence among the roughly twenty-five thousand Shi'ite émigrés from Lebanon who had settled in the lightly policed, generally lawless Triple Frontier region of Argentina, Paraguay, and Brazil. In 1998, FBI director Louis Freeh called the Triple Frontier a "free zone for significant criminal activity, including people who are organized to commit acts of terrorism."[144]

It hasn't improved since then, and Hizballah operatives there are widely thought to be involved in smuggling money to jihadis in the Middle East and directing jihad training camps elsewhere in South America. A Muslim leader in the Paraguayan city of Ciudad del Este said that the local Shi'ite mosques had "an obligation to finance" Hizballah.[145]

Interviewed in Ciudad del Este in 2007, Hizballah operative Mustafa Khalil Meri was adamant that if President George W. Bush attacked Iran, it would bring disaster upon him: "If he attacks Iran, in two minutes Bush is dead. We are Muslims. I am Hezbollah. We are Muslims, and we will defend our countries at any time they are attacked.... In [the] United States, there are many Arabs—in Canada, too. If one bomb [strikes] Iran, one bomb, [Bush] will see the world burning.... If an order arrives, all the Arabs that are here, in other parts in the world, all will go to take bombs, bombs for everybody if he bombs Iran."[146]

Meri and others like him were of particular concern to U.S. officials, because they could easily slip into the United States as Spanish-speaking tourists from South America, without anyone knowing they were Hizballah operatives on a mission to kill.

They are already active all over South America. Hizballah has a public presence in Chile, Argentina, El Salvador, Mexico, and many other countries in Central and South America.[147] Augusto Anibal Lima of Paraguay's Triborder Police noted that "the Paraguayan justice [ministry] and the national police have found propaganda materials for Hezbollah" all over South America.[148] And in October 2006, a Hizballah member left bombs outside the U.S. Embassy in Caracas; police safely detonated them, but the point was made: Hizballah was in Venezuela, and would be heard from again.[149]

A CIA report on Hizballah activity worldwide noted that the terror group had mounted operations not only in South America but also in the United States, the United Kingdom, Germany, Austria, Southern Europe, Spain, Cyprus, Thailand, and elsewhere.[150]

"By 2031, the total immigrant population of Canada will increase by 64 percent, and ... the number of Iranians will increase due to birthrate"

Iran did not work internationally only through Hizballah operatives and hired assassins. In July 2012, Hamid Mohammadi, the Iranian cultural affairs counselor at the Iranian Embassy in Ottawa, Ontario, Canada, gave a Farsi-language interview that caught the attention of counterterror officials in both Canada and the United States.

Mohammadi said that there were roughly five hundred thousand Iranians in Canada, and that number was rapidly growing: "By 2031, the total immigrant population of Canada will increase by 64 percent, and that the number of Iranians will increase due to birthrate." He noted with pride that Iranians in Canada had "preserved their strong attachments and bonds to their homeland," and exhorted Iranians in Canada to "resist being melted into the dominant Canadian culture." Some young Canadian-born Iranians, he said, already held "influential government positions," and others should strive to "occupy high-level key positions." Why? So that they could "be of service to our beloved Iran."[151]

What kind of service? David Harris, director of the international and terrorist intelligence program at Insignis Strategic Research in Ottawa, testified before a Canadian Senate committee that "Iran, with its nuclear weapons development, and thousands volunteering for suicide missions, has an aggressive presence in this very city [Ottawa], variously relying on, and victimizing, its expatriates."[152]

On August 9, 2012, Christine Williams, an influential Canadian journalist and an appointee of the Canadian government to the Canadian Race Relations Foundation, observed that "as a tight network of Iranian terrorists expands as a 'fifth column' in Canada, there have been calls to shut down the Iranian embassy there."[153] Added Harris, "Through espionage and subversion, the Embassy projects Tehran's will, relying, in part, on Iranian newcomers from among Canada's vast immigrant inflows to intimidate loyal Canadians of Iranian background, penetrate government and infrastructural interests and generally contribute to Tehran's influence in Canadian life."[154]

On September 7, 2012, Canada took note of this subversive activity, closing its embassy in Tehran and sending Iranian diplomats in Ottawa back to Iran. Foreign Affairs Minister John Baird dubbed Iran "the most significant threat to global peace and security in the world today" and charged

THE AYATOLLAH'S SPIT LIST

"Let's be clear. Islam is not our adversary. Muslims are peaceful and tolerant people and have nothing whatsoever to do with terrorism."

—Hillary Clinton[158]

"Islam is a religion that prevents men from waging war? I spit upon those foolish souls who make such a claim."

—the Ayatollah Khomeini[159]

that "the Iranian regime has shown blatant disregard for the Vienna Convention and its guarantee of protection for diplomatic personnel."[155] Baird criticized Iran's support for the al-Assad regime in Syria, its dismal human rights record, and its support for jihad terror groups as reasons for the decision to cut diplomatic relations, noting also that Iran "routinely threatens the existence of Israel and engages in racist anti-Semitic rhetoric and incitement to genocide."[156]

After leftist Prime Minister Justin Trudeau took office in late 2015, however, Canadian-Iranian relations began to thaw. Trudeau promised to reestablish full diplomatic relations with the Islamic Republic.[157]

Chapter Four

"ISRAEL WILL GO, IT MUST NOT SURVIVE, AND IT WILL NOT"
IRAN'S ALL-CONSUMING HATRED FOR ISRAEL

In November 2012, a huge billboard on Tehran's Niayesh highway depicted a missile with the legend, "Destination Tel Aviv."[1] It attracted little attention from the Iranians who drove by it. Over the previous three decades of living in the Islamic Republic, they had become accustomed to a steady barrage of bellicose anti-Israel rhetoric. From the moment the Iranian mullahs took power, they had been outspoken about their hostility to Israel. The Ayatollah Khomeini dubbed Israel "the Little Satan" and once declared, "this regime occupying Jerusalem must vanish from the page of time."[2]

The Islamic Republic was determined to make sure that happened. It set out to make good on its aggressive rhetoric in the early 1980s by creating Hizballah as a permanent force set against the Jewish state. During the 2006 Israeli-Hizballah conflict, Iranian forces directly aided Hizballah, and two

Did you know?

- According to the president of Argentina, the Obama White House urged her country to supply Iran with nuclear fuel

- The head of Iran's Revolutionary Guard claims Iran has missiles that can reach all of Israel

- Iran has pledged its support to "any group which confronts the Zionist regime" because Israel "must not survive"

- Iran-funded jihadis tried to assassinate Israeli Prime Minister Benjamin Netanyahu in January 2016 members of the Islamic Revolutionary Guards Corps were killed fighting alongside Hizballah in Lebanon.[3] Hundreds of Iranian soldiers aided Hizballah in firing missiles into Israel.[4]

Iran has pursued a proxy war against Israel through many different methods, including the use of friendly nations to help it camouflage its activities. In March 2009, Iran was shipping weapons to Gaza through Sudan—until Israeli forces carried out airstrikes against the shipments.[5] Two years later, Israeli commandos boarded a cargo ship flying the Liberian flag. On it they found, in containers that were labeled as carrying cotton and lentils, mortar shells and Chinese-made anti-ship missiles bound for Hamas. Instruction manuals were written in Farsi. The cargo had been loaded in the Syrian port of Latakia; then the ship had made its way to Turkey before attempting to pass by Israeli defenses and get its cargo to Hamas.[6]

On July 18, 2012, a caller to Bulgaria's tourist office warned that a group of Israeli tourists who were just arriving would be "welcomed by two bombs." When the tourists duly arrived at Bulgaria's Burgas International Airport, they boarded a bus to their hotel—and seven people were killed and over thirty more wounded when a bomb tore through that bus. Benjamin Netanyahu immediately pointed to the mullahs and accused them of carrying out terror attacks against Israelis all over the globe: "All signs point towards Iran. Over the last few months we have seen Iran's attempts to attack Israelis in Thailand, India, Georgia, Kenya, Cyprus and other countries. Exactly 18 years to the day after the horrendous attack on the Jewish Community Center in Argentina, deadly Iranian terrorism continues to strike at innocent people. This is a global Iranian terror onslaught and Israel will react firmly to it."[7]

Netanyahu's accusation was well founded. Bulgarian Interior Minister Tsvetan Tsvetanov announced in February 2013, "We have well-grounded reasons to suggest that the two [responsible for the bombing] were members of the militant wing of Hezbollah."[8] Europol Director Rob Wainwright concurred: "The Bulgarian authorities are making quite a strong assumption that this is the work of Hezbollah. From what I've seen of the case—from the very strong, obvious links to Lebanon, from the modus operandi of the terrorist attack and from other intelligence that we see—I think that is a reasonable assumption."[9] The mastermind of the attack was a member of Hizballah, traveling with a fake Michigan driver's license.[10]

Hizballah involvement meant Iranian involvement.

"If they (Jews) all gather in Israel, it will save us the trouble of going after them worldwide"

Hizballah's Hassan Nasrallah has said, "If they (Jews) all gather in Israel, it will save us the trouble of going after them worldwide."[11] Hizballah has certainly targeted Jews in Israel, but it has also taken the trouble to go after them worldwide. On March 17, 1992—in the Argentina attack Netanyahu was referring to—a jihad-martyrdom suicide bomber drove a truck filled with 220 pounds of TNT into the Israeli Embassy in Buenos Aires murdering twenty-nine people and wounding 242.[12]

Iran immediately denied any involvement in the bombing, but a number of facts cast that denial into doubt. A Muslim group called the Islamic Jihad Organization immediately claimed credit for the bombing, saying it had been perpetrated by a convert to Islam named Abu Yasser in order to avenge the killing of Hizballah leader Abbas Mussawi and his family, including his five-year-old son Hussein, in an Israeli air raid. "We hereby declare with all pride," said Islamic Jihad's statement, "that the operation of the martyr infant Hussein is one of our continuing strikes against the criminal Israeli enemy in an open-ended war which will not cease until Israel is wiped out of existence."[13]

But the Islamic Jihad Organization (IJO) was essentially just Iran client Hizballah operating under a different name. Journalist Ronen Bergman explained, "The Hizballah command in Beirut selected the Israeli Embassy in Buenos Aires as the best target for revenge for the Mussawi assassination. The Triple Frontier area—the border region shared by Argentina, Paraguay and Brazil—at the Iguazu Falls was the staging ground, due to its large population of Shi'ite immigrants from Lebanon who maintain close links with their families back home and are ready to help when necessary."[14]

The IJO had also carried out the bombing of the U.S. Marine barracks in Beirut in 1983. A key Hizballah leader, Imad Mughniyeh, was said to have been one of the principal planners of that attack and to have watched it happen with binoculars from the top of a building nearby. Hizballah's first Secretary-General, Subhi al-Tufayli, was also implicated in the barracks attack, as was Mohammad Hussein Fadlallah, a key Hizballah spiritual leader.[15]

On July 18, 1994, another jihad-martyrdom suicide bomber destroyed the Jewish-Argentine Mutual Association (AMIA) building in Buenos Aires, killing eighty-five people and wounding three hundred.[16] As years went by and no one was convicted of the attack, numerous accusations were made of cover-ups by Argentine investigators and authorities. Finally, in October 2006, Argentine state prosecutor Alberto Nisman formally charged Iran and Hizballah and called for the arrest of, among others, former Iranian President Hashemi Rafsanjani, charging that he had ordered the attack as revenge for Argentina's ending its nuclear cooperation with Iran.[17] Nisman's report alleged that Argentina was providing Iran with low-grade enriched uranium and that since powerful elements in both countries wanted these transactions to continue, both had an interest in covering up Iran's role in the bombings.[18]

Both Iran and Hizballah denied any involvement. In 2013, Argentine president Cristina Fernández de Kirchner struck a deal with the Islamic Republic to open a joint investigation of the bombing. Nisman, however, charged that this joint investigation was designed solely to divert attention from Iranians who had been accused of involvement in the case, and to quash arrest warrants for them.[19]

On January 14, 2015, Nisman accused President Fernández de Kirchner of negotiating secretly with the Iranians—offering to make the bombing investigation go away in exchange for favorable oil terms from Iran.[20] Nisman was scheduled to meet with Argentine officials on January 19 to give them the details of his accusations, but he was found dead that morning—shot to death in his bathtub.[21]

It seemed that some very powerful and ruthless people in Argentina did not want the details of Iran's role in the AMIA bombing—and Argentina's possible role in Iran's nuclear program—to come out.

The connection between Argentina and Iran's nuclear ambitions was further complicated on September 28, 2015, when Fernández de Kirchner, addressing the United Nations General Assembly, claimed that in 2010 Obama administration officials had exhorted her to provide nuclear fuel to the Iranians: "In 2010 we were visited in Argentina by Gary Samore, at that time the White House's top advisor in nuclear issues. He came to see us in Argentina with a mission, with an objective: under the control of IAEA, the international organization in the field of weapons control and nuclear regulation, Argentina had supplied in the year 1987, during the first democratic government, the nuclear fuel for the reactor known as 'Teheran.'" According to Fernández de Kirchner, the Obama administration, in order to smooth the way for the deal it was negotiating with Iran, wanted Argentina to supply the mullahs with fuel for their nuclear program.[22]

"The range of (our) missiles covers all of Israel today. That means the fall of the Zionist regime, which will certainly come soon."

As it acquired nuclear technology and murdered Jews worldwide, Iran continued to prosecute the war of words, as well—at which the Islamic

WHAT A DEAL!

"[White House advisor] Gary Samore had explained to our Minister of Foreign Affairs, Héctor Timerman, that negotiations were underway for the Islamic Republic of Iran to cease with its uranium enrichment activities or to do it to a lesser extent but Iran claimed that it needed to enrich this Teheran nuclear reactor and this was hindering negotiations. They [the Americans] came to ask us, Argentines, to provide the Islamic Republic of Iran with nuclear fuel. Rohani was not in office yet. It was Ahmadinejad's administration and negotiations had already started."[23]

—Argentine president Fernández de Kirchner

Republic's spokesmen were always adept. In August 2012, Brigadier General Gholamreza Jalali, the head of Iran's civil defense organization and a former commander of the Islamic Revolutionary Guards Corps, declared that "no other way exists apart from resolve and strength to completely eliminate the aggressive nature and to destroy Israel."[24]

The head of the Islamic Revolutionary Guards Corps, General Mohammad Ali Jafari, boasted in November 2014: "The range of (our) missiles covers all of Israel today. That means the fall of the Zionist regime, which will certainly come soon."[25]

In May 2015, Iran's state-run Fars News Agency falsely charged that former Israeli Defense Forces General Staff Chief Moshe Ya'alon had threatened that the IDF would target Lebanese civilians. In response, General Yahya Rahim Safavi, military advisor to Khamenei, issued a new threat: "Iran, with the help of Hezbollah and its friends, is capable of destroying Tel Aviv and Haifa in case of military aggression on the part of the Zionists. I don't think the Zionists would be so unintelligent as to create a military problem with Iran. They know the strength of Iran and Hezbollah."[26]

Since he became the Islamic Republic's Supreme Leader in 1989, the Ayatollah Khamenei has repeatedly reiterated the necessity of utterly destroying Israel. On December 4, 1990, he said, "Regarding the Palestine issue, the problem is taking back Palestine, which means disappearance of Israel."[27] He made it clear that this didn't just mean the Israeli land commonly termed "the occupied territories," but the entire state of Israel: "There is no difference between occupied territories before and after [the Arab-Israeli war of] 1967. Every inch of Palestinian land is an inch of Palestinians' home. Any entity ruling Palestine is illegitimate unless it is Islamic and by Palestinians. Our position is what our late Imam [Khomeini] said, 'Israel must disappear.'"[29]

Jews could still live in Palestine, though, if they accepted Islamic rule, which for them would mean second-class status as dhimmis, the "protected people" of the Islamic state: "The Jews of Palestine can live there, if they accept the Islamic government there. We are not against Jews. The issue is the illegal ownership of Muslims' homes. Muslim leaders, if they were not influenced by the world powers, could solve this important problem, but unfortunately have not been able to."[30]

IT'S ALWAYS THE JEWS

In a September 2013 interview with NBC News, President Hassan Rouhani labeled Israel "an occupier and usurper government" and claimed that it committed "injustice to the people of the region, and has brought instability to the region, with its warmongering policies."[28]

Again on August 19, 1991, Khamenei emphasized that Israel must be destroyed: "Solving the Palestinian problem entails destroying and eliminating the illegitimate government there, so that the true owners [of the land] can form a new government; Muslims, Christians, and Jews can live side by side.... Our view regarding the Palestine issue is clear. We believe the solution is destroying the Israeli regime. Forty years has passed [since establishment of the state of Israel], and if another forty years passes, Israel must disappear, and will."

One of the Supreme Leader's favorite terms for Israel was "cancerous tumor." In March 1994, Khamenei complained that "the United States and others support this cancerous tumor in the heart of Islamic nations."[31] Four months later, he again referred to Israel as "this cancerous tumor" and said that it had a "a terrorist government."[32] In June 2013, he ascribed the phrase to the Ayatollah Khomeini: "our magnanimous Imam is the person who never changed his mind about the Zionist regime; that 'the Zionist regime is a cancerous tumor that must be removed' are the Imam's words."[33]

On January 15, 2001, Khamenei declared, "It is the mission of the Islamic Republic of Iran to erase Israel from the map of the region."[34] On April 22 of the same year, he called for Muslim nations to support the jihad against Israel, predicting "that if even a portion of the Islamic world's resources is devoted to this path, we will witness the decay and eventual disappearance of the Zionist regime." Muslim nations should be willing to use their resources for Israel's destruction because the Jewish state was created, in Khamenei's view, in order to undermine them: on January 31, 2002, Khamenei complained that "the cancerous Zionist tumor" had been built by the U.S. and its allies "to use it against Islamic nations."[35]

In August 2012, Khamenei reiterated that Israel would soon vanish: "the fake Zionist (regime) will disappear from the landscape of geography. The light of hope will shine on the Palestinian issue, and this Islamic land will certainly be returned to the Palestinian nation."[37] In 2014, he returned to the same theme: "This barbaric, wolflike and infanticidal regime of Israel which spares no crime has no cure but to be annihilated."[38]

CALL IT THE KHAMENEI DOCTRINE

"From now on we will also support any nation, any group that confronts the Zionist regime, we will help them, and we are not shy about doing so. Israel will go, it must not survive, and it will not."
—Iran's Supreme Leader Khamenei, issuing a blanket promise of support to any nation that fights against Israel in a February 3, 2012, Friday sermon[36]

"9 key questions about elimination of Israel"

In November 2014, Iran's Supreme Leader codified and made public the strategy Iran had been pursuing to destroy Israel when he released a chart entitled "9 key questions about elimination of Israel" on Twitter.[39]

The first question was: "Why should the Zionist regime be eliminated?" The chart gave this answer, in marginal English: "During its 66 years of life so far, the fake Zionist regime has tried to realize its goals by means of infanticide, homicide, violence and iron fist while boasts about it blatantly."[40]

Next was: "What does elimination of Israel mean in the viewpoint of Imam Khomeini?" The answer: "The only means of bringing Israeli crimes to an end is the elimination of this regime. And of course the elimination of Israel does not mean the massacre of the Jewish people in this region. The Islamic Republic has proposed a practical & logical mechanism for this to international communities."[41]

That mechanism? "All the original people of Palestine including Muslims, Christians and Jews wherever they are, whether inside Palestine, in refugee camps in other countries or just anywhere else, take part in a public and organized referendum. Naturally the Jewish immigrants who have been persuaded into emigration to Palestine do not have the right to take part in this referendum."[42]

Such a referendum, stacked against Jewish Israelis, would result in the formation of a government that would "decide whether the non-Palestinian emigrants who have immigrated to this country over the past years can continue living in Palestine or should return to their home countries."[43] How they would be compelled to return to their "home countries," and what would happen if they would or could not do so, the Ayatollah did not say. In the meantime, in any case, there will be jihad warfare: "Up until the day when this homicidal and infanticidal regime is eliminated through a referendum, powerful confrontation and resolute and armed resistance is the cure of this ruinous regime."[44]

To this end, "the West Bank should be armed like Gaza and those who are interested in Palestine's destiny should take action to arm the people of the West Bank so that the sorrows and grieves of the Palestinian people will reduce in the light of their powerful hands and the weakness of the Zionist enemy."[45] This weaponry, however, should not be supplied for the purpose of a conventional war: "We recommend neither a classical war by the army of Muslim countries nor to throw migrated Jews at sea and certainly not an arbitration by UN or other international organizations."[46] Here again, however, Khamenei did not explain what would happen to Israeli Jews who wanted to stay, or had no means to leave.

The Supreme Leader let slip a hint that he was aware that Israeli's war is defensive, while that of the Palestinians is one of conquest, genocide, and annihilation, when he took the trouble to deny "[t]hat the rockets of Gaza led to the crimes of Israel," calling it "a wrong conclusion."[47] He didn't explain why.

Despite Khamenei's rejection of a "classical war by the army of Muslim countries against Israel" in 2014, in November of the next year the Islamic Revolutionary Guard Corps conducted a war game involving direct conflict between Iran and Israel. Thousands of IRGC paramilitary forces stormed a model that was supposed to represent the Al-Aqsa Mosque on the Temple Mount in Jerusalem (it was actually a replica of the Dome of the Rock, also on the Temple Mount, which dominates the Jerusalem skyline with its gold dome). One IRGC member went to the top of the replica dome and placed there two flags: one of Iran, and one of the color red, signifying martyrdom.[48]

"The hegemony of Iran will be promoted"

In a book he published in the summer of 2015, Khamenei expanded upon his plan to destroy Israel, revealing his grand strategy regarding the Jewish state. Iranian-born journalist Amir Taheri revealed that shortly after the nuclear deal was concluded Khamenei had published, in Farsi only, a lengthy book entitled *Palestine*. The jacket copy hailed the Supreme Leader as "the flagbearer of Jihad to liberate Jerusalem."[49] In the book, Khamenei once again called Israel a "cancerous tumour" and discussed its imminent "annihilation"—which he said must be brought about because of "well-established Islamic principles," such as the proposition that any land once ruled by Muslims belongs by right to Muslims forever, and must not be ruled by non-Muslims, as the Qur'an directs, "drive them out from where they drove you out" (2:191).[50]

According to Khamenei, Israel's wars against Muslim countries have made it into a "kaffir al-harbi," that is, an infidel at war with Islam. The Supreme Leader revealed one of his "most cherished wishes": to pray in Jerusalem after Israel had been conquered and destroyed.[51]

This conquest would not, he said once again, occur by means of "classical wars," nor would it result in a new genocide of the Jews. Rather, noted Taheri, "what he recommends is a long period of low-intensity warfare designed to make life unpleasant if not impossible for a majority of Israeli Jews so that they leave the country. His calculation is based on the assumption that large numbers of Israelis have dual nationality and would prefer emigration to the United States and Europe to daily threats of death."[52]

This "low-intensity warfare" would feature regular jihad terror attacks from Lebanon, Gaza, and the West Bank. This would lead to victories on the order of previous ones for which, Khamenei said, Iran was responsible: "We have intervened in anti-Israel matters, and it brought victory in the 33-day war by Hezbollah against Israel in 2006 and in the 22-day war between Hamas and Israel in the Gaza Strip."[53]

This constant pressure on Israel, Khamenei wrote, would lead to "Israel fatigue" in the United States and

IT'S ALWAYS THE JEWS

Israel, Khamenei says in *Palestine*, is a foremost "ally of the American Great Satan" and a principal exponent of the Americans' "evil scheme" to control "the heartland of the Ummah"—that is, the global Muslim community.

among Israel's other supporters in the international community, who would then cast about for "a practical and logical mechanism" to betray Israel into the hands of its enemies. "The solution," he wrote, "is a one-state formula," a State of Palestine that would be ruled by Islamic law but would allow non-Muslims—including even Jews if they have what the Supreme Leader called "genuine roots" in that area—to live there as dhimmis, the subjugated "People of the Book" under Islamic rule, denied basic rights.[54]

British Foreign Secretary Philip Hammond was sure that Khamenei didn't really mean it. Or, if he did, the Iranian regime as a whole didn't. Hammond, visiting Tehran in August 2015 to reopen the United Kingdom's Embassy there, claimed that Iranian President Rouhani had a "more nuanced approach" toward Israel.

OSTRICH ALERT

According to UK Foreign Secretary Hammond, Khamenei's "revolutionary sloganizing" should not be taken as an indication of "what Iran actually does in the conduct of its foreign policy. We've got to, as we do with quite a number of countries, distinguish the internal political consumption rhetoric from the reality of the way they conduct their foreign policy."[55]

But Hussein Sheikholeslam, a foreign affairs advisor to the speaker of the Iranian Parliament, Ali Larijani, brusquely dismissed Hammond's wishful thinking: "Our positions against the usurper Zionist regime have not changed at all; Israel should be annihilated and this is our ultimate slogan.... These powers admitted that the reason for their pressure on us is our position on Israel. We told them that we reject the existence of any Israeli on this earth."[56]

In the months after the nuclear deal was concluded, bellicose rhetoric came from Tehran in a steady drumbeat. In August 2015 Khamenei charged that Israel and the United States were making war against Islam itself, conspiring "against the Quran and not Shiism and Iran, because they know that the Quran and Islam are the center of awakening nations."[57] The Iranian people, he said, "have realized that their real stubborn enemy is the world arrogance and Zionism and that's why they chant slogans against the US and Zionism."[59]

The next month Khamenei took to Twitter to threaten Israel in broken English: "After negotiations, in Zionist regime they said they had no more concern about Iran for next 25 years; I'd say: Firstly, you will not see next 25 years; God willing, there will be nothing as Zionist regime by next 25 years. Secondly, until then, struggling, heroic and jihadi morale will leave no moment of serenity for Zionists."[60]

"We should mobilize the whole Islamic world for a sharp confrontation with the Zionist regime . . . if we abide by the Qur'an, all of us should mobilize to kill"

Still, Iranian Foreign Minister Mohammed Javad Zarif had insisted in March 2015 that the Islamic Republic doesn't hate Jews: "If you read the Book of Esther, you will see that it was the Iranian king who saved the Jews. If you read the Old Testament, you will see that it was an Iranian king who saved the Jews from Babylon. Esther has a town in Iran where our Jewish population, which is the largest in the Middle East, visits on a regular basis."[61]

Zarif was protesting too much: the declarations that Israel would soon be destroyed had come from Iranian leaders in a steady stream over many years. In 2008, Yahya Rahim Safavi, onetime commander of the Islamic Revolutionary Guard Corps, proclaimed, "With God's help the time has come for the Zionist

WHAT A DEAL!

Not long after the nuclear deal was concluded, Iran's Foreign Minister Mohammed Javad Zarif went to Lebanon, where he said that the agreement would help Iran target Israel. "Zarif said from Beirut that the nuclear agreement between Tehran and the world powers created a historic opportunity for regional cooperation to fight extremism and face threats posed by the Zionist entity."

—Hizballah's al-Manar TV station[58]

regime's death sentence."[62] In 2011, the commander of the paramilitary Basiji forces, Mohammad Reza Naqdi, warned Israelis, "We recommend them to pack their furniture and return to their countries. And if they insist on staying, they should know that a time [will] arrive when they will not even have time to pack their suitcases."[63]

Many other Iranian officials had said essentially the same thing. Said Ahmad Alamolhoda, a member of the Assembly of Experts, which chooses and supervises the Supreme Leader: "The destruction of Israel is the idea of the Islamic Revolution in Iran and is one of the pillars of the Iranian Islamic regime. We cannot claim that we have no intention of going to war with Israel."[65] Hojjat al-Islam Ali Shirazi, Khamenei's representative in the Islamic Revolutionary Guard Corps, said in 2013 that the end of Israel was imminent: "The Zionist regime will soon be destroyed, and this generation will be witness to its destruction."[66] Mohammad Ali Jafari, commander in chief of the Islamic Revolutionary Guard Corps, vowed in 2015, "The Revolutionary Guards will fight to the end of the Zionist regime.... We will not rest easy until this epitome of vice is totally deleted from the region's geopolitics."[67]

NOT THAT THIS HAS ANYTHING TO DO WITH ISLAM

"If we abide by real legal laws, we should mobilize the whole Islamic world for a sharp confrontation with the Zionist regime...if we abide by the Qur'an, all of us should mobilize to kill."

—Iran's "moderate" President Mohammad Khatami in 2000[64]

"We said 'hell no' to the overflights"

"The Zionist regime separated from America has no meaning, and we must not recognize Israel as separate from America." So said Islamic Revolutionary Guard Corps naval commander Ali Fadavi in September

2012.[68] But events did not always bear out his conspiratorial view of cooperation between the "Great Satan" and the "Little Satan."

In the midst of all the threats and boasts of the imminent destruction of Israel emanating regularly from Tehran, many Western policy analysts assumed during the presidency of George W. Bush that eventually the United States and Israel would coordinate a military attack on Iran's nuclear facilities.

In early 2008, the Israelis appeared ready to go it alone, but they needed materiel, and approval, from Washington. In secret meetings, Israeli authorities asked Bush administration officials for new bunker-buster bombs that would penetrate the defenses that the Iranians had built around their nuclear installations, along with equipment to enable their aircraft to refuel while flying from Israel to Iran and back, and most importantly of all, for permission to fly over Iraq to get to Iran.

A Bush White House official recounted, "We said 'hell no' to the overflights," and didn't give a straight answer to the other two requests. In January 2009, as Bush was preparing to turn over the presidency to Barack Obama, a spokesman for Robert Gates, the Secretary of Defense who was to continue in his job under the new president, said, "A potential strike on the Iranian facilities is not something that we or anyone else should be pursuing at this time."[69]

The Israelis had to look for other options.

"I don't know who took revenge on the Iranian scientist, but I am definitely not shedding a tear"

In 2010, researchers discovered the Stuxnet cyberweapon, which had infiltrated Iranian computer systems and ultimately destroyed a thousand of Iran's six thousand centrifuges. It was reportedly a joint American-Israeli effort that had the approval of even Barack Obama, who, according to the *Washington Post*, "was eager to slow [Iran]'s apparent progress toward building an atomic bomb without launching a traditional military attack, say current and former U.S. officials."[70]

The Israelis may have acted against the Iranian nuclear program in other ways as well. On January 12, 2010, Masoud Alimohammadi, an Iranian particle physicist, was on his way to work in Tehran when he was killed by a bomb that had been strapped to a motorcycle.[71] Then on November 29 of the same year, an Iranian nuclear scientist, Majid Shahriari, was also killed in Tehran when a motorcyclist placed a bomb on his car.[72] Another Iranian scientist, Darioush Rezaeinejad, was shot and killed in Tehran on July 23, 2011.[73] On November 12, 2011, Islamic Revolutionary Guards Corps commander Hassan Tehrani Moqaddam, who was deeply involved in Iran's missile program, and sixteen others were killed in a mysterious explosion at an Iranian missile base. A Western intelligence official advised, "Don't believe the Iranians that it was an accident."[74]

The Iranian nuclear facilities in Isfahan were hit by a similarly mysterious explosion on November 28, 2011. Iran's state-run Fars News Agency initially reported that an explosion had taken place, but then removed that report. The deputy governor of Isfahan insisted, "So far no report of a major explosion has been heard from any government body in Isfahan." Israeli officials, however, said that the explosion did take place, and was "no accident."[75]

The mysterious attacks continued: on January 11, 2012, Mostafa Ahmadi Roshan, deputy chief of Iran's uranium enrichment facility at Natanz, was killed in Tehran in the same way that Shahriari had been killed in 2010: motorcyclists placed a bomb on his car.[76]

In February 2012, an Israeli diplomat's car was destroyed in an explosion near the Israeli embassy in New Delhi, India, shortly after two men on bicycles threw something onto the car. Around the same time, officials of the Israeli embassy in Tbilisi, Georgia, thwarted an attempt to place a bomb on the car of an embassy official.[77]

Benjamin Netanyahu pointed his finger directly at Iran. "Today we witnessed two more terror attacks—in India and Georgia. Iran, which is behind these two attacks, is the world's largest terror exporter. The government of Israel and its security services will continue to cooperate with local authorities against Iran-sponsored global terror."[78] In another statement he accused Iran of targeting Jews worldwide: "Iran is behind these attacks; it is the largest exporter of terrorism in the world. In recent months, we have witnessed several attempts to attack Israeli citizens and Jews in several countries, including Azerbaijan, Thailand and others. Iran and its proxy Hezbollah were behind all of these attempted attacks."[79]

A foreign ministry official in Tehran shot back, "We categorically reject the accusations made by the Zionist regime. They are part of a propaganda war."[80] Nonetheless, the suspicions remained, especially after Indian police arrested an Indian citizen who worked for an Iranian publication in connection with the New Delhi bombing.[81]

Were the Iranians retaliating for attacks on nuclear scientists that had been carried out using similar methods? Certainly it was widely assumed that Israel was behind the attacks on the nuclear scientists (though there was also some speculation that the scientists were being targeted by the Islamic Republic itself for disloyalty). Some assumed that the United States was also involved; Obama administration officials, including Secretary of State Hillary Clinton, strenuously denied this.

But were the Israelis indeed targeting Iranian nuclear scientists for assassination in order to hamstring Iran's nuclear program? A spokesman for the Israeli military, Brigadier General Yoav Mordechai, said after the killing of Roshan, "I don't know who took revenge on the Iranian scientist, but I am definitely not shedding a tear."[82]

NBC News reported in 2012 that "deadly attacks on Iranian nuclear scientists are being carried out by an Iranian dissident group that is financed, trained and armed by Israel's secret service."[83] That dissident group was the

Mujahedin-e Khlaq (MEK), a group that is dedicated to an Islamic state in Iran but nonetheless opposes the ruling mullahs. Mohammad Javad Larijani, an aide to Khamenei, claimed that the Israelis partnered with the MEK because "Israel does not have direct access to our society. [The MEK], being Iranian and being part of Iranian society, they have…a good number of places…to get into touch with people."[84] The MEK, for its part, denied working with Israel.

Early in 2014 it was revealed that Barack Obama had pressured the Israelis to stop targeting Iranian nuclear scientists for assassination.[85] This was ironic, albeit not in the least surprising, since it was American inaction and Obama's solicitude for Iran and enabling of its nuclear program with his nuclear deal that would have been the primary impetus for Israel's resorting to unconventional ways to head off Iran's acquisition of nuclear weapons. For whatever reason, however, the killings stopped with Roshan.

Or at least they did on one side. In January 2016, several Hamas operatives were indicted for a plot to murder Benjamin Netanyahu—a plot that was unfolding as Iran resumed funding Hamas to the tune of tens of millions of dollars.[86]

"For them in this world is disgrace, and for them in the Hereafter is a great punishment"

Iran's hatred of Israel is rooted in its identity as an Islamic Republic. The Qur'an contains a great deal of material that can and does incite furious hatred for Jews, and a pious Muslim, Shi'ite or Sunni, sees Israel and modern Jews through a Qur'anic prism.

The Qur'an states that in the Torah is "guidance and light" (5:44) and asks why the Jews approach Muhammad to settle their disputes: "But how is it that they come to you for judgment while they have the Torah, in which is the judgment of Allah?" (5:43). It also asserts, however, that the Qur'an is "the Book in truth, confirming that which preceded it of the Scripture and as a criterion over it" (5:48).

The Jews, however, did not see the Qur'an as confirming their Scriptures, and did not convert to Islam en masse. The Qur'an explains this as a manifestation of their perversity and rebellion from Allah: "And when a messenger from Allah came to them confirming that which was with them, a party of those who had been given the Scripture threw the Scripture of Allah behind their backs as if they did not know" (2:101). Allah says of the Jews: "Is it not that every time they took a covenant a party of them threw it away? But most of them do not believe" (2:100).

According to the Qur'an, those Jews who did not accept Muhammad and Islam are "avid listeners to falsehood, listening to another people who have not come to you. They distort words beyond their usages" and are "the ones for whom Allah does not intend to purify their hearts." They face the divine wrath in this world as well as the next: "For them in this world is disgrace, and for them in the Hereafter is a great punishment" (5:41). They are disgraced everywhere they go: "They have been put under humiliation wherever they are overtaken, except for a covenant from Allah and a rope from the Muslims. And they have drawn upon themselves anger from Allah and have been put under destitution. That is because they disbelieved in the verses of Allah and killed the prophets without right. That is because they disobeyed and transgressed" (3:112).

The Jews even dare to claim that "Allah did not reveal to a human being anything." Allah instructs Muhammad to respond, "Say, 'Who revealed the Scripture that Moses brought as light and guidance to the people? You make it into pages, disclosing it and concealing much. And you were taught that which you knew not—neither you nor your fathers. Say, 'Allah.' Then leave them in their discourse, amusing themselves" (6:91).

Ultimately, and this punishment too is described in the Qur'an, Allah transforms disobedient Jews into apes and pigs (2:63–66; 5:59–60; 7:166).

Muslims should avoid such people: "O you who have believed, do not take the Jews and the Christians as allies. They are allies of one another. And whoever is an ally to them among you—then indeed, he is of them. Indeed, Allah guides not the wrongdoing people" (5:51). Now the Jews are accursed of Allah for rejecting the Qur'an: "And when there came to them a Book from Allah confirming that which was with them—although before they used to pray for victory against those who disbelieved—but when there came to them that which they recognized, they disbelieved in it; so the curse of Allah will be upon the disbelievers" (2:89). They are the worst enemies of the Muslims: "You will surely find the most intense of the people in animosity toward the believers the Jews.... " (5:82).

Iranian officials have also borrowed ancient blood libels against the Jews from Europe. In 2012, Iranian Vice President Mohammad Reza Rahimi claimed that the Talmud teaches "how to destroy non-Jews so as to protect an embryo in the womb of a Jewish mother."[87] And in April 2015, a website operated by Iranian Majlis member Ahmad Tavakkoli charged that "blood shedding by Jews is not a new theme.... By examining Jewish history in past centuries, it becomes evident that they insist on blood shedding and even bloodthirstiness based on their altered religion and teachings."[88]

Thus it was no surprise when Islamic Revolutionary Guards Corps Deputy Commander Brigadier General Hossein Salami in March 2014 articulated the destruction of Israel as a principal goal of the Islamic Republic: "Despite the geographical distance," he said, "we are attached to the hearts of the Palestinians. How is it that our slogans and goals are identical to the slogans and causes of the Palestinians? Why do we strive to become martyrs and risk our lives for the Palestinian cause? The answer is that the religion of Islam has designated this for us—this goal, this motivation, this belief, this energy—so that we, here, can muster all our energies in order to annihilate the Zionist entity, more than 1,400 kilometers away. We are ready for that moment in the future."[89]

"The Jews are currently subjecting us to an unprecedented trial"

Iranian leaders also portrayed Israel as the gray eminence behind virtually everything that went wrong, or threatened to go wrong, for Muslims. Enemies of the regime were branded Zionists, however implausibly. Pas-

NOT THAT THIS HAS ANYTHING TO DO WITH ISLAM

The enemies of the Muslims, the killers of the prophets, dishonest, evil, subhuman, and accursed of Allah—this is the Qur'an's picture of the Jews. Combine all that with the Qur'anic command to "kill them wherever you overtake them and expel them from wherever they have expelled you" (2:191), and one has come to the root of the implacable hostility among Muslims toward Israel—and the heart of the Islamic Republic of Iran's stance toward the Jewish state.

tor Yusef Nadarkhani, a convert from Islam to Christianity, was imprisoned and threatened with capital punishment for leaving Islam, a capital crime in Islamic law. But Gholam-Ali Rezvani, deputy governor general of the province of Gilan, where Nadarkhani was tried, denied that he was facing death because of apostasy: "The issue of crime and of capital punishment of this individual is not a question of faith or religion—in our system, one cannot be executed for changing their religion." Rather, Rezvani claimed in September 2011, Nadarkhani faced execution for being "a Zionist, a traitor and had committed security crimes."[90]

Going even further, in April 2013 one Iranian writer told a group of seminarians that the Jews controlled the United States by means of sorcery:

The Jews are currently subjecting us to an unprecedented trial. As you read in the Koran, Solomon ruled the world—and God ordered a group of sorcerers to come out against him. The Jews have the greatest powers of sorcery, and they make use of this tool. All the measures that have been brought against us originate with the Zionists. The U.S. is a tool in their hands. So far, they have not used the full [scope of] their sorcery against us. Sorcery was the final means to which they resorted during the Ahmadinejad era, but they were defeated. This ability of the Jews was eliminated by Iran. Five years ago they tried to oust Ahmadinejad.[91]

The same writer claimed in an article that the Jews "believe that it is possible to conquer nature and control the world, and even to control God's decisions, by using sorcery methods."[92]

The author of this anti-Semitic conspiracy fantasy was no marginal paranoiac: he was Mehdi Taeb, a prominent Iranian intellectual and close associate of Khamenei. The Supreme Leader himself, while favorably comparing Iranian democracy with the American variety, charged in June 2013 that the "U.S. president is being elected only from two parties while Zionist regime is controlling everything behind the scenes."[93]

Controlling everything behind the scenes how? By means of sorcery? Maybe. Islamic Republic of Iran Broadcasting (IRIB), Iran's state-run broadcaster, in the summer of 2014 broadcast a show featuring Valiollah Naghipourfar, a Muslim cleric and professor at Tehran University, who asked, "Can jinns be put to use in intelligence gathering?" Jinns are spirit beings whose existence is taken for granted in the Qur'an. That question naturally led Naghipourfar to a discussion of those accomplished sorcerers, the Jews: "The Jew is very practiced in sorcery. Indeed most sorcerers are Jews." The Zionist regime, he charged, used jinns against Iran.[94]

Jinns—and squirrels. The state-run Islamic Republic News Agency (IRNA) announced in July 2007, "In recent weeks, intelligence operatives have arrested 14 squirrels within Iran's borders. The squirrels were carrying spy gear of foreign agencies, and were stopped before they could act, thanks to the alertness of our intelligence services." Iranian police commander Esmaeil Ahmadi-Moqadam admitted that it was true: the Iranians had indeed arrested Zionist spy squirrels, although he grew testy when asked for details.[95] Jinns, squirrels, and pigeons: the Iranian newspaper Etemad Melli reported in late October 2008: "Early this month, a black pigeon was caught bearing a blue-coated metal ring, with invisible strings."[96] Suspicion fell on—who else?—Israel, of course.

Besides controlling the United States, the Israelis were also busy stirring up conflict between Sunnis and Shi'ites. Ayatollah Mohsin Qommi, the head of international affairs in the office of the Supreme Leader of the Islamic Revolution (that is, Khamenei) explained at a 2013 convention in Pakistan that "Shia-Sunni tension is created to benefit and defend the weak and illegitimate state of Israel."[97]

Not content with controlling the U.S. and stirring up Sunni-Shia strife, the Israelis were working to destroy Islam. At least that was the view of some Iranian officials. Iran's state-run Press TV editorialized in January 2014: "With Zionists more intent than ever on defiling one of Islam's holiest of holy, al-Aqsa Mosque, the very ground upon which, so many prophets of God, including Prophet Mohammed (PBUH), have walked upon, one should not ponder over whether Israel is working towards the building of its Third Temple but rather ask when it plans to destroy one of Islam's beacons."[98]

Not only one of Islam's beacons, but Islam itself: "Such men want to extradite [sic] Islam from its land and deny its very existence for it poses an inherent threat to their own belief system. As a religion of truth, the closing chapter of God's message onto Men, Islam requires no indoctrination as it is light by essence. It is such light which Israel seeks to annihilate as its forces only yearn for darkness."[99]

Khamenei echoed this analysis in May 2014 and added to Israel's agenda the prevention of Iran and the Shi'ites from taking a leading role in the

Islamic world: "The goal of the enemy is to bring Islam to its knees and prevent the Shiite community from becoming a role-model."[101]

Israel's baneful influence extended to all aspects of life in Iran. Mohammad-Reza Madani of Iran's Society for Fighting Smoking charged in 2010 that "some of the most famous cigarette brands worldwide including Marlboro, which accounts for the bulk of smuggled cigarettes [into the Islamic Republic] are tainted with [hazardous] nuclear materials." Who produced these poisonous cigarettes? "Philip Morris International, which is led by Zionists."[102]

Not just cigarettes, but drugs. In June 2012, Iran's vice president, Mohammad Reza Rahimi, accused "Zionists" of "inciting global drug trade and addiction in a bid to annihilate non-Jewish communities." He claimed that the Jews' control of the drug trade explained "why you cannot find a single addict among the Zionists." Expanding on that bit of hysterical nonsense, Rahimi issued a challenge: "The Islamic Republic of Iran will pay for any-

IT'S ALWAYS THE JEWS

When the Iranian Embassy in Beirut was bombed in November 2013 by Sunni jihadists, Iranian officials blamed their usual whipping boy. Iranian Foreign Ministry spokesman Marzieh Afkham said, "The Islamic Republic of Iran takes the Zionists and their mercenaries responsible for this action." Iran's Ambassador to Lebanon, Qazanfar Roknabadi, agreed: "Zionists have been behind the bombing." Ali Shamkhani, Secretary of Iran's Supreme National Security Council, maintained that despite the bombing, Iran would keep backing Hizballah: "These attempts will leave no impact on the course of Iran's continued support for the Islamic resistance movement." He said that the bombing indicated how "desperate Israel and the terrorist groups working in line with the interests of the Zionist regime in the region feel."[100]

body who can research and find one single Zionist who is an addict. They do not exist. This is the proof of their involvement in drugs trade."[103]

Only a trifle less hysterically, Khamenei warned participants in the International Quran Competition in 2014 that if they were not familiar with the Qur'an, they could travel a path of corruption that could lead them even to cooperating with Israel: "Intimacy with Quran is an indication that the heart is prepared to receive heavenly guide. Today, the greatest plight for Islamic world is ignoring the intimacy with Quran and subsequently, to remain unaware of the enemies' ruses." Those ruses were ignored at one's own peril: "Some parts of the Ummah ignore such policies, and they easily fall to the trap of fratricide or even cooperation with the Zionist Regime." The Supreme Leader exhorted them to see the Qur'an as the antidote: "The heavenly blessings and understanding Quranic criteria to know the enemies hinge upon close companionship of Quran."[104]

When Iran signed a preliminary nuclear agreement with Western powers in November 2013, Foreign Minister Mohammed Javad Zarif said the agreement was "a big success for Iran" and crowed that "all plots hatched by the Zionist regime to stop the nuclear agreement have failed."[105]

On July 14, 2015, the day the principal Iranian nuclear deal was concluded, a gleeful Iranian President Hassan Rouhani hailed it precisely because of Israel's opposition to it: "Today people in Lebanon and Palestine are happy because Zionists have tried to block this deal but failed." Rouhani told Iranians, "Do not be deceived by the propaganda of the usurper Zionist regime," for "the Zionist state has failed in its efforts" to stop the deal.[106]

The Zionist state did not fail, however, to put a roadblock in the way of Iranians hoping to travel to the U.S.—at least in the view of the Iranian regime. On December 18, 2015, after murderous jihad terror attacks in Paris and San Bernardino, California, Barack Obama approved an adjustment to the U.S. Visa Waiver Program prohibiting entry into the U.S. from Iraq, Syria, Sudan, and Iran without a visa. Zarif fumed that Iran's placement on

---

THE AYATOLLAH'S SPIT LIST

. . . .

"The attacks have nothing to do with Islam."
—UK Home Secretary Theresa May on the November 2015 jihad attacks in Paris, in which 130 people were murdered[110]

"Islam is a religion that prevents men from waging war? I spit upon those foolish souls who make such a claim."
—the Ayatollah Khomeini[111]

---

this list was "absurd," and added, "No Iranian nor anybody who visited Iran had anything to do with the tragedies that have taken place in Paris or in San Bernardino or anywhere else."[107] Iranian Foreign Ministry spokesman Hossein Jaber Ansari declared that the U.S. had only adopted this measure "under pressure from the Zionist lobby and currents opposed to the JCPOA."[108]

Then, on December 27, 2015, at the 29th International Islamic Unity Conference in Tehran, Rouhani decried disunity among Muslims, accusing the world's non-Muslim powers of using Islamic jihad groups to portray Islam as violent. The only beneficiary of Muslim disunity, he said, would be Israel. "Muslims have no option," he declared, "but to become more united."[109] He did not explain how or why tiny Israel had been able to become such a thorn in the side of the Islamic Republic, and the entire Muslim world.

Chapter Five

"I AM CYRUS, KING OF THE WORLD"

ONE OF THE WORLD'S GREAT CIVILIZATIONS

Unlike most Muslim countries (with notable exceptions such as Egypt and Iraq), Iran was a significant player on the global stage long before it accepted Islam, or became generally known as Iran. The history of the nation stretches back to the Bronze Age or before, and Iranians play a key role in ancient Greek history, as well as in the Bible.[1]

Iran was first unified under the rule of the Medes in the seventh century BC.[2] The Medes figure in biblical prophecy, with the prophet Isaiah declaring that they will be the instruments of God's wrath against Babylon: "Behold, I am stirring up the Medes against them, who have no regard for silver and do not delight in gold. Their bows will slaughter the young men; they will have no mercy on the fruit of the womb; their eyes will not pity children. And Babylon, the glory of kingdoms, the splendor and pride of the Chaldeans, will be like Sodom and Gomorrah when God overthrew them" (Isaiah 13:17–19).

Jeremiah agrees: "Sharpen the arrows! Take up the shields! The LORD has stirred up the spirit of the kings of the Medes, because his purpose concerning Babylon is to destroy it, for that is the vengeance of the LORD, the vengeance for his temple" (Jeremiah 51:11).

The land of the Medes was in the northwest region of present-day Iran; Babylon is a little over fifty miles south of Baghdad. Nearly three thousand years later, conflict still rages in the same area, still fueled by men who believe themselves to be instruments of the divine wrath.

The rivals of the great empires that were established in and around the land that is Iran today generally referred to those empires and their inhabitants as *Persian*, but among the people who lived within them they were always *Iranian*, a word that reflects the identity of the people there, along with many in India and Europe, as *Aryan*—a word that acquired horrific associations in twentieth-century Europe. In the twentieth century, also for the first time, the name of the country known variously as Persia and Iran became a point of contention.

"I am Cyrus, king of the world"

Mahmoud Ahmadinejad and the Ayatollah Khamenei were by no means the first Iranian rulers to have global ambitions. Their very first predecessor had the world on his mind as well. In the sixth century BC, Cyrus the Great established the Achaemenid empire, the first great Persian empire. He was known as the "king of kings," or in modern Farsi, *shahanshah*, Shah of Shahs. A clay cylinder discovered in the nineteenth century quotes the Persian king: "I am Cyrus, king of the world, rightful king, king of Babylon, king of Sumer and Akkad, king of the four quarters (of the earth)...."[3]

Unlike his remote successors in the Islamic Republic, however, Cyrus can plausibly be called a Zionist: he sponsored the return of Jews to their ancestral homeland, which would be named "Palestine" by the Romans six hundred years later. Because Cyrus allowed the Israelites to return to their land from exile in Babylon, the biblical prophet Isaiah hails him as the Lord's anointed and promises future success: "Thus says the Lord to his anointed, to Cyrus, whom he has taken by his right hand to subdue nations before him and strip the loins of kings, to force gateways before him that their gates be closed no more: I will go before you levelling the heights. I will shatter the bronze gateways, smash the iron bars. I will give you the hidden treasures, the secret hoards, that you may know that I am the Lord" (Isaiah 45:1–3).

ZIONISTS ANCIENT AND MODERN

• • •

When President Harry Truman extended official recognition to the newborn State of Israel in 1948, he happily wrapped himself in the mantle of the ancient Persian king, saying, "I am Cyrus."[4]

Cyrus amassed the first great global empire: his Achaemenid Persia was the world's first superpower, stretching from present-day Greece to Afghanistan and beyond in Central Asia, and lasting over two hundred years, until the middle of the fourth century BC, when it was conquered by Alexander the Great.[5] Today, Iranians engaged in a subtle form of dissent from the Islamic regime often name their children Cyrus, a towering figure in what Islamic hardliners dismiss as Iran's *jahiliyya*, its pre-Islamic period of ignorance.

"By the favor of Ahura Mazda"

One of Cyrus's illustrious successors, Darius, left behind inscriptions declaring his allegiance to what would soon be the religion of the Persians, until the coming of Islam: Zoroastrianism. "By the favor of Ahura Mazda," Darius is depicted as proclaiming, "I am of such a sort that I am a friend to right. I am not a friend to wrong. It is not my desire that the weak man should have wrong done to him by the mighty; nor is it my desire that the mighty man should have wrong done to him by the weak."[6]

Zoroaster, or Zarathustra, the prophet who gave his name to the religion, is a figure shrouded in myth. He probably lived in the middle of the second millennium BC, in northern Iran or Afghanistan. He taught that there was one supreme god, Ahura Mazda ("Wise Lord"), active in the world as Spenta Mainyu (the "Bounteous Principle"), opposed by Angra Mainyu (the "Destructive Principle"). Like the later Christianity and Islam, Zoroastrianism is a monotheistic religion teaching a set of ethical principles derived from a written scripture; Zoroastrians are one of the three principal religious groups, along with Jews and Christians, that are designated "People of the Book" in the Qur'an: those who have received legitimate revelations from Allah and then ignored or twisted their meanings. Along with the options of conversion or death, the Qur'an gives the "People of the Book" the opportunity to continue practicing their ancestral religions while submitting to Islamic hegemony and paying regular tribute (*jizya*) to the Muslims.

Zoroastrianism was devastated by the Islamic onslaught and is practiced today only by a small minority in Iran, along with a larger community in India; but it had considerable influence on the theological and ethical development of Christianity and Islam. Followers of Zoroastrianism were known as *magi*, the most famous of whom once followed a star to the birthplace of a baby many would come to believe was the promised savior of another monotheistic religion (Matthew 2:1–12).

"They are taught three things only: to ride, to use the bow and to speak the truth"

Achaemenid history is intertwined with that of classical Greece, one of the chief intellectual pillars of Western civilization. The Persian Wars were fought between 499 and 449 BC, as intellectual life in Athens was reaching its height. This was the era when Socrates and his faithful disciple Plato were laying the foundation for the West's philosophical tradition, even as the comic playwright Aristophanes mocked Socrates as a crank. Herodotus, "the father of history," gave the world its first historical account (as opposed to a year-by-year chronicle of events) in his *Histories* on the wars between Greece and Persia. Herodotus memorably said of Persian boys, "They are taught three things only: to ride, to use the bow and to speak the truth."[7] Thucydides, another key figure in the development of modern historiography, picked up where Herodotus left off.

Iran's modern threat to the United States and the West has an ancient antecedent: Athens was an oasis of civilization in a sea of savagery, flowering even as the Persians threatened the very existence of the city and its people.

In the fourth century BC, the Greeks, who had up to that point suffered several Persian invasions and occupations, gained the upper hand. Alexander the Great, who had been tutored by Aristotle, a disciple of Plato, began his great campaigns and, by 331 BC, numbered the Persian Empire among his conquests. After Alexander's sudden death, Persia fell to his general Seleucus—hence the Seleucid Dynasty that ruled Persia until the middle of the third century BC, diffusing the Greek language and Greek culture throughout the ancient land.

In 247 BC, King Arsaces I of Parthia, a region in northeastern Persia, revolted against the Seleucids and supplanted them with what became known as the Arsacid Empire, after its first Shah, or more commonly the Parthian Empire. This dynasty lasted nearly five hundred years, from 247 BC to 224 AD and saw a revival of ancient Iranian traditions, though there was no complete throwing-off of the Greek influence. The Parthian Empire

THANK THE GREEKS FOR PERSIA

• • •

To the ancient Athenians, and only to them, do we owe any knowledge of the Persian Wars at all; no Persian accounts have survived. The histories of Herodotus, Thucydides, and others such as Xenophon are among the considerable intellectual achievements of the Athenians, which unfolded against the backdrop of a protracted struggle for survival.

became the great rival to the Eastern ambitions of a new superpower on the global stage: the Roman Empire. The fault line between the Eastern Roman or Byzantine Empire, which in the fourth century became Christian, and the Zoroastrian Persian Empire was the line of demarcation between two immensely different and irreconcilably opposed civilizations and cultures. After centuries of Roman expansion, the Parthians stopped the Roman Empire from expanding eastward beyond the middle of modern-day Turkey. Centuries before the advent of Islam itself, the seeds were being sown for the division of the modern world—between the Christian or post-Christian West and the Islamic Middle East.

"His skin, stuffed with straw, and formed into the likeness of a human figure, was preserved for ages in the most celebrated temple of Persia"

It was the successor Persian empire, however, the Sassanid Empire, that did the most to set the stage for the coming of Muhammad and Islam. For eight centuries, from the first century BC to the seventh century AD, the Romans and Persians fought a series of costly and largely inconclusive wars that defined and confirmed each as the mortal enemy of the other. The Persians stung Rome's military pride when they captured the Roman emperor, Valerian, at the Battle of Edessa in 260 AD and held him prisoner for the rest of his life. The eighteenth century historian Edward Gibbon, in his *Decline and Fall of the Roman Empire*, recounts that Valerian's captor, the Shah Shapur I (Sapor), was disinclined to be magnanimous in victory, and even used the former emperor as a footstool: "The voice of history, which is often little more than the organ of hatred or flattery, reproaches Sapor with a proud abuse of the rights of conquest. We are told that Valerian, in chains, but invested with the Imperial purple, was exposed to the multitude, a constant spectacle of fallen greatness; and that whenever the Persian monarch mounted on horseback, he placed his foot on the neck of a Roman emperor."[8]

Shapur's pride was based upon his military success: he had taken much of Roman Armenia and Syria and considered himself to be the most powerful king in the world. Because he now ruled over a vast empire that included both Persians and non-Persians, he gave himself the title "King of kings of Iran and Aniran (non-Iran)."[9]

When Valerian died, Shapur's pride had not abated: "Notwithstanding all the remonstrances of his allies, who repeatedly advised him to remember the vicissitude of fortune, to dread the returning power of Rome, and to make his illustrious captive the pledge of peace, not the object of insult, Sapor still remained inflexible. When Valerian sunk under the weight of shame and grief, his skin, stuffed with straw, and formed into the likeness of a human figure, was preserved for ages in the most celebrated temple of Persia; a more real monument of triumph than the fancied trophies of brass and marble so often erected by Roman vanity."[10]

Having recounted this famous story, Gibbon immediately casts doubt upon it, believing Shapur incapable of this savagery: "The tale is moral and pathetic, but the truth of it may very fairly be called in question. The letters still extant from the princes of the East to Sapor are manifest forgeries; nor is it natural to suppose that a jealous monarch should, even in the person of a rival, thus publicly degrade the majesty of kings. Whatever treatment the unfortunate Valerian might experience in Persia, it is at least certain that the only emperor of Rome who had ever fallen into the hands of the enemy languished away his life in hopeless captivity."[11]

But whatever the fate of Valerian, the Romans were not definitively beaten. Under the emperors Carus in 283 and Galerius in 298 they sacked Ctesiphon, the Persian imperial capital. Galerius even captured the entire Persian imperial treasury, as well as the imperial harem and the Shah Narseh's wife and was able to dictate favorable terms that resulted in several decades of peace. When Narseh sent a representative to negotiate with

Galerius, the Roman emperor reminded the unfortunate envoy of how Shapur had treated Valerian and summarily dismissed him.[12]

"Shoulder Master"

The Roman victory was, however, not total. In the fourth century the Sassanid Empire experienced resurgence under the powerful and long-lived Shapur II, who reigned from 309 to 379. In a foreshadowing of the Arab-Persian divide that would find later expression in the Sunni-Shi'ite conflict, Arab invaders had entered Sassanid territory during the period of Persian weakness toward the end of the third century and beginning of the fourth. In the 320s, Shapur II fought back, leading Persian armies into the Arabian Peninsula, laying waste to numerous Arab tribes, and advancing as far as Medina.[13]

Shapur II was notably cruel to the Arabs, who called him *Dhu'l-aktaf,* "Shoulder Master," because of his practice of having the Arab prisoners' shoulders pierced so that they could be held together by a common rope run through the wounds.[14] To prevent future Arab incursions into Persia, he ordered a wall constructed, "the wall of the Arabs"—a tactic that the Israelis would also employ many centuries later, to the rage of Shapur's successors in the Islamic Republic.[15]

Shapur was hostile toward Christianity as it was the new religion of the Sassanids' great rival, the Roman Empire. When Armenia, which the Sassanids thought to be within their sphere of influence, converted to Christianity early in the fourth century, Shapur considered it an affront, and restarted the wars with the Romans in 337. By 350, however, an uneasy peace prevailed again, as neither side had been able to achieve a decisive victory. In the 360s, Shapur II withstood a full-scale challenge from the Roman Emperor Julian the Apostate, who marched on the Persian capital of Ctesiphon—a grand city that rivaled the splendor of Rome and Constantinople—but was unable to take it, and was killed while in the process of retreating.

Julian's successor, Jovian, in a position of weakness, recognized Persian rule over Armenia, Georgia, and other territories. This led to a period of peace that was strengthened in 387 when the Shah Shapur III and the Emperor Theodosius I agreed to a partition of Armenia, with the Romans controlling its Western and Christian portion and the Persians its Zoroastrian Eastern regions. Peace largely prevailed until 502, when the Persians asked the Romans for financial aid to help them repel barbarian tribes in the Caucasus and the Romans asked for territorial concessions in return.[16]

"Saving Christianity"

The wars resumed, but were never conclusive. In 532, the two empires concluded "the Eternal Peace," under the terms of which each gave up the occupied territories of the other and the Romans sent the cash-strapped Persians a huge shipment of gold. This tribute, however, did not secure eternal peace—it lasted only eight years. In 540, the Shah Khosrau I invaded Roman Syria and laid waste to the great city of Antioch, sending its people to Persia as slaves. The Romans regrouped, however, and stymied further Persian advances. But a Roman invasion of Armenia failed; in 545, the two sides concluded a five-year truce, during which the Romans agreed to make regular tribute payments of gold to the Persians. For the most part, this truce held in the ensuing years and led to the conclusion of a fifty-year peace treaty in 561.

But that fifty-year truce lasted only eleven years, followed by a series of further inconclusive conflicts. After the Persian general Bahram Chobin deposed the Shah Khosrau II, the Romans helped Khosrau regain his throne in 591, whereupon Khosrau ceded several territories back to the Romans, including half of Persian Armenia. In 602, however, after a rival murdered the Roman Emperor Maurice, Khosrau attacked again and conquered Roman holdings in Mesopotamia and the Caucasus. In 611, the Persians captured Syria and Jerusalem, from which they took what was believed to be the True

Cross of Christ back to Persia as a war prize, and entered Anatolia, the heartland of the Eastern Roman Empire. The Emperor Heraclius mounted a counter-attack that failed miserably, leading to the Persian conquest of Chalcedon, right across the Bosporus from Constantinople, as well as of Roman Palestine and Egypt.[17]

The Roman Empire, which had already seen its holdings in Western Europe completely overrun and the Western Roman Empire extinguished in 476, was on the brink of total collapse.

Heraclius sued for peace, but Khosrau, seeing total victory in his grasp, refused any negotiated settlement, preferring to fight on and destroy the Romans utterly. With his back to the wall, Heraclius began a new offensive against the Persians in 622, exploiting Byzantine naval power, which the Persians never adequately countered, as well as the element of surprise, to win a series of victories over Khosrau's troops.[18]

The Romans portrayed this as a war for "saving Christianity."[19] Heraclius carried an image of Christ as a military standard. The Roman emperor won victories over the Persians in Armenia and Azerbaijan, and then in Mesopotamia. Advancing as far as Ctesiphon, he was prevented from taking the Persian capital only by the Persians' destruction of the bridges that led into the great city. Kavadh II, the son of Khosrau II, overthrew and killed his father and then sued for peace. The Romans demanded that the Persians withdraw from all Roman territory they had occupied in previous wars dating back to 602, and return the True Cross to Constantinople. Kavadh, facing little choice, agreed.[20]

It was a crowning triumph for Heraclius. He had saved the Christian empire—or at very least postponed its destruction. This endless series of wars, however, particularly those between Heraclius and Khosrau, accomplished little more than to exhaust the resources of both combatants, thereby creating a power vacuum that could easily be exploited by newcomers on the scene. Those newcomers would be the Arabs, energized for large-scale conquest by the aggressive and militaristic exhortations and prophecies of a new prophet, Muhammad, and his new holy book, the Qur'an.

"Khosrau will be ruined, and there will be no Khosrau after him"

In his heyday, Khosrau had annexed Egypt, Jordan, Palestine, and Lebanon—all longstanding Byzantine territories—to the Persian Empire. When Kavadh agreed to return them to the Romans, Heraclius had few troops to spare to send. Islamic tradition holds that when in 631 Muhammad led his large Muslim force on a raid on Tabuk in northern Arabia, ostensibly part of the great Christian empire, they found that the Byzantine troops had withdrawn rather than engage them. Or perhaps there simply weren't enough Roman troops to man every garrison, and the soldiers had moved on to the next outpost, guarding the border as best they could.

According to Islamic tradition, Muhammad died in 632, and before his death he prophesied the destruction of both great empires, the Roman and the Persian, at the hands of the warriors of Islam: "Khosrau will be ruined, and there will be no Khosrau after him, and Caesar will surely be ruined and there will be no Caesar after him, and you will spend their treasures in Allah's Cause." He then cried out, "War is deceit."[21]

There was indeed no Khosrau after Khosrau, but no one need be carried away with enthusiasm for Muhammad's prognosticating abilities: the "prophecy" was actually composed a couple of centuries after the Arab conquest of Persia. Whether inspired by the aggressive commands of their new prophet or simply motivated by the age-old and universal desire for conquest, in 633 the Arabs moved against one of the two exhausted world powers and defeated the Persians in the Battle of al-Qadisiyah in Iraq in 636, laying the entire Persian Empire open for conquest.

"Only the Persians engaged in the task of preserving knowledge and writing systematic scholarly works"

The Arabs conquered Persia completely by 651, and added much of what is now Afghanistan and the surrounding areas by 674. Muslims believe that the second half of their prophet's prophecy, about the removal of Caesar, finally came to pass on May 29, 1453, when the Islamic armies of Mehmet the Conqueror finally broke through the defenses of Constantinople and brought the final remnant of the Roman Empire, the dominant world power for a millennium, to a bloody and ignominious end.

As they did in other lands they conquered, the Arabs made a clean sweep of the Persian Empire. Islam holds the achievements of all civilizations before their conquest by Muslims to be worthless trash, *jahiliyya*, products of the society of unbelievers. And so in the fourteenth century the pioneering Arab historian Ibn Khaldun had to ask, "Where are the sciences of the Persians that Umar ordered to be wiped out at the time of the conquest?"[22] The answer was that they had been obliterated at the hands of those who believed, as in a quip attributed to the Caliph Umar, that if books agreed with the Qur'an, they were superfluous, and if they disagreed with it, they were heretical—in either case, of no account.

Because of the harsh restrictions that Islam placed upon the practice of non-Muslim faiths, Zoroastrianism went into a steep and irreversible decline after the Arab conquest of Persia, and by the end of the eleventh century the Persians were almost completely Islamized. Persia, however, being a great civilization in its own right, exerted considerable influence over the nascent Arab empire, giving it much of its administrative structure.

WE DON'T NEED NO EDUCATION

• • •

According to Ibn Khaldun, a Muslim warrior approached Umar with a huge cache of Persian books, offering to distribute them among the Muslims. But Umar was disdainful: "Throw them into the water. If what they contain is right guidance, God has given us better guidance. If it is error, God has protected us against it."[23]

In fact, Persian was the official language of the Umayyad caliphate (661–750) until it was supplanted by Arabic toward the end of the seventh century—right around the time that there first begins to be mention in contemporary sources of the Arabs' claim to have a new prophet, a new holy book, and a new religion. Hajjaj ibn Yousef, the governor of Iraq who was responsible for the introduction of a great deal of what became standard Islamic practice, made a concerted effort to destroy the Zoroastrians' writings and kill all their priests, so that their history and doctrine would be largely obliterated.

Persia itself went into eclipse as the Umayyad caliphate enforced a strict Arab supremacism that demanded tribute from non-Arab Muslims and relegated them to second-class status. When the Abbasids overthrew the Umayyads in 750, however, they constructed the city of Baghdad and moved their capital there in 762, within the Persian intellectual and cultural milieu. In the ninth and tenth centuries, the Persians rebelled against Arab supremacism and made a concerted effort to preserve the Persian language and culture. In the eleventh century, the Seljuk Turks conquered Persia, and since they were not themselves Arabs, allowed for the continued reassertion of Persian identity, within a Sunni Muslim context.

The Persian influence over the Arabs and Islam was immense—so immense, in fact, that Arab historian Ibn Khaldun credited them even with the codification of the Arabic language, as well as of a great deal of Islamic tradition and law:

> Thus, the founders of grammar were Sibawayh and, after him, al-Farisi and Az-Zajjaj. All of them were of non-Arab (Persian) descent. They were brought up in the Arabic language and acquired the knowledge of it through their upbringing and through contact with Arabs. They invented the rules of (grammar) and made it into a discipline (in its own right) for later

(generations to use). Most of the hadith scholars who preserved traditions for the Muslims also were Persians, or Persian in language and upbringing, because the discipline was widely cultivated in Iraq and the regions beyond. Furthermore, all the scholars who worked in the science of the principles of jurisprudence were Persians. The same applies to speculative theologians and to most Qur'an commentators. Only the Persians engaged in the task of preserving knowledge and writing systematic scholarly works. Thus, the truth of the statement of the Prophet becomes apparent, "If scholarship hung suspended in the highest parts of heaven, the Persians would attain it."[24]

Persian philosophers, mathematicians, and scientists built on the works of Euclid and other sources from classical Greece, including writings of Aristotle lost to Europe until they were reintroduced from the Muslim world in the High Middle Ages. Omar Khayyam, a Persian geometrician who flourished around the turn of the twelfth century, was also a poet whose verses became familiar to the English-speaking world through Edward Fitzgerald's loose translation, *The Rubaiyat of Omar Khayyam*. Some of its best-known lines:

The Moving Finger writes; and, having writ,
Moves on: nor all thy Piety nor Wit
Shall lure it back to cancel half a Line,
Nor all thy Tears wash out a Word of it.

In 1219, about twenty years after the collapse of Seljuk rule in Persia, the Mongols invaded, laying waste to the country. They eventually converted to Islam and eased the harshness of their rule, but Persia had fallen on hard times, being dismembered in Mongol infighting and falling prey to a succession of foreign invaders.

By the dawn of the sixteenth century, Persia had been under the heel of foreign invaders—Arabs, Turks, and Mongols—for eight hundred years, with the exception of the Iranian Buyid dynasty in the tenth and eleventh centuries.

At the beginning of the sixteenth century, however, Persia's fortunes as an independent polity revived, in a most unexpected way.

"I belong to the religion of the 'Adherent of the Vali' and on the Shah's path I am a guide to every one who says: 'I am a Muslim'"

The reemergence of Persia as an independent entity had its roots in the establishment, two hundred years earlier, of the Safaviyya. Sheikh Safi od-Din of Ardabil in northwestern Iran, who gave the group its name, founded the Safavids as a religious order dedicated to preaching the ideals of Sufism, the mystical strain of Islam, at first within a Sunni perspective. It is not clear exactly how and when the Safavids adopted Shi'ite Islam, but the change appears to have arisen out of their challenge to both the Mongol invaders and the Turks for what the Safavids characterized as the rulers' corruption of Islam. The Safavids' Twelver Shi'ism, the strain of Shi'ite Islam that counts twelve successors of Muhammad as the leaders of the Muslim community, provided a counterpoint and standing critique to the Sunni Islam of the Mongols and Turks, whom the Safavids fought for the control of Persia.

The Safavids were first active in Anatolia and the southern Caucasus, as well as in some regions of Azerbaijan and northwestern Iran. Given that the political and social aspects of Islam emanate from its political aspects and are inseparable from them, it was perhaps inevitable that this order would not limit itself to preaching, but would begin to seek political power, as it did in the middle of the fifteenth century, when its leader Jonayd declared himself the "sultan" and began assembling a military force.

Jonayd fought against the rulers of the divided Persia of his time until he was killed in 1460 and succeeded by his son Haydar. In battling the Sunni rulers who held sway over various regions of Persia, Haydar offered Shi'ism to Iranians in order to distinguish himself from their present rulers and to rally and consolidate opposition to them. Like Constantine seeing a vision of the cross of Christ in the sky at the Battle of the Milvian Bridge, Haydar related that he had had a dream in which Ali, the great figure of the Shi'ites, visited him. On waking, Haydar devised a distinctive turban featuring twelve triangular pieces, commemorating the Imams of Twelver Shi'ism. Topping those was a red spike that led the Ottoman Turks to deride the Safavids as "redheads" (*qezelbas*), a term they soon adopted for themselves.[25]

Haydar was killed in 1488, but his movement was not. The *qezelbas* continued to make inroads against the other Persian rulers, so that by the time Haydar's fourteen-year-old son Ismail was proclaimed Shah in 1501, he ruled over a considerable expanse of Persian territory, and was to win much more. By 1508, he was the ruler of a united—and now Shi'ite—Persia.[27]

Ismail, like the Ayatollah Khomeini long after him, fancied himself a poet. In one of his verses he declared, "I belong to the religion of the 'Adherent of the Vali' and on the Shah's path I am a guide to every one who says: 'I am a Muslim.'"[28] Vali means governor or leader, and refers here to Ali ibn Abi Talib, the great hero of the Shi'ites. Ismail's poetry had a strong mystical bent: "Muhammad is made of light, Ali of Mystery. I am a pearl in the sea of Absolute Reality."[29]

SECRET DESIRES

• • •

A century and a half after Haydar, the Persian historian Eskander Beg noted that the Shi'ite leader had had simultaneous political and spiritual ambitions: "His secret aspiration was to have dominion over territories and subjects...inwardly, following the example of shaikhs and men of God, he walked the path of spiritual guidance and defence of the faith; outwardly, he was a leader sitting on the throne in the manner of princes."[26]

But there was much more than just mysticism in Ismail's poetry. Ismail not only proclaimed his allegiance as a Shi'ite to Muhammad and Ali; he also made sweeping, grandiose claims about himself:

> My name is Shah Ismail.
> I am on God's side: I am the leader of these warriors.
> My mother is Fatima, my father Ali:
> I am one of the twelve Imams.
> I took back my father's blood from Yazid.
> Know for certain that I am the true coin of Haydar
> Ever-living Khidr, Jesus son of Mary
> I am the Alexander of the people of this age.[30]

Fatima was Muhammad's daughter and Ali, her husband, was the founding figure of Shi'ite Islam. The twelve Imams were the twelve successors of Muhammad and members of his household who, in the view of Twelver Shi'ites, carry something of Muhammad's prophetic spirit. Yazid was the Sunni Umayyad caliph who defeated and killed Hussain, the son of Ali, in the Battle of Karbala in 680, solidifying the Sunni-Shi'ite split and giving Shi'ites an everlasting object of mourning. Khidr is a key figure of Sufi mysticism, described in Sufi literature as an encounter with the divine in human form, and based on the mysterious figure who teaches Moses three esoteric lessons in sura eighteen of the Qur'an. By identifying himself also with "Jesus, son of Mary," Ismail was not claiming to be the Son of God and Savior of Christianity, but the Muslim prophet who, in the Qur'an, prophesies the coming of Muhammad (61:6). Alexander was, of course, Alexander the Great, the foremost conqueror in Persian history.

Above all, however, Ismail proclaimed himself to be a bearer of the divine spark: "The Mystery," he wrote, "of 'I Am the Truth' is hidden in this my heart. I am the Absolute Truth [or 'Allah'] and what I say is Truth."[31]

Understandably, it was on this point that Shah Ismail I encountered some resistance from the Iranian religious authorities, foreshadowing the tensions between later shahs—including Mohammed Reza Pahlavi—and the mullahs. The Iranian jurist Jalal-al-Din Mohammad Davani is said to have once asked his students, "Who is the imam of the age?" They answered enthusiastically, "Shah Ismail!"—to Davani's disgust.[32]

While his divine or messianic pretensions gained little traction, Ismail did manage to impose Twelver Shi'ism upon the Persians, who up to that point had remained over 90 percent Sunni—although Sunni Islam was still prevalent enough that as late as 1743 the Sunni Persian ruler Nader Shah offered a peace settlement to the Ottoman Turks whereby Persia would remain Sunni.[33] But Persia was not even close to being wholly Sunni at the time of the offer, and it continued to become less so over time: eventually Shi'ite Islam became an essential element of the Persian identity, as it is to this day.

The Safavid Dynasty ruled Persia until 1722 and again from 1729 to 1736 and restored Persia to heights it had not attained since the days of Khosrau. In their heyday, the Safavids ruled an empire that stretched from the territory of modern-day Iran and Afghanistan all the way to Armenia and Georgia, Iraq and Kuwait. As Khosrau and his predecessors had been set against the Byzantines, so now the Safavids were the principal rivals of the Sunni Ottoman caliphate that had supplanted the Byzantines in Constantinople. Both empires were Muslim, but the civilizational divide between European and Persian culture continued. The Safavid empire reached its height under Shah Abbas I (1587–1629), who won numerous victories over the Ottomans and drove Portuguese adventurers out of the Persian Gulf.

"At night he was thinking of plunder and pillage, at dawn he was headless"

After Abbas I, however, Persia once again went into decline. The Ottomans occupied large portions of Persian territory and made slaves of numerous

Persians: the Sunni Ottomans considered the Shi'ite Persians to be heretics, and thus considered it permissible under Islamic law to enslave them.[34] The Russians under Czar Peter the Great went to war against Persia in 1722, capturing a great many of Persia's territories in the Caucasus. As a pretender to the Shah's throne set himself up in Isfahan, Persia was disintegrating: in 1724, the Ottomans and Russians concluded a treaty in Constantinople to divide Persia's lands between them.

Only a few years later, however, the Sunni Nader Shah defeated the Ottomans, restored the Safavid Dynasty, and regained the territory that the Persians had lost. He even compelled the Shi'ites to discard some of their practices that Sunnis found offensive—notably, the cursing of the first three caliphs after Muhammad, whom Shi'ites detested for having been chosen in place of their favorite, Ali.[35] But after a period of astonishing success, during which he even presented himself as a rival to the Ottomans as leader of the entire Islamic world, Nader Shah was defeated and killed in Dagestan in 1747. A poem that made the rounds in Persia recounted his swift reversal of fortunes:

> At night he was thinking of plunder of pillage
> At dawn he was headless, and his head, crownless
> At a turn of the deep blue sky
> Neither Nader remained nor a Naderite.[36]

Persia's fortunes followed those of Nader Shah. Chaos, and often Russian hegemony, prevailed. By 1779, however, a Persian warlord, Agha Mohammed Khan Qajar, became determined to shake off the Russian yoke and reunify Persia. He reconquered Armenia, Azerbaijan, Dagestan, and ultimately Georgia and was crowned shah in 1796, only to be assassinated the following year.[37] The Russians retook Georgia in 1799. Trying to recapture glories so recently won and then lost again, the Persians fought two costly wars with Russia early in the nineteenth century, resulting in the definitive loss of Armenia, Azerbaijan, Dagestan, and Georgia to the Russians.

A large population exchange went on during this period, with huge numbers of Muslims from the Caucasus moving south to Persia, while Armenian Christians in Persia relocated to Russia. This was often a brain drain for the Persians, with educated and relatively moneyed individuals being supplanted by populations of a lower level of education and attainment. Persia again went into decline, exacerbated by the Great Persian Famine of 1870, in which as many as two million perished.

"The most complete and extraordinary surrender of the entire industrial resources of a kingdom into foreign hands that has ever been dreamed of"

By the late nineteenth and early twentieth century, Western hegemony and the influence of Western Christian civilization were at their height in Persia, as they were in the senescent Ottoman Empire, Egypt, and elsewhere. As the famine continued to rage in 1872, the Qajar Shah Nassereddin's chancellor, Mirza Hosein Khan, concluded a sweeping agreement with Baron Paul Julius de Reuter, the British-based founder of the Reuters News Agency, giving him control over Persia's banking and customs, as well as permission to build a railway and exploit the nation's natural resources.

Nathaniel Curzon, a British official who later became Foreign Secretary, called it "the most complete and extraordinary surrender of the entire industrial resources of a kingdom into foreign hands that has ever been dreamed of, much less accomplished, in history."[38] A public outcry forced the cancellation of this particular agreement, but Persia nonetheless remained subject to British and Russian interests.

Nassereddin Shah complained in 1888, "Should I wish to go out for an excursion or a shooting expedition in the north, east and west of my country, I must consult the English, and should I intend to go south I must consult the

Russians."[39] Despite his complaints, Nassereddin Shah continued to sell off various Iranian resources to the British and Russians, as well as the Belgians.

The influence of Western ideas, no less than of Western governments and companies, was at an all-time high: Persians, impatient with autocracy, demanded a constitution. On December 30, 1906, Shah Muzaffareddin approved one, and died ten days later; his son Mohammed Ali Shah became a constitutional monarch, and the first Majlis, or parliament, was convened. Fazlollah Nuri, a Tehran cleric who was to become one of the Ayatollah Khomeini's heroes, was alarmed that the parliamentarians were actually making laws, and saw how democracy could lead away from strict adherence to Islamic law.

Nuri forced adoption of a Supplement to the Constitution that stipulated that a committee of five *mojtaheds*, Islamic jurists, would be empowered to "reject or repudiate any proposal that is at variance with the sacred laws of Islam."[43] This committee was duly constituted, although it never had any actual power until the Islamic Revolution of 1979. Nonetheless, its formation was indicative of the growing uneasiness of the clerical hierarchy as Western

THANK YOU FOR NOT SMOKING

Resentment against Nassereddin's concessions to foreign powers boiled over in 1890 when he granted a monopoly on tobacco to an English company, destroying Persia's indigenous tobacco industry.[40] Sayyid Ali Akbar Fal Asiri, a cleric in Shiraz, stood in the pulpit of his mosque with a drawn sword and cried out: "O people, you must ensure your women are not stripped. I have here a sword and a couple of drops of blood. Any foreigner who comes to Shiraz to monopolize the tobacco will have his belly ripped with this sword."[41] Muslim clerics in Tehran called for a smoking boycott—which the Shah's senior wife forced even him to observe. By 1892 Nassereddin Shah, longing for a smoke, canceled the monopoly. His cave-in to public pressure was a sign of the times.[42]

influence and power waxed in Persia. Nuri argued that no parliament was actually necessary, since Allah had already given the world all the laws it needed. No wonder Khomeini loved him.

Mohammed Ali Shah loved Nuri, too, for he had no taste for constitutionalism, and wanted to rule as an autocrat, like all shahs before him. A power struggle ensued; the constitutionalists won out, and Mohammed Ali Shah was deposed. In a sign of Persia's dual fascination with Islamic authenticity and Western secularism, the supporters of Western-style parliamentarianism and constitutional monarchy put Nuri on trial for "corruption in the land," an offense for which the Qur'an specifies the death penalty (5:33). He was duly executed, and is revered as a martyr by the Islamic Republic, which considers him one of its pioneering theorists.[45]

Then on May 26, 1908, the British struck oil in Persia, leading to a jockeying for power and influence there between the Russians and the British. Now all the elements of contemporary Iran were in place: oil wealth, deep resentment of foreign influence, and mullahs who believed the country should be ruled only by Islamic law.

But at first events continued to move along much as they had done, with foreigners asserting control over Persian resources. The Anglo-Persian Oil Company (APOC), which later became the Anglo-Iranian Oil Company (AIOC) and then British Petroleum (BP), concluded an oil deal with

NOT THAT THIS HAS ANYTHING TO DO WITH ISLAM

"These fireworks, receptions of ambassadors, these foreign manners, hurrahs, banners saying Long live! Long live! Long live! Long live equality! Long live fraternity! Why not write on one of them: Long live the holy law! Long live the Qur'an. Long live Islam."

—Fazlollah Nuri, martyred early-twentieth-century Tehran cleric who served as a model for the Ayatollah Khomeini[44]

the Persians at extraordinarily favorable terms for the British. During World War I, British, Russian and even Ottoman troops traversed ostensibly neutral Persia, which lay prostrate underneath their feet. After the war, amid fears of a Bolshevik takeover in Tehran, the British backed a takeover by a military officer, Reza Khan, to stave off the Russians. At first Reza Khan made himself prime minister and spoke of an Ataturk-style Western republic in Persia; but seeing how unpopular that idea was among Persians, in 1925 he deposed the shah and took his place, ending the Qajar dynasty and founding a new one he called Pahlavi, "heroic."[46]

Despite his abandonment of the idea of a republic, Reza Shah, like Ataturk in Turkey, admired Western secularism, as well as the nationalist movements that were at that time becoming more powerful in Italy and elsewhere in Europe. Also like Ataturk, he mandated Western clothing, including hats, which interfered with the prostrations of Islamic prayer, and disapproved of the hijab, the mandatory Islamic head covering for women. In 1936, his wife and two daughters appeared unveiled in public. Reza Shah stated, "The women of our country, because of their exclusion from society, have been unable to display their talent and ability. I might say they have been unable to do their duty toward their beloved country and people."[47]

The Shi'ite mullahs, whose power remained strong in the Persian countryside, were incensed by the movement toward secularism. In 1935, Iranian troops had to be called in to quell an uprising at an Islamic shrine in Mashhad. This militarism was a hallmark of Reza Shah's rule; the shah did not hesitate to resort to force to ensure that his will was carried out, even against the mullahs, whose opposition to the regime solidified.

"Dominion of the Aryans"

In 1935 Reza Shah mandated that his nation be henceforth referred to as "Iran." This was an ancient name for the land; in fact, the Sassanids' name for their empire was *Iranshahr*, the "Dominion of the Aryans." Throughout their history, Persians had referred to their land as Iran, and to themselves as Iranians. Some have suggested, though, that Reza Shah had more on his mind than just reasserting Iran's proud history, contending that what made the name appealing to the shah was its assertion of a connection to Aryanism that might win the nation Adolf Hitler's favor. The Iranian Ambassador to Nazi Germany is even said to have suggested the name change.[48]

Reza Shah, goes the charge, admired Hitler at very least as a counterweight to the British and Russians who oppressed his domains. But others deny that the name change had anything to do with Hitler at all, pointing out that Iranians had called themselves Iranians and their country Iran since time immemorial, with Persia being foreigners' appellation for the land. And the claim that Reza Shah admired Hitler was propaganda devised by the British, who disliked Reza Shah for opposing the extremely favorable terms they had made with his Qajar predecessors for access to Iranian oil.[49]

Undeniably, however, there was a deep-rooted sympathy among Iranians for Hitler and his goals, emanating from the Shi'ite Muslim contempt and hatred for Jews. Farajollah Parvizian, an Iranian who grew up in Tehran in the 1940s and 1950s, recalled that Muslims in the capital routinely derided and abused the city's "dirty Jews," and during World War II looked forward to the Nazi armies smashing through the Caucasus and entering Iran.[50]

The Nazis never came. Instead, the British and the Russians, who had vied with one another for hegemony in Iran for so long, invaded in 1941 in order to secure the use of Iran's oil supplies for the Allies. They used the pretext of Reza Shah's Nazi sympathies, despite the fact that he had opposed attempts to form a Nazi-style party in Iran.[51] Martial law was imposed. The invaders removed Reza Shah in favor of his callow young son, Mohammed Reza Pahlavi, who was at that time twenty-one years old. At first, few took the young new shah seriously. The Soviets blithely disregarded the Tehran Declaration they had signed in 1943 guaranteeing Iran's postwar territorial integrity and at the end of World War II established puppet regimes in northern Iran. Iranian Prime Minister Ahmad Ghavam warned the Soviets that their favorable oil concessions could be canceled if they continued to prop up these regimes, whereupon they withdrew their support for them in May 1946; the Iranians quickly crushed the nascent communist states and reclaimed their territory.[52]

"With God's blessing and the will of the people, I fought this savage and dreadful system of international espionage and colonialism"

Meanwhile, resentment was growing in Iran over the outrageously favorable terms under which the British enjoyed the use of Iranian oil: at the end of World War II, Britain still controlled a vast empire and was a world power, with tanks and battleships running on Iranian oil. Under the deal concluded with the British when oil was struck, between 1911 and 1950 the

NOT-SO-RIGHTEOUS GENTILES

Some Muslims in Tehran couldn't wait: during World War II, they approached the Jewish proprietor of a large Tehran department store with a curious request. The department store owner's son recounts, "In the area of our family's residence, there were many 'moderate' Muslim families. For the most part, the relationship between us was cordial for decades. However, it was during this time (news of Hitler's possible invasion) that two of the Muslim neighbors came to our home. One of them said to my father, 'when Hitler comes, we would like to have your dining room furniture.' The other said the same thing about our carpets. This was said matter-of-factly, knowing that if Hitler did come, all the Jews would be rounded up and taken away. Jews, already living as second-class citizens, were considered disposable. It was upsetting to think that the neighbors of many years had no concern whatsoever about our fate, but were happy to take advantage of the opportunity to take our possessions."[53]

Iranians received only 9 percent of the revenue from their own oil; the British received 36 percent.[54] In 1950, the AIOC earned 200 million pounds, of which Iran's share was only 16 million.[55] These ratios made the AIOC the most profitable British business operating anywhere in the world.[56] In stark contrast, the U.S. concluded a deal with Saudi Arabia providing for a fifty-fifty split of the oil proceeds.[57] Iranians noticed the disparity, and anger grew.

This anger made the reform-minded Mohammed Mossadegh prime minister in April 1951, after he vowed to confront the British and end the unjust oil arrangement.[58] He acted swiftly to do so, abrogating the deal with the AIOC and nationalizing the oil industry, to the rage of the British and the joy of huge numbers of Iranians. The move was massively popular inside Iran, leading a confident Mossadegh to demand of the Shah that he be allowed to name the Minister of War and Chief of Staff. The young Shah, seeing that this would give Mossadegh effective power over the entire government, refused, whereupon Mossadegh resigned.[59]

All the strata of Iranian society, from secular socialists to Muslim clerics, were outraged, and took to the streets: they loved how Mossadegh had faced down the British and claimed for Iran the oil revenue that was rightfully its own. After five days of this, the Shah backed down and reinstated Mossadegh as prime minister. Now even more popular than he was before, Mossadegh was granted emergency powers by the Majlis and stayed on course. He matched Britain's recalcitrance and growing hostility with his own, refusing to budge on the nationalization of the oil industry and finally breaking diplomatic relations with Britain after the British blocked all oil exports from Iran.[60]

The British, even further enraged, threatened military action, moving warships into place and imposing an economic embargo, including a boycott of Iranian oil, which weakened the Iranian economy but failed to break Mossadegh's resolve.[61] In a confidential memo, a British official explained why his government was being so high-handed and intransigent: "The first effect of nationalization would be to put control into Persian hands. Seen from the United Kingdom point of view the present problem was not solely one of the fate of a major asset. It concerns *the* major asset which we hold in the field of raw materials. Control of that asset is of supreme importance."[62]

As the crisis wore on, numerous compromise agreements were proposed. The British even signaled that they would accept nationalization as long as they retained de facto control.[63] However, the issue was control, and no fig leaf compromise could hide the fact that it would be in either Iranian or British hands; neither side would budge.

In August 1953, the British and their American allies had had enough and were unwilling to concede on the central point. They initiated an action to remove Mossadegh, nominally led by retired General Fazlollah Zahedi but directed by the CIA and the British spy service MI6. The head of the CIA's Near East and Africa division, Kermit Roosevelt Jr., contended that "the original proposal for AJAX [the code name for the operation] came from British Intelligence after all efforts to get Mossadegh to reverse his nationalization of the Anglo-Iranian Oil Company (AIOC) had failed. The British motivation was simply to recover the AIOC oil concession."[64]

The Shah was reluctant to go along, in light of Mossadegh's popularity, but when Roosevelt told him that Mossadegh was going to be removed whether he approved of it or not he acquiesced, dismissing Mossadegh and naming Fazlollah Zahedi prime minister.[65] The CIA/MI6 action against Mossadegh is commonly called a "coup," but under the Iranian constitution of the time, the Shah was completely within his rights to dismiss the prime minister and name another. Nonetheless, passions were running high. As demonstrations both for and against Mossadegh raged, the Shah briefly left the country, traveling to Baghdad and then Rome, but returned home as calm was restored.[66]

Abbas Ghaffari was the president of the American division of the National Iranian Oil Company (NIOC) from the 1960s until 1980. He was a key figure in the Iranian oil industry, overseeing Iranian dealings with the Organization of Petroleum Exporting Companies (OPEC) and the Shah's policies toward the U.S., Canada, and Mexico.[67] He was thus in a position to know aspects of the oil nationalization controversy that were not made known to the general public. Abbas Ghaffari died in 2015; his widow, Avideh Ghaffari, stated that Mossadegh was much more unpopular in Iran than he is now commonly portrayed to have been, particularly for his rule by emergency powers. "Mossadegh," she declared, "was a dictator; he was not the nice man that people describe today. This was one of the factors leading to his removal."[68]

Avideh Ghaffari also notes that initially the British were happy with Mossadegh and even with nationalization, which would have relieved the British of the expenses of production and given them the potential for increased profits. Mossadegh himself, she says, was an Anglophile, and the chief concern of the British was ensuring the Iranian oil supply for themselves by whatever means necessary.[69] Historian Ervand Abrahamian says of Mossadegh, "Although often depicted as an 'Anglophobe,' he was in fact an unabashed admirer of nineteenth-century British parliamentary government."[70]

The postwar British taste for socialism may have led to the mutual admiration between the British and Iranians. In 1946, the British Ambassador to Iran, Sir Reader Bullard, wrote that the Iranian communist Tudeh Party was "the only coherent political force in the country and is strong enough to nip in the bud any serious opposition since it has almost complete control of the press and of labour throughout the country."[71] That same year a British Parliamentarian remarked, "I cannot get it out of my mind that the Tudeh Party, though admittedly a revolutionary party, may be the party of the future which is going to look after the interests of the working man in Persia."[72] Mossadegh was not a member of the Tudeh Party, but that party, not surprisingly, welcomed and applauded his nationalization plan.

J. H. Bamberg, a historian of the Iranian oil industry, confirms that Mossadegh, ostensibly the great antagonist of the British, was actually offering them an arrangement that would have been highly favorable to them. "The AIOC," writes Bamberg, "paradoxically owed a large debt of gratitude to Dr. Mossaddeq who, having played with great effect on US fears of communism to wring concession after concession out of the British, was offered terms in February 1953 which would have left the Iranians in charge of their own oil industry and the AIOC with no more than a share in a consortium responsible for the international marketing of Iranian oil exports."[73] Historian Parviz Mina concluded that Mossadegh "succeeded in nationalizing Iranian oil but failed in making nationalization work for the benefit of his country."[74]

But the British were in a bind: having adopted a hostile and belligerent stance toward Mossadegh, they couldn't turn around and accept the favorable arrangements he was offering without a substantial loss of face. They were also concerned that Mossadegh, now in a state of open defiance against Britain for which the British were largely responsible, was moving Iran closer to the Soviet Union. When Winston Churchill replaced Clement Atlee as prime minister in 1950, the Tudeh Party fell out of favor with British officials, and with the Cold War in high gear, the British argued that removing Mossadegh was essential to preventing Iran from falling into the Soviet orbit. The Shi'ite clergy, although they favored nationalization as a step to lessening Western influence in Iran, feared a communist takeover as well, and so supported the coup.[75]

After having replaced Mossadegh as prime minister, Zahedi quickly negotiated a series of deals with the United States and Great Britain. The NIOC would own the oil fields and the machinery, but British Petroleum and other foreign companies would handle production and sales.[76]

Nonetheless, if one of the primary goals of the British in participating in the coup to remove Mossadegh was to preserve their oil monopoly, the operation was a massive failure for them. Before the whole incident, in 1950, the U.S. was one of the AIOC's biggest customers, buying up no less than 40 percent of its production.[77] After the coup, however, the U.S. was no longer just a customer; it had supplanted Britain as Iran's principal foreign partner. The Shah owed them his position, and also preferred their fair-mindedness, as evidenced by their fifty-fifty arrangement with the Saudis, over the exploitative British. Anthony Verrier of the British Secret Intelligence Service (SIS) noted, "Washington had decided that a policy of working with Britain to restore the Shah's powers and against Britain to increase America's stake in Middle East oil (they got 40 percent in the consortium that was subsequently formed) was, indeed, a sound combination of diplomacy and commerce."[78]

Mossadegh went on trial for treason. Defending himself against the charge, he insisted that he had acted for the benefit of Iran against a rapacious foreign power: "Yes, my sin—my greater sin and even my greatest sin is that I nationalized Iran's oil industry and discarded the system of political and economic exploitation by the world's greatest empire. This at the cost to myself, my family; and at the risk of losing my life, my honor and my property. With God's blessing and the will of the people, I fought this savage and dreadful system of international espionage and colonialism."[79]

He fought, but he lost. Mossadegh was found guilty of treason and placed under house arrest, under which he died in 1967. He declared, "I am well aware that my fate must serve as an example in the future throughout the Middle East in breaking the chains of slavery and servitude to colonial interests."[80] It did: the coup to remove him, as a manifestation of overpowering Western influence over Iran, became one of the chief points on the list of grievances that Iranians who opposed the Shah were assembling to show why his regime should be overthrown.

To stave off the supporters of Mossadegh and other dissenters, the U.S. funded a massive increase in the Shah's military and state security apparatus. At this point, to stay in power, the Shah had to become an authoritarian ruler, and with American help, he did. He banned Tudeh and Mossadegh's party and essentially ruled by fiat. In October 1973, the renowned Italian journalist Oriana Fallaci asked him, "Would you deny that you're a very authoritarian king?" The Shah replied, "No, I wouldn't deny it, because in a certain sense I am. But look, to carry through reforms, one can't help but be authoritarian."[81]

At the same time, paradoxically, the Shah tried to become genuinely popular, and succeeded to the degree that he noted with pride to Fallaci, "When I returned from America, I drove through the city in an open car, and from the airport to the palace I was wildly applauded by at least a million people overcome with enthusiasm.... Nothing has changed since the day I became king and the people lifted my car on their shoulders and carried it for three miles."[82] This was not altogether an exaggeration.

The Shah was determined to secularize and modernize Iran, but that very determination earned him the everlasting antagonism of the Shi'ite hierarchy and devout faithful, and he grew increasingly dependent on his security services to keep a lid on dissent. Influential voices in Iran were calling for a reform quite different from what the Shah had in mind, and ultimately, they would not be stifled.

THE AYATOLLAH'S SPIT LIST

"Many of them are deeply disturbing, truly horrifying and bear no relation whatsoever to the true practices and principles of the ancient venerable religion."
        —UK judge Michael Topolski, after viewing jihad videos[83]

"Islam is a religion that prevents men from waging war? I spit upon those foolish souls who make such a claim."
        —the Ayatollah Khomeini[84]

Chapter Six

"ISLAM SAYS, KILL THEM"
THE ISLAMIC REVOLUTION

Did you know?

- Marxist revolutionaries allied themselves with Shi'ite radicals against the Shah, helping to usher in the Islamic Republic
- The Ayatollah Khomeini said the Shah was destroying Islam in Iran—by giving women the vote
- The Shah spent more than $16 billion on a 2,500th anniversary celebration of the original Persian Empire, and offended pious Muslims by serving champagne
- The Iranians played Russian roulette with female hostages at the American Embassy

The Shah was serious about reforming and modernizing Iranian society. On October 8, 1962, he granted women the right to vote in elections for local councils and gave permission for those elected to take their oaths of office on any sacred book, not just the Qur'an—which meant that they didn't have to be Muslim.[1]

The secular and Western-oriented cast of the Shah's program did not endear him to Iranians who thought such influences were toxic. As the reforms proceeded, an Iranian writer named Jalal Al-e Ahmad wrote a book entitled Gharbzadegi and published it secretly for fear of the Shah's security services. In its English edition, that title was translated Weststruckness, but the term is actually more pejorative: "Westoxication," "Westitis," and "Occidentosis" are all valid renderings.[2]

In Gharbzadegi, Ahmad likened Western influence in Iran to a plague: "I say that gharbzadegi [Weststruckness] is like cholera. If this seems distasteful, I could say it's like heatstroke or frostbite. But no. It's at least as bad as sawflies in the wheat fields. Have you ever seen how they infest wheat? From within. There's a healthy skin in place, but it's only a skin, just like the shell of a cicada on a tree. In any case, we're talking about a disease. A disease that comes from without, fostered in an environment made for breeding diseases."[3]

TURN THAT NOISE OFF!

• • •

"We Weststruck people…don't know our own music and hear it as useless noise. We talk about symphonies and rhapsodies. We've turned our back on Iranian portraiture and miniatures.… We've laid Iranian architecture aside, with its symmetry, its ponds and fountains; its gardens, basements, bathhouses; and sash and latticed windows. We have closed our traditional gymnasiums and forgotten how to play polo."

—Jalal Al-e Ahmad in Gharbzadegi[5]

That "environment made for breeding diseases" was the Shah's Iran, prostrate before the West. Ahmad complained that Iranian cities "are just flea markets hawking European manufactured goods."[4] Iran's own culture was being lost.

The one aspect of Iranian life that Ahmad believed to be untouched by gharbzadegi was Shi'ite Islam, unmoved by fads and unchanged by trends.

The underground publication of Gharbzadegi in Iran was arranged for by Ali Shariati, a Shi'ite activist who was living in self-imposed exile in Paris at that time. Like Sayyid Qutb, the key theorist of the Muslim Brotherhood in Egypt, Shariati taught that the remedy for cultural colonization by the decadent West—as well as for the modern world's entrenched economic and political injustices and its ideological confusion—was Islam. He called upon Muslims to "launch a religious renaissance through which, by returning to the religion of life and motion, power and justice, will on the one hand incapacitate the reactionary agents of the society and, on the other hand, save the people from those elements which are used to narcotize them."

By "those elements which are used to narcotize them" Shariati meant the Islamic trappings of the Pahlavi regime, which only served to stifle the authentic Islam that could bring about freedom from Western hegemony: "By launching such a renaissance, these hitherto narcotizing elements will be used to revitalize, give awareness and fight superstition. Furthermore, returning to and relying on the authentic culture of the society will allow the revival and rebirth of cultural independence in the face of Western cultural onslaught."[6] In 1972, Shariati decried "the present Islam" as "a criminal Islam in the dress of 'tradition'" and argued that "the real Islam is the hidden Islam, hidden in the red cloak of martyrdom."[7]

That real Islam was Shi'ite Islam, the only form of Islam—in fact the only religion, ideology, or belief system of any kind—that had the power to remove tyrants, as it had at the time of the revolt against the Seljuk Turks and Mongols:

> The religious body of the Sunni sect, which had from the beginning become "the government's Islam," becomes a conglomeration of the most debased and prejudiced beliefs and harsh rules. It turns into a tool for the justification of the anti-human ways of rulers. It compromises with the autocratic regimes of the Ghaznavid and Seljuk Turks and the Mongols. It becomes an opiate for the masses, and an instrument for murder to be used against any thought or action that jeopardizes the interest of the strong and harms the landlords and feudal chiefs.
>
> This is what causes Shi'ism, during this period, to appear as the fountainhead of rebellion and the struggle of the downtrod-

den and oppressed masses, especially among the rural people. It flourished wondrously in multiple facets and directions, moderate or extreme, in the form of various movements of the masses against the powers of the day... Finally, the intellectual, moderate and rich school of the imamate, as the greatest flow of thought and culture, revolts when confronted by the religion and culture of the government.[8]

The idea that authentic Shi'ite Islam was "the fountainhead of rebellion and the struggle of the downtrodden and oppressed masses" was fanciful at best, but it had a powerful appeal in the Iran of the 1960s and 70s, when the Shi'ite clergy's objections to the Shah's secularist bent coalesced with Marxist critiques of the injustices of Iranian society. The poet Khosrow Golesorkhi epitomized the blend of the two. During his 1974 trial for a plot to kidnap the queen and crown prince, "Verily," Golesorkhi cried, "Life is belief and struggle! I begin my statement with a saying of Master Hosein, the great martyr of the Middle Eastern proletariat. Though I am a Marxist-Leninist, I came to social justice through the teachings of Islam and then came to socialism."[9]

Hosein, or Hussain, was the son of Ali whose death at the hands of Umayyad Sunni forces in the Battle of Karbala in 680 marks the formal beginning of the divide between Sunni and Shi'ite Islam. To call Hussain, killed in a struggle for power with the Umayyad caliph Yazid, "the great martyr of the Middle Eastern proletariat" was an audacious anachronism and recasting of history, but it resonated in the political climate of early-1970s Iran. For the opponents of the Shah, Hussain was an exemplar who had challenged the unjust regime of Yazid, just as the Shi'ite Leftists were challenging the modern-day Yazid, Mohammed Reza Pahlavi.

"God Almighty, in addition to revealing a body of law, has laid down a particular form of government"

Granting women the right to vote had aroused the ire of a little-known ayatollah named Ruhollah Khomeini, who told a colleague, "The son of Reza Khan has embarked on the destruction of Islam in Iran. I will oppose this as long as the blood circulates in my veins."[10] He and two other ayatollahs sent telegrams to the Shah, making clear their opposition to the law on religious grounds. The Shah wrote back addressing the ayatollahs as "hojjat al-Islam," a lesser ranking of the Shi'ite clergy that signified that he didn't recognize them as ayatollahs. "I wish you success in your guidance of the populace," he wrote more diplomatically, but added praise for their "non-interference" in politics.[11]

After the ayatollahs wrote to the Shah's prime minister, Asadollah Alam, and didn't receive an answer, Khomeini wrote to the Shah again. Taking up the Shah's wish for the clerics' success in "guidance of the populace," Khomeini wrote, that the "heretic Alam does not listen to God's word, the constitution, the law of the Majlis, the orders of Your Majesty, the advice of the clergy or the demands of the people."[12] He said that the prime minister and his colleagues, "with their anti-Islamic and anti-constitutional actions, are weakening the foundations of the nation and

NOT THAT THIS HAS ANYTHING TO DO WITH ISLAM

"Your Majesty's statement is in line with the hadith of the Prophet: 'When heresy appears among my people the alem [theologian] must enlighten them, otherwise God's damnation will be upon him.'"

—the Ayatollah Khomeini to Shah Reza Pahlavi[13]

monarchy" and called on Alam to "repent of the insult he has committed against the holy Qur'an."

Khomeini and his colleagues instructed Shi'ite clergy all over the country to denounce the government. Several weeks later, the Shah relented: Alam announced that candidates for local councils would have to be Muslims, that oaths must be sworn on the Qur'an only, and that the Majlis would decide the question of women's suffrage.[14] Khomeini was still dissatisfied, telling supporters, "Don't think that they will give up. They are readying themselves for a new assault on Islam. Be prepared, strengthen your ties and expect a new move."[15]

That "new move" came in January 1963, when the Shah announced a series of reforms he called the White Revolution, including distributing land to the poor and allowing women not only to vote but also to run for office. Khomeini declared, "What is happening is a calculated plot against Iranian independence and the Islamic nation, and it is threatening the foundation of Islam."[16] He and other Shi'ite clergy called for demonstrations, which so unnerved the Shah that on January 24, 1963, during a presentation on the glories of land reform, he gave an impromptu speech attacking the ayatollahs and their allies as "a stupid and reactionary bunch whose brains have not moved...stupid men who don't understand and are ill-intentioned...they don't want to see this country develop."[17]

Tensions continued to increase. In a sermon on June 3, Khomeini addressed the Shah as "you wretched, miserable man," called upon him to "listen to my advice, listen to the clergy's advice, not to that of Israel" and warned him to "learn a lesson from the experience of your father"—that is, that he could be toppled from power and exiled, as was Reza Shah.[18] "Shall I declare you, Mr. Shah, to be a heathen so that you are chased out of this country?"[19]

Khomeini's warning was prophetic, though it didn't seem so at the time. Instead of the Shah, it was Khomeini who was exiled, after he had been

arrested and freed from prison and had resumed his
opposition to the Shah. In an October 27, 1964, speech
he decried the fact that Americans "enjoy legal immu-
nity with respect for any crime they may commit in
Iran. If some American's servant, some American's
cook, assassinates your marja' [model for emulation,
that is, an ayatollah] in the middle of the bazaar, or
runs over him, the Iranian police do not have the right
to apprehend him! Iranian courts do not have the right
to judge him! The dossier must be sent to America, so
that our masters there can decide what is to be done!"[22]

Khomeini added, "Let the American President
know that in the eyes of the Iranian people, he is the
most repulsive member of the human race today
because of the injustice he has imposed upon the
Muslim nation. Today the Qur'an has become his
enemy, the Iranian nation has become his enemy. Let
the American government know that its name has

> ## IT'S ALWAYS THE JEWS
>
> "Israel does not want the
> Qur'an to be in this kingdom.
> Israel does not want the rules
> of Islam to be in this country."
> —Khomeini, blaming the
> Jewish state for the Shah's
> modernizing policies[20] and
> calling on Shah Reza Pahlavi
> to "listen to my advice, listen
> to the clergy's advice, not to
> that of Israel"[21]

been ruined and disgraced in Iran. Those wretched deputies in the Majlis
begged the government to ask 'our friends' the Americans not to make such
impositions on us, not to turn Iran into a colony. But did anyone listen?"[23]

The Shah's security services did. After this speech they sent Khomeini
into exile, thereby confirming, in the eyes of many Iranians, every charge
the ayatollah had made. Khomeini's exile did nothing to quell the restive-
ness in Iran. The principal ideas that led up to Iran's Islamic Revolution—
resentment of the Western influence in Iran and resurgent Islam—were very
much in ferment; even from outside the country, Khomeini remained one
of their principal exponents.

Khomeini's key contribution to that ferment was the argument that since
Shi'ite Islam, as Shariati and other Marxism-oriented Shi'ites maintained,

held the key to establishing a just society, it stood to reason that Shi'ite clerics should be the rulers. In exile in Iraq in 1970, the ayatollah articulated this view in a series of lectures, calling it *velayat-e faqih* (guardianship of the jurist). The lectures were quickly published in book form as Islamic Government, a small volume that circulated clandestinely in the Shah's Iran.

Islam, Khomeini argued, had not just given mankind a set of laws. "A body of laws alone," said Khomeini, "is not sufficient for a society to be reformed. In order for law to ensure the reform and happiness of man, there must be an executive power and an executor. For this reason, God Almighty, in addition to revealing a body of law (i.e., the ordinances of the shari'a), has laid down a particular form of government together with executive and administrative institutions."

Where were these divinely ordained executive and administrative institutions to be found? Khomeini argued that clerical rule, which many dismissed as an unacceptable innovation in Islam, was mandated by the example of Muhammad himself, whom the Qur'an declared to be the supreme model for Muslims (33:21): "The Most Noble Messenger (peace and blessings be upon him) headed the executive and administrative institutions of Muslim society. In addition to conveying the revelation and expounding and interpreting the articles of faith and the ordinances and institutions of Islam, he undertook the implementation of law and the establishment of the ordinances of Islam, thereby bringing into being the Islamic state."[24]

So, following the example of Muhammad, modern-day Shi'ite clerics should rule Iran and make it an Islamic state. Khomeini catalogued the numerous benefits of rule by clerics, asking rhetorically, "What is the good of us asking for the hand of a thief to be severed or an adulteress to be stoned to death when all we can do is recommend such punishments, having no power to implement them?"[25] Once clerics had that power, they could save society from all manner of ills: "If the ordinances of Islam are to remain in effect, then, if encroachment by oppressive ruling classes on the rights of the weak is to be prevented, if ruling minorities are not to be permitted to plunder and corrupt the people for the sake of pleasure and material interest, if the Islamic order is to be preserved and all individuals are to pursue the just path of Islam without any deviation, if innovation and the approval of anti-Islamic laws by sham parliaments are to be prevented, if the influence of foreign powers in Islamic lands is to be destroyed—government [by clerics] is necessary."[26]

Allah would express his will through his clerics. The general failure of majority-Muslim countries to implement rule by Islamic clerics had been destructive to the religion itself: "Indeed it is precisely because the just fuqaha have not had executive power in the lands inhabited by Muslims and their governance has not been established that Islam has declined and its ordinances have fallen into abeyance."[28]

> ## ANSWERING TO A HIGHER AUTHORITY
>
> • • •
>
> "The fundamental difference between Islamic government, on the one hand, and constitutional monarchies and republics, on the other, is this: whereas the representatives of the people or the monarch in such regimes engage in legislation, in Islam the legislative power and competence to establish laws belongs exclusively to God Almighty."
> —the Ayatollah Khomeini[27]

Working against this decline, Khomeini gave sermons in exile that were captured on cassette tape and smuggled back into Iran, where they found a ready audience among those who believed, as did the ayatollah, that the Shah's rule was un-Islamic and that he must be overthrown.[29]

"Rest in peace, for we are well awake"

The armed struggle that led up to the Islamic Revolution began on February 8, 1971, when the Marxist Iranian People's Fedai Guerrillas struck a police outpost in the town of Siahkal on the Caspian Sea in an operation to free two of their members who had been jailed there; three policemen were killed. Thirteen of the group's members were rounded up and executed in March.[30] Not to have their thunder stolen, the Shi'ite Leftists of the People's Mujahedin swung into action, planning their own series of guerrilla attacks, only to be foiled by the Organization of Intelligence and National Security, the Shah's secret police and security organization, which was known by its Persian acronym, SAVAK. SAVAK executed much of the leadership of the People's Mujahedin in May 1972, but the fuse had been lit: violence, followed by repressive crackdowns that only fueled resentment and led to more violence, increasingly became a hallmark of the resistance to the Shah.[31]

The Shah himself, meanwhile, was only giving more fuel to the forces that opposed him. From October 12 to 16, 1971, the Shah's regime celebrated the twenty-five-hundredth anniversary of the founding of the Persian Empire. Leaders from all over the globe attended the extraordinarily opulent celebration in the ancient city of Persepolis, although the Shah was annoyed that Queen Elizabeth II did not come. The Shah's government put the cost of the festivities at $16.6 million, which was extravagant enough, but opponents of the regime maintained that it had actually been significantly more expensive.[32]

Iranians were not allowed to attend, stoking resentment of the regime that was exacerbated by harsh preventative measures taken by SAVAK to make sure that Iranian revolutionaries of whatever ideology did not trouble the assembled heads of state. Worst of all, the Shah toasted the anniversary with the finest champagne, Dom Perignon Rose 1959 (Möet Chandon).[33] His Shi'ite critics took careful note of his un-Islamic choice of beverage.

Equally un-Islamic was the Shah's paying his respects to a pre-Islamic Persian ruler. At the Persepolis celebrations, he approached the tomb of Cyrus the Great and intoned,

O Cyrus, great King, King of Kings, Emperor of the Achaemenians, monarch of the land of Iran. I, the Shahanshah of Iran, offer thee salutations from myself and from our nation....

Cyrus, we gather today around the tomb in which you eternally rest to tell you: Rest in peace, for we are well awake and we will always be alert in order to preserve your proud legacy.

We promise to preserve forever the traditions of humanism and goodwill, with which you founded the Persian Empire: traditions which made our people be the carrier of message transmitted everywhere, professing fraternity and truth.[34]

For the Shah, this was not just empty grandiosity: Mohammed Reza Pahlavi had a vision of leading a resurgent Persian Empire that would rival the United States and the Soviet Union as a world power. As oil prices skyrocketed, greatly increasing Iran's national revenue (and the Shah's personal fortune), former Prime Minister Alam, still a minister of the Royal Court and the Shah's close friend, praised him for becoming foremost among the leaders of Middle Eastern nations. The Shah, however, was still unsatisfied: "But I have so many more aspirations. To be first in the Middle East is not enough. We must raise ourselves to the level of a great world power. Such a goal is by no means unattainable."[35] In October 1973 he told Oriana Fallaci that he could only get along with U.S. President Richard Nixon "if I'm sure that he's treating me as a friend. In fact, as a friend who within a few years will represent a world power."[36] He insisted that "to say [Iran] will rank among the five greatest and most powerful countries in the world isn't going too far at all. Thus Iran will find itself at the same level as the United States, the Soviet Union, Japan, and France."[37]

In 1977, the Shah even published a book entitled *Towards a Great Civilization*, in which he sketched out Iran's pathway to become a great power. "To take the Iranian nation to the age of 'the great civilization' is my greatest

EVERYTHING UNTIL NOW HAS BEEN LEADING UP TO ME

As grandiose as Cyrus proclaiming himself "king of the world, rightful king, king of Babylon, king of Sumer and Akkad, king of the four quarters (of the earth)," the Shah saw himself as ushering in the greatest era of Iran's history: "The great civilization toward which we are now moving is not just a chapter in the history of this land. It is its greatest chapter; an ideal with which thousands of years of Iran's development must inevitably end up, and which in turn must be the dawn of a new era in our national life."[39]

A new era in Iran's national life was indeed about to dawn, and could not be staved off.

wish.... The goal which I have determined for my own nation is undoubtedly highly ambitious and lofty, but it is not one that would be impossible for the nation, given its plentiful material and spiritual possibilities, and its abundant mental and moral resources. If such a goal looks beyond the normal limit, it is because to try and achieve a lesser ideal is essentially not worthy of our nation."[38]

"Playing games with the dignity of God's prophet"

In March 1976, the Shah once again—just as five years earlier when he served champagne at Persepolis—demonstrated how tone deaf he was to his people's commitment to Islam. He replaced the Islamic hijri calendar, which marked the years from Muhammad's emigration to Medina and first assumption of political and military power in the year 622 AD, with a new calendar that counted from 559 BC, when Cyrus the Great first took the throne. In a flash Iran went from the year 1355, in Islam's lunar calendar, to the Persian imperial year 2535.[40]

Khomeini, furious, issued a fatwa forbidding use of the new calendar, which had accomplished nothing but to reinforce the Shi'ite revolutionaries' contention that the Shah's regime was not just un-Islamic but an actual enemy of Islam, determined to counter the religion's influence in Iran. The calendar, the ayatollah fumed, was "the worst thing this man has done during his reign, playing games with the dignity of God's prophet, worse even than the massacres."[41]

The worst thing the Shah did during his reign was followed later that year by the worst thing that happened to him: Jimmy Carter was elected president of the United States. Carter immediately announced that a primary focus of his presidency would be the defense of human rights worldwide. The Shah appeared to sense what was coming, musing to Prime Minister Alam, "Who knows what sort of calamity he may unleash on the world?"[42] Early in 1977 the Shah tried to stave off that calamity, announcing that SAVAK would no longer torture prisoners; he even opened up his prisons to visits from the Red Cross.[43]

Instead of welcoming these gestures, the Shah's opponents greeted them with contempt, seeing them as indications that he was dancing to Carter's tune. They took advantage of the relaxation of state control to denounce the Shah's repressive tactics and demand more relaxation: from October 10 to 19, 1977, the Iranian Writers Association in Tehran organized "Ten Nights" of readings by famous Iranian writers, who used the large platform this afforded them to denounce the Shah's regime and to call for the freedom of speech and an end to state censorship in Iran.[44]

The end of repressive measures was not forthcoming, at least not immediately. On October 23, 1977, just four days after the conclusion of the Ten Nights, the Ayatollah Khomeini's son and assistant, Mostafa Khomeini, was found dead of a heart attack at his home in Najaf, Iraq, where his father was in exile.[45] Mostafa was forty-six. His death followed the death on June 19 of Ali Shariati in England at the age of forty-three, also from a heart attack.[46]

Did both these prominent foes of the Shah's regime just happen to have weak hearts? Or did Mostafa Khomeini and Shariati owe their deaths more to SAVAK than to leaky valves? Many Iranians believed that SAVAK, and the Shah, were indeed responsible—and so if SAVAK had indeed killed the pair in order to weaken the opposition to the Shah, their actions had exactly the opposite effect.

The Shah met Carter for the first time in Washington on November 15, 1977. Police dispersed anti-Shah demonstrators with tear gas, which the wind carried to the White House's South Lawn, where the Shah and Carter were standing with their wives, Queen Farah and Rosalynn Carter. Photos of the four wiping tears from their eyes were featured in the international media, and widely taken as an omen. Queen Farah was outraged, certain that there was "a desire on the part of the new administration to embarrass us."[47]

In the months ahead, Carter would give her numerous reasons to think so.

"Mohammed Reza Pahlavi was emotionally wrecked, if not psychologically broken"

In January 1978, seminarians in Qom rioted over a newspaper article that had criticized Khomeini; police killed several of the students, although exactly how many was a matter of dispute. Forty days later, as mosques all over Iran held memorial services for the students who had been killed, demonstrations against the government began. In Tabriz, the demonstration became a riot and some of the protesters were killed. When memorial services were held for them forty days later on March 29, more demonstrations were held and more protesters killed, with the cycle repeating itself yet again forty days later.[48]

In response, the Shah decided that concessions, rather than repression, would calm the protests, and promised freedom of speech and free elections for the Majlis in 1979. He fired officials whom he deemed responsible for the deaths in the riots and even replaced the head of SAVAK with a general who had a gentler reputation.[49] The situation seemed to have been pacified, but only briefly. In the Iranian city of Abadan on August 19, at least 470 people were killed at a movie theater when the doors were barred and fires set. Khomeini blamed the Shah, sparking massive protests against him; only long after the Islamic Revolution did it come to light that Islamic jihadists, not the Shah's men, set the fire, hoping to ignite the opposition to his regime.[50] And it worked.

Protests and riots in which people were killed increased all over Iran. The Shah tried more concessions, appointing a reformist prime minister, legalizing opposition political parties, cracking down on corruption among government officials, allowing for freedom of the press, and releasing political prisoners. To appease the Shi'ite hardliners, he abolished the hated Cyrus the Great calendar and closed nightclubs, which they regarded as dens of iniquity.[51]

It was too late. In early September, hundreds of thousands of protesters demonstrated against the Shah in Tehran. Finally, on Friday, September 8, 1978, the Shah imposed martial law in Tehran and other key cities and banned all street demonstrations. Defying the order, thousands of protesters showed up in Tehran's Zhaleh Square. Police ordered them to disperse; when they did not do so, the police fired into the crowd, killing fifty-eight people in what became known as Black Friday. Most Iranians blamed the Shah, but he was just as horrified as everyone else. One of his government ministers later recalled, "Mohammed Reza Pahlavi was emotionally wrecked, if not psychologically broken, by the events of Black Friday."[52]

"A bastard of conscience"

As all these events unfolded, Jimmy Carter offered no help to his ostensible ally the Shah. Instead, he dithered, his administration riven by disagreement between those who wanted the United States to act to keep the Shah in power and those who, like U.S. Ambassador to Iran William

Sullivan, preferred to make some accord with Khomeini in hopes that he would consent to becoming the figurehead leader of a secular constitutional republic.

Confusion reigned. Ultimately, the Carter White House abandoned the Shah to his fate, in part because neither the president nor any of his staff could decide exactly what to do instead—but mostly because many in the Carter administration admired Khomeini and didn't want to do anything to harm him or his movement.

In contrast, Carter was ambivalent about the Shah: "When the Shah came here to visit in November of 1977, my first year in office, I knew that he had been an intimate friend of six presidents before me and a staunch ally that provided stability in that region of the world. But I knew also that SAVAK, his secret military service, had attacked some student demonstrators."[54] The human rights president would not and could not support such a regime.

The Shah, quite understandably, felt betrayed. "The fact that no one contacted me during the crisis in any official way," he recounted later, "explains everything about the American attitude. I did not know it then—perhaps I did not want to know—but it is clear to me now that the Americans wanted me out."[55]

The Americans did nothing as the situation continued to deteriorate. The day after Black Friday, workers in Tehran began going on strike; other workers followed suit, and the strikes quickly became a nationwide phenomenon, while demonstrations also continued. Crowds chanted, "Islam, Islam, Khomeini, we will follow you."[56] As the chaos spread, the Shah's

THREE-ALARM
OSTRICH ALERT

Andrew Young, the U.S. ambassador to the United Nations, said, "Khomeini will eventually be hailed as a saint."

Ambassador William Sullivan saw him as a man of peace: "Khomeini is a Gandhi-like figure."

Carter advisor James Bill declared the ayatollah a "holy man" of "impeccable integrity and honesty."[53]

government increased pressure on Iraq to exile Khomeini. Saddam Hussein was only too happy to be rid of the charismatic Shi'ite cleric, and so on October 5, 1978, Khomeini left, only to be turned away by Kuwait and to settle ultimately in France, despite his reluctance to live, "so to speak, among heathens."[57] Among those heathens, he became a darling of the Western media, which began eagerly shining light on events in Iran, thereby hastening the demise of the Shah's regime.

On November 5, which came to be known as "The Day Tehran Burned," rioters, egged on by mullahs who preached about the evils of the West, targeted symbols of Western power such as the British Embassy, as well as outposts of secular pleasures such as movie theaters, along with Iranian government and police installations.[58]

The next day, the Shah appointed a military government, but addressed the nation in conciliatory terms on television, saying, "I, too, have heard the message of the revolution of you, the Iranian people. I am the guardian of the constitutional monarchy which is the divine duty entrusted the Shah by the people. After all the sacrifices that you have made, I pledge that in future the Iranian government will be founded in the Basic Law, social justice and the people's will and know nothing of despotism, tyranny and corruption.... You should know that in the revolution of the Iranian people against colonialism, tyranny and corruption, I am beside you; and in the defense of our territorial integrity, national unity and Islamic religious observances, in the establishment of basic freedoms and the realization of the wishes and ideals of the Iranian people, I will be by your side...this revolution cannot but be supported by me, the king of Iran."[59] Humbling himself, he used the word for "king," not "king of kings," shahanshah, which he had preferred up to this point.

Khomeini, however, was in no mood for conciliation. He compared the Shah to a cat trying to lure mice out of their hiding places with soothing words, only to kill them when they emerged, and he renewed his call for the Shah to be overthrown.[60] He could be confident that few Iranians would be taken in by the Shah's speech. The Shah had been in power since 1941 and had never—at least since the removal of Mossadegh—respected the limitations of constitutional monarchy. Why should anyone believe that he was going to start now? He denounced colonialism, and yet he had been the chief architect of America's influence in Iran, for which Khomeini had been skewering him for years; tyranny, although his regime had grown increasingly authoritarian since the early 1950s; and corruption, although he and his family had been among the primary beneficiaries of the sharp rise in oil prices in the early 1970s.

And so from France, Khomeini continued to lead the opposition to the regime, sending a steady stream of cassette tapes of his sermons into Iran—sermons that preached the duty of Shi'ites to revolt against oppressors. He called for protests during the Islamic sacred month of Muharram, which fell between December 2 and December 30, 1978. On December 2, two million protesters heeded his call and took to the streets of Tehran, demanding that the Shah step down and Khomeini be allowed to return to Iran.

The protests grew quickly. Within a week, nine million protesters had taken to the streets. On December 28, 1978, the Shah appointed secular opposition leader Shahpour Bakhtiar prime minister, and announced that he and his family would be going on "vacation" outside Iran, with a referendum scheduled for three months hence on whether Iran would keep its Shah or become a republic.

On January 4, 1979, Jimmy Carter traveled to Guadeloupe in France for a summit meeting with French President Valery Giscard d'Estaing, British Prime Minister James Callaghan, and West German Chancellor Helmut Schmidt. Carter told the three that the U.S. was withdrawing all support for the Shah and backing Khomeini. "I was horrified," recalled Giscard, at this abandonment of an ally. "The only way I can describe Jimmy Carter is that he was a 'bastard of conscience.'"[61]

On January 16, 1979, a tearful Mohammed Reza Pahlavi and his family left Iran.[62] Their promised return never happened; after two and a half millennia, the Persian monarchy was over.

"I shall kick their teeth in"

Two weeks later, on February 1, Khomeini returned to Iran after fourteen years of exile. Where the Shah had been tearful, Khomeini was studiously stoic. As Khomeini's plane neared Iran, Peter Jennings of ABC News asked him, "Ayatollah, would you be so kind as to tell us how you feel about being back in Iran?" He replied, "Nothing"—in Persian, hichi. His translator, amazed, responded, *"Hichi?"* Khomeini was adamant: *"Hich ehsasi nadaram"*—"I don't feel a thing."[63] More emotional was the massive and adoring throng of several million people that greeted him at the Tehran airport. The crowd was so huge that the roads were absolutely blocked and Khomeini could not proceed by car; he had to be carried from the airport by helicopter.[64]

He was ready to assert his power. Of Bakhtiar's government, he said, "I shall kick their teeth in. I appoint the government, I appoint the government in support of this nation." On February 4, he named his own prime minister, Mehdi Bazargan, demanding loyalty to him on the theory of clerical rule.[65]

Bakhtiar resisted, but the military refused to support his government, which collapsed on February 11, 1979. In Iran today, February 11 is "Islamic Revolution's Victory Day," a national holiday marked by chants of "Death to America" and "Death to Israel."[66]

Khomeini held a referendum on March 30 and 31 on whether to establish an Islamic Republic—the announced results were that 98.2 percent of Iranians had voted yes.[67] He established the Islamic Revolutionary Guards Corps and suppressed opposition groups.[68] He pushed through a new constitution solidifying the Islamic character of the state; it, too, was made

NOT THAT THIS HAS ANYTHING TO DO WITH ISLAM

. . . .

"As a man who, through the guardianship [velayat] that I have from the holy lawgiver [the Prophet], I hereby pronounce Bazargan as the Ruler, and since I have appointed him, he must be obeyed. The nation must obey him. This is not an ordinary government. It is a government based on the shari'a. Opposing this government means opposing the shari'a of Islam and revolting against the shari'a, and revolt against the government of the shari'a has its punishment in our law...it is a heavy punishment in Islamic jurisprudence. Revolt against God's government is a revolt against God. Revolt against God is blasphemy."

—the Ayatollah Khomeini, explaining why Iranians would have to accept his choice for prime minister[69]

subject to a referendum. But even before it could be voted upon, Khomeini had made abundantly clear that the Islamic Republic would consider the United States a mortal enemy when he enabled the storming of the U.S. Embassy in Tehran. American diplomats would be held hostage for well over a year.

"Jimmy Carter is too much of a coward to confront us militarily"

The immediate pretext for the invasion of the Embassy was Jimmy Carter's reluctant decision to allow the gravely ill Shah to enter the United States on October 23, 1979, for medical treatment. Carter presciently asked his advisors, "What are you guys going to advise me to do if they overrun our embassy and take our people hostage?"[70] They did just that on November 4, 1979, when a group calling itself the Muslim Student Followers of the Imam's Line (that is, Khomeini's line) entered the embassy compound and took the skeleton staff of sixty-six that was still serving there after the fall of the Shah hostage.[71]

Khomeini was delighted, dubbing the hostage-taking "the Second Revolution."[72] He told a reporter, "I regard the occupation of the American

Embassy as a spontaneous and justified retaliation of our people."[73] He explained that the hostage crisis would assist the Islamic Republic in consolidating power: "This action has many benefits. The Americans do not want to see the Islamic Republic taking root. We keep the hostages, finish our internal work, then release them. This has united our people. Our opponents do not dare act against us. We can put the constitution to the people's vote without difficulty, and carry out presidential and parliamentary elections. When we have finished all these jobs we can let the hostages go."[74]

Khomeini wasn't worried about the Americans interfering with his timetable: "Jimmy Carter is too much of a coward to confront us militarily."[76] At Thanksgiving 1979, the Iranians freed thirteen black and female hostages, but Khomeini said that the Embassy had been a "den of espionage and those professional spies will remain as they are until Mohammed Reza Pahlavi is returned to be tried and until he has returned all that he has plundered. However, as Islam has a special respect towards women, and the blacks who have spent ages under American pressure and tyranny and may have come to Iran under pressure, therefore, mitigate their cases if it is proved that they have not committed acts of espionage."[77] One more hostage was freed in the summer of 1980, when he became dangerously ill. The other fifty-two remained in captivity for 444 days, until January 20, 1981.[78]

One hostage recounted, "During the first part of our captivity, our hands were tied very tightly, and on the second day of captivity, a number of hostages and myself were tied around the ambassador's dining room table." He said that the captors played Russian roulette with two of the female hostages "to get information from us. They put a bullet in the chamber,

A LITTLE LIGHT BEDTIME READING

. . .

The papers from the American Embassy in Iran were seized and published in sixty-six volumes entitled *Documents from the Nest of Spies.*[75]

spun the chamber, and they clicked the trigger off on a couple of the girls."[79] The Iranians repeatedly threatened to execute all the hostages, and the hostages believed that they were eminently capable of doing so.[80]

Meanwhile, Carter was proving Khomeini right: he did seem to be "too much of a coward" to do anything effective to rescue the hostages. When he did attempt to do so, with Operation Eagle Claw in April 1980, the mission was a miserable failure. Engine failure put some of the helicopters needed for the mission out of action; a crash killed eight U.S. military personnel.[81] The abject failure and apparent amateurishness of the operation epitomized the Carter administration's impotence in the face of repeated provocations from the nascent Islamic Republic—and true to form, Khomeini ascribed its failure to the hand of Allah and labeled it a victory for Islam.

The hand of Allah was not so much in evidence, however, in November 1980, when Ronald Reagan overwhelmingly defeated Carter's bid for reelection. One of Reagan's campaign themes had been that he would deal with the Iranians much more firmly than Carter had, and the Iranians clearly knew that Ronald Reagan was not too much of a coward to confront them militarily: they freed the hostages on January 20, 1981, the day Reagan took office.

"Allah did not create man so that he could have fun"

Khomeini continued to ensure that the Islamic Republic would be Islamic, and nothing but. He declared, "What the nation wants is an Islamic Republic. Not just a Republic, not a democratic Republic, not a democratic Islamic Republic. Do not use the word 'democratic' to describe it. That is the Western style."[82] Indeed, there was nothing democratic about his regime. Khomeini embarked on a reign of terror, executing his political foes in large numbers and shutting down opposition newspapers and magazines.[83] He told secularists, "The 'clog-wearer and the turbaned' have given you a chance. After each revolution several thousand of these corrupt elements are executed in public and burnt and the story is over. They are not allowed to publish newspapers.... We will close all parties except the one, or a few which act in a proper manner.... We all made mistakes. We thought we were dealing with human beings. It is evident we are not. We are dealing with wild animals. We will not tolerate them any more."[84]

The sharia state that Khomeini constructed gave Iranians neither democracy nor equality of rights under the law. In 1985, Sa'id Raja'i-Khorassani, the Permanent Delegate to the United Nations from the Islamic Republic of Iran declared that "the very concept of human rights was 'a Judeo-Christian invention' and inadmissible in Islam.... According to Ayatollah Khomeini, one of the Shah's 'most despicable sins' was the fact that Iran was among the original group of nations that drafted and approved the Universal Declaration of Human Rights."[85]

"Those who study Islamic Holy War will understand why Islam wants to conquer the whole world"

Some Iranians became disillusioned with the Islamic Republic, but the costly war that Iran and Iraq fought between 1980 and 1988, ending essentially in a stalemate and bringing military and economic catastrophe to both sides, only strengthened Khomeini's hold on power. Tensions between Iraq and Iran had been increasing for years, until finally, on September 22, 1980, Saddam Hussein's Iraq invaded the Islamic Republic.

THE REVOLUTION LOSES A SUPPORTER

· · ·

"Around 1984 or 1985 I was becoming disillusioned. I saw a fascism and political tyranny emerging in Iran. Anyone who asked questions was branded 'antirevolutionary' and 'against Islam.'... A certain faction in Iran has turned religion into ideology, faith into fascism. It promised us heaven, but it created a hell on earth."

—Akbar Ganji, a young Iranian who originally supported the Islamic Revolution and at one point even joined its intelligence service[86]

Saddam was alarmed by Khomeini's talk of exporting the Islamic Revolution to other countries, particularly because he himself was a Sunni at the head of a secular regime in a country that had a Shi'ite majority—and bordered the Islamic Republic. He hoped that his invasion would cause the Iranian people to turn against the mullahs and topple their fledgling regime; instead, it ended up strengthening their regime, particularly since the hated U.S. was aiding Saddam with weaponry and large amounts of cash.

The Iranian regime generally framed the conflict in Sunni-Shi'ite terms. A 1981 offensive was dubbed Operation Eighth Imam; in 1986 the Iranians named another Operation Karbala-4, harking back to the Battle of Karbala in 680, which marked the formal beginning of the Sunni-Shi'ite schism. Khomeini insisted that the war was a struggle for the very soul of Islam.

Sunni states neighboring Iraq knew that when Khomeini said that the war was one of "Islam versus blasphemy," he meant "Shi'ite versus Sunni," and took heed: the Saudis sent billions to Saddam to finance the Iraqi war effort. Like Stalin suddenly finding the Orthodox church useful during World War II, Saddam himself began to be photographed at prayer, hoping to counterbalance the Iranians' appeal to Islam.

As the war dragged on, the Islamic Republic became an increasingly poor, dangerous, tightly controlled totalitarian state. Yet the regime didn't blink. Khomeini had thundered that fighting was an Islamic duty: "Jihad or

NOT THAT THIS HAS ANYTHING TO DO WITH ISLAM

"It is our belief that Saddam wishes to return Islam to blasphemy and polytheism.... if America becomes victorious...and grants victory to Saddam, Islam will receive such a blow that it will not be able to raise its head for a long time.... The issue is one of Islam versus blasphemy, and not of Iran versus Iraq."

—the Ayatollah Khomeini, explaining the stakes in the Iran-Iraq War[87]

Holy War, which is for the conquest of [other] countries and kingdoms, becomes incumbent after the formation of the Islamic State in the presence of the Imam or in accordance with his command. Then Islam makes it incumbent on all adult males, provided they are not disabled or incapacitated, to prepare themselves for the conquest of countries so that the writ of Islam is obeyed in every country in the world.... Islam's Holy War is a struggle against idolatry, sexual deviation, plunder, repression and cruelty.... But those who study Islamic Holy War will understand why Islam wants to conquer the whole world."[88] The goal of this conquest would be to establish the hegemony of Islamic law.

Khomeini had no patience for those who insisted that Islam was a religion of peace:

IT'S ALWAYS THE JEWS

Even though Israel was not involved in the Iran-Iraq War, it was always on the Iranians' minds: one of their operations was called Operation Tariq al-Quds (Operation Jerusalem Way); another, Operation Beit ol-Moqaddas (Operation Jerusalem).

Those who know nothing of Islam pretend that Islam counsels against war. Those [who say this] are witless. Islam says: Kill all the unbelievers just as they would kill you all! Does this mean that Muslims should sit back until they are devoured by [the unbelievers]? Islam says: Kill them [the non-Muslims], put them to the sword and scatter [their armies]. Does this mean sitting back until [non-Muslims] overcome us? Islam says: Kill in the service of Allah those who may want to kill you! Does this mean that we should surrender [to the enemy]? Islam says: Whatever good there is exists thanks to the sword and in the shadow of the sword! People cannot be made obedient except with the sword! The sword is the key to Paradise, which can be opened only for the Holy Warriors! There are hundreds of other [Qur'anic] psalms and Hadiths [sayings of the Prophet] urging

Muslims to value war and to fight. Does all this mean that Islam is a religion that prevents men from waging war? I spit upon those foolish souls who make such a claim.[89]

As Iranians became increasingly war-weary, even the days of Mohammed Reza Pahlavi began to look good in retrospect: a joke circulated in Iran in which a man who was about to become an Islamic martyr and enter Paradise pressed Khomeini for details of what Paradise was like. "Well," replied the Ayatollah, "there's always wonderful weather in paradise. There are lots of trees and the water is very pure." Asked for more, he added, "All the foods, including the finest meat and lots of fruit, are available. People have only one job and there are many ways to engage in pleasure." And? "There's no tension with anyone and everybody's happy." Pressed for still more about what Paradise is like, the joke has Khomeini saying, "Well, it's very much like the time of the Shah."[90]

Under the Islamic Republic, Iran had become a totalitarian sharia backwater, the embodiment of a notorious statement of Khomeini: "Allah did not create man so that he could have fun. The aim of creation was for mankind to be put to the test through hardship and prayer. An Islamic regime must be serious in every field. There are no jokes in Islam. There is no humor in Islam. There is no fun in Islam. There can be no fun and joy in whatever is serious. Islam does not allow swimming in the sea and is opposed to radio and television serials. Islam, however, allows marksmanship, horseback riding and competition."[91]

There was no fun in Islam, or in Iran either.

"I never saw my father laugh. I think you are the only person in this world who made him laugh.'"

Oriana Fallaci ventured into the nascent Islamic Republic in 1979 to interview the Ayatollah Khomeini. To secure the interview, Fallaci had to "marry" her interpreter (to avoid the "scandal" of their being alone in a room together) and wear a chador. During the interview, she complained about the oppression of women in Iran, and Khomeini growled, "Our customs are none of your business. If you do not like Islamic dress, you are not obliged to wear it. Because Islamic dress is for good and proper young women."[92]

To that, the famously feisty Fallaci replied, "That's very kind of you, Imam. And since you said so, I'm going to take off this stupid, medieval rag right now. There. Done. But tell me something...."[93] And the interview continued. Fallaci later recounted, however, that more had happened than what appeared in the published interview when she cast off her chador. "At that point, it was he who acted offended. He got up like a cat, as agile as a cat, an agility I would never expect in a man as old as he was, and he left me. In fact, I had to wait for twenty-four hours (or forty-eight?) to see him again and conclude the interview."[94]

Before she was allowed to continue, Khomeini's son Ahmed told Fallaci that the imam was quite angry over what had happened the previous day, so she had better avoid the subject of chadors. When the interview resumed, Fallaci accordingly immediately asked him about chadors. "First he looked at me in astonishment. Total astonishment. Then his lips moved in a shadow of a smile. Then the shadow of a smile became a real smile. And finally it became a laugh. He laughed, yes. And, when the interview was over, Ahmed whispered to me, 'Believe me, I never saw my father laugh. I think you are the only person in this world who made him laugh.'"[95]

Khomeini, Fallaci recalled, was "the most handsome old man I had ever met in my life. He resembled the 'Moses' sculpted by Michelangelo." He was, she said, "not a puppet like Arafat or Qaddafi or the many other dictators I met in the Islamic world. He was a sort of Pope, a sort of king—a real leader. And it did not take long to realize that in spite of his quiet appearance he represented the Robespierre or the Lenin of something which would go very far and would poison the world. People loved him too much. They saw in him another Prophet. Worse: a God."[96]

"The sooner we get all those other hostages out of Beirut, the better. Do whatever it has to take, Bill."

Up until the Iranian nuclear deal, the Islamic Republic of Iran and the United States had maintained a relationship of almost unremitting hostility, with a few notable exceptions. The most notorious of those exceptions is the curious episode in 1985 and 1986 that almost brought down the presidency of Ronald Reagan: the Iran-Contra Affair.

It all started when Hizballah kidnapped and murdered CIA agent William Buckley after 444 days of captivity and torture. When CIA director William Casey told Reagan that Buckley was dead, Reagan was silent for a while, and then said, "The sooner we get all those other hostages out of Beirut, the better. Do whatever it has to take, Bill."[97]

What followed was a clandestine deal to circumvent the embargo on selling arms to Iran in order to facilitate the release of American hostages held by Hizballah. Lieutenant Colonel Oliver North, a National Security Council official, developed a plan whereby the U.S. would secretly sell arms to Iran in exchange for the release of the hostages, with some of the proceeds going to the Nicaraguan anti-Communist guerrillas, the Contras—clandestinely also, since Congress had prohibited funding them. In the course of these dealings, several hostages were freed.[98]

When the scheme was discovered, it immediately became a partisan political issue in the U.S., with Democrats trying to use it to diminish Reagan and destroy his presidency. On November 13, 1986, Reagan explained in a nationally televised address, "For 18 months now we have had underway a secret diplomatic initiative to Iran. That initiative was undertaken for the simplest and best of reasons: to renew a relationship with the nation of Iran, to bring an honorable end to the bloody 6-year war between Iran and Iraq, to eliminate state-sponsored terrorism and subversion, and to effect the safe return of all hostages." He insisted, "The United States has not made concessions to those who hold our people captive in Lebanon. And we will not. The United States has not swapped boatloads or planeloads of American weapons for the return of American hostages. And we will not."

Reagan did acknowledge, however, that "during the course of our secret discussions, I authorized the transfer of small amounts of defensive weapons and spare parts for defensive systems to Iran. My purpose was to convince Tehran that our negotiators were acting with my authority, to send a signal that the United States was prepared to replace the animosity between us with a new relationship.... At the same time we undertook this initiative, we made clear that Iran must oppose all forms of international terrorism as a condition of progress in our relationship. The most significant step which Iran could take, we indicated, would be to use its influence in Lebanon to secure the release of all hostages held there."[99]

However, after initially denying that the U.S. had traded arms for hostages, Reagan said on national television on March 4, 1987, "A few months ago I told the American people I did not trade arms for hostages. My heart and my best intentions still tell me that's true, but the facts and the evidence tell me it is not." Referring to the findings of an investigatory commission, he continued, "As the Tower board reported, what began as a strategic opening to Iran deteriorated, in its implementation, into trading arms for hostages. This runs counter to my own beliefs, to administration policy, and to the original strategy we had in mind."[100]

Reagan's popularity plummeted, although it rebounded later. Fourteen administration officials were indicted for their role in these dealings, and eleven were convicted; all those convicted had their convictions overturned on appeal or were pardoned by President George H. W. Bush.[101]

IT ALL DEPENDS ON WHOSE OX IS BEING GORED

In one of the ironies of American politics, many of those that were most vocal in their indignation over the Iran-Contra Affair—the Democratic Party and media organs such as the New York Times and the Washington Post—were the loudest in applause of Barack Obama's nuclear deal three decades later.

Not just Iran-Contra

Despite the huge embarrassment that the Iran-Contra Affair was to the U.S. government, quiet contacts between the U.S. and the Islamic Republic continued over the years. In January 2003, the Bush administration, about to invade Iraq, agreed to bomb Iraqi bases of the Iranian dissident group the Mujahedin-e Khalq (MEK). According to a National Defense Research Institute monograph, this was in return for "Iranian support for subsequent reconstruction efforts and cooperation in rescuing downed pilots."[102]

On April 15, 2003, General Richard B. Myers, chairman of the Joint Chiefs of Staff, stated that the U.S. had bombed some MEK camps and added, "We're still interested in that particular group. How that will affect U.S.-Iranian relationships, I think we're going to have to wait until more time goes by."[103] In May 2003, the U.S. disarmed the MEK.[104]

U.S.-Iran talks revolving around the MEK evidently continued, with Time magazine reporting in October 2003 that "Tehran has offered to repatriate some al-Qaeda suspects if the U.S. cracks down on the People's Mujahedin (m.e.k.), a group of Iranian exiles in Iraq who want to overthrow Iran's mullocracy."[105]

The U.S. got nothing from these deals. It had duly bombed the MEK camps, but Iran did not support reconstruction efforts in Iraq, did not cooperate in rescuing downed pilots, and never repatriated any al-Qaeda suspects.

Another notable secret contact between the U.S. and Iran came in 2008, when presidential candidate Barack Obama sent Ambassador William G. Miller, who had been stationed in Iran while the Shah was in power, to Tehran. His mission, according to Michael Ledeen of the Foundation for the Defense of Democracies, was "to assure the mullahs that [Obama] was a friend of the Islamic Republic, and that they would be very happy with his policies."[106] This was no mere rumor. Ledeen has said, "Ambassador Miller has confirmed to me his conversations with Iranian leaders during the 2008 campaign."[107]

Obama's presidency confirmed that it was true: the mullahs would be very happy with his policies.

THE AYATOLLAH'S SPIT LIST

In January 2016 in Philadelphia, a convert to Islam named Edward Archer shot and seriously wounded police officer Jesse Hartnett and then explained: "I follow Allah. I pledge my allegiance to the Islamic state. That is why I did what I did."[108]

Philadelphia Mayor Jim Kenney then said at a press conference: "In no way shape or form does anyone in this room believe that Islam or the teaching of Islam has anything to do with what you've seen on the screen.... It is abhorrent. It is terrible and it does not represent the religion or any of its teachings. This is a criminal with a stolen gun who tried to kill one of our officers. It has nothing to do with being a Muslim or following the Islamic faith."[109]

"Islam is a religion that prevents men from waging war? I spit upon those foolish souls who make such a claim."

—the Ayatollah Khomeini[110]

Chapter Seven

"THE MIDDLE EAST IS GOING TO HAVE TO OVERCOME THAT"
SHI'ITE ISLAM AND THE SUNNI-SHI'ITE JIHAD

According to Islamic tradition, the Sunni-Shi'ite split goes back to the period immediately following the death of Muhammad, the prophet of Islam. That tradition holds that he died after a sudden and brief illness in the year 632. Ever since then, Muslims have been arguing over what kind of leadership he envisioned for the community he left behind.

Muhammad had no son, and so there was no obvious candidate for his successor. Upon his death, the Muslim community chose his companion Abu Bakr to succeed him as caliph—the successor of Muhammad as the military, political, and spiritual leader of the Muslims. But not everyone welcomed this choice, although Abu Bakr was Muhammad's father-in-law, the father of his child bride Aisha, and had been one of his most fervent and indefatigable followers. One group among the Muslims thought that the leadership instead belonged by right to Ali ibn Abi

Did you know?

- Sunnis and Shi'ites originally split over who was Muhammad's rightful successor
- Muhammad's favorite wife opposed one candidate because he had encouraged Muhammad to have her stoned for adultery
- Taqiyya, religious deception, is at the very heart of Shi'ite Islam—according to its highest authorities
- The Shi'ites believe that the Twelfth Imam, born in the ninth century and hidden since then, will return in the end times
- Shi'ite eschatology may lead Iran to nuke Israel

Talib, Muhammad's cousin, son-in-law and one of his first followers, and after him only to another member of the prophet's household (*ahl ul-bayt*). Indeed, this group claimed that Muhammad himself had designated Ali to be his successor.

Ali had been a member of Muhammad's household since his early childhood. According to Muhammad's first biographer, Ibn Ishaq, when Ali was around five years old a famine hit Mecca and Ali's father was in desperate straits. Muhammad took the lad into his home and raised him; Ibn Ishaq relates that when Muhammad received his prophetic call, the ten-year-old Ali became his first male follower (Muhammad's wife Khadija had become the first Muslim of all). Muhammad and Ali would pray together to the god who was delivering messages to Muhammad.[1]

The party of Ali (*shiat Ali*, or Shi'ites), based their insistence that it was the will of the prophet of Islam himself that Ali lead the Muslims on certain statements of Muhammad.[2] A hadith, or saying of Muhammad, that is accepted by both Sunni and Shi'ite Muslims depicts the Muslim prophet asking Ali, "Will you not be pleased that you will be to me like Aaron to Moses? But there will be no prophet after me."[3] This did suggest that Ali was to be Muhammad's successor, for in the Qur'an, Moses tells Aaron, "Take my place among my people" (7:142).

Other hadiths make Ali's claim to be Muhammad's successor absolutely clear and undeniable, but only Shi'ites tend to accept these traditions as authentic. One depicts Muhammad saying, "He who wishes to live as I have lived and to die as I will die, and enter the Garden of Eternal Bliss which Allah has promised me—let him take Ali as his leader (*wali*), because Ali will never lead you away from the Path of Truth, nor will he take you into error."[4]

In another, Muhammad expands upon the Qur'an's dictum that "whoever obeys the Messenger [that is, Muhammad] has obeyed Allah" (4:80) to include Ali: "He who obeys me will have obeyed Allah, and he who disobeys me will have disobeyed Allah. And he who obeys Ali will have obeyed me, and he who disobeys Ali will have disobeyed me."[5]

Still another account that Shi'ites cherish has a group of Muslims on a journey with Muhammad toward the end of his life. When the Muslims stopped at a place called Ghadir Khumm, Muhammad is said to have announced "For whomever I am his *Mawla* then Ali is his *Mawla*."[6] Shi'ites argue that by this, Muhammad meant that Ali would assume his leadership of the Muslim community, for the word *Mawla* in the Qur'an generally is used of Allah and means "master," "protector," or "lord"—the one who is in charge. The Qur'an addresses Allah (or rather, has Allah addressing himself, since he is supposed to be the sole speaker in the Muslim holy book): "You are our protector [*Mawla*], so give us victory over the disbelieving people" (2:286). It also says, "But Allah is your protector [*Mawla*], and he is the best of helpers" (3:150), "Then they his servants are returned to Allah, their true Lord [*Mawla*]" (6:62), and "There, every soul will be put to trial for what it did previously, and they will be returned to Allah, their master [*Mawla*], the Truth, and lost from them is whatever they used to invent" (10:30).

Lord, protector, master: this would seem to be fairly conclusive in establishing that Muhammad meant for Ali to be the leader of the Muslims, but Sunnis dispute that conclusion. The great medieval Sunni jurist Ibn Taymiyya, a favorite of Osama bin Laden, dismissed the very idea that Muhammad said this, contending that this hadith was "one of the reports which were narrated by the scholars and concerning whose authenticity the people disputed."[7]

Islam Question and Answer, a popular Sunni website supervised by the Saudi hardline Sheikh Muhammad Saalih al-Munajjid, on the other hand, concedes that the statement might really be authentic, but says that even if so, it "cannot under any circumstances be taken as evidence to support what the extremists added to the hadeeth to prove that Ali (may Allaah be pleased with him) takes precedence over all the other Sahaabah [Companions of Muhammad], or to slander the Sahaabah and accuse them of usurping his rights."[8]

A scholar on the website suggested that Muhammad's statement meant that "whomever I took as a friend, Ali will also take him as a friend as opposed to an enemy, and whomever I used to love, Ali will also love him." In other words, Ali is not the leader of the Muslims. Another insisted, with Jesuitical casuistry, that "it is incorrect to interpret the mawla as referring to the imam who conducts the affairs of the believers, because the only person who was in charge of the Muslims' affairs during the lifetime of the Prophet (peace and blessings of Allaah be upon him) was the Prophet himself and no one else, so the word mawla must be interpreted as referring to love, the bonds of Islam and so on."[9] This interpretation simply begs the question of whether Muhammad intended by these words to designate a successor.

"It is not befitting that a group, among whom is Abu Bakr, be led by other than him"

A fuller version of the Ghadir Khumm story has Muhammad offering prayers and then taking Ali's hand while declaring, "One who has me as his master has Ali as his master. O Allah! Befriend the one who befriends him (Ali) and be the enemy of one who is his enemy."

The story goes on to note that after Muhammad said this, one of his closest companions, Umar ibn al-Khattab, approached Ali and said: "O Ibn Abi Talib! Congratulations, you have become the master of every male and female believer, morning and evening."[10]

That fuller version reveals why Sunnis have good reason to regard such traditions with skepticism: Umar became the caliph after Abu Bakr's death in 634, just two years after Muhammad died. If Umar had seen and heard Muhammad declare that "one who has me as his master has Ali as his master" and had even himself hailed Ali as "the master of every male and female believer" just a few years earlier, how could he have agreed to become caliph? Why didn't he defer to Ali, in accord with Muhammad's wishes?

Muhammad's youngest and favorite wife, Aisha, who was eighteen years old at the time of Muhammad's death, denied that he had ever said anything about passing on his authority to Ali, heaping contempt upon the very idea: "When did he appoint him by will? Verily when he died he was resting against my chest and he asked for a wash-basin and then collapsed while in that state, and I could not even perceive that he had died, so when did he appoint him by will?"[11]

To be sure, the partisans of Ali regarded Aisha's testimony as just as suspect as she regarded theirs. Not only was she Abu Bakr's daughter; she hated Ali with a passionate intensity. Several years before Muhammad died, she had been accused of adultery. The accusation greatly troubled Muhammad, who was genuinely fond of her; Ali, however, told Muhammad with a pitiless lack of gallantry: "O Allah's Messenger! Allah does not put you in difficulty, and there are plenty of women other than she."[12] In other words, if Aisha needed to be stoned to death, no problem: there were plenty of other fish in the sea.

Exonerated by Muhammad's reception of a Qur'anic revelation that demanded four witnesses to establish a charge of adultery (24:4, 24:13), Aisha never forgot or forgave Ali's slight. As the Muslims deliberated on who should succeed Muhammad, she quoted the prophet of Islam as saying, "It is not befitting that a group, among whom is Abu Bakr, be led by other than him."[13] And indeed, Abu Bakr, not Ali, became the first caliph.

How could both sides have quoted Muhammad in support of their man? How could Muhammad have said that both Ali and Abu Bakr should lead the Muslims? Perhaps the prophet of Islam changed his mind from day to day; more likely, however, the partisans of each man fabricated these traditions to buttress the claim of their candidate for the leadership. There are no contemporary records of Muhammad; everything we know about him comes from over 125 years after his death. In the eighth and ninth centuries, hadiths depicting Muhammad saying or doing something that supported a Muslim faction's doctrine or practice were fabricated by the hundreds of thousands, by parties on all sides of various issues.

Consequently, the hadith literature is filled with contradictory material: in one hadith Muhammad says one thing, and in another he says its opposite. The hadiths claiming that Muhammad at various times endorsed both Ali and Abu Bakr as his successor constitute just one example of this phenomenon.

And so who Muhammad really appointed to succeed him, if he appointed anyone at all, is lost in the mists of time, like virtually everything else about the life of the prophet of Islam.

"The only reason I have fought against them was so that they should adhere to the authority of this Book"

Ali was passed over for the leadership of the Muslims three times. He finally became caliph in the year 656 but faced challenges to his rule so severe that his caliphate came to be known as the period of the First Fitna (disturbance)—a time of chaos and civil war. Aisha, still smarting over Ali's casual willingness to see her killed so many years before, even organized an armed revolt against Ali. At the Battle of the Camel in Basra on November 7, 656, she directed her forces from the back of a camel, on which she was sitting fully veiled and concealed inside a howdah. Ali, victorious perhaps because of his superior freedom of movement, magnanimously spared her life.

This act of mercy, however, won him no supporters among his enemies.[14] Soon Muawiya, the governor of Syria, claimed the caliphate; he and Ali fought in 657 in the Battle of Siffin, a village on the banks of the Euphrates

River in Syria. A much later account that is almost certainly legendary nonetheless reflects certain facets of the Sunni-Shi'ite conflict that continue to this day.

Addressing Muawiya's forces, Ali is supposed to have piously invoked the Qur'an: "I have given you time so that you might revert to the truth and turn to it in repentance. I have argued against you with the Book of God and have called you to it, but you have not turned away from oppression or responded to truth."[15] Speaking to his own men on the eve of battle, he sounded similarly pious notes: "Tomorrow you will meet the enemy, so lengthen the night standing in prayer, make abundant recitation of the Qur'an, and ask God for help and steadfastness."[16]

The battle was hotly contested and protracted; finally, when it looked as if victory was in sight for Ali, one of Muawiya's commanders, Amr ibn al-As, offered his chief a plan: his forces would raise aloft copies of the Qur'an and proclaim, "Their contents are to be authoritative in our dispute."

Amr was sure that if Muawiya appealed to the Qur'an to arbitrate his dispute with Ali, Ali would have to accept, giving Muawiya's weary forces time to rest and regroup while the scholars perused the holy text. If Ali dared to refuse, his own men would see that refusal as impious.[17] And so Muawiya's men raised up copies of the Qur'an on their lances and called out to Ali's men, "This is the Book of God between us and you."

The party of Ali (shiat Ali) answered, "We respond to the Book of God, and we turn in repentance to it." But Ali didn't halt the fight, crying out, "Servants of God, keep on fighting your enemies, for you have truth and right on your side."

This was a canny move. Ali motivated his men by claiming that Muawiya was ignorant of the true religion, calling his enemies "men without religion and without qur'an."[18] He justified his fighting on by charging that the raising up of copies of the Qur'an was just a ruse: "They do not exalt them and do not know what it is that they contain. They have raised them up to you

THESE KIDS TODAY

• • •

"I know them better than you, for I was with them both as children and as men, and they were the worst of children and the worst of men."[20]

—Ali, speaking to his followers about Muawiya and his supporters

only to deceive you, to outwit you, and to trick you." He insisted, "The only reason I have fought against them was so that they should adhere to the authority of this Book, for they have disobeyed God in what He has commanded and forgotten His covenant and rejected His Book."[19]

Nonetheless, both sides finally agreed to arbitration based on the Qur'an, as explained by Muawiya: "You will send a man from among you whom you find acceptable, and we will send a man from among us, and we will impose upon them that they act according to what is in the Book of God, not opposing it. Then we will follow what they agree upon."[21]

And so the arbitration commenced. Meanwhile, however, a third party in this dispute registered their disapproval of the entire process. The Khawarij, or Kharijites, were an especially fervent and violent party of Muslims that had initially supported Ali but ultimately broken with him. At this point they complained to Ali that Muawiya and his supporters had "always rejected our appeals when we summoned them to the Book of God."[22] Thus they considered Muawiya and his followers heretics who "should be killed or repent," pressing Ali on what they considered to be a violation of the Qur'an's command, a contradiction of his promises to abide by the word of Allah's Book.[23] The Kharijites were saying that Muawiya should not be negotiated with, but simply fought—as the Qur'an commanded. They were angry with Ali for submitting to arbitration instead.

Ultimately the arbitration was inconclusive anyway. Muawiya returned to Syria and maintained an uneasy peace with Ali. But the Kharijites, enraged at what they considered to be the deviation of both parties from obedience to the Qur'an, murdered Ali in 661. At that point, Muawiya became caliph.

The story is full of legendary elements. This battle, and the subsequent arbitration, are supposed to have taken place only eight years after Uthman codified the contents of the Qur'an and distributed the standardized copy to the provinces. It is extremely unlikely that Muawiya's men would have had copies of the Qur'an in such proliferation that they could raise them on their lances, and unlikely that they would have risked damage to the Muslim holy book by doing so. Actually, there is no contemporary record of the Qur'an's actually existing at that time. The significance of the abortive truce and arbitration between Ali and Muawiya is that it shows why the Sunni-Shi'ite split is intractable: both sides still claim to be the true followers of the Qur'an and the sole authentic exponents of Islam. Both sides claim that the other's piety is feigned and deceptive—that they aren't genuine Muslims at all.

Meanwhile, the murder of Ali by the Khawarij was the first of several serious defeats that resonate within the Shi'ite consciousness to this day. Shi'ites, always much smaller in numbers than the Sunnis, have all too often experienced failure and defeat at the hands of the majority community, in a way that Sunnis never have. This has given Shi'ite spirituality a particular cast, marked by sentimentality and a keen sense of loss and mourning. Indeed, until the advent of the Islamic Republic of Iran, Shi'ite theology was marked by a sense of defeat, as defeats came so often that they began to appear inevitable. Only with the coming of the Islamic Republic did a sense of victory arising from the ashes of defeat become combined with a new and lethal aggressiveness.

Muawiya made the caliphate into a family dynasty; in 680, his son, Yazid I, succeeded him. However, Ali's own son, Hussain, was not willing to accept Yazid's authority, and in the year 680 he stood at Karbala in Iraq against Yazid's forces, which vastly outnumbered the *shiat Ali*. Hussain and his six-month-old son were both killed—but Hussain's followers refused to accept Yazid's authority, and the split in the Muslim community became permanent: the *shiat Ali* and the majority Sunnis went their separate ways, with both sides condemning and cursing the other as heretical.

"The man in front"

Aside from the question of the leadership, there are no significant doctrinal differences between the Sunni and Shi'ite camps, but that difference over the leadership of the Muslim community involves much more than just the question of who should be in charge. The two camps have vastly different ideas of the nature of that authority. For the Sunnis, the caliph was the man in charge, who must be obeyed: "You should listen to and obey your Imam," a hadith depicts Muhammad as saying, "even if he was an Ethiopian (black) slave whose head looks like a raisin."[24] ("Imam" in this context means the ruler of the Muslims, a usage that later was common only among Shi'ites.) But duty to obey him didn't mean that he was anything more than just a man.

The Shi'ites, by contrast, believe that their Imams have much more than just earthly authority over the Muslims: like Muhammad himself, they possess nothing less than divine knowledge of Allah's will. This is the concept of *isma*, "protection."

"Imam" means "leader" or "the man in front." In Sunni Islam, an imam is the prayer leader in the local mosque, the man who stands in front of the others. In Shi'ite Islam, by contrast, the word is used in a much more restrictive sense. It refers primarily to Ali and his successors—those who succeeded Muhammad and were the rightful caliphs. All of these enjoyed the *isma* that Allah gave to the prophets, as is explained

MORE INFALLIBLE THAN THE POPE

• • •

Isma includes not only infallibility—freedom from error—but also impeccability—freedom from sin. It is given by Allah, in the Shi'ite view, to protect the community of believers from going astray. *Isma* was given first to the prophets before Muhammad, and then to Muhammad himself and his household, including the Imams who led the community after his death.

in the Qur'an (4:64): if the prophets were not infallible, the reasoning goes, how could they guide the people to the truth of Allah? "And We did not send any messenger except to be obeyed by permission of Allah." Shi'ites reason that if Allah sent the prophets to be obeyed, he must have protected the messenger from sin and the message from error.[25]

Shi'ites also point to the many Qur'an verses (3:32; 3:132; 4:13; 4:59; 4:69; 4:80; 5:92; 8:1; 8:20; 8:46; 9:71; 24:47; 24:51; 24:52; 24:54; 24:56; 33:33; 47:33; 49:14; 58:13; 64:12) that tell Muslims to obey the Messenger—that is, Muhammad. In many of these, Allah demands that the Muslims obey Muhammad in the same breath as demanding obedience to himself: "O you who have believed, obey Allah and obey the Messenger and those in authority among you" (4:59). One verse actually equates the Muslim prophet with Allah: "He who obeys the Messenger has obeyed Allah" (4:80). The Shi'ites contend that Allah never would have said such a thing if Muhammad had not been infallible.

The Qur'an also tells Muslims, "So be patient for the decision of your Lord and do not obey from among them a sinner or ungrateful" (76:24). If Muslims must obey the Messenger, but Muslims are not to obey those who are sinners or ungrateful, it follows that the Messenger can be neither a sinner nor ungrateful.

For the Shi'ites, that establishes that Muhammad is infallible, possessing of *isma*, for he does not "speak from inclination," but rather delivers "a revelation revealed" (Qur'an 53:3–4). But what about after his death? As far as Shi'ites are concerned, the same reasoning still holds true for those whom Allah has chosen to lead the community. Allah has established them in authority over the community, and that means he has made them *ma'sum* (infallible), for otherwise his call to the people to obey "those in authority among you" (4:59) would be pointless.

The Imams accordingly possess some of the light of Muhammad; if Muhammad is the seal of the prophets (Qur'an 33:40)—which both Sunnis and Shi'ites understand to mean that he is the last prophet—then this infallibility must pass to the post–prophetic era leaders of the community, the Imams. Shi'ites hold that when Muhammad designated Ali as his successor at Ghadir Khumm, Allah revealed this Qur'anic verse: "This day I have perfected for you your religion and completed My favor upon you and have approved for you Islam as religion" (5:3).

The Shi'ite scholar Allamah Sayyid Muhammad Husayn Tabatabai explains: "The obvious meaning of this verse is that before that particular day the infidels had hopes that a day would come when Islam would die out, but God through the actualization of a particular event made them lose forever the hope that Islam would be destroyed. This very event was the cause of the strength and perfection of Islam and of necessity could not be a minor occasion such as the promulgation of one of the injunctions of the religion. Rather, it was a matter of such importance that the continuation of Islam depended upon it."[26] The enemies of Islam, who had hoped that the religion would die, were foiled at Ghadir Khumm, where "their wishes were brought to nought and the Prophet presented Ali as the guide and leader of Islam to the people. After Ali the heavy and necessary duty of guide and leader was left upon the shoulders of his family."[27]

Indeed, says Tabatabai, "it is not necessary for a prophet (nabi) always to be present among mankind, but the existence of the Imam, who is the guardian of Divine religion, is on the contrary a continuous necessity for human society."[28] That kind of talk leads Sunnis to accuse Shi'ites of idolatry and Shi'ites to see Sunnis as lacking in faith—Sunnis, not believing in the infallibility of their caliphs, hold to the idea that Allah protected his prophets, particularly Muhammad, from error, but after Muhammad's death effectively abandoned his community by allowing for the possibility that it could fall into error. The Imamate, in the Shi'ite view, guarded the community against that possibility.

The only catch to this neatly thought-out little system is that, according to the dominant strain of Shi'ite Islam, there hasn't been an Imam in the world for over eleven hundred years.

"Ali held his peace for the sake of the unity of Islam"

The official religion of the Islamic Republic of Iran is Twelver Shi'ism. This refers to the belief of the Shi'ite sect that dominates Iran: that there were twelve legitimate caliphs, or successors, of Muhammad. The twelve successors of Muhammad recognized by Twelver Shi'ites are known as the Imams; each possessed infallibility. Ali was the first, followed by eleven others, until the line ended in the year 874. Ali's being the first means, of course, that Shi'ites do not accept the legitimacy of the first three caliphs after Muhammad's death: Abu Bakr, Umar, and Uthman, who, according to Islamic tradition, ruled the Muslim community between 632 and 656, when Ali finally became caliph.

Shi'ites believe that during all those years Ali was the rightful ruler of the Muslims and that Abu Bakr, Umar, and Uthman were usurpers, but Ali did not forcefully assert this authority for the sake of preserving the unity of the Muslim community. And for Shi'ites, Ali's patience and forbearance are admirable. Shi'ites, historically minority communities in most countries aside from Iran, Iraq, and Bahrain, and denied political power even when they have formed a substantial portion of the population, have often had occasion to emulate those virtues.

LIKE PATIENCE ON A MONUMENT

• • •

"Ali held his peace for the sake of the unity of Islam and gave his support to the government of those people. Throughout his 25 years' wait, this hero who had cut down his enemies with his sword ... had to keep silent and remain inactive. He saw his house attacked and his wife insulted, but maintained a silence which he described succinctly when he said that for nearly 25 years he had had 'dust in his eyes and thorns in his mouth.'"[29]

—Ali Shariati

A NATION OF MARTYRS?

Ali's dying words contain the seed of the Shi'ite idea that salvation comes through martyrdom and can be found even in the moment of death—a pair of assumptions that, as deeply rooted beliefs in the Islamic Republic of Iran, could have catastrophic consequences for those whom the Iranian mullahs deem their enemies, as well as for the world at large. If it held true for Ali, would it not also hold true for Shi'ite Iran? Might national salvation come through national martyrdom—that is, a terrible military defeat or even nuclear annihilation, brought on as retaliation for an Iranian nuclear strike?

But there was a great deal more about Ali worthy of emulation. Ali Shariati, the Iranian Shi'ite revivalist and political theorist who died mysteriously in England in 1977, wrote that Ali "laid out a path, a permanent model for humankind, he has shown man once and for all the perfect example of a man."

(Note that Shariati said this not about Muhammad, whom the Qur'an designates as an "excellent example" (33:21), but about Ali. In Shi'ite Islam, Muhammad is so exalted and honored as to become somewhat remote. Ali is much more approachable and accessible.) "That is how he became an Imam," Shariati continued, "otherwise he would have been nothing but a failed governor, rejected by all, and both he and his line would have been annihilated. For an Imam is one who goes ahead, to show man the direction to take, at all times. That is why he refused the rank of victorious leader, which would have been extinguished at his death, and preferred instead the role of Imam, which led him to retreat, after refusing any compromise, but which extended his life beyond death. We see that every day he is more alive, that we have ever greater need for him, and hearts that are vibrant for humanism, liberty, justice and purity…turn ever more towards him and his Imamate."[30]

This "humanism, liberty, justice and purity" were not exactly what Westerners might assume was meant by the terms. According to Shi'ite legend, as Ali was being stabbed to death, he cried out, "By the God of the Ka'ba! I swear it, I am saved and victorious!"[31]

"I don't know Ali as God, but neither do I know him to be separate from God"

The high regard for Ali, combined with the idea of the Imam possessing infallibility, Shi'ite Islam's mystical bent, and the embattled position Shi'ites have been in for most of the history of Islam—with Ali being their unifying figure and rallying point—have led to an *extremely* high view of who exactly Ali is in some circles. In 1988 one Persian villager told a visitor that Muhammad had said, "I don't know Ali as God, but neither do I know him to be separate from God."[32]

That villager was neither ignorant nor eccentric. Some Shi'ite texts—certainly outside of mainstream Shi'ism, but nonetheless widely circulated—quote Ali saying, "I am the Sign of the All-Powerful. I am the First and the Last. I am the Manifest and the Hidden. I am the Face of God. I am the Hand of God. I am the Side of God. I am he who in the Gospel is called Elijah. I am he who keeps the secret of God's Messenger."[33] Offshoots of the Shi'ites such as the Alawites and Druze are said to worship Ali as a deity, but they remain highly secretive about the specifics of their beliefs for fear of Sunni persecution.

Even in the face of denials from mainstream Shi'ites, the idea that they deify and worship Ali remains a feature of Sunni anti-Shia polemic to this day. The Sunni website Discovering Islam states that "the way the Shia elevate the status of Imam Ali is very similar to the way Christians elevate the status of prophet Jesus and worship him.... Some Shia (particularly the Ismaelis & Arab Alawis) believe Ali is God; while others reject this. However, many of the Twelver Shia even though they don't believe Imam Ali is

God, yet they assign to Imam Ali some of God's functions and attributes. For example, they say that Imam Ali is the one who determines who will go to Hell and who will go to Paradise. This is one of the most serious blasphemies because it constitutes 'Shirk' (associating partners with God) which is the most serious sin in Islam."[34]

Sunnis claim that Shi'ites deny worshiping Ali because they are engaging in deliberate and religiously-sanctioned deception: *taqiyya*.

"*Taqiyya* is our religion and the religion of our fathers; he who has no *taqiyya* has no religion"

In the decade and more of Islamic jihad that the United States has experienced since 9/11, several Islamic terms have become widely known among non-Muslims, particularly among those concerned about jihad terror and the encroachments of Sharia supremacists in the West. One of these is *taqiyya* (literally "fear" or "caution"), which is generally taken to mean a blanket Islamic permission for Muslims to lie to non-Muslims in order to further the goals of Islam.[35]

That definition is not actually all that far off from the truth. The concept of *taqiyya* as such is specifically Shi'ite, developed during the time of the sixth Imam, Jafar al-Sadiq, in the middle of the eighth century, when the Shi'ites were being persecuted by the Sunni caliph al-Mansur. *Taqiyya* allowed Shi'ites to pretend to be Sunnis in order to protect themselves from Sunnis who were killing Shi'ites. Until the advent of the Shah Ismail I and the Safavids, *taqiyya* was an important element of Shi'ite survival, for Sunnis, in the majority almost everywhere, would not infrequently take it upon themselves to cleanse the land of those whom they referred to as Rafidites, that is, rejecters—those who rejected the caliphates of Abu Bakr, Umar, and Uthman.

Some Shi'ite thinkers turned the secrecy that had become a necessity into a virtue. The medieval Shi'ite scholar Ali ibn Musa ibn Tawus, who died in 1266, taught that Allah had revealed Shi'ism secretly, and it was incumbent upon the believers to practice it in secret. At the end of days, Allah will admit them secretly into Paradise.[36] Some secrets were never to be revealed under any circumstances. The fifth imam, Muhammad al-Baqir, who died in 732, once gave a book to one of his disciples, telling him, "If you ever transmit any of it, my curse and the curse of my forefathers will fall upon you."[37]

The sixth Imam, Jafar al-Sadiq, who died in 765, had a servant who was suspected of having revealed some of the secrets of the faith. The Imam lectured, "Whoever propagates our tradition is like someone who denies it.... Conceal our doctrine and do not divulge it. God elevates in this world one who conceals our doctrine and does not divulge it and he turns it in the next world into a light between his eyes which will lead him to Paradise. God abases in this world one who divulges our tradition and our doctrine and does not conceal it, and in the next world he removes the light from between his eyes and turns it into darkness which will lead him to hell. *Taqiyya* is our religion and the religion of our fathers; he who has no *taqiyya* has no religion."[38]

Other Imams also emphasized the cardinal importance of *taqiyya*, apparently not only because Shi'ites were under constant threat from Sunnis, but because Shi'ite Islam contained doctrines that must stay hidden from outsiders. Some sayings of the Imams include, "He who has no *taqiyya* has no faith"; "he who forsakes *taqiyya* is like him who forsakes prayer"; "he who does not adhere to *taqiyya* and does not protect us from the ignoble common people is not part of us"; "nine tenths of faith falls within *taqiyya*"; "*taqiyya* is the believer's shield (*junna*), but for *taqiyya*, God would not have been worshipped."[39]

ADDING INSULT TO INJURY

If a Sunni wants to insult Shi'ites, he calls them *rafida*—"rejectors"—for rejecting the caliphates of Abu Bakr, Umar and Uthman. If a Shi'ite wants to insult Sunnis, he calls them *nasibi*—"haters"—for hating Ali and the Imams who followed him. Certainly the appellation *nasibi* could be applied to both sides.

HOW TO KEEP A SECRET

The required concealment wasn't always easy even for the Imams: al-Baqir, who died in 732, told one of his followers no fewer than seventy thousand secret hadiths, that is, traditions of Muhammad's words and deeds, with the strict charge that he pass them on to no one. After he died, the unfortunate recipient of this largesse confessed to al-Baqir's successor, Jafar al-Sadiq, that the secret was burning within him. Al-Sadiq told him to go out into the desert, dig a hole, and shout the hadiths into it; the man did so, and felt better.[40] What happened to those hadiths is not recorded.

The elements of this secret tradition are, understandably, not entirely clear. Some, including Sunnis engaged in anti-Shi'ite polemic, say that the Shi'ites have additional chapters of the Qur'an. These are supposed to deal, at least in part, with the special prerogatives of Ali. But this cannot be taken as certain, since, because of the nature of *taqiyya*, what the Shi'ites possess has been concealed.[41]

Although they do not use the term *taqiyya*, Sunnis have doctrines of deception as well. The Qur'an teaches that deception is allowed, so this is not a solely Shi'ite concept: "Let not believers take disbelievers as allies rather than believers. And whoever does that has nothing with Allah, except when taking precaution against them in prudence" (Qur'an 3:28). A Muslim is not to take Muslims as friends unless he has "a fear of them" and is only feigning friendship to protect himself.

The Twelve Imams

A hadith that both Sunnis and Shi'ites accept has Muhammad saying, "Islam will continue to be triumphant until there have been twelve Caliphs."[42] Shi'ites, not surprisingly, claim that this was a prophecy of their Twelve Imams, while Sunnis find different explanations, pointing out that the history of the twelve Shi'ite Imams is hardly one of Islam continuing to be triumphant. Indeed, it is a virtually unbroken record of loss and defeat.

In 941 the last of the Twelfth Imam's Special Deputies, Ali Ibn Muhammad Samari, claimed to have received a letter from the Twelfth Imam, telling him, "Death will come to you within the next six days. So you complete your works and do not nominate any person after you. The sequence of special deputies will come to an end and the Major Occultation will commence with your demise."[43] The period of the Twelfth Imam's speaking through the Special Deputies was the "Minor Occultation."

Shi'ites believe that the Major Occultation, in which the Twelfth Imam is alive but hidden upon the earth, continues to this day. The Twelfth Imam himself explained in his letter to Samari that "the reappearance will occur only with the permission of Allah, after a prolonged period and after the hearts of people are hardened."[44]

"At that time you shall be severely examined and you shall be differentiated and sieved. There will be famines"

Shi'ite Islam, embattled for most of its history, developed tendencies toward secrecy and esoteric observance that were only exacerbated by the disappearance of the Twelfth Imam as such a young child. Not surprisingly, he is a figure shrouded in mystery. Shi'ite Muslims hold that only unbelievers utter the name of the Twelfth Imam. Pious Shi'ites are to refer to him as "the Proof from Muhammad's family."[45] Indeed, the Twelfth Imam is depicted as cursing those who utter his name in the presence of a crowd.[46]

Compounding the sense of mystery is the fact that no one knows exactly when the Twelfth Imam is going to come out of the Major Occultation. The Sixth Imam, Jafar al-Sadiq, is supposed to have said, "Those who fix a time

THE SAD HISTORY OF THE TWELVE SHI'ITE IMAMS

1. **Ali ibn Abi Talib**, the first and greatest of the Imams and the foremost hero of the Shi'ites, was in the Shi'ite view the rightful leader of the Muslims from Muhammad's death in 632 until his own death in 661, although from 632 to 656 the usurper caliphs held this authority instead. Ali, according to Tabatabai, "had no shortcomings from the point of view of human perfection."[47] His "courage was proverbial" and he was also "without equal in religious asceticism and the worship of God."[48] Ali was followed by his sons.

2. **Hasan ibn Ali**, was the elder son of Ali and his wife Fatima, Muhammad's daughter. He laid claim to the caliphate when his father was murdered in 661, but Muawiya quickly displaced him. Shi'ites invoke a hadith that depicts Muhammad referring to his grandchildren Hasan and Hussain, who succeeded Hasan as the Imam of the Shi'ites, as his own children and saying that they were "Imams whether they stand up or sit down"—that is, whether they actually ruled over the Muslims or not.[49] For the most part, they did not. Hasan, it is said, died in Medina in 670, poisoned by Muawiya.

3. **Hussain ibn Ali**, the younger brother of Hasan, lived quietly until 680, when Muawiya's son Yazid became caliph and demanded an explicit avowal of obedience from him. Hussain refused and went out with a small group of followers to meet Yazid's forces in battle at Karbala in Iraq in 680. He was killed there—as he held the Qur'an in one hand and a sword in the other, according to pious legend. His death marked the end of Shi'ite hopes to lead all the Muslims and the beginning of the formal split between Sunnis and Shi'ites. Shi'ites feel this defeat keenly, and to this day mark the anniversary of Hussain's death as Ashura, the Day of Remembrance. On Ashura, the tenth day of the Muslim month of Muharram, Shi'ite men often march in processions to honor Hussain while flagellating themselves or cutting themselves with knives to express their regret at not being able to save him.

4. **Ali ibn Hussain al-Sajjad**, also known as Zayn al-Abidin, was Hussain's son, ill on the day of the Battle of Karbala and thus not killed or captured there. The Umayyad caliph did imprison him several times, however, after which he lived quietly in Medina, devoting himself to prayer and writing spiritual works that won renown among the Shi'ites, especially his *al-Sahifat al-sajjadiyyah*, "The Psalm of the Household of the Prophet."[50] He died in 712.

5. **Muhammad ibn Ali al-Baqir** is known for formulating numerous Shi'ite legal traditions. He died in Medina in 732.[51]

6. **Jafar ibn Muhammad al-Sadiq** was able to teach Shi'ite Islam more openly than his immediate predecessors because of the conflict among the Sunnis between the Umayyads and the Abbasids. Once the Abbasids gained power, however, the Abbasid caliph Mansur cracked down on Jafar's activities and ultimately, in 757, had him poisoned. Jafar had continued al-Baqir's legal work; his contribution there is so great that the Shi'ite school of jurisprudence is called Jafari after him.[52]

7. **Musa ibn Jafar al-Kazim** faced persecution from the Abbasid caliphs al-Mansur and the putatively tolerant Harun al-Rashid, who had him imprisoned in Baghdad, where he died from poisoning in 799.[53]

8. **Ali ibn Musa al-Rida** led revolts against the Sunni hierarchy that so unnerved the caliph al-Ma'mun that he named al-Rida his successor, hoping that this would heal the schism and quell the revolts. Al-Rida accepted, but other counsel prevailed; alarmed at al-Rida's popularity (or so go the Shi'ite accounts, anyway), al-Ma'mun reconsidered his invitation and ultimately had al-Rida poisoned in 817, settling the question of whether or not the Shi'ite Imam would succeed the Sunni caliph once and for all.[54]

9. **Muhammad ibn Ali al-Taqi** participated in efforts to heal the Sunni-Shi'ite breach. He married al-Ma'mun's daughter and was allowed to return to the Imams' traditional home in Medina. However, al-Ma'mun's successor, al-Mu'tasim, ordered him back to Baghdad, where in 835 he, too, was poisoned, making it clear that, once again, a Shi'ite Imam would not succeed a Sunni caliph.[55]

10. **Ali ibn Muhammad al-Naqi** was allowed to live and teach in Medina for a time, but was ultimately called to Samarra by the Abbasid caliph al-Mutawakkil, who was otherwise famous for mistreating Jews and Christians. Al-Mutawakkil had al-Naqi likewise mistreated, ridiculed, and tortured until he also was poisoned to death in 868.[56]

11. **Hasan ibn Ali al-Askari** lived under house arrest in Samarra until his death, also by poisoning, in 874. Shi'ite tradition holds that the prophecy that the twelfth Imam would be the Mahdi, the savior figure of Islam awaited by both Sunnis and Shi'ites, was widely

known—so that al-Askari was kept under wraps lest he father a son who could claim that title.[57] Shi'ites believe, however, that he managed to have a son anyway, although there are differing traditions about who his wife was and where she was from, and no one is sure how she got to the Imam under the watchful eyes of the Sunnis. Nonetheless, the Shi'ites revere the couple's offspring, the awaited Twelfth Imam:

12. **Muhammad ibn Hasan al-Mahdi** was just four years old when his father was killed. Soon after his father was killed, he disappeared—or, in the Shi'ite view, he went into "Occultation," unable to be seen by ordinary human eyes. Four men who came to be known as his Special Deputies claimed to be in contact with him, and they led the Shi'ite community for the next seventy years.

for it are liars. We have not timed what has passed and we will not time what is to come."[58]

Nonetheless, he did give some specifics about the conditions that would have to prevail for the Twelfth Imam to return. Speaking of the Shi'ites in general, Jafar al-Sadiq said, "That time (of reappearance) shall not come to pass but after you have become despondent and hopeless. No, I swear by Allah, till you are separated from each other. No, I swear by Allah, till you are severely tested. No, I swear by Allah, till the time that the unfortunate ones become unfortunate, while the fortunate ones become fortunate."[59]

The sixth Imam spoke a great deal about how much the Shi'ites would have to be tested before the Twelfth Imam appeared again. During the Major Occultation, he said, "those who remain attached to their religion will be like those who rub their hands on a thorny branch."[60] And, "What will be your condition at that time when you shall be without an Imam or guide and you will be disgusted with each other? At that time you shall be severely examined and you shall be differentiated and sieved. There will be famines.

A person will become a ruler in the morning and put to death in the evening."[61]

The return of the Twelfth Imam, said his sixth predecessor, would come at a time when the Shi'ites were experiencing persecution to a terrible, unprecedented degree: One contemporary of the sixth Imam recounted "Once I came to Imam Ja'far Sadiq and there were some people with him. While we were talking with each other, he turned to us and said: 'What are you talking about? How far! How far! That which you look forward to will not be until you are tested. How far! That which you look forward to will not be until you are sieved. How far! That, which you look forward to, will not be until you are sifted. That which you look forward to will not be except after despair. That which you look forward to will not be until he who is to be wretched becomes wretched, and he who is to be happy becomes happy.'"[62]

How severe would this test be? Jafar al-Sadiq said that the Twelfth Imam's return "will not occur till two-third population of the world is not destroyed."[63] Presumably, then the Twelfth Imam will return when one-third of the world's population has been destroyed.

This time of massive death and destruction, however, will herald the consummation of all things. A prophecy attributed to no less an authority for Shi'ites than Ali himself says, "In the last period of time, the Almighty Allah will raise a man among the illiterate masses whom he will support by his angels and protect his helpers, help him through his signs and he will conquer the whole world. All would enter the fold of religion willingly or unwillingly. He would fill the earth with justice, equity and proof. No disbeliever will remain without accepting faith. During his rule, even the wild beasts would become tame. And the earth will through up its vegetation. Blessings will descend from the sky. The treasures buried in the earth will be exposed and he would rule the world for forty years. Fortunate would be one who lives till that time and hears his speech."[64]

As the Twelfth Imam conquers the whole world and fills it with justice and equity, he will do away with all earthly governments. A Shi'ite tradition details the glories of those days, when this community that has suffered so much loss and defeat will finally emerge victorious:

> The Imam who will create a world state will make the ruling nations pay for their crimes against society. He will bring succor to humanity. He will take out the hidden wealth from the breast of the earth and will distribute it equitably amongst the needy deserving. He will teach you simple living and high thinking. He will make you understand that virtue is a state of character which is always a mean between the two extremes, and which is based upon equity and justice. He will revive the teaching of the Holy Qur'an and the traditions of the Holy Prophet after the world has ignored them as dead letters.... He will protect and defend himself with resources of science and supreme knowledge. His control over these resources will be complete. He will know how supreme they are and how carefully they will have to be used. His mind will be free from desires of bringing harm and injury to humanity. Such a knowledge to him will be like the property which was wrongly possessed by others and for which he was waiting for the permission to repossess and use. He, in the beginning, will be like a poor stranger unknown and uncared for, and Islam then will be in the hopeless and helpless plight of an exhausted camel who has laid down its head and is wagging its tail. With such a start he will establish an empire of God in this world. He will be the final demonstration and proof of God's merciful wish to acquaint man with the right ways of life.[65]

Muhammad, in a hadith, calls this salvific figure a member of his household, as Shi'ites insist on regarding the Imams: "Were there remaining but one day of the duration of all time, God would send forth a man from the people of my house, who will fill the earth with equity as it has been filled with oppression."[66]

"An atomic bomb would not leave any thing [sic] in Israel but the same thing would just produce damages in the Muslim world"

The emphasis on the Twelfth Imam only returning at a time of immense persecution of the Shi'ites has given rise to speculation that the leaders of the Islamic Republic might try to hasten his return by provoking that persecution. The Iranian leader Ali Akbar Hashemi Rafsanjani, who was President of Iran from 1989 to 1997 and remains influential in the Iranian government, said in December 2001, "If a day comes when the world of Islam is duly equipped with the arms Israel has in possession, the strategy of colonialism would face a stalemate because application of an atomic bomb would not leave any thing [sic] in Israel but the same thing would just produce damages in the Muslim world."[67] It could also, with millions of Muslim dead, bring the Twelfth Imam out of Occultation.

The Iranian leadership clearly takes the prophecies regarding the Twelfth Imam very seriously. Mahmoud Ahmadinejad, president of Iran from 2005 to 2013, had a highway built between Tehran and the Shi'ite holy city of Qom, approaching the Iraqi city of Samarra—the city in which the Twelfth Imam disappeared and from which he will return. The highway is apparently intended for the Twelfth Imam himself, so that immediately after he does come out of Occultation, he can make his way to Tehran quickly and begin to wage global war against the enemies of the Shi'ites.

MADDER THAN MAD

. . .

The Cold War deterrence strategy of Mutually Assured Destruction has no teeth in a situation in which one side welcomes death—sure not only that Allah will reward martyrdom, but that large scale carnage will hasten the consummation of all things and the final victory of its party over not just one but all of its enemies.

Ahmadinejad also made frequent pilgrimages to the Jamkaran Mosque near Qom, where in the year 984 a man said he had seen a vision of the Twelfth Imam. At the place where the Twelfth Imam is said to have become visible long enough for the man to see him stands the "Well of Requests," to which Iranians make pilgrimages, tying strings on the metal grids covering the well to symbolize the prayers they are sending to the Imam Mahdi. The Jamkaran Mosque exploded in popularity as a pilgrimage site only in the 1990s—in large part, no doubt, because of the preoccupation of the leaders of the Islamic Republic with the Twelfth Imam.[68]

The Supreme Leader Khamenei said in June 2014, "The coming of Imam Zaman is the definite promise by Allah."[69] Imam Zaman is Imam of the Time, a title of the Twelfth Imam. He said that the very existence of the Islamic Republic was a sign that the Twelfth Imam was soon to return: "Who would have thought that in this sensitive region and in this important country, with a regime [run by Shah Pahlavi] and supported by the international powers, a revolution based on religion and Sharia would take place?"[70]

The fact that such a revolution did happen was a sign that Allah was working toward the conclusion of the great story of the human race: "The caravan of humanity from the day of creation has been moving through the windings of the hard maze [of life]…to reach an open path, [and] this open path is that of the time of the coming of Imam Mahdi. The awaiting for the coming is a hopeful and powerful wait, providing the biggest opening for the Islamic society."[71]

But, Khamenei said, for the Twelfth Imam actually to return would require some changes, including "regional preparedness." The Islamic

GET OUT OF THAT SEAT. IT'S RESERVED FOR THE HIDDEN IMAM

Eagerly anticipating that moment, Ahmadinejad always saved a seat for the Twelfth Imam at his cabinet meetings. And when he addressed the United Nations General Assembly in 2005, he declared that his address had been the occasion of a miracle from Imam Mahdi: "A person told me that when I started to say 'in the name of God,' 'a halo of light surrounded you and you were protected by a fence of light until the end of your speech.' I felt it myself as well. I felt the atmosphere was changed and people did not blink for the 27 or 28 minutes of my address."[72]

Republic, in any case, "without a doubt will be connected to the worldwide revolution of Imam Mahdi."[73]

In light of former president Rafsanjani's words about nuclear war ("application of an atomic bomb would not leave any thing [sic] in Israel but the same thing would just produce damages in the Muslim world")[74] and the prophecies about the persecution that would trigger the Twelfth Imam's return, Khamenei's term "regional preparedness" took on a decidedly ominous cast. Might the mullahs actually be willing to nuke Tel Aviv and take a retaliatory nuclear strike that could kill tens of millions of Iranians?

If it would hasten the Mahdi's coming, why not?

"They've completed a case against the Hidden Imam, and closed it also for his arrest"

As far as Mahmoud Ahmadinejad was concerned, the U.S. government knew about all this—and was working furiously to head off the return of the Twelfth Imam.

American research on the Twelfth Imam, said Ahmadinejad, was devoted to preventing his return: "To quote a friend, they've completed a case against the Hidden Imam, and closed it also for his arrest. The only [evidence] they lack is his picture."[76]

Why would the United States want to arrest the Twelfth Imam? Because, Ahmadinejad explained, the Americans see the Imam Mahdi as a threat to their "empire," and the "evil" U.S. government would stop at nothing to preserve that empire. "It is really a government established by Satan," he explained, "to prevent reaching God and the Hidden Imam.... This evil government knows that its end will come if the Hidden Imam reappears."[77]

Ahmadinejad did admit that "some in Iran laugh about these comments."[78]

Yes, and some outside Iran as well.

"There's still a tendency to see these things in Sunni-Shia terms. But the Middle East is going to have to overcome that."

The age-old character of the Sunni-Shi'ite split, as well as the high emotions among Shi'ites over the death of Hussain, made the division appear unbridgeable, and there were no ecumenical talks between Sunni and Shi'ite leaders aimed at healing it. Western analysts, generally unfamiliar with Islamic theology and the history of the schism, tended to underestimate its virulence. Secretary of State Condoleezza Rice complained in January 2007, "There's still a tendency to see these things in Sunni-Shia terms. But the Middle East is going to have to overcome that."[79]

It won't be easy. The enmity between Sunnis and Shi'ites is one of the oldest hatreds in the world, and it burns today with greater intensity than it has for centuries.

Since each believes that the other has departed from the truth of Islam, and each (particularly the Shi'ites) nurses centuries-old grudges over ancient wrongs done to them, this split is not ever going to be "overcome." Saddam Hussein kept a lid on it in Iraq by brute force, but now that he is gone and a Shi'ite government is in power there, the Sunnis are determined to wrest control back from them, and the Shi'ites and their Iranian patrons are just as determined to keep it. With Iran's increasing Middle Eastern adventurism, the split is more bitter than it has been in centuries, and shows no signs of healing.

The Sunni-Shi'ite divide, coupled with Islam's death penalty for heresy, is a recipe for endless warfare—until the Mahdi returns and reveals whether he has come as the Sunni or the Shi'ite version.

"Our dignity has been pawned away"

On January 2, 2016, the Saudi government executed the dissident Saudi Shi'ite cleric Nimr al-Nimr, pushing tensions between Shi'ite Iran and Sunni Saudi Arabia higher than they had been since 1987, when several hundred Iranian pilgrims were killed in clashes with Saudi forces.

Shi'ites make up 10 percent of Saudi Arabia's population, mostly in the Eastern Province, the region of the country that is just across the Persian Gulf from Iran and close to majority-Shi'ite Bahrain. Saudi Shi'ites have long complained of discrimination, and al-Nimr was their champion. In a 2009 Friday sermon, he roared, "Our dignity has been pawned away, and if it is not…restored, we will call for secession. Our dignity is more precious than the unity of this land."[80]

That was enough for the Saudis to regard him as a dangerous enemy of the state, and al-Nimr, never a shrinking violet, compounded their suspicions with a nonstop stream of incendiary rhetoric. In June 2012, he rejoiced in the death of Saudi Crown Prince Nayef:

> Who are those tyrants? It's all nonsense. So what if they have money and power?
>
> Where is Nayef's army now? Will it protect him from the Angel of Death? Where are his intelligence agencies? Where are his officers? Can they protect him from the Angel of Death? He will be eaten by worms and suffer the torments of Hell in his grave....
>
> Don't you see that the Qur'an says: "On that day shall the believers rejoice"? Why shouldn't we be happy at the death of the man who imprisoned and killed our children? This is the man who spread fear and terror, so why shouldn't we rejoice?
>
> Allah be praised! May He take their lives, one after the other—the Saud, Khalifa, and Al-Assad dynasties.
>
> The sons of Abd Al-Aziz [al-Saud] will rule this land until Judgment Day—that's what Nayef declared. Let's see how he rules it.... Let him rule it from the grave. It is a reckless, tyrannical regime.
>
> Who is the Saud clan? They are killing our brothers in Bahrain. If any good can become of them, let them liberate Palestine from the Zionists, rather than [bully] half a million Bahrainis— good defenseless people.
>
> The [Saud clan] says that they are the "lions of the Sunna." You, the lions of the Sunna? Pffff...Nonsense. They said: "We are the lions of the Sunna facing Iran." Don't make me laugh. You? Facing Iran? The day Saddam entered Kuwait, you all fled and brought the US to defend you.[81]

Al-Nimr's imprisonment and ultimate execution infuriated the Iranians and became the occasion for a new flare-up in Sunni-Shi'ite tensions. On the day his execution was announced, Shi'ites protested in the Eastern Province and Bahrain; in Tehran, protesters stormed the Saudi Embassy, smashing furniture and breaking windows, and ultimately setting fire to part of the embassy compound.[82]

Khamenei vowed "divine vengeance" for al-Nimr's death.[83] Ayatollah Ahmad Khatami, a powerful Iranian cleric, said, "I have no doubt that this pure blood will stain the collar of the House of Saud and wipe them from the pages of history. The crime of executing Sheikh Nimr is part of a criminal pattern by this treacherous family...the Islamic world is expected to cry out and denounce this infamous regime as much as it can."[84] Iranian Foreign Ministry spokesman Hossein Jaber Ansari warned, "The Saudi Government supports terrorist movements and extremists, but confronts domestic critics with oppression and execution...the Saudi Government will pay a high price for following these policies."[85]

Iraq's former prime minister, Nuri al-Maliki, a Shi'ite and client of Iran, likewise predicted the end of the House of Saud: "We strongly condemn these detestable sectarian practices and affirm that the crime of executing Sheikh al-Nimr will topple the Saudi regime."[86] Hizballah's Hassan Nasrallah agreed: "This blood that has been shed will spell the end of the [Saud] regime and clan."[87]

Taking note of all this, Saudi Arabia broke off diplomatic relations with Iran.[88]

"Great sign of Allah"

The career path for Iranian mullahs is clearly marked, from talib ilm (young seminarian) to grand ayatollah ("sign of Allah").

Beyond the Grand Ayatollahs is the Imam—that is, the Twelfth Imam who is the object of Shi'ite longing. However, during his tenure as Supreme Leader of the Islamic Republic, the Ayatollah Khomeini was commonly referred to as "the Imam" Khomeini—a usage he did not discourage.

STEPS ON THE IRANIAN CLERICS' CAREER PATH

1. **Talib ilm:** When a young man in Iran decides on a career in the Shi'ite clergy, he may go to seminary in the great seminary town of Qom. There he becomes a *talib ilm*, a student of sacred knowledge, at the very bottom of the Shi'ite clerical pecking order. (If he gets discouraged or overwhelmed with his studies, however, a *talib ilm* can always find relief in a temporary marriage.)[89]

2. **Mojtahed:** A seminary graduate is a *mojtahed*: a jurist, officially authorized to teach and interpret Islamic sacred law. A young *mojtahed* may now become a mullah, the head of a local mosque. (Although any Muslim cleric can be referred to as a mullah, in Iran and its environs the term is often used for the local cleric, equivalent to a parish priest.)

3. **Mubellegh al risala:** A mojtahed who gains respect for his religious rulings and begins to amass a following will likely come to be known as a *mubellegh al risala*, "carrier of the message."

4. **Hojjat al-Islam:** Shi'ite clerics who rise higher in the ranks may earn the designation *hojjat al-Islam*, "authority on Islam." Shah Mohammed Reza Pahlavi subtly insulted the Ayatollah Khomeini when he addressed him in 1963 as "hojjat al-Islam," a notch below ayatollah—rather like addressing Pope Francis as "Bishop Bergoglio."

5. **Ayatollah:** The title *ayatollah* means "sign of Allah," and is an even more exalted designation than it appears to be at first glance, in light of the fact that Muslims refer to the verses of the Qur'an as *ayat*, or "signs"—that is, signs of the presence and power of Allah. In effect, then, the title ayatollah equates these exalted clerics, of whom there are very few in the world, with the very verses of the divine and perfect book.

6. **Grand Ayatollah:** To be a "great sign of Allah" is to have attained the highest possible rank among Iranian clerics. There are usually only five or six Grand Ayatollahs worldwide, but in keeping with the Shi'ite taste for concealment, their exact number is difficult to ascertain.

For Shi'ites, this was an astonishing audacity, and a testimony to the immense respect that Khomeini enjoyed among Iranians. Calling him the Imam was tantamount to equating him with the exalted and infallible leaders of Shi'ite Islam, and even hinting that he could himself be the long-awaited Twelfth Imam. This extraordinary exaltation is completely understandable: Khomeini, after all, presided over and in large part brought about one of the very few periods of victory that the Shi'ites had ever enjoyed in the long centuries since Hussain, Qur'an in hand, was cut down by the pitiless forces of Yazid nearly thirteen hundred years earlier.

Not good enough for Rita Hayworth

Twelver Shi'ism is the official religion of the Islamic Republic, but in Iran there are also a few thousand Ismaili Shi'ites. (There are many more around the world.) The Ismailis teach the seventh Imam was not Musa ibn Jafar al-Kazim, but his older brother Ismail ibn Jafar (hence the name Ismailis). The sixth Imam, Jafar al-Sadiq, had actually designated Ismail as his successor, but Ismail died before Jafar; the Ismailis believed that the Imamate then devolved not to Musa, but to Ismail's son Muhammad ibn Ismail. They argue that since the Imams are infallible, Jafar's designation of Ismail as his successor was not nullified by Ismail's death, and that the line was meant to continue through his descendants.

One Shi'ite sect, the Seveners, believed that Muhammad ibn Ismail went into "occultation," much as Twelvers believe of the Twelfth Imam, and that the line ends there. That group, however, has died out, whereas another group of Ismailis, known as the Nizaris, believe that there has been no Occultation at all and that the Imamate continues to this day. (The name "Nizaris" comes from yet another dynastic dispute farther down the line.)

Ismaili Shi'ism gained international attention in 1949, when Aly Khan, the son of the Aga Khan III, the forty-eighth Imam of the Nizari Ismailis, married movie star Rita Hayworth. (Aly Khan, a renowned international playboy, was born in Italy but claimed royal lineage from the Iranian Shah Fath Ali Qajar, who died in 1834, and thus he was often referred to in the tabloids as Prince Aly Khan.)

THE AYATOLLAH'S SPIT LIST

"Authentic Islam and the proper reading of the Koran are opposed to every form of violence."

—Pope Francis[91]

"Islam is a religion that prevents men from waging war? I spit upon those foolish souls who make such a claim."

—the Ayatollah Khomeini[92]

The marriage was rocky, and Hayworth filed for divorce in 1951. Aly Khan offered Hayworth a million dollars to raise their daughter, Yasmin Khan, as a Muslim, but Hayworth refused.[90]

Chapter Eight

"IN IRAN, NOTHING IS WHAT IT SEEMS"
LIFE INSIDE THE ISLAMIC REPUBLIC

I n March 2015, Thomas Erdbrink, the Tehran bureau chief for the *New York Times*, who had lived in Iran for twelve years, called it a "mysterious and isolated country."

As one might expect of life inside a theocratic dictatorship, he said that attending sermons at Friday prayers in Tehran was a good way to obtain clues about the mindset of Iran's leadership: "Working here is like walking a tightrope, but a reporter can do much more than one might expect. There is no problem for me and a colleague to visit the Friday prayer session. If you want to know what's going on in the minds of the religious leaders, you should come here and listen carefully."[1]

"In Iran, nothing is what it seems"

Even that, however, was no sure indicator as to the direction that Iranian policymakers might be taking. In the land of taqiyya, where a religious

Did you know?

- The most popular yearly celebration in Iran is the Zoroastrian spring festival
- Though alcohol is illegal, the Islamic Republic recently announced plans for 150 alcohol treatment centers
- Iran executed 1,084 people in 2015, more than any other country
- Since the Islamic Revolution, 90 percent of Iran's Jews have left the country

autocracy had supplanted a secular one to the enthusiastic approval and then increasing disillusionment of the Iranian people, Erdbrink cautioned, "In Iran, nothing is what it seems."[2]

One notable aspect of nothing's being what it seems to be in Iran is the persistence of non-Muslim practices in the Islamic Republic. The mullahs have been in power since 1979, but most Iranians are keenly aware that Iran has a rich history that stretches back long before Khomeini took power, and also long before Persia was conquered by Islam.

Journalist Ramita Navai has observed:

> Despite the revolution, Iranians are inordinately proud of the great Persian empire, and it's still part of the culture. The biggest festival in Iran is Persenia, which is Zoroastrian. It's the first day of spring and has nothing to do with religion. Although it's interesting, because the state has got involved with these pagan, Zoroastrian traditions and has tried to hijack them and claim them for their own. Like the early Christians did with pagan, Celtic mythology.
>
> So, for example, at Persian New Year, you set a table called haftsin. People lay out seven objects all starting with the letter sīn.... Most secular Iranians will also put out a book of Hafiz's poetry. But the state encourages Iranians to put the Koran on the table.
>
> There is also chaharshanbeh souri, a fire festival celebrated on the last Tuesday night of the year. Bonfires are lit in the hope that fire and light will bring health and happiness. Young Iranians go crazy, setting off fireworks and jumping over the fires while reciting an old Zoroastrian saying. It's a bit like Guy Fawkes night, in England. The state always gets nervous about

this fire festival. But try as they might, they haven't been able to stamp it out. It's an ancient Zoroastrian tradition.[3]

"It is astonishing that the West cultivates an ever-closer alliance with a theocratic regime widely known for its abysmal human rights record"

In light of many Iranians' openness to un-Islamic activity, the Islamic Republic has been in varying degrees a brutal authoritarian regime since its inception. Iran may be, as Erdbrink said, a "mysterious and isolated country," but it is not so mysterious that the repressive character of the Islamic Republic is in any way unclear.

Even a true believer has said as much: in 2002, Dawud Salahuddin, the American convert to Islam who murdered Iranian dissident Ali Akbar Tabatabai in Washington in 1980 for the Islamic Republic and has lived in Iran ever since, expressed his disenchantment to American journalist Ira Silverman: "The Iranians of my immediate association turned out to be far from paragons of virtue. The corruption here among the highest levels of the mullahs is incredible—it includes financial malfeasance, gross human-rights violations, extrajudicial murder, and two systems of justice, one for the mullahs, and one for citizens." When making plans to meet Silverman, he wrote in an e-mail, "If you don't see me at the airport, it means I am either dead or under arrest."[4]

Salahuddin survived, however, and worked for several years at Press TV, a media organ of the Islamic Republic. Yet he continued to express discontent. In 2009, when asked about whether Press TV was dedicated to genuine journalism rather than propaganda, Salahuddin replied, "No, I don't think Press TV is about [real journalism]. By its nature, state journalism is not journalism. They have some programs on there that might be, but generally it's not."[5]

The Islamic Republic is an extraordinarily oppressive regime. The savage punishment of death by stoning remains alive and well in the Islamic Republic. The case of one woman, Sakineh Mohammadi Ashtiani, gained international attention after she was sentenced in 2006 to be stoned to death for adultery and conspiracy to murder her husband. After a great deal of media pressure on the Islamic Republic, she was ultimately pardoned and freed in 2014.[6]

But the Iranians continue to sentence others to be stoned to death: in December 2015, a woman identified only by her initials, "A. Kh.," was sentenced to be stoned for aiding in the murder of her husband.[8] In November 2008, the Iranian Supreme Court upheld the sentence of death by stoning for a woman identified as Afsaneh R., who had been convicted of adultery. Afsaneh R. also received a second death sentence for murdering her husband with the help of her lover, but the stoning sentence was specifically

WHAT A DEAL!

"Whether or not one supports the nuclear deal with Iran, it is astonishing that the West cultivates an ever-closer alliance with a theocratic regime widely known for its abysmal human rights record and aggressive behavior in the region. They hang men for the 'crime' of writing poems; or engaging in peaceful protest; or loving someone of the same sex. Women are stoned for being raped and Iranian law even allows for juvenile executions. Iran is averaging three hangings per day at the moment and remains a pariah state with no regard for human life. In a despicable form of moral myopia, the gold rush for business, as the international sanctions regime begins to unravel, has made Western governments blind to the suffering of ordinary Iranians at the hands of the Ayatollahs."

—Julie Lenarz of Britain's Human Security Center in December 2015[7]

confirmed for the adultery offense alone. Her lover, meanwhile, was sentenced to one hundred lashes for the adultery and fifteen years in prison for the murder.[9]

Maryam Nayeb Yazdi, a Canadian-Iranian human rights activist, noted, "The rate of executions in Iran has not decreased in the last few years, it has increased. Although stoning has become more rare in Iran, such sentences are still being issued by Iranian judges. The probability of a stoning sentence to be carried out is slim due to the international sensitivity of the issue, there is a great chance her sentence may be 'converted' to death by hanging."[10]

Mohammad-Javad Larijani, chief of the Islamic Republic's Human Rights Council, had no patience with those who charged that stoning people to death was barbaric. In April 2014 he said, "We are not ashamed of stoning or any of the Islamic decrees. No one has the right to tell a judge to avert some sentences because the United Nations gets upset. We should firmly and seriously defend the sentence of stoning."[11] To those who charged that such punishments violated the human rights of the victim, Larijani said, "Retaliation and punishment are beautiful and necessary things. It's a form of protection for the individual and civil rights of the people in a society. The executioner or the person administering the sentence is in fact very much a defender of human rights. One can say that there is humanity in the act of retaliation."[12]

Given such attitudes, it is not surprising that other similarly draconian punishments are also common in Iran. According to an Iranian dissident group, the National Council of Resistance of Iran (NCRI), in August 2015 an Iranian court sentenced a twenty-seven-year-old man, identified only by his first name, Hamed, to have his eyes gouged out. This sentence came after Hamed admitted that in March 2011, he injured the eye of another man in an altercation over a car crash. "It was around midnight," he recounted, "and I was sitting at home when my mother called me and said that my father had gotten into a car accident. I rushed to the scene to help my dad, but I really didn't intend to injure anyone's eye."[13]

But he did, and so he was liable to be blinded, as the Qur'an itself commanded: "And We ordained for them therein a life for a life, an eye for an eye, a nose for a nose, an ear for an ear, a tooth for a tooth, and for wounds is legal retribution" (5:45). While that Qur'anic verse echoes the Old Testament, it is worth noting that no government in the world today blinds people on the basis of faith in the Bible.

The Iranians carried out another punishment from the Qur'an that same month, when they amputated the right hand and left foot of a prisoner identified by the suitably Kafkaesque moniker of Rahman K.[14] The unfortunate K. had apparently been found guilty of "spreading corruption on earth," the grab-bag offense for which double amputation is offered as one penalty in the Qur'an: "Indeed, the penalty for those who wage war against Allah and His Messenger and spread upon earth corruption is none but that they be killed or crucified or that their hands and feet be cut off from opposite sides..." (5:33).

"There isn't a corner of Tehran where you don't find booze"

The strict enforcement of Islamic orthodoxy in Iran has led to a culture of hypocrisy. Nothing is what it seems to be in Iran because the Islamic Republic was imposed upon a people who had lived under secular law for decades, during which time many Iranians developed a taste for numerous freedoms that were not available to them under the strictures of Shi'ite Islam.

As in all authoritarian and totalitarian regimes, rather than become virtuous, many Iranians instead outwardly conformed to the mullahs' rules but then retreated into areas where they thought it safe to indulge in vices that could get them jail terms or worse if discovered. In indulging in some now-illegal activities, they were recalling an earlier, freer Persia.

Islam brought an enforced sobriety to two peoples that had been known for their love of wine: the Arabs and the Persians. The Iranian city of Shiraz gave the world the variety of grape that has lent its name to a beloved wine. And despite centuries of Islam and decades of the Islamic Republic, Iranians still have a healthy appreciation for the grape.

Long after Islam had overwhelmed the region, the twelfth-century Persian poet Mujir Baylaqani expressed some ambivalence about what had become the faith of almost all of his countrymen: "In one hand the Qur'an, in the other a wineglass, / sometimes keeping the rules, sometimes breaking them. / Here we are in this world, unripe and raw, / not outright heathens, not quite Muslims."[15]

Probably the most quoted poetic reference to wine in English is from Edward Fitzgerald's translation of the Persian poetry of Omar Khayyam, who wrote around the same time: "A Book of Verses underneath the Bough, / A Jug of Wine, a Loaf of Bread—and Thou."

IN VINO VERITAS

"To wine-drinking they are very much given.... and they are wont to deliberate when drinking hard about the most important of their affairs, and whatsoever conclusion has pleased them in their deliberation, this on the next day, when they are sober, the master of the house in which they happen to be when they deliberate lays before them for discussion: and if it pleases them when they are sober also, they adopt it, but if it does not please them, they let it go: and that on which they have had the first deliberation when they are sober, they consider again when they are drinking."

—Herodotus, describing the Persians of fifth century BC in terms that would confirm the worst fears of any true believer in the Islamic Republic

Two centuries later, another Persian poet, Hafez (Khwāja Samsu d-Dīn Muhammad Hāfez-e Sīrāzī), wrote, "What drunkenness is this that brings me hope? Who was the cup-bearer and whence the wine?"[16]

But the teetotalers eventually won out, or appeared to, courtesy of the Ayatollah Khomeini. Alcoholic drinks have been banned in Iran since 1979, with manufacture, possession, and drinking of alcohol classified as crimes against Allah. Offenders face lashes and recidivists are threatened with the death penalty; nonetheless, the underground Iranian party scene has thrived to such an extent that in June 2015 the Iranian Health Ministry revealed plans to open no fewer than 150 outpatient alcohol treatment centers.[17]

Ramita Navai, who was born in Iran, observed, "Many people in Iran drink. There isn't a corner of Tehran where you don't find booze. Yet of course you have to lie about it, otherwise you'll get in trouble. So you need to lie, either to circumvent the laws or to avoid being judged by society."[18]

"The regime has created an atmosphere of absolute terror"

Another recurring feature of authoritarian regimes is that periods of relaxation of the laws alternate with repressive re-imposition of strict enforcement. The Islamic Republic began a new wave of strict enforcement of Shi'ite morality in 2007, with a hundred and fifty thousand people detained in the spring alone for wearing un-Islamic clothing. Students at Amir Kabir University in Tehran were arrested for disputing the Shi'ite principle of *isma*, infallibility, even as applied to Muhammad, the prophet of Islam, and the Ayatollah Khamenei. Abbas Milani, director of the Iranian studies program at Stanford University, remarked at the time, "People don't want to come to conferences, they don't even want to talk on the phone. The regime has created an atmosphere of absolute terror."[19]

That terror extended to matters that everyone except Islamic morality police would consider utterly trivial. In April 2007, the Islamic regime banned Western hairstyles. Police issued a statement saying, "In an official order to barbershops, they have been warned to avoid using Western hair styles and doing men's eyebrows."[20] Mohammad Eftekharifard, leader of the Iranian barbers' union, said police had commanded the union to "exercise specific regulations in barbershops that work under its supervision," to make sure they didn't offer Western-style haircuts. "Currently," Eftekharifard explained, "some barbershops apply make-up and use (hair) styles that are in line with those in European countries and America." But now, "an official order has been sent to the union...not to apply make-up on men's faces (or) do eyebrows...and hence the barbers are not allowed to do these things."[21]

That August, morality police in Tehran shut down twenty-four barber shops and hairdressing salons for offering Western styles. One woman's salon was closed for employing a man, flouting the Islamic Republic's laws about the public separation of the sexes. Men whose hairstyles were deemed un-Islamic were forced not only to get new haircuts, but to turn in their barbers.[22]

Then in June 2008, Iranian police closed thirty-two clothing stores and hairdressers for purveying un-Islamic styles and goods. According to the Associated Press, "during the crackdown, police stop women in the streets, issuing them warnings or even arresting them if their garb is deemed unsuitable. Men are also targeted for having long hair and other styles deemed too Western. But the shutting of shops appeared to be a new step, aimed at stopping the selling of shorter coats and lighter headscarves. The pro-reform daily *Kargozaran* reported Monday that police were questioning women and men [about] where they bought their clothes or had their hair done, then targeting the shops."[23]

The mullahs were happy to clear up any confusion over what was allowed and what wasn't. In June 2010, Iran's culture ministry released a catalogue of acceptable Islamic haircuts, "in order to avoid inappropriate hairstyles and encourage an Islamic culture."[24] Jaleh Khodayar, organizer of the "Modesty and Veil Festival," explained, "These hairstyles are inspired by the Iranians' complexion, culture and religion, and Islamic law."[25]

The Islamic regime resorted to repression on unpredictable occasions. In the spring of 2014, young people around the world began posting videos of themselves on YouTube, dancing to the American pop singer Pharrell Williams's hit song "Happy." But when six young Iranians, including three unveiled women, posted their version, they were swiftly arrested.

Tehran police chief Hossein Sajedinia explained, "After a vulgar clip which hurt public chastity was released in cyberspace, police decided to identify those involved in making that clip." There was nothing actually against "public chastity" about the clip, which just featured people dancing. "Following a series of intelligence and police operations and after

THE FASHION POLICE

A man could get in trouble not just for having the wrong haircut, but for wearing a necktie. One of the earliest decrees of the Islamic Republic banned ties: they were a manifestation of *gharbzadegi*, toxic Western influence. But some Iranian dandies persisted in wearing them, so that in May 2008, Iranian Customs Deputy Director Asgar Hamidi, who was also chief of the government program for the "development of culture, modesty, and headdress," felt he had to point out that ties "contradict the nature of Iranian culture."[26] He proclaimed, "We must adopt serious actions in order to put an end to the importation of ties. We must change import laws to that end." Like deranged Shi'ite comedians, members of the Islamic Revolutionary Guard Corps patrolled the streets carrying scissors, ready to cut off any necktie they saw.[27]

coordinating with the judiciary," Sajedinia continued, "all the suspects were identified and arrested."[28] The offenders, according to Iran's ISNA news agency, "confessed to their criminal acts."[29] They were swiftly released, but the incident doubtless remains in their police files and will form part of the case against them should they run afoul of the guardians of morality again.

The Islamic Republic usually makes use of sticks to enforce Islamic morality upon Iranian citizens, but occasionally resorts to carrots—and sometimes uses both at the same time. In 2012, at the International Book Fair in Tehran, the organizers of the event presented flowers to every woman entering the Fair who was dressed in the proper Islamic manner, including a hijab. Those not deemed to be dressed appropriately were beaten and prevented from entering.

The director of the Book Fair, Bahman Dari, was furious at the brutality and issued a statement declaring, "We shall not tolerate the physical harassment of women on our territory, and will deal with those responsible."[30] But what he could do about it, when the perpetrators were the religious police, he did not say.

"Do your best to ensure that your daughters do not see their first blood in your house"

The Civil Code of the Islamic Republic of Iran stipulates that "marriage before the age of majority is prohibited."[31] However, it also states: "the age of majority for boys is fifteen lunar years and for girls nine lunar years," and that "marriage before puberty by the permission of the Guardian and on condition of taking into consideration the ward's interest is proper."[32]

The Ayatollah Khomeini himself married a ten-year-old girl; he was twenty-eight at the time.[33] She became pregnant at age eleven, although that pregnancy ended with a miscarriage. Khomeini called marriage to a girl before her first menstrual period "a divine blessing," and advised the faithful:

NOT THAT THIS HAS ANYTHING TO DO WITH ISLAM

. . . .

The Islamic Republic has set the "age of majority" for purposes of marriage at nine years old for girls because Muhammad, the prophet of Islam and supreme model that Muslims must emulate, consummated his marriage with his wife Aisha when she was nine (and he was fifty-four).

"Do your best to ensure that your daughters do not see their first blood in your house."[34]

In February 2016, the United Nations Committee on the Rights of the Child (CRC) stated that it was "seriously concerned" that child marriage was becoming more common in Iran, and that an increasing number of "girls at the age of 10 years or younger…are subjected to child and forced marriages to much older men."[35] It called upon Iran to "repeal all legal provisions that authorise, condone or lead to child sexual abuse."[36]

The UN committee also decried an Iranian law mandating that wives must "fulfill sexual needs of their husbands at all times."[37] This, too, like all Iranian laws, was derived from Islamic sharia law: Muhammad is said to have warned wives that if they refused their husbands sex under any circumstances, the angels would curse them.

"The Imams have said that whoever makes love legitimately has in effect killed an infidel"

Sometimes the Islamic Republic's hypocrisy is wrapped in legality and even Shi'ite piety. In Iran today, sex outside of marriage can end in arrest, or a large fine.[38] There is, however, the Shi'ite Muslim practice of temporary marriage, *siqeh* or *mutah*, which is simply a marriage contract with an expiration date; a fig leaf of morality placed over what is in reality simply prostitution.

The mullahs justify temporary marriage by their reading of Qur'an 4:24, which begins by stipulating that Muslim men may not have sexual relations with married women except "those your right hands possess"—that is, slave girls. The Qur'an follows this with a passage that allows men to have sexual relations provided that they "seek them with your property"—that is, compensate the women for their labors. "And lawful to you are beyond these, that you seek them with your property, desiring chastity, not unlawful sexual intercourse. So for whatever you enjoy from them, give them their due compensation as an obligation. And there is no blame upon you for what you mutually agree to beyond the obligation. Indeed, Allah is ever knowing and wise."

Shi'ite divines read this passage as authorizing marriages contracted by means of payment ("give them their due compensation as an obligation") for a specified and limited time ("the obligation").

In Iran and Shi'ite southern Iraq, "temporary wives" are commonly found in seminary towns where young men are on their own for the first time. They're also popular among men who aren't wealthy enough to pay the dowry that would allow them to enter into a permanent marriage.

Temporary marriage has the full and enthusiastic backing of the Islamic Republic. In June 2007, Interior Minister Mostafa Pourmohammadi said on state-controlled Iranian television, "Temporary marriage is God's rule. We must aggressively encourage that.... We have to find a solution to meet the sexual desire of the youth who have no possibility of marriage." One young Iranian cab driver expressed his delight with the institution: "I have no money to set up a matrimonial life. I don't want prostitutes. What should I do with my sexual needs?"[39]

Early in the twentieth century, the Shi'ite student Aqa Najafi Quchani rejoiced in the sexual release that temporary marriage provided, comparing a session with a temporary wife to the delights of waging jihad against infidels: "Fortunately, the woman was at home and I married her for a while.

RESISTANCE IS FUTILE

• • •

"The only way to get rid of temptation is to yield to it."

—Oscar Wilde, inadvertently describing the Shi'ite practice of temporary marriage

When I had quietened [sic] my desire and enjoyed the pleasure of the flesh from my lawful income, I gave the woman the *qeran* [an old Iranian monetary unit].... It is reported that the Imams have said that whoever makes love legitimately has in effect killed an infidel. That means killing the lascivious spirit. It is obvious that when a *talabeh* [student] has no problem with the lower half of his body he is happier than a king."[40] Aqa Najafi Quchani had engaged in "killing the lascivious spirit" not by resisting it but by giving in to it.

And note that, searching for a comparison for how positively beneficial it is for him to have "made love legitimately" rather than indulged in fornication, he refers to the highest authorities in Shi'ite Islam, the Imams, and their assertion that "whoever makes love legitimately has in effect killed an infidel."

That comparison was not eccentric, in Iran. A century later, one Muslim cleric noted that it came from the central figures of Shi'ite Islam, the twelve imams. In 2012, Iranian cleric Hossein Dehnavi produced a DVD, "The Art of Making Love," which became a hot seller in Tehran. It was simply a video of a speech he had given to a group of newlyweds, entitled, "Improving the Skill of Making Love: The Peace and Pleasure in Matrimonial Life."[41]

"According to our religion," said Dehnavi, "eshqbazi [lovemaking] is a form of worship." He echoed Aqa Najafi Quchani's comparison of sex to jihad warfare: "We have quotes from the 12 Imams saying that having sex with your wife is just like jihad, fighting for the sake of Allah." Dehnavi meant this as a positive thing, adding, "Unfortunately, some people believe sexual relationships are ugly. No, it is not an ugly behavior in Islam, it is a divine behavior and it is even a religious obligation to properly make love."[42]

It is not, however, divine behavior or a religious obligation to recognize the rights of Iran's temporary wives. In March 2012 the Majlis considered a bill that would have required men to register temporary marriages, which under the present system are as ephemeral as snowflakes. Registration would have allowed the women and children involved in temporary marriages to claim some legal rights—but the measure was voted down.[43]

"There is no oppression. But there are limitations."

As the Persian Empire was home to people of many creeds and cultures, so, too, is the Islamic Republic—but in the latter, the hegemony of Islam and Islamic culture is diligently guarded.

The Qur'an commands Muslims to fight "the People of the Book"—that is, Jews, Christians, and Zoroastrians—until they "pay the jizya with willing submission and feel themselves subdued" (9:29). If they do so, they are guaranteed protection (*dhimma*) under Islamic law: they can live as non-Muslims as long as they submit to Islamic hegemony. This is a precarious existence, as the "protected people" (dhimmis) have always been subject to the whims of their Muslim masters. In Shi'ite Persia, according to historian Laurence D. Loeb, "from the beginning of the seventeenth century, through 1925, Jewish survival was in constant danger, as Iranian hostility toward them increased.... The proclamation of Shi'a Islam as the state religion has greatly contributed to the suffering of Iranian Jewry. The Shi'a clergy has frequently led hostile action against Jews."[44] Persian Jews were frequently subjected to forced conversion to Islam, pogroms, beatings, expulsion, restrictions on travel, and more.

Hitler did not invent the concept of an identifying badge for Jews; Jews were first made to wear such a badge in the ninth century by the Sunni Abbasid caliph al-Mutawakkil; later in Persia, the Shah Abbas I (1571–1629) mandated it as well. "The badge of shame," according to Loeb, "was an identifying symbol which marked someone as a *najas* [unclean] Jew and thus to be avoided. From the reign of Abbas I until the 1920s, all Jews were required to display a badge."[46]

It was Reza Shah who ended the requirement that Jews wear this identifying badge; during his reign and that of his son, as Iran secularized, life for Jews in Iran improved considerably, although this improvement was not universal: in some areas of Iran Jews were made to wear distinctive yellow patches on their clothing as late as 1950.[47]

With the advent of the Islamic Republic, Jews in Iran saw the writing on the wall, particularly when Habib Elghanian, a prominent Jewish leader, was executed for "contacts with Israel and Zionism."[48] With the Shi'ite clergy, which had a long history of persecuting Jews, now running the country, Jews began to stream out of Iran. The Jewish community in the Islamic Republic of Iran, down from between eighty and a hundred thousand in 1979 to only around ten thousand today, lives relatively unmolested

A HARD RAIN'S A-GONNA FALL

The idea that Jews were unclean led to a prohibition on their venturing out while it was raining, lest rainwater might splash off a Jew and hit a Muslim, thereby rendering him unclean. One Iranian Jew recounted, "When I was a boy, I went with my father to the house of a non-Jew on business. When we were on our way home it started to rain. We stopped near a man who had apparently fallen and was bleeding. As we started to help him up, a Muslim *akhond* (theologian) stopped and asked me who I was and what I was doing. Upon discovering that I was a Jew, he reached for a stick to hit me for defiling him by being near him in the rain. My father ran to him and begged the *akhond* to hit him instead. The surprised *akhond* did not hit anyone and we were permitted to continue homeward."[45]

by Iranian authorities, as long as they know their place and tolerate the periodic chants of "Death to Israel."

The Jews who still remain in Iran take the long view. Iranian Jewish leader Ciamak Morsadegh maintains, "We are not tenants in this country. We are Iranians, and we have been for 30 centuries."[49] Haroon Saketi, a Jewish merchant in Isfahan, declares, "There is a distinction between us as Jews and Israel. We consider ourselves Iranian Jews, and it has nothing to do with Israel whatsoever. This is the country we love."[50]

Dr. Siamak Moreh Sedgh, the Jewish member of the Majlis (recognized religious minorities get seats in the Iranian Parliament, even in the Islamic Republic), has said that "compared to Europe, synagogues here are one of the safest places."[51] According to Sedgh, "Iran is the country of unbelievable paradoxes. You can find that there is the greatest Jewish community in the Middle East in Iran, in the country with the greatest political problem with Israel."[52] The head of the Tehran Jewish Committee, Homayoun Sameyah Najafabadi, has noted that this safety comes at the price of numerous forms of discrimination: "There is no oppression. But there are limitations."[53]

These limitations come in many forms. Jews are barred from certain government positions. Explains Moreh Sedgh, "It's not a problem that affects our day-to-day life, but we think that people with good knowledge and a high degree of ability, from a religious minority, can help the country to be a better country."[54]

Jewish schools must have Muslim principals. Says Najafabadi, "We have five schools, and the principals in all of them are Muslim. There's no enmity. They're very cooperative. But it's kind of insulting."[55] Inheritance laws favor converts to Islam over relatives who do not convert. Other laws reflect the Islamic view that non-Muslim lives simply aren't worth as much as Muslim lives: Maurice Motamed, who has previously served as the Iranian Parliament's Jewish representative, points out that "under Sharia...if a Muslim kills a Jew, there will be blood money payment. But if a Jew kills a Muslim, the penalty is execution."[56]

Tehran Jewish restaurateur David Shumer is not exercised about these issues: "I have a car, and a job. Everything I have is here. Why not?" He keeps photos of Khomeini and Khamenei on the wall of his restaurant.[57]

"The deviant Baha'i sect"

While the Iranian leadership reserve their sharpest rhetorical barbs for Israel, they are far harsher to a group of "heretics" in Iran than they are to Iran's Jews. Ahmed Shaheed, the United Nations special rapporteur on Iran, wrote in 2013 about "the difficult situation of recognized and unrecognized religious minorities," saying that non-Muslim communities "continue to report arrests and prosecution for worship and participation in religious community affairs."[59]

The Bahais bear the brunt of this persecution. A senior Iranian cleric, Ayatollah Bojnourdi, has declared, "Only Baha'is 'who cooperate with Israel' or 'advocate against Islam' are not entitled to citizenship rights, and...they still have human rights even though they cannot take advantage of 'privileges,' such as going to university in Iran."[60]

The Bahai faith in Iran is a phenomenon going back over 150 years. On May 22, 1844, a twenty-four-year-old Persian merchant named Siyyid Ali Muhammad Shirazi declared that he was the Mahdi, the long-awaited Twelfth Imam finally returned. He called himself The Bab, ("The Gate"), and quickly amassed a significant following—significant enough to unnerve the Shi'ite clergy to the degree that he was tried and executed in 1850. Before he was killed, however, he promised that there would soon come another messenger from Allah; several years later, another Persian, Mirza Husayn Ali Nuri, declared that he was that man and was hailed as Bahaullah, the glory of Allah.

Today Bahaullah's followers, who are known as Bahais, number about three hundred thousand in the Islamic Republic of Iran, where they are generally subjected to harsh treatment: the Shi'ite hierarchy regards them as heretics, as they appear to transgress against the Qur'an's declaration that Muhammad is the "seal of the prophets" (33:40), which both Sunnis and Shi'ites generally take to mean that there will be no prophets or messengers from Allah after Muhammad.

The Islamic Republic recognizes the People of the Book—Jews, Christians, and Zoroastrians—as legitimate religious minorities, but not Bahais. When Khomeini first took power, he had numerous Bahais imprisoned and even killed. Like Jews in Nazi Germany, they were expelled from universities, and the Shi'ite government seized billions of dollars in property and businesses owned by Bahais. A lawyer who had defended some Bahais commented, "The government has set up a system where Baha'is are not allowed to build up financial strength."[61]

The situation for Bahais did not improve over the years. In July 2013, Khamenei commanded Iranians to avoid dealing with Bahais.[62] An October 2015 United Nations report on the human rights situation in the Islamic Republic noted that "at least 74 members of the Baha'i community were detained" and that some had been prosecuted "for their association with the Baha'i Institute for Higher Education (BIHE)." Seventeen Bahais were imprisoned for the crime of "membership of the deviant Baha'i sect with the goal of taking actions against the security of the country" and "collaboration with the BIHE."

Meanwhile, "the authorities allegedly continue to summon, interrogate and arrest Baha'is, and close down businesses belonging to adherents of that faith." There were also reports of "the destruction of the cultural sites and of the property of Baha'i community members. This apparently includes the demolition on 22 April of a home owned by imprisoned Baha'i community leader, Jamaloddin Khanjani. Officials reportedly made repeated allegations regarding the property's deed and construction since Mr. Khanjani's arrest, threatening the family with demolition of their ancestral home and restrictions on their agricultural lands."[63]

Heiner Bielefeldt, the UN Special Rapporteur on freedom of religion or belief, said that the Iranian government's treatment of Bahais was "really one of the most obvious cases of state persecution. It's basically state persecution, systematic and covering all areas of state activities, the various systems from family law provisions to schooling, education, security."[64]

Adherents of Persia's oldest religion arguably fare even worse.

"Sinful animals who roam the earth and engage in corruption"

In Iran today there are between thirty-five thousand and ninety thousand members of Persia's ancestral religion, Zoroastrianism. Exact figures are hard to come by, as many Zoroastrians conceal their religion for fear of running afoul of the mullahs. The Islamic Republic has been particularly tough on the Zoroastrians: when it came to power, a Shi'ite mob stormed the Zoroastrian fire temple in Tehran and tore down a portrait of the prophet Zoroaster, replacing it with one of Khomeini and warning the Zoroastrians who were present that the Imam's picture had to stay there, or else. Zoroastrian schools have likewise been filled with pictures of Khomeini and Khamenei, as well as with images of Qur'an verses denouncing unbelievers. Once Iranian Zoroastrians get through those schools, they're barred from attending universities.[65]

In November 2005, Ayatollah Ahmad Jannati of the Council of Guardians of the Constitution denounced Zoroastrians as "sinful animals who roam the earth and engage in corruption"; this language was ominous, as the Qur'an directs that those who spread corruption on the earth are to be crucified or their hands and feet amputated on opposite sides (5:33).[66] Kourash Niknam, the Zoroastrian member of the Majlis, said in 2006 that being a Zoroastrian in Iran was like being a foreigner in one's native land: "We don't have the right to make programmes about our religion. I have no platform on radio or television to go and speak about Zoroastrianism. We cannot get any budget for building a new fire temple when mosques are being built one after another."[67] Yet although many Zoroastrians have left Iran, one declared his determination to stay: "Why should we leave? This is our mother country. Iranian culture is wonderful. Western culture is stress, stress, stress."[68]

Despite the difficulties Zoroastrians face in the Islamic Republic, however, Zoroastrianism's status as the original religion of Iran makes it particularly attractive to young people who are disgusted with the Islamic regime. Some Iranians see the excesses and violence of the Islamic Republic as manifestations of Islam and take up Zoroastrianism as a sign of their rejection not only of the regime but of the premises upon which it is built. Exact numbers are impossible to find, as Shi'ite Muslims who convert to Zoroastrianism in the Islamic Republic are taking their lives in their hands. But it is happening: one Iranian Shi'ite cleric said in a sermon, "The biggest threat of all is when our young Shia Muslims convert to Zoroastrianism."[69]

"Christians are enemies who are a major threat to the state"

There are about three hundred fifty thousand Christians in Iran, and the presence of Christianity there dates back to the beginning of the Christian faith itself. But for the most part, throughout pre-Islamic Persian history Christianity has been seen as an alien faith, the religion of the Romans, who were the Persians' great rivals for hundreds of years. With the advent of

Islam, that antagonism only deepened, and since the Islamic Republic supplanted the secular and Western-oriented Shah in 1979, Christians have had a tougher time in Iran than they have for centuries.

When Mahmoud Ahmadinejad became president in 2005, he vowed, "I will stop Christianity in this country."[70] Shortly thereafter, a convert to Christianity named Ghorban Tori was kidnapped and murdered. Hours after his killers threw his body in front of his house, police arrived and searched the house for contraband Christian material. Raids on the homes of nearby Christians followed.[71]

When Hassan Rouhani was making his successful run for the presidency of Iran in 2013, there appeared to be a light at the end of the tunnel for Christians, as he declared: "All ethnicities, all religions, even religious minorities, must feel justice."[72] What he meant by justice, however, apparently was more in line with Sharia than with Western ideas.

The Christian organization Open Doors notes that Christian proselytizing is strictly forbidden in Iran, "especially when it occurs in Persian languages—from evangelism to Bible training, to publishing Scripture and Christian books or preaching in Farsi. In 2014, at least 75 Christians were arrested. More Christians were sentenced to prison and pressure on those detained increased, including physical and mental abuse."[73]

The UN's Ahmed Shaheed has noted, "As of 1 January 2015, at least 92 Christians remain in detention in the country allegedly due to their Christian faith and activities. In 2014 alone, 69 Christian converts were reportedly arrested and detained for at least 24 hours across Iran. Authorities reportedly continued to target the leaders of house churches, generally from Muslim backgrounds. Christian converts also allegedly continue to face restrictions in observing their religious holidays."[74]

Christian activist Marlene Mathew has stated that "the Iranian government actively pursues Christian ministers and believers, placing them in prison under trumped up political charges, or simply killing them in accordance with their law. These people are innocent and need to be set free.... In recent weeks the Iranian government has openly declared that 'Christians are enemies' who are a major threat to the state."[75] She adds, "Iran has one of the highest number of spies per capita in the world, believers are often in fear of speaking openly lest they awaken the wrath of the religious police."[76]

An Iranian-American pastor, Saeed Abedini, was arrested while working at an orphanage in Iran in 2012 and sentenced to eight years in prison, where guards and other prisoners have beaten him. His wife Naghmeh Abedini reported, "Saeed's life is continuously threatened not only because he is an American, but also because he is a convert from Islam to Christianity." Leaving Islam is a capital offense according to Islamic law, which puts Abedini in continuing danger. Said Naghmeh Abedini, "The times they have moved him in and out of solitary and the times they have threatened him, they said 'You will stay here longer than the eight years and your only key to freedom is if you deny your Christian faith and you return to Islam.' The guards have said that, officials have said that continuously."[77] On January 16, 2016, Abedini was released along with four other American prisoners that the Iranians had been holding; in return, Barack Obama pardoned (or stopped the prosecutions of) twenty-one Iranians who were accused of illegally helping Iran advance its nuclear program.[78]

Iranian officials also demanded that another imprisoned pastor who had converted from Islam to Christianity return to Islam in order to avoid the death penalty. Pastor Youcef Nadarkhani was arrested in 2009 for apostasy, a crime in the Islamic Republic. He was also accused of another crime: proselytizing for Christianity among Muslims. He was ultimately acquitted and released after arguing that he had never been a practicing Muslim, but he remains in danger. Pastor Firouz Sadegh-Khandjani, a Member of the Council of Elders for the Church of Iran, explained, "In Iran about 18 years ago, they had released a pastor, but then came and assassinated him and his bishop later. We cannot stop the pressure."[79]

Sometimes Christians can awaken the wrath of the government simply by being Christians. As Easter 2015 approached, according to the NCRI, "the Iranian regime's State Security Forces (police) sent threatening letters to churches in the city of Urumiyeh warning them against holding gatherings for Easter celebrations. According to the directive sent by the force's Office of Public Building, Christians have only been allowed to hold Easter celebrations in their homes."[80] In June 2015 an Iranian court sentenced eighteen converts from Islam to Christianity to prison on charges that included evangelism. Morad Mokhtari, a convert who left Iran in 2006, said of converts to Christianity that "Iranian religious authorities prefer that they leave Iran because the authorities can't control them. Just their name is evangelism. Imagine someone says he's a Christian and has a Muslim name."[81]

In some cases, even leaving Iran is not enough. In October 2011 a group calling itself the Unknown Soldiers of the Hidden Imam sent emails to eleven converts from Islam to Christianity who had left Iran, telling them that they were "not hidden from the acute eyes of the Unknown Soldiers" and must return to Islam; "otherwise, according to the Fatwa given by Mahdi the Hidden Imam," they must be killed.[82]

Some of the institutionalized mistreatment of non-Muslims in the Islamic Republic must be ascribed to the inequalities taught in Islamic law. A leading Shi'ite authority in Iran, Sheikh Sultanhussein Tabandeh, actually defended the idea that a non-Muslim's life was worth less than that of a Muslim in his 1970 critique of the United Nations' Universal Declaration of Human Rights, *A Muslim Commentary on the Universal Declaration of Human Rights*:

> Thus if [a] Muslim commits adultery his punishment is 100 lashes, the shaving of his head, and one year of banishment. But if the man is not a Muslim and commits adultery with a Muslim woman his penalty is execution.... Similarly if a Muslim deliberately

murders another Muslim he falls under the law of retaliation and must by law be put to death by the next of kin. But if a non-Muslim who dies at the hand of a Muslim has by lifelong habit been a non-Muslim, the penalty of death is not valid. Instead the Muslim mur-

NOT THAT THIS HAS ANYTHING TO DO WITH ISLAM

"The penalties of a non-Muslim guilty of fornication with a Muslim woman are augmented because, in addition to the crime against morality, social duty and religion, he has committed sacrilege, in that he has disgraced a Muslim and thereby cast scorn upon the Muslims in general, and so must be executed."
—prominent Iranian cleric Sheikh Sultanhussein Tabandeh[84]

derer must pay a fine and be punished with the lash.... Since Islam regards non-Muslims as on a lower level of belief and conviction, if a Muslim kills a non-Muslim...then his punishment must not be the retaliatory death, since the faith and conviction he possesses is loftier than that of the man slain.... Islam and its peoples must be above the infidels, and never permit non-Muslims to acquire lordship over them.[83]

"By beginning the new year with an execution spree, Iran is signaling that it will continue to defy the international community and basic standards of human rights"

The Islamic Republic was not much less perilous for ordinary Shi'ite Muslims. In 2015, the Iranian government executed 1,084 people—more than any other country in the world. That was up from 753 in 2014, which was itself a record. And the mullahs began 2016 by executing twenty-five

people during the first week of the year, including thirteen on January 6 alone.

Indeed, there have been several times in recent years when hopes among Western observers that the Islamic Republic was moderating were raised. President Hassan Rouhani was widely touted as a moderate, but this massive number of executions has taken place during his tenure. Iran has had moderate presidents before: Mohammad Khatami, the president of Iran from 1997 to 2005 and more credible as a reformist than Rouhani, won worldwide praise for trying to give the Islamic Republic a more human face. *New York Times* reporter Elaine Sciolino gushed that Khatami was a "larger-than-life figure" who "invited comparisons to Nelson Mandela, Vaclav Havel, and Bill Clinton," despite the fact that he echoed the Islamic Republic's familiar libel that Israel was a "racist Zionist regime."[86]

Whatever the sincerity or effectiveness of Khatami's reformist impulses, he was succeeded as president by Mahmoud Ahmadinejad, who was notorious for his Islamic rigidity and bellicosity toward Iran's perceived enemies, and then by the *faux*-moderate Rouhani. Khatami backed Rouhani's bid for the presidency, a fact that did a great deal to burnish the perception that Rouhani was a moderate. The new president, however, surprised friend and foe alike: by February 2015, the Iranian media had been prohibited even to mention Khatami's name.[87]

Khatami had run afoul of his colleagues by backing Mir Hossein Mousavi and Mehdi Karroubi, two Iranian politicians who had been under house arrest since 2011; Hassan Rouhani had promised to end the house arrest of dissidents but reneged.[88] Mousavi and Karroubi were the leaders of Iran's Green Movement, a call for reform in the Islamic Republic that began in mid-June 2009 with massive demonstrations following the reelection of hardliner Ahmadinejad. As many as a million people took to the streets to protest that the election—

THE AYATOLLAH'S SPIT LIST

"Perversion of Islam is the source of a lot of the problems in the Middle East."

—former British Prime Minister Tony Blair[89]

"Islam is a religion that prevents men from waging war? I spit upon those foolish souls who make such a claim."

—the Ayatollah Khomeini[90]

in which the incumbent Ahmadinejad won nearly 62 percent of the vote to Mousavi's 34 percent (and 1 percent for Karroubi)—had been fixed.

The demonstrations roused hopes among many in the West that the Islamic Republic would fall. It did not. But the Green Revolution nevertheless shook the Islamic Republic to its core, and its shockwaves are still reverberating today.

Chapter Nine

"I WILL NOT SUBMIT TO THIS DANGEROUS CHARADE"
IRAN'S GREEN REVOLUTION

O n June 20, 2009, as protests engulfed Tehran, a twenty-six-year-old woman named Neda Agha-Soltan got out of a car at a protest site and was almost immediately shot dead, most likely by the Basiji, the Islamic Republic's fearsome paramilitary militia.[1] Someone standing nearby captured her killing on cell phone video, and suddenly an aghast world saw the inhumanity of Iran's Islamic regime up close.[2]

In death Neda—young, beautiful, and so senselessly and brutally murdered—became the symbol of the Iranian people's resistance to the Islamic Republic. Outrage grew when Islamic Republic officials barred mosques from holding any memorial services for Neda and even threatened her family if anyone showed up at her burial to mourn her. Soona Samsami, executive director of the Women's Freedom Forum in Iran, said, "They were

Did you know?

- Iran's Council of Guardians ruled that the fact that there were more votes than voters in some districts wasn't an indication of election fraud
- Members of the Palestinian terror group Hamas helped enforce the violent crackdown on peaceful protesters in Iran
- Virgins in Iranian prisons are forcibly "married" to a guard before being executed

threatened that if people wanted to gather there the family would be charged and punished."[3]

The protests in Iran captured the imagination of the West's fashionably leftist glitterati. Joan Baez sang "We Shall Overcome" in English and Farsi and issued a statement:

> To the People of Iran:
>
> In you the world sees the power of nonviolence. We hear it in the roar of your silence and see it in your eyes as you sit down peacefully in the face of terror. We are moved by your courage and inspired by your sacrifices. I am fortunate to be alive to witness this movement. I send you my prayers, love, and support.[4]

Just as she had been in the heady days of the early 1960s, Baez was a trendsetter. Jon Bon Jovi recorded a version of "Stand By Me," also in English and Farsi, and U2 dedicated a performance of "Sunday, Bloody Sunday" to the Iranian protesters.[5] The *New York Times* enthused that "Iran has morphed in the global consciousness, to the point that U2 and Madonna have adopted the cause of Iranian democracy."[6]

Western observers on both the Left and the Right hailed the protests and held high hopes for them. Counterterror analyst Ryan Mauro summed up those hopes when he wrote, "The struggle of the Iranian people is a quintessential liberal cause. The Iranian people are nonviolently protesting their unjust suppression of every type of right a human deserves."[7]

Some even hoped that the protests would ultimately lead to the toppling of the Islamic Republic. Leftist journalist and political analyst Robert Fisk proclaimed that "the very existence of the Islamic regime may now be questioned openly in a nation ever more divided between reformists and those who insist on maintaining the integrity of the 1979 revolution."[8]

There was no doubt that the Green Revolution placed the Islamic Republic in a more precarious position than it had been since its inception. But even the name of the protest movement indicated that it was not precisely what its Western boosters so fervently believed it was or hoped it would become: a democracy movement that would bring an end to the Islamic Republic. It was called the Green Revolution simply because green was the chosen color of Iranian politician Mir Hossein Mousavi's presidential campaign: the demonstrations began not as protests against the legitimacy of the Islamic Republic itself, but only against the reelection of President Mahmoud Ahmadinejad over Mousavi in an election that Iranians widely believed was fraudulent. There is scant indication that the Green Revolution was ever anything more than a movement against the corruption of the Islamic Republic, rather than a challenge to its very existence.

"I will not submit to this dangerous charade"

The protests started eight days before Neda Agha-Soltan was murdered, on June 12, 2009, when the Islamic Republic held its tenth presidential election, with Ahmadinejad seeking a second term. Although no one can run for president of the Islamic Republic without the approval of the Supreme Leader, which severely limits the range of Iran's political spectrum, those who were hoping for reform threw their support to two candidates: Mousavi, who had served as prime minister of Iran until 1989, when the position was abolished, and Mehdi Karroubi, a Muslim cleric and veteran Iranian politician who had served as speaker of Iran's parliament.

Journalist Laura Secor, covering the election results at a gathering of Iranian expatriates in New York, noted that on election day the reformists' confidence was high: "From 3:30 P.M. until 4:15 P.M., the scene at the Hyatt was festive, despite the news earlier in the day that the reformist headquarters had been sacked and prominent reformists arrested."[9]

The reformists had good reason to be confident. According to Secor, "Government polls (one conducted by the Revolutionary Guards, the other by the state broadcasting company) that were leaked to the campaigns allegedly showed ten- to twenty-point leads for Mousavi a week before the election; earlier polls had them neck and neck, with Mousavi leading by one per cent, and Karroubi just behind."[11]

The announced results, however, refuted those polls more decisively than any polls had been refuted since Truman defeated Dewey. Officially, Ahmadinejad won in a landslide of FDR-esque proportions with nearly 63 percent of the vote, garnering over eleven million more votes than Mousavi. Karroubi, despite having run second to Mousavi in the polls, gained less than 1 percent of the vote. Mousavi didn't even carry his hometown.[12]

HIGH HOPES

. . .

"Everyone had a story about a relative who had never voted before, who was a royalist or an all-purpose skeptic, who was wearing green in the streets or simply casting a vote for Mousavi. There was only one way this could go. Turnout, we heard, was over eighty per cent."

—Laura Secor, reporting on the 2009 Iranian presidential election for the *New Yorker*[10]

Supreme Leader Khamenei was delighted: "The 12 June election was an artistic expression of the nation, which created a new advancement in the history of elections in the country. The over 80 percent participation of the people and the 24 million votes cast for the president-elect is a real celebration which with the power of almighty God can guarantee the development, progress, national security, and the joy and excitement of the nation."[13]

Iranians and others immediately began to question the results. One woman who supported Mousavi declared, "It's a fraud. I can't believe it. Last night we celebrated victory. And this morning Ahmadinejad was the winner."[14] Secor reported that "a trusted Iranian source based in Canada" told her that "3,400 Iranian expatriates voted in Ottawa. It took the volunteers there six hours to count those votes. Meanwhile, the Interior Ministry in Tehran claims to have counted five million votes before the polls closed in Tehran, and ten million half an hour later."[15] The official results would mean that "urban Iranians who voted for the reformist ex-president Mohammad Khatami in 1997 and 2001 have defected to Ahmadinejad in droves"—something that was extraordinarily unlikely, given the repression that characterized Ahmadinejad's first term.[16]

The historian of Iran Michael Axworthy reports that "a defector from the Basiji told a Channel 4 journalist later that they had received instructions through their chain of command that the supreme leader had decided that Ahmadinejad should win the election, and they should do all that was necessary to ensure he did. On the day, blank ballots and the ballots of illiterates and others were filled in for Ahmadinejad, irrespective of the actual wishes of voters; some ballot boxes were counted, but then all were sent back to 'the centre' with most still uncounted."[17]

Ominously, the Iranian Interior Ministry, which was counting the votes, issued a statement warning that those who approached the Interior Ministry building would be shot.[18] But there were other places to protest, and the protests began almost immediately. Riots engulfed Tehran on Saturday, June 13, the day after the election, and stretched into Sunday and beyond. Protesters from all walks of life burned tires and threw rocks at police, chanting "Down with dictatorship!" and "Give me my vote back!"[19] Others dared to chant, "The President is committing a crime and the Supreme Leader is supporting him."[20] Some shouted "Death to the dictator!," "Down with Khamenei!," and even "Death to Khamenei!"—an astonishing show of defiance toward the Supreme Leader.[21]

Candidate Karroubi termed the results "engineered."[22] He declared that "the results of the 10th presidential election are so ridiculous and so unbelievable that one cannot write or talk about it in a statement. It is amazing that the people's vote has turned into an instrument for the government to stabilize itself."[23]

Another candidate, avowed hardliner and former Islamic Revolutionary Guards commander Mohsen Rezai, agreed that the results were fraudulent.[24] He said he had won between 3.5 and 7 million votes, but the official tally gave him only 680,000.[25] Leading reform candidate Mousavi tried to hold a press conference, but police wouldn't allow journalists to attend. Then he issued a statement declaring, "I will not submit to this dangerous charade" and detailing an extensive string of irregularities with the election.[26] His campaign's newspaper, the *Green Word*, claimed that no fewer than ten million votes were "untraceable," as they were not attached to any Iranian's identification number—a clear indication that they had been fabricated.[27]

Mousavi formally protested the results to the Council of Guardians, a powerful body of twelve Shi'ite clerics with authority over elections, among other matters: "I have submitted my official formal request to the Council to cancel the election result. I urge you, the Iranian nation to continue your nationwide protests in a peaceful and legal way."[28] He asked for official permission for the protests: "We have asked officials to let us hold a nationwide rally to let people display their rejection of the election process and its results."[29]

That permission was not forthcoming. Iran's National Security Council warned Mousavi to "refrain from provoking illegal rallies.... It is your duty not to incite and invite the public to illegal gatherings; otherwise, you will be responsible for its consequences."[30] By nightfall on Saturday, June 13, both he and Karroubi were under house arrest.[31]

Their followers stayed busy. On that same day, Mousavi supporters launched denial-of-service (DDoS) attacks against government websites and posted on Twitter and Facebook ways that others could join in the cyber-attacks. The demonstrators also used Twitter and Facebook to communicate with one another and coordinate activities. Regime officials responded by completely shutting down the Internet in Iran.[32]

"On Friday's election, the people of Iran emerged victorious"

In a speech on June 19, Khamenei brushed aside all claims that the election had been rigged. "Some supporters of candidates should know that the Islamic Republic would not cheat and would not betray the votes of the people," he insisted. "The legal mechanism for elections would not allow any cheating."[33] He warned that if the protesters didn't disperse and end their challenges to the election results, they would be "responsible for bloodshed and chaos."[34] At that, Rezai withdrew his protest, but Mousavi and Karroubi stood firm.[35] Mousavi told his followers, "I am ready for martyrdom."[36]

The victorious candidate, meanwhile, called Iran's elections a "model of democracy," unacceptable only to "Western oppressors."[37] Ahmadinejad complained that by playing up the demonstrations, the international media had "launched the heaviest propaganda and psychological war against the Iranian nation,"[38] claiming that "all political and propaganda machines abroad and sections inside the country have been mobilized against the nation."[39]

Ahmadinejad boasted that "the people of Iran inspired hope for all nations and created a source of pride in the nation and disappointed all the ill wishers. This election was held at a juncture of history."[41] What kind of juncture? "There were two options. Either to return to the old days or continue our leap forward towards high peaks...and progress. Fortunately, the people voted for that last option."[42] Sounding very much like a victorious American politician,

JUST SORE LOSERS

• • •

Ahmadinejad dismissed the demonstrations as "not important from my point of view," explaining, "Some believed they would win, and then they got angry. It has no legal credibility. It is like the passions after a soccer match.... The margin between my votes and the others is too much and no one can question it. In Iran, the election was a real and free one."[40]

he declared piously, "On Friday's election, the people of Iran emerged victorious."[43] Like a member of the U.S. Congress who had survived charges of scandal, he said in a victory speech the Sunday night after the election, "We are hopeful. Now it's time to move on and continue to build our great Iran."[44]

The Council of Guardians conducted a perfunctory investigation. On June 29, 2009, after a recount of just 10 percent of the votes that had been cast, Council of Guardians spokesman Abbas Ali Kadkhodaei announced that there had been "no tangible irregularity" in the election, and that even the fact that in some districts the number of votes cast exceeded the number of voters was no indication of fraud. Kadkhodaei closed the door on any further investigations: "After this, the file will be closed and from today on in the presidential election, the file has been closed."[45]

"There have been many other police and members of the security forces arrested because they have shown leniency toward the protesters"

Iranian authorities dealt brutally with the protesters. Police on motorcycles swung truncheons at demonstrators.[46] Militiamen from Ansar Hizballah, a hardline group in Iran, set on the protestors with batons, screaming "Allahu akbar" as they began administering beatings to those who dared to protest the election results.[47]

After a week of demonstrations, the crackdown got even worse. On June 20, Iranian General Esmaeil Ahmadi Moghadam went on state television to issue a threat: "We acted with leniency, but I think from today on, we should resume law and confront more seriously. The events have become exhausting, bothersome and intolerable. I want them to take the police cautions seriously because we will definitely show a serious confrontation against those who violate rules."[48] On June 22, the Islamic Revolutionary Guards warned protesters to "be prepared for a resolution and revolutionary confrontation with the Guards, Basiji and other security forces and disciplinary forces."[49]

These were not empty words. Basiji militiamen set on the protesters with clubs and electric prods.[50] The regime used tear gas and water cannons against the demonstrators.[51] One witness recounted that the streets were hazardous even for non-protesters: "It was not possible to wait and see what happened. At one point we saw several riot police in black clothes walk towards a group of people who looked like passers-by. Suddenly they pulled out their batons and began hitting them without warning."[52] Another witness recalled the savagery of the Basiji: "I saw one group of about 100 people who began chanting 'Death to the dictator' on one of the side streets. The Basijis attacked them and beat them really bad."[53]

Morteza Alviri, a former major in the Iranian army and a Karroubi campaign official, reported by phone from the middle of the protests, "Commando troops are beating the people. I even saw they beat an old lady. They were beating her to a pulp."[54]

In a quid pro quo for the funding they received from Iran, Hamas members traveled to Iran to aid in the crackdown. One protester told a *Jerusalem Post* reporter on June 16, "The most important thing that I believe people outside of Iran should be aware of is the participation of Palestinian forces in these riots."[55] Another recounted, "My brother had his ribs beaten in by those Palestinian animals. Taking our people's money is not enough, they are thirsty for our blood too." He remarked bitterly that Ahmadinejad "tells us to pray for the young Palestinians, suffering at the hands of Israel," and said he hoped that Israel would "come to its senses" and confront the Palestinians.[56] There were other reports of "Arab militias" participating in the crackdown as well.[57]

The Iranian government acknowledged that it arrested four thousand people during the protests.[58] And Neda Agha-Soltan wasn't the only protester to be shot in the streets. In September 2009, Mousavi's camp asserted that 72 people had been killed in the protests; the Iranian government acknowledged only half as many deaths.[59] The actual number of casualties is likely to have been 150 or more.[60] Police officers and other officials who showed kindness to the protesters were punished, as one member of the Basiji recounted: "There have been many other police and members of the security forces arrested because they have shown leniency toward the protesters out on the streets, or released them from custody without consulting our superiors."[61]

This militiaman had himself been imprisoned during the Green Movement for the crime of freeing a thirteen-year-old boy and a fifteen-year-old girl from custody. "They were so young. They looked like children and I knew what would happen to them if they weren't released." Freeing the girl, he said, was what "really got me in trouble."[62]

He had previously worked as a prison guard, he said, and "I was given the 'honor' to temporarily marry young girls before they were sentenced to death." According to the militiaman, this was because in Iran it was illegal to execute a virgin. "I could tell that the girls were more afraid of their 'wedding' night than of the execution that awaited them in the morning. And they would always fight back, so we would have to put sleeping pills in their food. By morning the girls would have an empty expression; it seemed like they were ready or wanted to die. I remember hearing them cry and scream after [the rape] was over. I will never forget how this one girl clawed at her own face and neck with her fingernails afterwards. She had deep scratches all over her."[63]

The Islamic Republic's leadership encouraged the brutality with fiery maximalist rhetoric. On June 26, 2009, in a sermon at Tehran University that was broadcast throughout the nation, a senior cleric, Ayatollah Ahmad Khatami (not to be confused with the reformist former president, Mohammad Khatami), called for the protesters to be killed as enemies of Allah: "Anybody who fights against the Islamic system or the leader of Islamic society, fight him until complete destruction. Anyone who takes up arms to fight with the people, they are worthy of execution. We ask that the judiciary confront the leaders of the protests, leaders of the violations, and those who are supported by the United States and Israel strongly, and without mercy to provide a lesson for all."[64] He said that the protesters were "at war with God" and should consequently be "dealt with without mercy."[65]

The British, said Khatami, were responsible for stirring up a great deal of this trouble: "In this unrest, Britons have behaved very mischievously and it is fair to add the slogan of down with England to slogan of down with USA."[66] The jubilant crowd responded by chanting "Death to Israel."[67] (The scapegoating wasn't just verbal: two days after Khatami blamed the British, nine Iranians who worked at the British Embassy in Tehran were arrested.[68])

Khatami even claimed that Neda Agha-Soltan had not been killed by government forces, but by her fellow demonstrators: "The proof and evidence shows that they have done it themselves and have raised propaganda against the system. I say hereby that these deceitful media have to know that the ordeal will be over and shame will remain for them."[69]

"I think we, in retrospect, handled it pretty well"

The Islamic regime's treatment of the protesters drew tepid murmurs of dissent from world leaders. Vice President Joe Biden expressed guarded concern about "the way they're suppressing crowds, the way in which people are being treated," but said that the U.S. government had no choice but to accept the election results "for the time being," even though "there's an awful lot of questions about how this election was run. We don't have enough facts to make a firm judgment."[70]

Secretary of State Hillary Clinton issued a statement that was the epitome of a politician's non-statement: "We are monitoring the situation as it unfolds in Iran, but we, like the rest of the world, are waiting and watching to see what the Iranian people decide."[71] French Foreign Minister Bernard Kouchner was unhappy with what he termed Iran's "somewhat brutal reaction" to the protests.[72] The European Union stated that it was "concerned about alleged irregularities."[73]

But no response was more tepid than Barack Obama's. A White House statement issued immediately after the election praised "the vigorous debate and enthusiasm that this election generated, particularly among young Iranians," and tut-tutted about "reports of irregularities."[74] The president's words in a June 16 interview were a bit stronger: "When you've got 100,000 people who are out on the streets peacefully protesting, and they're having to be scattered through violence and gunshots, what that tells me is the Iranian people are not convinced of the legitimacy of the election."[75]

But then in response, Mojtaba Samareh Hashemi, a top aide to Ahmadinejad, issued a threat to the Obama administration: "I hope in the case of the elections they realize their interference is a mistake, and that they don't repeat this mistake. They'll certainly regret this. They'll have problems reestablishing relations with Iran."[77]

And Obama took the hint, saying on June 17, "It is not productive, given the history of US-Iranian relations to be seen as meddling—the US president, meddling in Iranian elections."[78] Yet on June 20, as the protests raged and the Islamic Republic's violent crackdown was in full swing, Obama issued a statement that sounded a lot like "meddling":

OSTRICH ALERT

"And my hope is that the regime responds not with violence, but with a recognition that the universal principles of peaceful expression and democracy are ones that should be affirmed."

—President Barack Obama[76]

The Iranian government must understand that the world is watching. We mourn each and every innocent life that is lost. We call on the Iranian government to stop all violent and unjust actions against its own people. The universal rights to assembly and free speech must be respected, and the United States stands with all who seek to exercise those rights.

As I said in Cairo, suppressing ideas never succeeds in making them go away. The Iranian people will ultimately judge the actions of their own government. If the Iranian government seeks the respect of the international community, it must respect the dignity of its own people and govern through consent, not coercion.

Martin Luther King once said—"The arc of the moral universe is long, but it bends toward justice." I believe that. The international community believes that. And right now, we are bearing witness to the Iranian peoples' belief in that truth, and we will continue to bear witness.[79]

This was a curious statement. Obama seemed to have missed the fact that the Islamic Republic's Constitution—based on the Qur'an and Sharia law rather than "universal rights"—did not guarantee its citizens the rights to either assembly or free speech. And in fact, despite his bold statement that "the United States stands with all who seek to exercise those rights," he did nothing to make that "stand" anything more than empty words.

Shortly thereafter, President Obama said he was "appalled and outraged" by the Iranian government crackdown—but he still took no action. Even his words, however, annoyed Ahmadinejad: "Mr Obama made a mistake to say those things... your question is why he fell into this trap and said things that previously Bush used to say. Do you want to speak with this tone? If that is your stance then what is left to talk about? ... I hope you avoid interfering in Iran's affairs and express your regret in a way that the Iranian nation is informed of it."[80] Obama did not apologize, but he didn't do anything to support the Green Revolution demonstrators, either.

In an August 2009 interview Secretary of State Clinton defended the Obama administration's failure to do anything significant to support the protesters by arguing that too much visible support from the Great Satan would have hurt their cause: "We did not want to get between the legitimate protests and demonstrations of the Iranian people and the leadership. And we knew that, if we stepped in too soon, too hard, the attention might very well shift and the leadership would try to use us to unify the country against the protesters. And that was—it was a hard judgment call. But I think we, in retrospect, handled it pretty well."[81]

Clinton elaborated her defense of the administration's hesitancy in an October 2011 interview: "At the time the most insistent voices we heard from within the Green Movement and the supporters from outside of Iran were that we, the United States, had to be very careful not to look like what was happening inside Iran was directed by or in some way influenced by the United States, when in fact it was an organic uprising by people who knew their election had been stolen, who saw the hypocrisy and the betrayal in the regime for what had been promised. So we were torn. I will tell you it was a very tough time for us, because we wanted to be full-hearted in favor of what was going on inside Iran, and we kept being cautioned that we would put people's lives in danger, we would discredit the movement, we would undermine their aspirations."[82]

If this argument seemed superficially persuasive, it fell apart in light of the fact that the Obama administration had enthusiastically supported protesters and opposition forces in Libya, Egypt, and Syria, even when they knew those forces were led by Muslim Brotherhood and even al-Qaeda operatives.[83] Those groups gladly accepted American money and weapons, never showing any hesitation over the possibility that someone might think that their movements were "directed by or in some way influenced by the United States."

Nevertheless, Clinton even went so far as to place the blame for the U.S. inaction on the Green Revolution demonstrators themselves: "I think if something were to happen again, it would be smart for the Green Movement or some other movement inside Iran to say, 'We want the voices of the world. We want the support of the world behind us.'"[84]

But they had done just that, asking Obama—whose administration was lending legitimacy to the Iranian government by soliciting the Islamic Republic's leadership for a deal on its nuclear program—to pick one side or the other. On November 4, 2009, Hate America Day in Iran (the anniversary of the takeover of the U.S. Embassy in 1979), Green Revolution protesters shouted, "Obama, Obama, you are either with us or with them"—that is, the Islamic regime.[85]

But the administration continued with the same ineffective posturing it had been indulging in since the protests began. In the August 2009 interview, Clinton had claimed that the Obama administration was not completely unsupportive of the protesters: "Now, behind the scenes, we were doing a lot, as you know. One of our young people in the State Department got twittered, you know, 'Keep going,' despite the fact that they had planned for a technical shutdown. So, we were doing a lot to really empower the protesters without getting in the way. And we're continuing to speak out and support the opposition."[86]

How grateful the Iranians must have been for the support of their social media friends at the State Department—as they were being bludgeoned and shot in the streets.

In September 2015, back on the presidential campaign trail, Clinton reversed her 2009 claim that the Obama administration had handled the Green Revolution "pretty well." Without admitting error or failure as Secretary of State, she said that the U.S. had been "too restrained in our support of the protests in June 2009," and vowed, "That won't happen again."[87]

But Clinton had been at the helm of the State Department for four years as the Obama administration assiduously courted the Islamic Republic—a courtship that culminated in the nuclear deal. And it seems that her infamously tenuous relationship with the truth may explain her claim that the Green Revolution protesters had wanted the United States not to intervene. Only in January 2016 did a *Wall Street Journal* exposé reveal that "Iranian opposition leaders secretly reached out to the White House in the summer of 2009 to gauge Mr. Obama's support for their 'green revolution.'"[88] According to officials inside the administration, the demonstrations had "caught the White House off guard."[89]

Pressed to support the demonstrators, Obama vacillated: "Let's give it a few days."[90] One official who was present at meetings about the Green Revolution explained, "It was made clear: 'We should monitor, but do nothing.'"[91]

Why? Because Obama was trying to open a channel of communication with the Supreme Leader. Just before the Iranian election, he had sent a friendly letter to Khamenei.[92] He ordered the CIA to do nothing to aid the Green Revolution.[93]

WHAT A DEAL!

"If you were working on the nuclear deal, you were saying, 'Don't do too much'" to support the demonstrators."

—senior National Security official Michael McFaul[94]

So for the sake of an agreement that strengthened the Islamic Republic militarily and economically, and threatened the peace of the Middle East and the entire world, Obama condemned the Green Revolution demonstrators to torture, death, and newly virulent oppression.

"What we've seen from the performance of officials . . . is nothing but shaking the pillars of the Islamic Republic of Iran's sacred system"

Despite all the high hopes the Green Revolution raised in the West, however, there were numerous indications that it was never a movement for democracy, and that while the protesters hated the corruption and repressiveness of the Iranian regime, they were not questioning the idea of an Islamic Republic as such.

Opposition presidential candidate Mousavi himself certainly wasn't. After warning that he would not "surrender to this manipulation," he added, "The outcome of what we've seen from the performance of officials...is nothing but shaking the pillars of the Islamic Republic of Iran's sacred system and governance of lies and dictatorship."[95]

Clearly he didn't want the pillars of "Iran's sacred system" to be shaken; he just wanted a less corrupt Islamic Republic. Mousavi was an unlikely figurehead for a reform movement from the beginning: during the 2009 presidential campaign, he described himself as a "reformist who refers to the principles" of the Islamic revolution—a significant reservation.[96] He strongly supported Iran's nuclear program, insisting it was peaceful.[97]

Mousavi did, however, make some serious gestures toward reform. Just under two weeks before the election, on May 30, 2009, he said at a campaign rally, "We should reform laws that are unfair to women"—a statement that drew cheers from the many Iranians who despise the morality police that patrol Iran's streets enforcing the Islamic dress code for women.[98] He promised to advocate for a bill that would call for revising "discriminatory and unjust regulations" against women.[99] His wife, Zahra Rahnavard, spoke at the same rally, saying: "We should prepare the ground for an Iran where women are treated without discrimination. We should reform laws that treat women unequally. We should empower women financially, women should be able to choose their professions according to their merits, and Iranian women should be able to reach the highest level of decision-making bodies."[100]

And as the demonstrations raged, Rahnavard spoke of reforms more sweeping than any her husband had ever backed publicly: "People are tired of dictatorship. People are tired of not having freedom of expression, of high inflation, and adventurism in foreign relations. That is why they wanted to change Ahmadinejad."[101]

What Mousavi meant by laws that were "unfair to women" was unlikely to have been the same as what Western feminists might have meant by the same words. As Laura Secor reported in the *New Yorker*, he was "no liberal," but had nonetheless emerged as "the vehicle for a groundswell of youthful democratic sentiment—meaning whatever his personal views or background, if Mousavi became president, he would carry with him the same social forces and the same expectations as "moderate" President] Khatami, who was fatefully paralyzed between the demands of his supporters and the constraints of his superiors."[102]

The hopes and expectations of Khatami's reformist supporters had been largely dashed during his presidency; there is little indication, with Khamenei still wielding the ultimate power, that a Mousavi presidency would have been significantly different. Even as the Green Revolution was in its first week, a spokesman for Mousavi admitted, "People say that Mousavi won't change anything as he is part of the establishment. That is correct to a degree because they wouldn't let anyone who is not in their circle rise to seniority."[103] Even Barack Obama noticed that, as George Wallace said of the Republicans and Democrats in 1968, "there wasn't a dime's worth of difference" between the two chief claimants for the Iranian presidency: "It's important to understand that, although there is amazing ferment taking place in Iran, the difference between Ahmadinejad and Mousavi in terms of their actual policies may not be as great as has been advertised."[104]

Even as the protests raged on June 21, Mousavi called the Basiji, which was beating and brutalizing protestors, "our brothers" and "protectors of our revolution and regime."[105]

Mousavi's stance had been consistent throughout his political career. In 1987, when he was prime minister, he sounded for all the world like his future nemesis, Mahmoud Ahmadinejad: "If today Islamic forces from all the Islamic countries are waking up, they are indeed bound in unity. If we witness resistance in Lebanon, and if world arrogance and the Arch-Satan [the U.S.] and Zionism are being gradually repulsed, this is because of the existence of Islam.... We can in no way return to American culture and our nation will never do so. The people have stood against any move to this end and will continue to stand."[106]

"Certainly, if in early Islam the goodness was in the sword, in our time the goodness is in artillery, tanks, automatic guns and missiles"

Likewise, the Green Revolution's spiritual leader, Grand Ayatollah Hussein Ali Montazeri, who died in December 2009, didn't sound the slightest bit different from Khomeini or Khamenei when railing against the U.S. and Israel:

> YOU SAY YOU WANT A REVOLUTION?
>
> . . .
>
> "The experience of the Islamic Republic of Iran is a good experience for the world. We do not think this revolution belongs just to our own country; rather we deem it a momentous movement among the world's people."
>
> —"reform" candidate and Green Movement leader Mir Hossain Mousavi[107]

Very soon through a billion strong march by all the Muslims of the world, we can liberate beloved Jerusalem, destroy usurping Israel, and place the destiny of Islam and the Muslims in their own hands.... The Muslims should clearly recognize the main danger to Islam and the Islamic lands, which is the United States and international Zionism...One cannot fight against the United States and Zionism merely by holding meetings and chanting slogans. The ulema of Islam and all the Muslims should make some serious decisions...There are more than 300 verses in the Koran about jihad, which are unfortunately forgotten, and about 60 books of Islamic jurisprudence are devoted to political issues, economics, judicial matters, punishments, and similar subjects. In view of this it is regrettable that the enemies of Islam and the colonialists succeeded in influencing the thoughts and attitudes of Muslims and of the ulema and Islamic writers and preachers. These enemies took away from them their Islamic character, and said that religion is separate from politics.... He [Muhammad] did not sit in a corner and merely pray, although all his prayers would have been answered. On the contrary, he [Muhammad] carried out an uprising and had about 80 military clashes. He [Muhammad] called on the Muslims to arise, and he established a just government and powerfully implemented Allah's laws, injunctions, and justice among the people.... In the Mahdi's occultation period, jihad is not to be abandoned; even if occultation lasts for a hundred thousand years, Muslims have to defend and fight for the expansion of Islam. Certainly, if in early Islam the goodness was in the sword, in our time the goodness is in artillery, tanks, automatic guns and missiles.[108]

NOT EXACTLY GLORIA STEINEM

"You see, if people around the world want to say certain things about women for example being equal to men in matters of inheritance or legal testimony, because these issues pertain to the very letter of the Qur'an, we cannot accept them…in Iran we cannot accept those laws that are against our religion…on certain occasions that these laws contradict the very clear text of the Qur'an, we cannot cooperate."

—Green Revolution spiritual leader Hussein Ali Montazeri[109]

Green Revolution protesters shouted "Allahu akbar," an odd slogan for the movement if its goal was really to establish Jeffersonian democracy with the freedom of speech and the equality of rights of all people before the law—since Islamic law denies both of those principles.[110] On Twitter (protesters having found ways to circumvent the government Internet shutdown), some urged their comrades to carry copies of the Qur'an to demonstrations.[111] According to the *Economist*, "Protesters have deliberately dressed modestly, enlisting religious symbolism to appeal to the notions of injustice and redemption that lie at the heart of Shia Islam."[112]

Yet all this is not conclusive in itself: the protesters may have been trying to counter the mullahs' attempt to depict them as pro-Western allies of the Great Satan. What's more, Islam and the Qur'an had inspired a revolution in Iran in recent memory, and they remained the only cultural touchstones the demonstrators had to draw upon to give their revolution some context. "Allahu akbar" had become a rallying cry for protesters during the uprisings against the Shah, even among secular Iranians; the Green Revolution protesters may have been linking their movement to the revolution that had toppled Pahlavi, as a similar attempt to face down tyranny—putting the mullahs in the place of the hated Shah. Appeals to Islamic principles had had a profound resonance in 1979; the demonstrators may have calculated that they would again in 2009—and that invoking them would embarrass the Islamic regime.

But even allowing for the constraints of the Islam-dominated environment in which they had to operate, it is hard to see how, with leaders like Mousavi and Montazeri, a successful Green Revolution would have resulted in anything more significant than the removal of some corrupt officials and the reform of certain electoral procedures. It is unlikely that Green Revolution leaders would have ended the Islamic Republic, and inconceivable that they would have returned Iran to the secularizing, modernizing, and Western-oriented path of Mohammed Reza Pahlavi.

Indeed, the Green Revolution's "Seven-Point Manifesto," issued just days after the demonstrations began, delineates an agenda that would have left the Islamic Republic substantially intact. The demonstrators called for, in the words of their manifesto:

1. Stripping Ayatollah Khamenei of his supreme leadership position because of his unfairness. Fairness is a requirement of a supreme leader.

2. Stripping Ahmadinejad of the presidency, due to his unlawful act of maintaining the position illegally.

3. Transferring temporary supreme leadership position to Ayatollah Hussein-Ali Montazery until the formation of a committee to reevaluate and adjust Iran's constitution.

4. Recognizing Mir Hossein Mousavi as the rightfully elected president of the people.

5. Formation of a new government by President Mousavi and preparation for the implementation of new constitutional amendments.

6. Unconditional release of all political prisoners regardless of ideology or party platform.

7. Dissolution of all organizations—both secret and public—designed for the oppression of the Iranian people, such as the Gasht Ershad (Iranian morality police).[113]

Presumably, since "fairness is a requirement of a supreme leader," a new, fairer Supreme Leader would have been chosen, and the Islamic Republic would have continued. Still, it would have been at very least a marginal improvement over the Islamic Republic of Khamenei and Ahmadinejad.

There is no doubt that in their secret hearts, and whispered among themselves, many Iranians devoutly wished that the Green Revolution had not only succeeded but gone farther and definitively ended the cruelty and tyranny of the Islamic regime.

As the demonstrations began, the man who made the Islamic Republic possible, former President Jimmy Carter, demonstrated once again the touching naivety that characterized his entire political career, expressing confidence that everything was going to be all right.[114] Instead, the tyranny of the regime and its cruel repression of its opponents only worsened, with Green Revolution leaders frequently menaced, when they weren't being kept under house arrest.

OSTRICH ALERT

Jimmy Carter on the 2009 presidential election in Iran: "I think this election has bought out a lot of opposition to [Ahmadinejad's] policies in Iran, and I'm sure he'll listen to those opinions and hopefully moderate his position."[115]

Surprise! He didn't.

On June 6, 2010, the twenty-fifth anniversary of the Ayatollah Khomeini's death, his grandson Hassan Khomeini, who was known to be a reformist, was heckled and jeered off the stage by pro-regime thugs at a commemoration ceremony.[116] The thugs confronted presidential candidate Mehdi Karroubi, who was also there, and screamed at him, "Death to hypocrites."[117] When Green Revolution supporters planned a rally commemorating the election and its aftermath on June 12, 2010, the election's first anniversary, Mousavi and Karroubi canceled the rally just a few days before that date, saying it had to be called off for the "safety of the people."[118] Shortly after that, regime

THE AYATOLLAH'S SPIT LIST

"They are vicious killers and murderers who have perverted one of the world's great religions."
—Barack Obama, March 23, 2016, speaking about the Islamic State[120]

"Islam is a religion that prevents men from waging war? I spit upon those foolish souls who make such a claim."
—the Ayatollah Khomeini[121]

hoodlums attacked Karroubi's car while chanting "Dirty," "Corrupt," "American stooges."[119]

Just a few years later, with the nuclear deal, the Americans gave the regime that hired those hoodlums the biggest boost it had ever received.

Chapter Ten

"IF YOU WANT PEACE, PREPARE FOR WAR"
WHAT CAN BE DONE ABOUT IRAN

There are two ways the decades-long hostility between the Islamic Republic of Iran and the United States of America could be ended:

1. War.
2. The reestablishment of friendly relations.

A third possibility, that the tense relationship that has prevailed now for over forty years between Iran and the U.S. will continue indefinitely, is extraordinarily unlikely given Iran's ongoing bellicosity, repeated declarations of wanting war with the United States, and escalating nuclear program. As we have seen, the guardians of the Islamic Republic have repeatedly insisted that they want war with the United States, and that it is inevitable, and that they will win. Most analysts have dismissed all this as empty braggadocio, or even as the furious rhetoric of a dying regime. By all accounts, the Iranian military would be no match for that of the United States, and most assume that an actual war between the United States and the Islamic Republic would be almost as one-sided and brief as the American incursion into Iraq that toppled Saddam Hussein and his regime in three weeks.

After that, of course, things did not go so well, and if U.S. forces were to enter Iran, topple the mullahs, and attempt to establish a secular republic, things would not go well for them in Iran, either. The bitter experience of Iraq has led many who initially supported that conflict to oppose any military intervention into Iran, and there are abundant reasons for thinking it unwise to enter the Islamic Republic—not least the fact that the Iranian population has been fed a steady diet of virulent anti-Americanism since 1979, and anti-Western sentiment was the focus of discontent with the Shah's regime before then. Nowadays, many Iranians who hate the Islamic regime love America out of a spirit of defiance, but it would be unwise in the extreme for any American analysts to assume that U.S. troops would be welcomed into Iran as liberators.

Today no one is speaking about military intervention into Iran anyway, aside from the reminders by Obama and Kerry that the military option is "still on the table"; no one really believes it ever was during the entire Obama presidency. Few believe that the nuclear deal will bring about any lasting peace, and many are concerned that it has made Iran more aggressive and bellicose than ever. Whether the United States wants to go to war with Iran or not, the fact is that Iran has effectively been at war with the United States since 1979. Besides its hostile rhetoric, it has treated U.S. military personnel as agents of a hostile power (witness the blindfolding and holding at gunpoint ten U.S. Navy sailors in January 2016) and plotted terror attacks in the United States and all over the world in service of its interests and ambitions.

As long as the mullahs are in power, none of that is going to stop. As long as the U.S. is governed by weak presidents who wish to pretend that the gap between America and the Islamic Republic can be bridged with negotiations and concessions, Iran will not choose the path of peace, but will become even more aggressive.

On the other hand, a serious president who wants to defend the United States and its allies, and preserve the world in peace as much as possible will follow a different path:

1. Negotiate if you must, but understand with whom you're dealing. The Obama administration was committed as a matter of policy to the idea that Islam is a religion of peace; if anyone ever explained the concept of taqiyya to Obama or Kerry, they would undoubtedly have dismissed it as an "Islamophobic" fiction, an insult to their Shi'ite negotiating partners. The idea that the Iranian leadership adheres to a religion that values and even reveres dishonesty in the service of self-protection, and that this might influence the Iranians' behavior in the nuclear negotiations, would have been dismissed contemptuously by every American diplomat who participated in those negotiations.

Unfortunately, however, it is true, and so the provisions of the nuclear deal that mandate weeks of notice before inspections, and even allow the Iranians to conduct their own inspections, render the whole agreement hollow—and dangerous. If there are to be any future negotiations with the Islamic Republic, American negotiators would do well not to be as naïve and complacent as their predecessors, and to make sure that every provision of any agreement is genuinely verifiable.

2. Respond to provocations with strength. When Ronald Reagan was elected president of the United States, the Islamic Republic took notice. They had treated Jimmy Carter with gleeful condescension, storming the U.S. Embassy and taking hostages, and mocking his efforts to find a solution to the hostage crisis. But they released the hostages on January 20, 1981, the day Reagan was inaugurated president. Reagan's team played no role in the negotiations with Iran over the hostages; it didn't have to. The Iranians knew that here was a man quite different from Carter: a man of conviction, courage, and strength of character, who was certain to move against them decisively. Reagan believed in "peace through strength," and, in fact, strategists since ancient times have warned, "If you want peace, prepare for war."

The Iranians responded to weakness with contempt, but to strength with respect. But this lesson has not been learned. After the Iranians seized the Navy boats in 2016, Obama administration officials first tried to ascribe the whole incident to a mechanical failure and then praised the Iranians for their willingness to resolve the matter swiftly. To a culture and mindset that reveres strength and despises weakness, all that was an unrivalled indication of weakness, to be answered with increased assertiveness and aggression.

3. Fight the ideological war. Iranian rallies routinely feature the chant, "Death to America." John Kerry tried to explain this away by saying that he was unaware of any concrete plans that the Iranians actually had to destroy America. That was beside the point. Kerry was sure that all the differences between the U.S. and Iran could be negotiated away. With the Obama administration's unshakeable dogma about Islam being peaceful, neither Kerry nor any other administration official dared challenge the Islamic Republic's ideology, or even study why destroying America and Israel is so important to the mullahs. During the Cold War, the U.S. responded energetically to the Soviet Union's attempts to export communism around the world, not least by challenging the very premises of the communist ideology. Today, Iran is dedicated to spreading Islam, including its vision of political Islam, around the world, and no one in any leadership position in the West dares confront this or try to explain why a government that does not establish an official religion is superior to an Islamic state, or why the freedom of speech and the equality of rights of all people before the law are better than Islamic shari'a law.

4. Support Iranian dissidents. If the U.S. actually did defend the principles upon which it was founded, numerous Iranians would see it as a champion and turn more decisively away from the Islamic Republic. The Green Movement is by no means a movement for genuine republican government, but it indicates that there is immense discontent with the regime inside Iran. There is no doubt that the Islamic Republic is a criminal regime, a rogue state—why isn't the United States trying to encourage and capitalize upon this discontent?

5. Undermine the Islamic Republic in other non-military ways. A de facto state of war exists now between the U.S. and Iran. The alternative to eventual war between the U.S. and Iran, the reestablishment of friendly relations, can only come about if the Islamic Republic falls—or if the Ayatollah Khamenei gets his wish, and America falls and is replaced by a regime more to the mullahs' liking. The idea that America will fall is wildly fanciful; that the Islamic Republic will, not so much. An American president worth his or her salt will work to bring about the fall of the Islamic Republic as energetically as the Iranians are working to undermine U.S. interests worldwide.

This wouldn't be to the benefit of America alone, or even of the free world alone. The Iranians are the children and heirs of one of the oldest civilizations on earth. Their country has been one of the greatest in the world, and has the potential to be again, if the scourge of dogmatism, totalitarianism, and government brutality were removed from their land. They deserve better than the Islamic Republic. As do we all.

ACKNOWLEDGMENTS

Thanking those to whom one is in intellectual debt is always a risky endeavor for me. If I were to do it justice, the list would run longer than this book itself and try the patience of even the most gratitude-avid readers. What's more, in the nature of my work, I encounter a great many people who alert me to important facts or clarify essential truths for me but who do not, for a variety of reasons (in this case not least the vengefulness and long reach of the Islamic Republic of Iran), wish to be named. Their contribution to whatever is good about this book, and my appreciation for their help, however, is undimmed by their need to remain anonymous.

So many people gave me valuable information; if this book contains any material that is enlightening or revelatory, it is due to them. Former CIA operations officer Clare Lopez helped me locate and verify astounding information about Iran's role in plotting and carrying out the September 11,

2001, jihad terror attacks. Iran's involvement in 9/11 is unknown to most Americans and shocked me as much as I believe it will shock most readers. Without Clare Lopez none of the astonishing evidence of Iran's 9/11 machinations would be in this book, and she deserves all the credit for it.

The Canadian journalist Christine Williams, meanwhile, alerted me to the Islamic Republic's use of its embassy in Canada (among others) as a base for espionage and worse and explained to me the controversy that led to the (late, lamented) Harper government's closure of Iran's Ottawa Embassy. Her investigative work helped provide an impetus to that closing, and so I could not have had a better guide to help me navigate that unfamiliar territory.

I also must thank Pamela Geller for her valuable remarks on portions of the book, and above all for introducing me to one of the two notable Iranians who assisted me immensely, Avideh Ghaffari. Ms. Ghaffari and another native Iranian, Dr. Farajollah Parvizian, gave me vital assistance, including extraordinary insight into daily life in Iran, the nature of the Islamic Republic, and much more—most notably a firsthand view of some of the key events of Iran's modern history. Their recollections of events differ from the standard histories that predominate today, sometimes sharply, and often in intriguing and compelling ways that shine a light on the inconsistencies in the received account. I will always be indebted to them for their patience and for the time they gave to me to help ensure I was recounting events accurately.

After doing the research, of course, I had to write the book. Primarily responsible once again, as she has been for my last two books as well, for whatever shape, order, coherence and readability that might be found in these pages is the indefatigable Elizabeth Kantor, the extraordinary editor at Regnery Publishing whose deft hand takes my clouded prose and turns it pellucid. Were she to have become a surgeon, I am sure that at this stage in her life she would be performing the most agonizingly complex forays into repairing the brain and heart with a skill and aplomb that would leave the objects of her attentive care revitalized and their relatives awestruck; as things stand, I am grateful for her surgery on my writings, leaving nary a scar and a happily readable patient.

A round of applause is likewise due to Hugh Fitzgerald, the towering genius who is, I am proud to say, my Jihad Watch colleague and one of the most brilliant, erudite, and witty writers on the planet today. Hugh looked over this manuscript when it was rough-hewn and indelicate and taught it some manners. It is a cleaner, clearer, sharper book because of his acuity and keen eye.

This is the ninth of my books to be published by Regnery Publishing. Marji Ross and Harry Crocker, as well as longtime publicist Patricia Jackson and my recently-departed (the company, not this world) and much-missed publicist Rachel Williams, have been patient, understanding, helpful, and kind to me to a superlative degree. Patient, understanding, helpful, and kind, meanwhile, don't begin to describe Maria Ruhl, whose assistance with the typesetting and especially the index were way above and beyond the call of duty, and a welcome reminder that there are still many, many good people in our world of darkening clouds. I am prouder than ever for my long association with Regnery, the nation's leading conservative publisher, especially in these difficult days of Obama.

I cannot let an Acknowledgments page go by without thanking my friend Jeffrey Rubin, who brought me to Regnery so long ago, and for years served as the chief inspiration, motivator, and guide for my writing efforts. Jeff, long may you wave.

It takes a village, as Hillary Clinton famously said, and I am honored to live in my largely online one, with so many people who have in so many and various ways helped me along the way.

NOTES

Chapter One: "The Ultimate Screwing": The Iran Nuclear Deal

1. Andrea Mitchell, Abigail Williams, and Cassandra Vinograd, "Iran Nuclear Deal: Tehran, World Powers Agree to Historic Pact," NBC News, July 14, 2015.
2. Ibid.
3. Erin McClam, "Iran Nuclear Deal: President Obama Says Deal Makes World 'Safer and More Secure,'" NBC News, July 14, 2015.
4. Mitchell, Williams, and Vinograd, "Iran Nuclear Deal."
5. Jeffrey Goldberg, "Kerry Warns Congress about Risk of 'Screwing' the Ayatollah," *Atlantic*, August 5, 2015.
6. Ibid.
7. Ari Yashar, "Iran Launches Haifa Missile Strike Game on Nuke Deal Deadline," Israel National News, July 11, 2015.
8. Ali Wambold, "Fatal Flaw in the Iran Deal," *New York Sun*, August 11, 2015.
9. "Iran's Khamenei Hails His People for Demanding Death to America and Israel," Times of Israel, July 18, 2015.
10. Patrick Goodenough, "Iran's Supreme Leader Posts Photo of Himself Trampling Israeli Flag: 'The Zionist Regime Is Doomed,'" CNS News, July 13, 2015.

11. Ibid.
12. "Iran's Khamenei Hails His People."
13. Ibid.
14. Ibid.
15. Ibid.
16. "Sectarian, Tribal Wars Protecting Israel: Leader," Press TV, July 18, 2015.
17. Ibid.
18. Jordan Schachtel, "Iran Dictator Calls for Muslim World to Unite and Destroy Israel, Says USA Created ISIS," Breitbart, July 19, 2015.
19. Ibid.
20. Ibid.
21. "Kerry Says Iran Vow to Defy U.S. Is 'Very Disturbing,'" Reuters, July 21, 2015.
22. "We Will Not Let Americans Gain Influence: Iran's Khamenei," Reuters, August 17, 2015.
23. Ibid.
24. "Netanyahu Accuses Iran of Trying to 'Conquer the Entire Middle East' amid Looming Nuclear Deal," Fox News, March 29, 2015.
25. Adam Kredo, "Iran: 'We Will Trample Upon America,'" Washington Free Beacon, July 20, 2015.
26. Robert Spencer, "Iran's Supremo Tweets Picture of Obama Committing Suicide," Jihad Watch, July 25, 2015.
27. "Iran Hits Out at Kerry's 'Empty Threats,'" AFP, July 25, 2015.
28. Adam Kredo, "Iran: Nuke Deal Permits Cheating on Arms, Missiles," Washington Free Beacon, July 27, 2015.
29. Ibid.
30. Tim Hume, "Iran Test-Fires New Generation Long-Range Ballistic Missiles, State Media Report," CNN, October 11, 2015.
31. Arthur MacMillan, "Iran Conducts New Missile Tests Defying US Sanctions," Agence France-Presse, March 8, 2016.
32. Jon Gambrell, "Iran Fires 2 Missiles Marked with 'Israel Must Be Wiped Out,'" Associated Press, March 9, 2016.
33. Elad Benari, "Iran: The Americans Had 'No Option' Besides a Deal," Israel National News, September 12, 2015.
34. Ibid.
35. Amir Taheri, "Obama Just Made Iran's Brutal Regime Stronger," *New York Post*, January 24, 2016.
36. Betsy Woodruff, "Ted Cruz Compares Obama to Neville Chamberlain and Iran to Nazi Germany," Slate, March 3, 2015.

37. Samuel Kleiner and Tom Zoellner, "Republicans' 'Munich' Fallacy," *Los Angeles Times*, July 20, 2015.

38. Melissa Clyne, "Ben Stein: Iran Deal Makes Chamberlain's Pact with Nazis Seem Trivial," Newsmax, July 14, 2015.

39. Joint Comprehensive Plan of Action, Vienna, July 14, 2015, p. 1.

40. "Neville Chamberlain—Peace In Our Time," YouTube, https://www.youtube.com/watch?v=FO725Hbzfls.

41. Dan Murphy, "Is the Iran Nuclear Deal like Munich 1938? Not Really," *Christian Science Monitor*, July 22, 2015.

42. Kleiner and Zoellner, "Republicans' 'Munich' Fallacy."

43. James Fallows, "The Central Question: Is It 1938?," *Atlantic*, March 3, 2015.

44. Goldberg, "Kerry Warns Congress."

45. "Iran Says Will Ban US Experts from UN Nnuclear Inspections," Associated Press, July 30, 2015.

46. "Khamenei's Advisor Ali Akbar Velayati: Inspectors Will Not Be Allowed into Iranian Military Sites," Middle East Media Research Institute (MEMRI), July 31, 2015.

47. Michael R. Gordon, "John Kerry Wins Gulf States' Cautious Support for Iran Deal," *New York Times*, August 3, 2015.

48. Guy Benson, "Wow: AP Confirms Secret Side Deal Allows Iran to Inspect Itself at Key Nuclear Site," Townhall.com, August 19, 2015.

49. Ibid.

50. Patrick Goodenough, "WH 'Confident' in IAEA's Reported Plan to Let Iran Inspect Its Own Suspect Nuclear Site," CNS News, August 20, 2015.

51. Ibid.

52. Andrea Mitchell, "'Side Deal' Allows Iran to Inspect Its Own Military Site," NBC News, August 19, 2015.

53. Ibid.

54. Katie Sullivan, "Conservative Media Run with Flawed AP Report to Claim Iran Will Conduct Inspections on Its Own Facilities," Media Matters, August 20, 2015.

55. Ibid.

56. Kelsey Davenport and Daryl G. Kimball, "The P5+1 and Iran Nuclear Deal Alert, July 30," Arms Control Association, July 30, 2015.

57. Mitchell, "'Side Deal.'"

58. Shadia Nasralla, "IAEA Says Report Iran to Inspect Own Military Site Is 'Misrepresentation,'" Reuters, August 20, 2015.

59. Teresa Welsh, "IAEA Disputes Report That Iran Will Inspect Its Own Military Site," *U.S. News & World Report*, August 20, 2015.

60. Patrick Goodenough, "WH 'Confident' in IAEA's Reported Plan to Let Iran Inspect Its Own Suspect Nuclear Site," CNS News, August 20, 2015.

61. George Jahn, "Correction: Iran-Nuclear story," Associated Press, August 28, 2015.

62. Cheryl Rofer, "How the AP Got the Iran Inspections Story Wrong," War on the Rocks, August 24, 2015.

63. International Atomic Energy Agency, "Implementation of the NPT Safeguards Agreement and Relevant Provisions of Security Council Resolutions in the Islamic Republic of Iran," derestricted November 18, 2011, p. 10.

64. Kimberly Dozier, "Satellites Show Mystery Construction at Iran's Top-Secret Military Site," Daily Beast, February 8, 2016.

65. Rofer, "How the AP Got the Iran Inspections Story Wrong."

66. Joint Comprehensive Plan of Action, p. 3.

67. Ibid., p. 9.

68. Elizabeth Chuck, "Benjamin Netanyahu to Lester Holt: Iran Nuclear Deal Poses Threat to U.S., Israel," NBC News, July 15, 2015.

69. Joint Comprehensive Plan of Action, p. 43.

70. Goldberg, "Kerry Warns Congress."

71. "Journalist Offers Inside Look at Modern Life in Iran," PBS NewsHour, March 24, 2015.

72. Joint Comprehensive Plan of Action, p. 3.

73. Patrick Goodenough, "Iran Deal Includes Loophole in Sanctions 'Snapback' Mechanism," CNS News, July 14, 2015.

74. Joint Comprehensive Plan of Action, p. 15.

75. Joint Comprehensive Plan of Action, p. 15.

76. Joint Comprehensive Plan of Action, p. 20.

77. Joint Comprehensive Plan of Action, p. 20.

78. Joint Comprehensive Plan of Action, p. 20.

79. Adam Kredo, "Former Israeli Ambassador: Iran to Get $700 Billion in Sanctions Relief," Washington Free Beacon, July 22, 2015.

80. Nicole Duran, "Obama Admits Iran Deal Could Fund terror," *Washington Examiner*, July 15, 2015; Chuck Ross, "Obama Admits Iran Will Likely Use Sanctions Relief Money to Fund Military, Terrorism [VIDEO]," Daily Caller, August 5, 2015.

81. Nicole Duran, "Obama Admits Iran Deal Could Fund terror," *Washington Examiner*, July 15, 2015; Chuck Ross, "Obama Admits Iran Will Likely Use Sanctions Relief Money to Fund Military, Terrorism [VIDEO]," Daily Caller, August 5, 2015; "Obama Admits Some Unfrozen Iran Cash Will Fund Terror," AFP, August 5, 2015.

82. Raf Sanchez, "Barack Obama Admits Iran Nuclear Deal Will Mean More Money for Terror Groups," *Telegraph*, August 5, 2015.

83. Avi Issacharoff, "Boosted by Nuke Deal, Iran Ups Funding to Hezbollah, Hamas," Times of Israel, September 21, 2015.

84. David Lawder, "Iran to Receive $1.7 Billion from the US in a Claim Settlement," Reuters, January 17, 2016; Joel Schechtman and Yeganeh Torbati, "White House Dropped $10m Claim in Iran Prison Deal," AOL.com, January 27, 2016.

85. Maayan Groisman, "Iran Offers Financial Reward for Families of Potential Palestinian 'Intifada Martyrs,'" *Jerusalem Post*, February 24, 2016.

86. Michael Rubin, "White House Making Up Iran Data?," *Commentary*, March 6, 2016.

87. Ibid.

88. Armin Rosen, "John Kerry Just Gave a Stirring Defense of the Iran Deal—but Left Open Some Major Questions," Business Insider, August 11, 2015.

89. "Phony Fatwa? Group Claims Iranian Anti-Nuke Edict Cited by Obama a Hoax," Fox News, September 30, 2013.

90. Bradford Thomas, "Obama: Iran Won't Pursue Nuclear Weapons Because It's 'Contrary to Their Faith,'" Real Clear Politics, February 9, 2015.

91. A. Savyon and Y. Carmon, "Renewed Iran-West Nuclear Talks—Part II: Tehran Attempts to Deceive U.S. President Obama, Sec'y of State Clinton with Nonexistent Anti-Nuclear Weapons Fatwa By Supreme Leader Khamenei," Middle East Media Research Institute, April 19, 2012.

92. Savyon and Carmon, "Renewed Iran-West Nuclear Talks."

93. Ibid.

94. "'Atomic Weapons against Islam,' Says Ahmadinejad as Israel Warns World Powers Not to Waver in Iran Talks," al-Arabiya, May 23, 2012.

95. Savyon and Carmon, "Renewed Iran-West Nuclear Talks."

96. "Iran Leader Rules Out Nuclear Bomb, Will Pursue Energy," Reuters, August 30, 2012.

97. "'Atomic Weapons against Islam.'"

98. Savyon and Carmon, "Renewed Iran-West Nuclear Talks."

99. Ibid.

100. "John Kerry: US Welcomes Ayatollah Khamenei's Fatwa against N. Weapons," Fars News Agency, March 22, 2014.

101. Savyon and Carmon, "Renewed Iran-West Nuclear Talks."

102. Ibid.

103. Michael Eisenstadt and Mehdi Khalaji, "Nuclear Fatwa Religion and Politics in Iran's Proliferation Strategy," The Washington Institute for Near East Policy, September 2011.

104. "Fatwas from Leader's Office in Qom," http://www.khamenei.de/fatwas/further.htm.

105. Savyon and Carmon, "Renewed Iran-West Nuclear Talks."

106. Juan Cole, "Yes, MEMRI, There Is a Fatwa from Khamenei Forbidding Nukes," Informed Comment, April 22, 2012.

107. Cole, "Yes, MEMRI, There Is a Fatwa from Khamenei."

108. National Iranian American Council, "Staff and Board of Directors," http://www.niacouncil.org/site/PageServer?pagename=About_staff_board; Sam Nunberg, "Iranian Regime Loses to Legal Project in Federal District Court," Legal Project, September 18, 2012.

109. Michael Rubin, "Is NIAC the Iran Lobby?," Commentary, February 8, 2013.

110. Sam Nunberg, "A Response to NIAC's Deceitful Fundraising Letter," FrontPageMagazine.com, January 9, 2013.

111. Adam Kredo, "Sanctioning Iran's American Allies: NIAC Ordered to Pay Nearly $200K in Legal Fees," Washington Free Beacon, April 22, 2013.

112. Savyon and Carmon, "Renewed Iran-West Nuclear Talks."

113. Ibid.

114. Ibid.

115. Amir Taheri, "How Bad Is the Iran Deal? Let's Count the Ways," New York Post, September 5, 2015.

116. "Interview with James Robbins of BBC," U.S. Department of State, July 14, 2015.

117. Rosen, "John Kerry Just Gave a Stirring Defense."

118. See chapter seven.

119. Shreeya Sinha and Susan Campbell Beachy, "Timeline on Iran's Nuclear Program," New York Times, April 2, 2015.

120. "'Atomic Weapons against Islam.

121. Jordan Schachtel, "Iran Dictator Calls for Muslim World to Unite and Destroy Israel, Says USA Created ISIS," Breitbart, July 19, 2015.

122. Ali Akbar Dareini, "Iranian Hardliner: The Supreme Leader Opposes the Nuclear Deal," Associated Press, August 15, 2015.

123. Sam Wilkin and Bozorgmehr Sharafedin, "Iran Parliament Approves Nuclear Deal Bill in Victory for Rouhani," Reuters, October 13, 2015.

124. "Iran Deal 'Adoption Day': US Approves Conditional Sanctions Waivers," Reuters, October 18, 2015.

125. Ibid.

126. Ibid.

127. Ibid.

128. Amir Taheri, "Obama Will Be the Only Person Sticking to Iran Deal," *New York Post*, October 11, 2015.

129. Ibid.

130. Ibid.

131. A. Savyon and Y. Carmon, "The Iranian Majlis Has Not Approved the JCPOA but Iran's Amended Version of It," Middle East Media Research Institute (MEMRI), October 13, 2015.

132. Amir Taher, tweet, https://twitter.com/AmirTaheri4/status/653865739229745152.

133. Savyon and Carmon, "The Iranian Majlis Has Not Approved the JCPOA."

134. Ibid.

135. Taheri, "Obama Will Be the Only Person."

136. Ibid.

137. Ibid.

138. Y. Carmon and A. Savyon, "Khamenei Capitulates to Pragmatic Camp, Accepts JCPOA without the Preconditions He Outlined in October 2015 Letter to President Rohani," Middle East Media Research Institute (MEMRI), February 3, 2016.

139. "Iran Demands Closure of UN Nuclear Watchdog Probe," Agence France-Press, November 29, 2015.

140. "UANI: IAEA Report Verifies Existence of Iranian Nuclear Weapons Program," United against Nuclear Iran, December 4, 2015.

141. Amir Taheri, "Obama Will Be the Only Person."

142. George Jahn and Bradley Klapper, "US, EU Lift Sanctions against Iran amid Landmark Nuke Deal," Associated Press, January 16, 2016.

143. Ibid.

144. Ibid.

145. Steve Guest, "John Kerry: 'The World Is Safer Today' because of the Iran Nuke Deal [VIDEO]," Daily Caller, January 18, 2016.

146. Ibid.

147. Adam Kredo, "Iran Accuses U.S. of Breaching Nuke Deal," Washington Free Beacon, March 3, 2016.

148. Michael Rubin, "Iran and the Murder in Vienna," *Commentary*, July 13, 2015.

149. "Iranian Political Analyst Mohammad Sadeq Al-Hosseini: If Not for the Geneva Deal, Obama Would Have Had to Kiss Nasrallah's and Khamenei's Hands to Prevent the Annihilation of Israel," Middle East Media Research Institute (MEMRI), December 11, 2013.

150. Ibid.

151. Ibid.

152. Ibid.

153. Ibid.

154. Ronald Rolheiser, "Our Muslim Brothers and Sisters," Angelus: The Tidings Online, December 3, 2015.

155. Amir Taheri, *Holy Terror: Inside the World of Islamic Terrorism* (Adler & Adler, 1987), 241–43.

156. David Samuels, "The Aspiring Novelist Who Became Obama's Foreign-Policy Guru," *New York Times*, May 5, 2016.

157. Ibid.

158. Ibid.

159. Ibid.

160. Ibid.

161. Ibid.

162. Ibid.

163. Ibid.

Chapter Two: "We Welcome War with the US": Iran's Ambition to Conquer the World for Islam

1.   Patrick Goodenough, "Kerry: 'I Have No Specific Knowledge of a Plan by Iran to Actually Destroy Us,'" CNS News, July 29, 2015.

2.   Ibid.

3.   Ibid.

4.   Ibid.

5.   Ibid.

6.   Nick Gass, "Kerry to Iran: Stop 'Death to America' Chants," Politico, July 24, 2015.

7.   "'Death to America' Stands Despite Nuclear Deal: Iran MPs," Agence France-Presse, November 2, 2015.

8.   Ibid.

9.   Ibid.

10.   Elizabeth Chuck, "Benjamin Netanyahu to Lester Holt: Iran Nuclear Deal Poses Threat to U.S., Israel," NBC News, July 15, 2015.

11.   Stuart Winer, "Netanyahu: Iran Wants to 'Take Over the World,'" Times of Israel, July 7, 2015.

12.   Justin Raimondo, "Bibi's Bombast Bamboozles Boehner—And No One Else," Antiwar.com, July 17, 2015.

13. Juan Cole, "No, Mr. Netanyahu, Iran Isn't Trying to Take Over the World & It Isn't ISIL," Informed Comment, July 13, 2015.

14. S. Noble, "Clinton Reaches Out to an Iranian Front Group for Campaign Donations," Independent Sentinel, February 20, 2016.

15. Ali Wambold, "Fatal Flaw in the Iran Deal," *New York Sun*, August 11, 2015.

16. Ibid.

17. "Iranian President-Elect Mahmoud Ahmadinejad: 'Is There Art That Is More Beautiful, More Divine, and More Eternal than the Art of Martyrdom?,'" Middle East Media Research Institute (MEMRI), July 25, 2005.

18. Patrick Goodenough, "Ayatollah: America Is the Source of the Region's Problems, Not the Solution," CNS News, November 2, 2015.

19. Bruce Thornton, "The President's Looking-Glass Islamic World," FrontPageMag.com, July 10, 2015.

20. Reza Kahlili, *A Time to Betray: The Astonishing Double Life of a CIA Agent Inside the Revolutionary Guards of Iran* (Simon and Schuster, 2010), 236.

21. Elaine Sciolino, *Persian Mirrors: The Elusive Face of Iran* (Free Press, 2000), 14.

22. "IRGC Deputy Commander Hossein Salami: If Muslims Unite, US Political Breathing Space Will Be Limited," MEMRI, February 1, 2014.

23. "IRGC Deputy Commander Hossein Salami: If Muslims Unite, US Political Breathing Space Will Be Limited," MEMRI, February 1, 2014.

24. "Iranian General: Obama, EU Leaders Should Convert to Islam for Peace," TheTower, December 29, 2014.

25. Kellan Howell, "Iran's Ayatollah Ali Khamenei Urges Islamic Unity against Real Enemies: U.S. and Israel," *Washington Times*, August 22, 2015.

26. Ibid.

27. "Iranian Supreme Leader Khamenei in Article Marking Hajj: 'The Idols Will Be Shattered,'" Middle East Media Research Institute (MEMRI), September 24, 2015.

28. Ibid.

29. "Jihad Culture Should Be Developed Among Muslim Nations—Leader," Bernama, June 15, 2011.

30. "Qom Friday Prayer Leader: 'The Islamic Revolution Shaken [sic] the Foundations of the Order Imposed by the West,'" Ahlul Bayt News Agency, September 6, 2014.

31. "Obama: Lifting of Sanctions Will Increase Iran's Ability to Finance Terrorists," *Jerusalem Post*, July 24, 2015.

32. "Iran's Offensive Power to Stun US: IRGC Commander," Tasnim News Agency, January 25, 2014.

33. "Iranian Military Official: 'We Laugh' When US Threatens to Attack," *Jerusalem Post*, August 12, 2015.

34. Ibid.

35. Joshua Levitt, "Khamenei Tells Winners of Quran Competition: Ignoring Holy Book Can Lead to 'Cooperation with Zionist Regime,'" Algemeiner, June 3, 2014.

36. "On Iranian Revolution Day 2014, Commander of IRGC Navy Says: The Americans Will Understand When Their Warships with Over 5,000 Crew Aboard Sink to the Depths of the Sea and They Have to Search for Their Bodies," Middle East Media Research Institute (MEMRI), February 27, 2014.

37. Ibid.

38. Ibid.

39. Ibid.

40. Ibid.

41. Elad Benari, "Iran Threatens to Annihilate Israel if U.S. Attacks," Israel National News, May 30, 2014.

42. "Iran News Round Up May 6, 2014," AEI IranTracker, May 6, 2014; Richard Kemp and Chris Driver-Williams, "Killing Americans and Their Allies: Iran's Continuing War against the U.S. and the West," Jerusalem Center for Public Affairs, March 2015.

43. Ibid.

44. Ibid.

45. "Deputy Commander Says IRGC Will Chase US Troops Even to Gulf of Mexico in Case of Attack," Fars News Agency, October 12, 2015.

46. "Iran's Revolutionary Guard Conducts Military Drill against Replica US Carrier," Fox News, February 25, 2015.

47. Ibid.

48. Nasser Karimi, "Iran Test Fires New Weapon in Naval Drill," Associated Press, February 27, 2015.

49. "Iran Warns to Set Fire to Enemy's Economic, Political Interests in Case of War," Fars News Agency, September 3, 2015.

50. "'Kayhan': The White House Will Be Destroyed in Under 10 Minutes if the U.S. Attacks Iran," Middle East Media Research Institute (MEMRI), July 10, 2015.

51. Ibid.

52. Ibid.

53. Ibid.

54. Ibid.

55. Ibid.

56. Ibid.

57. "Iran Warns to Set Fire to Enemy's Economic, Political Interests."

58. Ibid.

59. "Deputy Commander Says IRGC Will Chase US Troops Even to Gulf of Mexico."

60. Ibid.

61. Adam Kredo, "Iranian Warships Confront U.S. Navy on 'Daily Basis,'" Washington Free Beacon, September 8, 2015.

62. David Rutz, "Earnest on Navy Incident: These Kinds of Iranian Hostilities Are Why Obama Made Nuclear Deal," Washington Free Beacon, January 12, 2016.

63. Reena Flores, "Biden: Iran Didn't Want or Get Apology for Boats Incident," CBS News, January 13, 2016.

64. Ibid.

65. Ibid.

66. Ibid.

67. Ibid.

68. Michele Keleman, "Secretary Kerry Highlights Diplomacy in Freeing U.S. Sailors Held by Iran," NPR, January 14, 2016.

69. Adam Kredo, "Iran: 'American Sailors Started Crying After Arrest,'" Washington Free Beacon, January 16, 2016.

70. Ibid.

71. "Iran Says Seizure of U.S. Boats a Lesson to 'Troublemakers' in Congress," Reuters, January 13, 2016.

72. Tal Kopan, "John Kerry: Sailors Footage Made Me 'Angry,'" CNN, January 18, 2016.

73. Robert Spencer, "Khamenei Praises Islamic Revolutionary Guards Who Captured US Sailors, Crows about 'Americans with Hands on Heads,'" Jihad Watch, January 24, 2016.

74. "Iran Gives Medals for Capture of U.S. Sailors," Reuters, January 31, 2016.

75. Justin Fishel, "Iran Mocks US Sailors in Revolution Day Parade," ABC News, February 11, 2016.

76. Ahmed Vahdat, "Iran to Build a Statue of Captured US Sailors," Telegraph, March 18, 2016.

77. "On Iran's Islamic Revolution Day, IRGC Officials Slam U.S.," Middle East Media Research Institute, February 22, 2016.

78. Ibid.

79. Ibid.

80. Ibid.

81. Ibid.

82. Ibid.

83. Kimberly Kagan, "Iran's Proxy War against the United States and the Iraqi Government," Institute for the Study of War and The Weekly Standard, August 20, 2007, p. 1.

84. Carol L. Bowers, "Iran Playing 'Destabilizing Role' in Iraq, Crocker Says," American Forces Press Service, September 11, 2007; Richard Kemp and Chris Driver-Williams, "Killing Americans and Their Allies: Iran's Continuing War against the U.S. and the West," Jerusalem Center for Public Affairs, March 2015.

85. Bowers, "Iran Playing 'Destabilizing Role' in Iraq, Crocker Says."

86. Ibid.

87. "US Iraq Deaths Due to Iran Groups: Envoy," Al Arabiya, August 27, 2010.

88. Kagan, "Iran's Proxy War against the United States," p. 1.

89. Brian Bennett, "Iran Raises the Heat in Afghanistan," *Time*, February 22, 2008; Kemp and Driver-Williams, "Killing Americans and Their Allies."

90. Ibid.; Bennett, "Iran Raises the Heat in Afghanistan."

91. Ibid.

92. Thomas Joscelyn, "State Department: Iran Supports Taliban, Iraqi Militants," Long War Journal, August 6, 2010; Kemp and Driver-Williams, "Killing Americans and Their Allies."

93. Ira Silverman, "An American Terrorist," *New Yorker*, August 5, 2002.

94. Ibid.

95. Ibid.

96. Ibid.

97. Ibid.

98. Michael Isikoff, "Last Man to See Robert Levinson before He Vanished Denies Involvement in Disappearance," NBC News, December 14, 2013.

99. "Iranian Bomb Plotter Was Well-Known Texas Used Car Salesman," *New York Post*, October 12, 2011.

100. Chris Boyette, "Iranian-American Gets 25 Years in Plot to Kill Saudi Ambassador," CNN, June 2, 2013.

101. Charlie Savage and Scott Shane, "Iranians Accused of a Plot to Kill Saudis' U.S. Envoy," *New York Times*, October 11, 2011; Kemp and Driver-Williams, "Killing Americans and Their Allies."

102. Boyette, "Iranian-American Gets 25 Years."

103. "Timeline: Alleged Plot to Kill Saudi Ambassador," CNN, October 11, 2011.

104. Ibid.

105. Ibid.

106. Ibid.

107. Richard Weizel, "Man Who Sent Details on U.S. Jets to Iran Sentenced to Eight Years," Reuters, October 23, 2015.

108. Ibid.

109. Ibid.

110. Ibid.

111. "2 Via Rail Terror Plotters Sentenced to Life in Prison," CBC News, September 23, 2015.

112. Diane Mehta, "Via Rail Terror Suspect Asks Jury to Use Qur'an to Judge Him," The Canadian Press, March 4, 2015; Edward Prutschi, "Via Rail Terrorist Chiheb Esseghaier Fit to Be Tried," *Toronto Sun*, July 14, 2015.

113. Mehta, "Via Rail Terror Suspect Asks Jury."

114. Thomas Joscelyn, "Report: Senior al Qaeda Facilitator 'Back on the Street' in Iran," Long War Journal, January 31, 2014; Kemp and Driver-Williams, "Killing Americans and Their Allies."

115. Mark Hosenball, "Canada Train Plot Suspect Traveled to Iran: U.S. officials," Reuters, April 25, 2013; Kemp and Driver-Williams, "Killing Americans and Their Allies."

116. Hosenball, "Canada Train Plot Suspect."

117. Joscelyn, "Report: Senior al Qaeda Facilitator 'Back on the Street.'"

118. Ibid.

119. Ibid.

120. Mehta, "Via Rail Terror Suspect Asks Jury."

121. "Treasury Designates Iranian Ministry of Intellligence [sic] and Security for Human Rights Abuses and Support for Terrorism," U.S. Department of the Treasury, February 16, 2012; Kemp and Driver-Williams, "Killing Americans and Their Allies."

122. "Treasury Designates Iranian Ministry of Intellligence [sic] and Security for Human Rights Abuses."

123. Ibid.

124. Hassan Nasrallah, Al-Manar, September 27, 2002 (BBC Monitoring). Quoted in Deborah Passner, "Hassan Nasrallah: In His Own Words," Committee for Accuracy in Middle East Reporting in America (CAMERA), July 26, 2006.

125. Sara Carter, "Iran Aggressively Recruiting 'Invisible Army' of Latin American Converts to Infiltrate U.S. Through 'Soft Belly' of the Southern Border," Blaze, September 3, 2013.

126. *United States of America vs. Mahmoud Youssef Kourani*, Indictment, United States District Court, Eastern District of Michigan, Southern Division, November 19, 2003.

127. Terry Jeffrey, "A Question about Hizballah and Mexico," TownHall.com, January 28, 2004.

128. *United States of America vs. Mahmoud Youssef Kourani.*

129. Jeff Carlton, "Security Chief Says Terrorists Have Been Arrested on Texas Border," Associated Press, September 12, 2007; Kemp and Driver-Williams, "Killing Americans and Their Allies."

130. Hilary Leila Krieger, "FBI: Hizbullah Avoiding Attacks on US," *Jerusalem Post*, April 12, 2007.

131. "U.S. Acts on Groups Aiding Hezbollah," Associated Press, July 24, 2007.

132. Ibid.

133. "U.S. District Court Rules Iran Behind 9/11 Attacks," Mellon Webster & Shelly, December 23, 2011.

134. Ibid.

135. Ibid.

136. Ibid.

137. Ibid.

138. Kenneth R. Timmerman, "Iran's Dirty 9/11 Secrets," FrontPage Magazine, September 8, 2011.

139. Ibid.

140. "U.S. District Court Rules Iran Behind 9/11 Attacks."

141. Timmerman, "Iran's Dirty 9/11 Secrets."

142. Ibid.

143. United States District Court, Southern District of New York, Second Affidavit of Kenneth R. Timmerman, May 10, 2010.

144. Ibid.

145. Ibid.

146. "U.S. District Court Rules Iran Behind 9/11 Attacks."

147. United States District Court, Southern District of New York, Affidavit of Clare M. Lopez and Dr. Bruce D. Tefft, March 26, 2010.

148. "U.S. District Court Rules Iran Behind 9/11 Attacks."

149. "9/11 Lawsuit: Federal Court Awards $7 Billion in Final Judgment against Iran and Hezbollah," Winder & Counsel, n.d., http://www.winderfirm.com/library/9-11-lawsuit-federal-court-awards-7-billion-in-final-judgment.cfm; Kenneth Timmerman, email to author, April 6, 2016.

150. Daniel Beekman, "Terrorism Victims Win Right to Seize $500M Midtown Office Tower Linked to Iran after Long Legal Battle," *New York Daily News*, April 2, 2014.

151. Timmerman, "Iran's Dirty 9/11 Secrets."

152. "Iranians Hacked New York Dam And Banks, Says US," Sky News, March 24, 2016.

153. Ibid.

154. "Commentators on Arab TV: Obama Supports Iran because His Father Was a Shiite," Middle East Media Research Institute (MEMRI), March 25, 2015.

155. Ibid.

156. Michael W. Chapman, "Arab TV Commentators Claim Obama Supports Iran because His Father Was a Shiite," CNS News, April 17, 2015.

157. Sarah Lyons-Padilla and Michele Gelfand, "Want to Stop Islamic Terrorism? Be Nicer to Muslims," *Washington Post*, November 24, 2015.

158. Amir Taheri, *Holy Terror: Inside the World of Islamic Terrorism* (Adler & Adler, 1987), 241–43.

Chapter Three: "Wherever a Movement Is Islamic, Populist, and Anti-American, We Support It": Iran's Middle East Adventurism

1. Jonathan Beck, "Iran Deal Worse than Israel Feared, Netanyahu Says," Times of Israel, March 29, 2015.

2. Ibid.

3. Robin Wright and Peter Baker, "Iraq, Jordan See Threat to Election from Iran," *Washington Post*, December 8, 2004.

4. Juan Cole, "Is Iran Conquering the Middle East?," *Nation*, March 30, 2015.

5. Amir Taheri, "Iran Publishes Book on How to Outwit US and Destroy Israel," *New York Post*, August 1, 2015.

6. "Iran Responsible for 1983 Marine Barracks Bombing, Judge Rules," CNN, May 30, 2003.

7. Mohsen Milani, "Why Tehran Won't Abandon Assad(ism)," *Washington Quarterly*, Fall 2013, p. 81.

8. "The Hezbollah Program: An Open Letter, February 16, 1985," in Itamar Rabinovich and Jehuda Reinharz, editors, *Israel in the Middle East: Documents and Readings on Society, Politics, and Foreign Relations, Pre-1948 to the Present*, 2nd ed. (Brandeis University Press, 2007), 424.

9. Ibid., 424.

10. Adam Shatz, "In Search of Hezbollah," *New York Review of Books*, April 29, 2004.

11. "Iran Responsible for 1983 Marine Barracks Bombing."

12. Gordon Thomas, "William Buckley: The Spy Who Never Came in from the Cold," Canada Free Press, October 25, 2006.

13. Ibid.

14. Ibid.

15. "The Hezbollah Program: An Open Letter," p. 427.

16. Shatz, "In Search of Hezbollah."

17. "'Hezbollah Freed Our Country,'" *Spiegel*, July 26, 2006.

18. Shatz, "In Search of Hezbollah."

19. Greg Myre and Steven Erlanger, "Israeli Forces Enter Lebanon after 2 Soldiers Are Seized," *New York Times*, July 12, 2006.

20. Ronny Sofer, "US: Syria, Iran behind Kidnapping in North," Ynet News, July 12, 2006.

21. "Ahmadinejad: World Will Soon Witness the Demise of Israel," Iran Focus, July 13, 2006.

22. "Ahmadinejad to Assad: Israeli Strike on Syria Would Be like Attack on Entire Islamic World," Reuters, July 13, 2006.

23. "Iran Warns Israel of 'Unimaginable Losses' If Syria Hit," Agence France-Presse, July 16, 2006.

24. "Khamenei: Israel a 'Tumor,' Hezbollah Will Never Disarm," Iran Focus, July 16, 2006.

25. Ibid.

26. "No Part of Israel Is Safe, Iranian Lawmaker Says," Associated Press, July 18, 2006.

27. Aaron Klein, "War Dead Flown to Iran," *New York Sun*, July 24, 2006.

28. "Iran: Israel Doomed to 'Destruction,'" Associated Press, July 23, 2006.

29. "Hizbullah Envoy in Iran: We'll Leave No Place Safe for Israelis," Associated Press, July 24, 2006.

30. "FBI Eyes Hizbollah in US as Tensions with Iran Rise," Reuters, July 19, 2006.

31. "Iranian President Ahmadinejad on IRINN TV: 'Lebanon Is the Scene of an Historic Test, Which Will Determine the Future of Humanity,'" Middle East Media Research Institute (MEMRI), July 23, 2006.

32. Ibid.

33. Edward Wong, "U.S. Ambassador Says Iran Is Inciting Attacks," *New York Times*, August 12, 2006.

34. "Hezbollah Declares 'Historic Victory,'" Associated Press, August 15, 2006.

35. Mohsen Milani, "Why Tehran Won't Abandon Assad(ism)," *Washington Quarterly*, Fall 2013, 85.

36. "Report: Hezbollah Enlisting West Bank Youth to Carry Out Terror Attacks against Israel," *Jerusalem Post*, August 30, 2015.

37. Ibid.

38. Ibid.

39. Ibid.

40. Amir Taheri, "Obama Will Be the Only Person Sticking to Iran Deal," *New York Post*, October 11, 2015.

41. Cynthia Blank, "Hezbollah Calls for Intifada to 'Save Al Aqsa,'" Israel National News, October 18, 2015.

42. Hezbollah Leader Lauds Palestinian 'Sublime Jihad Spirit' against Israel," *Jerusalem Post*, November 7, 2015.

43. Hanin Ghaddar, "Iran Won Lebanon: The Arms Are above Everyone and Everything," Now, February 4, 2016, https://now.mmedia.me/lb/en/commentaryanalysis/566574-iran-won-lebanon.

44. Myra Abdallah, "Looking beyond the Release of Michel Samaha," Now, January 15, 2016, https://now.mmedia.me/lb/en/reportsfeatures/566493-looking-beyond-the-release-of-michel-samaha.

45. Ghaddar, "Iran Won Lebanon."

46. "Le Secuestran al Hijo, le Matan al Esposo y Ahora la 'Levantan'; Es Precandidata del PRD en Guerrero," *Proceso*, March 10, 2015.

47. Umberto Bacchi, "Mexico Female Mayoral Candidate Beheading: Drug Violence Continues after Bosses' Arrests," International Business Times, March 13, 2015.

48. Ibid.

49. Doris Gómora, "Hezbollah Is Working with Mexican Cartels: U.S.," *Universal*, March 30, 2015.

50. Ibid.

51. Ibid.

52. Eldad Beck, "Hezbollah's Cocaine Jihad," Israel National News, December 29, 2012; Michael Martinez, "Feds Raid Drug 'Super Tunnel' with Railway on U.S.-Mexico Border," CNN, October 24, 2015.

53. Rebecca Anna Stoil, "Ties between Hezbollah and Mexican Drug Cartels Revealed," *Jerusalem Post*, December 15, 2011.

54. Jason Ryan, "Lebanese Drug Lord Charged in US: Links to Zetas and Hezbollah," ABC News, December 13, 2011.

55. Stoil, "Ties between Hezbollah and Mexican Drug Cartels."

56. Gómora, "Hezbollah Is Working with Mexican Cartels."

57. Ryan, "Lebanese Drug Lord Charged in US."

58. Jay Solomon, "U.S. Moves against Hezbollah 'Cartel,'" *Wall Street Journal*, April 23, 2013

59. Ryan, "Lebanese Drug Lord Charged in US."

60. Stoil, "Ties between Hezbollah and Mexican Drug Cartels."

61. Solomon, "U.S. Moves against Hezbollah 'Cartel.'"

62. Columb Strack, "Syrian Government No Longer Controls 83% of the Country, *Jane's Intelligence Review*, August 23, 2015.

63. Mohsen Milani, "Why Tehran Won't Abandon Assad(ism)," *Washington Quarterly*, Fall 2013, 79–80.

64. Ibid., 80.

65. Ibid.

66. Geneive Abdo, "How Iran Keeps Assad in Power in Syria," *Foreign Affairs*, August 25, 2011.

67. Dexter Filkins, "The Shadow Commander," *New Yorker*, September 30, 2013.

68. Will Fulton, "How Deeply Is Iran Enmeshed in Syria?," U.S. Institute for Peace, The Iran Primer, May 6, 2013.

69. Milani, "Why Tehran Won't Abandon Assad(ism)," 81.

70. Farhad Pouladi, "Iran and Syria Sign Pact against 'Common Threats,'" Agence France Press, June 16, 2006.

71. Ibid.

72. Ibid.

73. Ibid.

74. Ibid.

75. "Iran, Syria Vow United Front to Thwart U.S. and Israel," *Haaretz*, February 18, 2007.

76. Fulton, "How Deeply Is Iran Enmeshed in Syria?"

77. Ibid.

78. Ibid.

79. "Iran-Backed Hezbollah Warns It May Intervene in Syria War," NBC News, May 1, 2013.

80. Abdo, "How Iran Keeps Assad in Power in Syria."

81. "Iran-Backed Hezbollah Warns It May Intervene in Syria War."

82. Dexter Filkins, "The Shadow Commander," *New Yorker*, September 30, 2013.

83. Fulton, "How Deeply Is Iran Enmeshed in Syria?"

84. "Iraq Says It Can't Halt Arms to Syria," Reuters, July 13, 2013.

85. Geneive Abdo, "How Iran Keeps Assad in Power in Syria," *Foreign Affairs*, August 25, 2011.

86. "Sanaa: Shiite Suicide Bomb Attack Leaves 15 Dead and Over 50 Injured," Asia News, September 29, 2014; "Yemen's Last Jews Eye Exodus after Militia Takeover," Reuters, February 15, 2015.

87. "Sanaa: Government and Shia Rebels Reach Peace Deal," Asia News, September 22, 2014.

88. "Sanaa: Shiite Suicide Bomb Attack."

89. Ahmed al-Haj, "Yemen's Shiite Rebels Attack Home of Islamist Politician South of Sanaa, Clashes Kill 12," Associated Press, October 18, 2014.

90. Josh Levs, Nick Paton Walsh, and Laura Smith-Spark, "Yemen's President 'Has No Control' As Houthi Rebels Storm Palace," CNN, January 20, 2015.

91. Ibid.

92. Ibid.

93. Yara Bayoumy and Mohammed Ghobari, "Iranian Support Seen Crucial for Yemen's Houthis," Reuters, December 15, 2014.

94. Ibid.

95. Ibid.

96. Ibid.

97. Ibid.

98. "Yemen Crisis: Houthi Rebels 'Announce Takeover,'" BBC, February 6, 2015.

99. Greg Botelho and Hakim Almasmari, "Official: Houthis Seize U.S. Embassy Vehicles, Marines' Weapons at Airport," CNN, February 11, 2015.

100. "Hadi, a Once-Quiet Leader of a Fractious Yemen, Strikes Defiant Pose by Reclaiming Presidency," Associated Press, February 22, 2015.

101. "142 Dead in Yemen Mosque Bombings Claimed by IS," Agence France Presse, March 20, 2015.

102. Ibid.

103. "Worshippers Chant 'Death to America' at Moment of Houthi Mosque Bombing in Yemen," Middle East Media Research Institute (MEMRI), March 20, 2015.

104. "U.S., British Forces Out in Yemen, Raising Terror Fears," CNN, March 23, 2015.

105. Robert Spencer, "NYT: Houthis Scream 'Death to America' but 'Don't Mean It Literally,'" Jihad Watch, February 12, 2015.

106. Ibid.

107. "U.S., British Forces Out in Yemen, Raising Terror Fears."

108. Ahmed Al-Haj and Hamza Hendawi, "Turmoil in Yemen Escalates As Saudi Arabia Bombs Rebels," Associated Press, March 26, 2015.

109. "Saudi Arabia Enlists Imams In Yemen War," Vocativ, March 29, 2015.

110. "Yemen: Al-Qaeda Announces 'Jihad against Shiites,'" Middle East Confidential, April 6, 2015.

111. "Fighting in Central Aden, Mosques Call for Jihad: Residents," *Daily Star* (Lebanon), April 8, 2015.

112. Johnlee Varghese, "Yemen: Isis in New Video Says 'We have Arrived' to 'Cut the Throats of Houthis,'" International Business Times, April 24, 2015.

113. "At least 4 Americans Reportedly Held by Yemen's Rebels," Fox News, May 31, 2015.

114. "Dozens Killed and Injured in Sanaa Mosque Blasts," Middle East Eye, June 17, 2015.

115. "Fistfight Breaks Out at Yemen Peace Talks," Reuters, June 18, 2015.

116. Ibid.

117. Alim Gelyastanov, "10 Facts About Iran Sponsoring Terrorism," Bankable Insight, n.d.

118. "Hamas 2010 Budget Mainly 'Foreign Aid' from Iran," World Tribune, January 5, 2010.

119. Thomas Erdbrink, "Iranian Missiles in Gaza Fight Give Tehran Government a Lift," *New York Times*, November 21, 2012.

120. Ibid.

121. Ibid.

122. Ibid.

123. Ibid.

124. Alexandra Olson, "US, UK Urge UN Probe of Israeli Rocket Seizure," Associated Press, March 20, 2014.

125. Con Coughlin, "Iran 'Is Intensifying Efforts to Support Hamas in Gaza,'" *Telegraph*, April 4, 2015.

126. Con Coughlin, "Iran Rekindles Relations With Hamas," *Wall Street Journal*, April 21, 2015.

127. "Iran Has Stopped Giving Us Money, Top Hamas Official Says," Times of Israel, July 28, 2015.

128. Jack Moore, "Iran Ceases Financial Aid to Hamas in Gaza, Official Claims," *Newsweek*, July 28, 2015.

129. "Iran Underlines Strong Support for Palestinian Hamas," Fars News Agency, August 26, 2015.

130. Adam Kredo, "Iran: Nuclear Deal Will Enable Support for Terrorism," Washington Free Beacon, August 25, 2015.

131. Ibid.

132. L. Todd Wood, "Hamas, ISIS Terrorists Arrested for Attempted Netanyahu Slaying Were Backed by Iran," *Washington Times*, January 9, 2016.

133. William Booth, "Iran's Post-Sanctions Windfall May Not Benefit Hamas," *Washington Post*, August 31, 2015.

134. Moore, "Iran Ceases Financial Aid."

135. Avi Issacharoff, "Hamas Rejects Iran Offer of Funding in Return for Backing in Saudi Row," Times of Israel, January 15, 2016.

136. Taheri, "Obama Will Be the Only Person."

137. "Iran," in "Chapter 3: State Sponsors of Terrorism Overview," U.S. Department of State, Bureau of Counterterrorism, Country Reports on Terrorism 2014, http://www.state.gov/j/ct/rls/crt/2014/239410.htm.

138. Elhanan Miller, "Iran Said to Pull Islamic Jihad's Funding over Group's Neutrality on Yemen," Times of Israel, May 26, 2015.

139. "Iran," in "Chapter 3: State Sponsors of Terrorism Overview."

140. Ibid.

141. Ibid.

142. Lisa Daftari, "Probe: Spain's 'Podemos' Party May Have Been Given 5 Million Euros by Iran Regime," Foreign Desk, January 12, 2016.

143. Ibid.

144. Pablo Gato and Robert Windrem, "Hezbollah Builds a Western Base," Telemundo and MSNBC, May 9, 2007.

145. Ibid.

146. Ibid.

147. Ibid.; Ronen Bergman, *The Secret War with Iran: The 30-Year Clandestine Struggle against the World's Most Dangerous Terrorist Power* (Simon and Schuster, 2008), 172.

148. Gato and Windrem, "Hezbollah Builds a Western Base."

149. Ibid.

150. Bergman, *The Secret War with Iran*; "Terrorist Designations of Hizballah Operatives Meliad Farah, Hassan el-Hajj Hassan, and Hussein Atris," U.S. Department of State, April 28, 2015.

151. "Envoy's Call to Iranians in Canada Raises Fear of Terror recruitment," Fox News, July 9, 2012.

152. Ibid.

153. Christine Williams, "Shut Down Iran's Embassy in Canada," Gatestone Institute, August 9, 2012.

154. Ibid.

155. Ian Austen, "Canada Closes Tehran Embassy and Orders Iran Envoys to Leave," *New York Times*, September 7, 2012.

156. Ibid.

157. Daniel Lak, "Canada and Iran Ease into a New Friendship," Al Jazeera, January 27, 2016.

158. Guy Benson, "Hillary: Muslims 'Have Nothing Whatsoever to Do with Terrorism,'" Townhall, November 20, 2015.

159. Amir Taheri, *Holy Terror: Inside the World of Islamic Terrorism* (Adler & Adler, 1987), 241–43.

Chapter Four: "Israel Will Go, It Must Not Survive, and It Will Not": Iran's All-Consuming Hatred for Israel

1. Thomas Erdbrink, "Iranian Missiles in Gaza Fight Give Tehran Government a Lift," *New York Times*, November 21, 2012.

2. Ethan Bronner, "Just How Far Did They Go, Those Words against Israel?," *New York Times*, June 11, 2006; "Iran to Examine Holocaust Evidence," Al Jazeera, September 3, 2006.

3. Aaron Klein, "Report: Iranian Soldiers Join Hizbullah in Fighting," World Net Daily, July 24, 2006.

4. Ibid.

5. "Report: Israel Carried Out 3 Attacks on Sudan Arms Smugglers," *Haaretz*, March 28, 2009.

6. Yaakov Katz, "Navy Intercepts Ship with Iranian Arms Bound for Hamas," *Jerusalem Post*, March 15, 2011.

7. "'All Signs Point to Iran,'" Washington Free Beacon, July 18, 2012.

8. "Bulgaria Implicates Hezbollah in Fatal Bus Bombing," Associated Press, February 5, 2012.

9. Ibid.

10. Nicholas Kulish and Eric Schmitt, "Hezbollah Is Blamed in Attack on Israeli Tourists in Bulgaria," *New York Times*, July 19, 2012.

11. "Hassan Nasrallah: In His Own Words," Committee for Accuracy in Middle East Reporting in America (CAMERA), July 26, 2006.

12. William R. Long, "Islamic Jihad Says It Bombed Embassy; Toll 21," *Los Angeles Times*, March 19, 1992; "Patterns of Global Terrorism: 1992," Office of the Secretary of State, April 30, 1993.

13. Long, "Islamic Jihad Says It Bombed Embassy; Toll 21."

14. Ronen Bergman, *The Secret War with Iran: The 30-Year Clandestine Struggle Against the World's Most Dangerous Terrorist Power* (Simon and Schuster, 2008), 172.

15. Matthew Levitt, "The Origins of Hezbollah," *Atlantic*, October 23, 2013.

16. "Iran Charged over Argentina Bomb," BBC, October 25, 2006.

17. Ibid.; Pablo Gato and Robert Windrem, "Hezbollah Builds a Western Base," Telemundo and MSNBC, May 9, 2007.

18. Gareth Porter, "Argentina's Iranian Nuke Connection," Inter Press Service, November 15, 2006.

19. "Prosecutor Who Accused Argentine President Fernández of Whitewashing Iranian Involvement in AMIA Bombing Found Dead," World Jewish Congress, January 19, 2015.

20. Ibid.

21. Ibid.

22. Taylor Tyler, "Argentine President: Obama Administration Tried to Convince Us to Give Iran Nuclear Fuel," HNGN, September 30, 2015.

23. Taylor Tyler, "Argentine President: Obama Administration Tried to Convince Us to Give Iran Nuclear Fuel," HNGN, September 30, 2015.

24. Herb Keinon and Joanna Paraszczuk, "Khamenei: Zionist Regime Will Disappear from Map," *Jerusalem Post*, August 15, 2012.

25. Mehrdad Balali, "Khamenei Tells Iran Armed Forces to Build Up 'Irrespective' of Diplomacy," Reuters, November 30, 2014.

26. Simon Tomlinson, "Iran Threatens to 'Rain Down 80,000 missiles' on Israel after Jewish State's Defence Minister Is Misquoted as Saying He Intended to Hurt Lebanese Civilians and Children," MailOnline, May 22, 2015.

27. Akbar Ganji, "Ayatollah Khamenei and the Destruction of Israel," *Boston Review*, November 1, 2013

28. F. Brinley Bruton, "EXCLUSIVE: Iran President Blames Israel for 'Instability,' Calls for Peace," NBC News, September 19, 2013.

29. Ganji, "Ayatollah Khamenei and the Destruction of Israel."

30. Ibid.

31. Ibid.

32. Ibid.

33. Ibid.

34. Jeffrey Goldberg, "The Iranian Regime on Israel's Right to Exist," *Atlantic*, March 9, 2015; Joshua Teitelbaum and Michael Segall, "The Iranian Leadership's Continuing Declarations of Intent to Destroy Israel, 2009–2012," Jerusalem Center for Public Affairs, 2013.

35. Ganji, "Ayatollah Khamenei and the Destruction of Israel."

36. Ibid.

37. Herb Keinon and Joanna Paraszczuk, "Khamenei: Zionist Regime Will Disappear from Map," *Jerusalem Post*, August 15, 2012.

38. Goldberg, "The Iranian Regime."

39. Antonia Molloy, "Iran's Supreme Leader Ayatollah Khamenei Outlines Plan to 'Eliminate' Israel," *Independent*, November 10, 2014.

40. Ibid.

41. Ibid.

42. Ibid.

43. Ibid.

44. Ibid.

45. Ibid.

46. Ibid.
47. Ibid.
48. Ali Akbar Dareini, "Iran Guard Simulates Capture of Al Aqsa Mosque," Associated Press, November 21, 2015.
49. Amir Taheri, "Iran Publishes Book on How to Outwit US and Destroy Israel," *New York Post*, August 1, 2015.
50. Ibid.
51. Ibid.
52. Ibid.
53. Ibid.
54. Ibid.
55. "'Israel Should Be Annihilated,' Senior Iran Aide Says," *Times of Israel*, August 25, 2015.
56. Ibid.
57. Itamar Sharon, "Khamenei Urges Islamic Unity against Real Enemies: US and Israel," *Times of Israel*, August 22, 2015.
58. "Iran Says the Nuke Deal Will Help It Target Israel," *New York Post*, August 13, 2015.
59. Sharon, "Khamenei Urges Islamic Unity."
60. "Khamenei: Israel Won't Survive Next 25 Years," *Times of Israel*, September 9, 2015.
61. Goldberg, "The Iranian Regime"; Michael Wilner, "Zarif Says iran an Historic Haven of the Jewish People," *Jerusalem Post*, March 5, 2015.
62. Ibid.
63. Ibid.
64. Goldberg, "The Iranian Regime."
65. Ibid.
66. Ibid.
67. Ibid.
68. "Iran Says It Treats Israeli Military Threats as American," Reuters, September 5, 2012.
69. David E. Sanger, "U.S. Rejected Aid for Israeli Raid on Iranian Nuclear Site," *New York Times*, January 10, 2009.
70. Ellen Nakashima and Joby Warrick, "Stuxnet Was Work of U.S. and Israeli Experts, Officials Say," *Washington Post*, June 2, 2012.
71. James Meikle, "Iran: Timeline of Attacks," *Guardian*, January 11, 2012.
72. Ibid.
73. Ibid.
74. "'Don't Believe Iran Blast Was an Accident,'" Ynet News, November 14, 2011.

75. "Report: Blast at Isfahan Damaged Nuclear Facility," Ynet News, November 30, 2011.

76. Dudi Cohen, "Tehran Blast Kills Nuclear Scientist," Ynet News, January 11, 2012.

77. Aviel Magnezi, "Israeli Missions in India, Georgia Targeted, Associated Press, February 13, 2012.

78. Moran Azulay, "Netanyahu: Iran Responsible for Attacks on Israeli Embassies," Ynet News, February 13, 2012.

79. Indrani Bagchi, "Israel Embassy Car blast: Indian Intelligence Hints at Iran's Hand," *Times of India*, February 14, 2012.

80. Ibid.

81. "Indian Journalist Held for Attack on Israeli Envoy," BBC, March 7, 2012.

82. Julian Borger, "Who Is Responsible for the Iranian Nuclear Scientists Attacks?," *Guardian*, January 12, 2012.

83. "Obama Pushes Israel to Stop Assassinations of Iran Nuclear Scientists—Report," RT, March 2, 2014.

84. Ibid.

85. Ibid.

86. L. Todd Wood, "Hamas, ISIS Terrorists Arrested for Attempted Netanyahu Slaying Were Backed by Iran," *Washington Times*, January 9, 2016.

87. Larry Cohler-Esses, "How Iran's Jews Survive in Mullahs' World," Forward, August 18, 2015.

88. Ibid.

89. "IRGC Deputy Commander Hossein Salami: We Are Ready to Annihilate the Zionist Entity in the Future," Middle East Media Research Institute (MEMRI), March 11, 2014.

90. "Iran Pastor Guilty of Being a 'Zionist, Traitor': Official," Agence France-Presse, September 30, 2011.

91. "Iranian Official: The Jews Use Sorcery against Iran," Middle East Media Research Institute, MEMRI, April 28, 2013.

92. Ibid.

93. "Khameini [sic]: U.S. elections controlled by 'Zionists,'" Jewish Telegraph Agency, June 15, 2013.

94. Azadeh Moaveni, "Iran Cleric: Jews Use Sorcery to Spy," Daily Beast, July 5, 2014.

95. Dudi Cohen, "Iranians Arrest 14 Squirrels for Spying," Ynet News, July 14, 2007.

96. "Iran Arrests Pigeons 'Spying' on Nuclear Site," *Telegraph*, October 20, 2008.

97. "Ayatollah Moshin Qommi: Global Imperialism Masterminds Shia-Sunni Riots to Save Israel," Ahlul Bayt News Agency, September 30, 2013.

98. Catherine Shakdam, "Zionists Planning to Annihilate Islam," Press TV, January 18, 2014.

99. Ibid.

100. Adam Kredo, "Iran Blames Israel for Beirut Embassy Bombing," Washington Free Beacon, November 19, 2013.

101. "Commander: Muslim Infighting Result of Arrogant Powers' Plotting," Fars News Agency, May 18, 2014.

102. "Iranian Official: Marlboro Tainted with Pig Blood & Nuclear Matter," PressTV, July 30, 2010.

103. "'Zionists to Blame for World Drug Trade,'" Ynet News, June 27, 2012.

104. Joshua Levitt, "Khamenei Tells Winners of Quran Competition: Ignoring Holy Book Can Lead to 'Cooperation With Zionist Regime,'" *Algemeiner*, June 3, 2014.

105. Gavriel Fiske, "Trumpeting Deal, Iranians Say Agreement Stymies 'Zionist Plot,' Times of Israel, November 24, 2013.

106. "Hailing Deal, Rouhani Slams 'Usurper Zionist Regime,'" *Times of Israel*, July 14, 2015.

107. "Iran Blames Israeli Lobby for U.S. Visa Changes," Reuters, December 22, 2015.

108. Ibid.

109. Iranian President Rouhani: Israel the Only Beneficiary of Islamic Disunity," *Jerusalem Post*, December 27, 2015.

110. James Forsyth, "Theresa May: The Paris Attacks 'Have Nothing to Do with Islam,'" *Spectator*, November 16, 2015.

111. Amir Taheri, *Holy Terror: Inside the World of Islamic Terrorism* (Adler & Adler, 1987), 241–43.

Chapter Five: "I Am Cyrus, King of the World": One of the World's Great Civilizations

1. Michael Axworthy, *A History of Iran: Empire of the Mind* (Basic Books, 2008), 2.

2. Ibid., 5.

3. Ibid.,13.

4. Jeffrey Goldberg, "The Iranian Regime on Israel's Right to Exist," *Atlantic*, March 9, 2015.

5. Axworthy, *A History of Iran*, 12–16; Homa Katouzian, *The Persians: Ancient, Medieval and Modern Iran* (Yale University Press, 2009), 35.

6. Axworthy, *A History of Iran*, 19.

7. Herodotus, *The Histories*, trans. Aubrey de Selincourt, rev. ed. (Penguin Books, 1972), 57.

8. Edward Gibbon, *The History of the Decline and Fall of the Roman Empire*, chapter ten.

9. A. Shapur Shabazi, "Sasanian Dynasty," *Encyclopedia Iranica*, 2005, http://www.iranicaonline.org/articles/sasanian-dynasty.

10. Edward Gibbon, *The History of the Decline and Fall of the Roman Empire*, chapter ten.

11. Ibid.

12. Timothy D. Barnes, *Constantine and Eusebius* (Harvard University Press, 1981), 18.

13. Daniel T. Potts, "Arabia ii. The Sasanians and Arabia," *Encyclopaedia Iranica*, 2012, http://www.iranicaonline.org/articles/arabia-ii-sasanians-and-arabia.

14. Touraj Daryaee, *Sasanian Persia: The Rise and Fall of an Empire* (I.B.Tauris, 2013), 16.

15. Touraj Daryaee, "Shapur II," *Encyclopaedia Iranica*, 2009, http://www.iranicaonline.org/articles/shapur-ii.

16. A. Shapur Shabazi, "Byzantine-Iranian Relations," *Encyclopedia Iranica*, 1990, http://www.iranicaonline.org/articles/byzantine-iranian-relations.

17. Ibid.

18. Ibid.

19. A. Shapur Shabazi, "Sasanian Dynasty," *Encyclopedia Iranica*, 2005, http://www.iranicaonline.org/articles/sasanian-dynasty.

20. Ibid.

21. Muhammed Ibn Ismail Al-Bukhari, *Sahih al-Bukhari: The Translation of the Meanings*, trans. Muhammad Muhsin Khan (Darussalam, 1997), vol. 4, book 56, no. 3027, p. 3030.

22. Ibn Khaldun, *The Muqaddimah: An Introduction to History*, trans. Franz Rosenthal, ed. and abridged by N. J. Dawood (Princeton University Press, 1967), 39.

23. Ibid., 373.

24. Ibid. 429–430.

25. Roger M. Savory and Ahmet T. Karamustafa, "Esma il I Safawi," *Encyclopedia Iranica*, 1998, http://www.iranicaonline.org/articles/esmail-i-safawi#ii.

26. Ibid.

27. Ibid.

28. Andrew J. Newman, *Safavid Iran: Rebirth of a Persian Empire* (I.B.Tauris, 2012), 13.

29. Ibid.

30. Axworthy, *A History of Iran*, 133.

31. Newman, *Safavid Iran*, 13.

32. Savory and Karamustafa, "Esma il I Safawi."

33. Katouzian, *The Persians*, 136.

34. Axworthy, *A History of Iran*, 151.

35. Ibid., 155.

36. Katouzian, *The Persians*, 132.

37. Ibid., 140.

38. James Buchan, *Days of God: The Revolution In Iran and Its Consequences* (Simon & Schuster, 2012), 8.

39. Ibid., 10.

40. Nikki Keddie, *Religion and Rebellion in Iran: The Tobacco Protest of 1891–92* (Frank Cass, 1966), 38.

41. Buchan, *Days of God*, 14.

42. Ibid.

43. Ibid., 17.

44. Ibid., 18.

45. Ibid., 18–19.

46. Ibid., 24–25.

47. Ibid., 34.

48. Ehsan Yarshater, "When 'Persia' Became 'Iran,'" *Iranian Studies*, vol. XXII, No.1, 1989; Ali N. Ansari, *Modern Iran Since 1921: The Pahlavis and After* (Longman, 2003), 65–66.

49. Avideh Ghaffari, interviews with the author, January 25–26 and February 7, 2016.

50. Farajollah Parvizian, interview with the author, May 9, 2003.

51. Ansari, *Modern Iran Since 1921*, 72.

52. Ervand Abrahamian, *A History of Modern Iran* (Cambridge University Press, 2008), 111; William R. Polk, *Understanding Iran* (Palgrave Macmillan, 2009), 110.

53. Farajollah Parvizian, interview with the author, February 26, 2016.

54. Abrahamian, *A History of Modern Iran*, 111; Polk, *Understanding Iran*, 110.

55. Ibid., 175.

56. Stephen Kinzer, *All the Shah's Men: An American Coup and the Roots of Middle East Terror* (John Wiley & Sons, 2003), 2.

57. Polk, *Understanding Iran*, 175.

58. Kinzer, *All the Shah's Men*, 2.

59. Abrahamian, *A History of Modern Iran*, 117–18.

60. Ibid.

61. Polk, *Understanding Iran*, 178.

62. Abrahamian, *A History of Modern Iran*, 119.

63. Ibid., 119.

64. Polk, *Understanding Iran*, 179.

65. Ibid.,180–182; Katouzian, *The Persians*, 252–53.

66. Polk, *Understanding Iran*, 180–82; Katouzian, *The Persians*, 252–53.

67. "Abbas Ghaffari (1925–2015)," Ghaffaris.com, http://ghaffaris.com/abbas-ghaffari-1925-2015/.

68. Avideh Ghaffari, interviews with the author, January 25–26 and February 7, 2016.

69. Ibid.

70. Abrahamian, *A History of Modern Iran*, 114.

71. Ibid., 109.

72. Abrahamian, *A History of Modern Iran*, 109.

73. Parviz Mina, "Oil Agreements in Iran," *Encylopedia Iranica*, July 20, 2004, http://www.iranicaonline.org/articles/oil-agreements-in-iran.

74. Ibid.

75. Vali Nasr, *The Shia Revival* (W. W. Norton & Company, 2007), 124.

76. Polk, *Understanding Iran*, 182.

77. Ibid., 178.

78. Gholam Reza Afkhami, *The Life and Times of the Shah* (University of California Press, 2009), 194.

79. "Dr. Mohammad Mossadegh Biography," The Mossadegh Project, http://www.mohammadmossadegh.com/biography/.

80. Ibid.

81. Oriana Fallaci, *Interview with History*, trans. John Shepley (Houghton Mifflin, 1976), 273.

82. Ibid., 273.

83. Anthony Joseph, "ISIS Supporter Who Threatened to Behead a Police Officer When His Stash of 'Grotesque' Execution Videos Was Uncovered Is Jailed for Two-and-a-Half Years," MailOnline, October 30, 2015.

84. Amir Taheri, *Holy Terror: Inside the World of Islamic Terrorism* (Adler & Adler, 1987), 241–43.

Chapter Six: "Islam Says, Kill Them": The Islamic Revolution

1.   Baqer Moin, *Khomeini: Life of the Ayatollah* (St. Martin's Press, 1999), 75.

2.   Valentine M. Moghadam, *Modernizing Women: Gender and Social Change in the Middle East* (Lynne Rienner Publishers, 2003), 158–59.

3.   Jalal Al-e Ahmad, *Gharbzadegi [Weststruckness]*, trans. John Green and Ahmad Alizadeh (Mazda, 1997), 11.

4.   Ibid., 75.

5.   Ibid., 169.

6.   Ali Shariati, *Where Shall We Begin?*, part 7, http://www.shariati.com/english/begin/begin7.html.

7.   Ali Shariati, *Red Shi'ism: The Religion of Martyrdom/Black Shi'ism: The Religion of Mourning*, http://www.shariati.com/english/redblack.html.

8.   Ibid.

9.   James Buchan, *Days of God: The Revolution In Iran and Its Consequences* (Simon & Schuster, 2012), 121–22.

10.   Moin, *Khomeini*, 75.

11.   Ibid., 76.

12.   Ibid, 77–78.

13.   Ibid.

14.   Ibid., 78.

15.   Ibid., 80.

16.   Ibid., 84.

17.   Ibid., 88.

18.   Moin, *Khomeini*, 104.

19.   Taheri, *The Spirit of Allah*, 139.

20.   Ibid., , 138.

21.   Moin, *Khomeini*, 122.

22.   Ibid.

23.   Ibid., 123.

24.   Ruhollah Khomeini, "Islamic Government," in *Islam and Revolution: Writings and Declarations of Imam Khomeini*, trans. Hamid Algar (Mizan, 1981), 40.

25.   Taheri, *The Spirit of Allah*, 163.

26.   Khomeini, "Islamic Government," 54.

27.   Ibid., 55.

28.   Ibid., 80.

29.   Homa Katouzian, *The Persians: Ancient, Medieval and Modern Iran* (Yale University Press, 2009), 317.

30.   Buchan, *Days of God*, 115.

31.   Ibid., 116.

32.   Ibid., 113.

33. "The Persepolis Celebrations: Unforgettable Glitter," *From Tehran to Persepolis: All the Glitter of the Empire*, http://www.angelfire.com/empire/imperialiran/persepolis4.html.

34. Ibid.

35. Katouzian, *The Persians*, 270.

36. Oriana Fallaci, *Interview with History*, trans. John Shepley (Houghton Mifflin, 1976), 280.

37. Ibid., 281.

38. Katouzian, *The Persians*, 271.

39. Ibid.

40. Buchan, *Days of God*, 142.

41. Ibid., 142.

42. Michael D. Evans, "35 Years Ago: An Iranian Revolution Thanks to Jimmy Carter," Blaze, February 11, 2014.

43. Buchan, *Days of God*, 143.

44. Ibid., 145.

45. Moin, *Khomeini*, 184.

46. Katouzian, The Persians, 298.

47. Buchan, *Days of God*, 146.

48. Katouzian, *The Persians*, pp. 314–15.

49. Buchan, *Days of God*, 155–56.

50. Jasmin S. Kuehnert, "The Theater of Horror: From Aurora to Abadan," Academic Exchange, July 26, 2012.

51. Joseph Kraft, "Letter from Iran," *New Yorker*, December 18, 1978.

52. Buchan, *Days of God*, 170–71.

53. Oliver North, "Avoiding a Jimmy Carter Moment," Townhall, February 4, 2011; Sheda Vasseghi, "Where's Jimmy? A Past President Goes Silent on his Iran Legacy," World Tribune, August 6, 2009.

54. Vasseghi, "Where's Jimmy?"

55. Mehran Kamrava, *The Modern Middle East: A Political History Since the First World War*, 3rd ed. (University of California Press, 2013), 150.

56. Michel Foucault, "What Are the Iranians Dreaming [Rêvent] About?," *Le Nouvel Observateur*, October 16–22, 1978, in Janet Afary and David B. Anderson, *Foucault and the Iranian Revolution: Gender and the Seductions of Islamism* (University of Chicago Press, 2005).

57. Buchan, *Days of God: The Revolution In Iran and Its Consequences* (Simon & Schuster, 2012), 170–71.

58. Ibid., 187–88.

59. Ibid., 190–91.

60. Ibid., 191.

61. Evans, "35 Years Ago."

62. Katouzian, *The Persians*, 322.

63. Elaine Sciolino, *Persian Mirrors: The Elusive Face of Iran* (Free Press, 2000), 55.

64. Moin, *Khomeini*, 201.

65. Ibid., 204.

66. "Iran Marks 25th Anniversary of Islamic revolution," CBC News, February 11, 2004.

67. Shaul Bakhash, *The Reign of the Ayatollahs: Iran and the Islamic Revolution* (Basic, 1990), 73.

68. Ibid.

69. Moin, *Khomeini*, 204

70. Buchan, *Days of God*, 261.

71. Mark Bowden, *Guests of the Ayatollah: The Iran Hostage Crisis: The First Battle in America's War with Militant Islam* (Grove/Atlantic, 2006), 70.

72. Buchan, *Days of God*, 257.

73. Ibid., 265.

74. Moin, *Khomeini*, 228.

75. Buchan, *Days of God*, 266.

76. Korey Willoughby, "Temptation," *Daily Iowan*, November 28, 1979.

77. "Iran to Free women, Black Hostages," *Washington Star-News*, November 18, 1979.

78. "Iran Hostage Crisis Fast Facts," CNN, December 25, 2015.

79. "Russian Roulette Played with Hostages," Associated Press, January 21, 1981.

80. Bowden, *Guests of the Ayatollah*, 203.

81. Stuart L. Koehl and Stephen P. Glick, "Why the Rescue Failed," *American Spectator*, July 1980.

82. Sciolino, *Persian Mirrors*, 68.

83. Bakhash, *The Reign of the Ayatollahs*, 111, 221–22; Moin, *Khomeini*, 219–20.

84. Ibid., 219.

85. Taheri, *The Spirit of Allah*, 20, 45.

86. Afshin Molavi, *The Soul of Iran: A Nation's Struggle for Freedom* (W. W. Norton and Company, 2005), 156.

87. Daniel Brumberg, *Reinventing Khomeini: The Struggle for Reform in Iran* (University of Chicago Press, 2001), 133.

88. Amir Taheri, *Holy Terror: Inside the World of Islamic Terrorism* (Sphere, 1987), 225–26.

89. Ibid., 226–27.

90. Robin Wright, *The Last Great Revolution: Turmoil and Transformation in Iran* (Knopf Doubleday, 2010), 29.

91. Taheri, *The Spirit of Allah*, 263–64.

92. Oriana Fallaci, "An Interview with Khomeini," *New York Times*, October 7, 1979.

93. Ibid.

94. Margaret Talbot, "The Agitator: Oriana Fallaci Directs Her Fury toward Islam," *New Yorker*, June 5, 2006.

95. Ibid.

96. Ibid.

97. Gordon Thomas, "William Buckley: The Spy Who Never Came in from the Cold," Canada Free Press, October 25, 2006.

98. "Excerpts From the Tower Commission's Report," http://www.presidency. ucsb.edu/PS157/assignment%20files%20public/TOWER%20EXCERPTS.htm.

99. Ronald Reagan, "Address to the Nation on the Iran Arms and Contra Aid Controversy," Reagan Library, November 13, 1986, https://www.reagan.utexas. edu/archives/speeches/1986/111386c.htm.

100. Ronald Reagan, "Address to the Nation on the Iran Arms and Contra Aid Controversy," Reagan Library, March 4, 1987, https://www.reaganlibrary. archives.gov/archives/speeches/1987/030487h.htm.

101. Paula Dwyer, "Pointing A Finger at Reagan," *Business Week*, June 23, 1997.

102. Jeremiah Goulka, Lydia Hansell, Elizabeth Wilke, and Judith Larson, "The Mujahedin-e Khalq in Iraq: A Policy Conundrum," National Defense Research Institute, Rand Corporation, 2009, 37.

103. Douglas Jehl, "U.S. Bombs Iranian Guerrilla Forces Based in Iraq," *New York Times*, April 17, 2003.

104. Stephen E. Atkins, *Encyclopedia of Modern Worldwide Extremists and Extremist Groups* (Greenwood Publishing Group, 2004), 212.

105. Adam Zagorin and Scott Macleod, "So Who's Talking To Iran?," *Time*, October 27, 2003.

106. Michael Ledeen, "Obama's Latest Big Lie: 'We Have No Strategy,'" PJ Media, August 29, 2014.

107. Ibid.

108. Aubrey Whelan, Mari A. Schaefer, Jeremy Roebuck, and Stephanie Farr, "Police: Gunman who shot cop pledged allegiance to the Islamic State," Philly. com, January 8, 2016.

109. "Mayor Kenney On Officer Shooting: 'It Has Nothing to Do with Being Muslim,'" CBS, January 8, 2016.

110. Amir Taheri, *Holy Terror: Inside the World of Islamic Terrorism* (Adler & Adler, 1987), 241–43.

Chapter Seven: "The Middle East Is Going to Have to Overcome That": Shi'ite Islam and the Sunni-Shi'ite Jihad

1. Ibn Ishaq, *The Life of Muhammad: A Translation of Ibn Ishaq's Sirat Rasul Allah*, trans. A. Guillaume (Oxford University Press, 1955), 159–61.
2. Allamah Sayyid Muhammad Husayn Tabatabai, *Shi'ite Islam*, trans. Seyyed Hossein Nasr, 2nd ed. (State University of New York Press, 1977), 41.
3. Muhammed Ibn Ismail Al-Bukhari, *Sahih al-Bukhari: The Translation of the Meanings*, trans. Muhammad Muhsin Khan, vol. 5, book 64, no. 4416 (Darussalam, 1997).
4. Al-Hakim, *al-Mustadrak*, vol. 3, 128; "Imam 'Ali ibn Abi Talib," Shiavault, http://www.shiavault.com/books/inquiries-about-shi-a-islam/chapters/8-imam-ali-ibn-abi-talib.
5. Al-Hakim, 221; "Imam 'Ali ibn Abi Talib."
6. *Jami al-Tirmidhi*, vol. 1, book 46, no. 3713, Sunnah.com, http://sunnah.com/urn/635920.
7. "The Status of the Hadeeth, 'If I Am Someone's Mawla Then Ali Is His Mawla Too' and Its Meaning," Islam Question and Answer, https://islamqa.info/en/26794.
8. Ibid.
9. Ibid.
10. Ahmad ibn Hanbal, "Refutation of the Article 'How to Approach the Shia Brothers," Musnad, 4:281, "ShiaPen, http://www.shiapen.com/comprehensive/refutation-of-how-to-approach-the-shia-brothers.html.
11. Al-Bukhari, *Sahih al-Bukhari*, vol. 4, book 55, no. 2741.
12. Ibid., vol. 5, book 64, no. 4141.
13. *Jami al-Tirmidhi*, vol. 1, book 46, no. 3673.
14. *The History of al-Tabari*, Volume XVI: The Community Divided, trans. Adrian Brockett (State University of New York Press, 1997), 52–166, *passim*.
15. Muhammad ibn Jarar Al-Tabari, *The History of al-Tabari*. Vol. xvii, "The First Civil War," trans. G. R. Hawting (State University of New York Press, 1996), 29.
16. Ibid., 34.
17. Ibid., 78.
18. Ibid., 79.
19. Ibid.

20. Ibid.

21. Ibid., 82.

22. Ibid., 101.

23. Ibid.

24. Al-Bukhari, *Sahih al-Bukhari*, vol. 9, book 93, no. 7142.

25. Tabatabai, *Shi'ite Islam*, 144.

26. Ibid., 178.

27. Ibid., 179.

28. Ibid., 185.

29. Yann Richard, *Shi'ite Islam: Polity, Ideology and Creed*, trans. Antonia Nevill (Blackwell, 1995), 17.

30. Ibid., 17.

31. Ibid., 19.

32. Ibid., 21.

33. Ibid.

34. "Sunni vs. Shia," Discovering Islam, http://www.discoveringislam.org/sunnis_vs_shia.htm.

35. Etan Kohlberg, "Taqiyya in Shi'i Theology and Religion," in Hans Gerhard Kippenberg and Guy G. Stroumsa, eds., *Secrecy and Concealment: Studies in the History of Mediterranean and Near Eastern Religions* (Brill, 1995), 345.

36. Ibid., 351.

37. Ibid., 370.

38. Ibid., 355–56.

39. Ibid., 373.

40. Ibid., 357–58.

41. Ibid., 363.

42. Muslim ibn al-Hajjaj, *Sahih Muslim*, trans. Abdul Hamid Siddiqi, rev ed. (Kitab Bhavan, 2000), no. 4480.

43. "The Fourth Special Deputy: Ali Ibn Muhammad Samari (r.a.)," al-Islam.org, http://www.al-islam.org/special-deputies-association-imam-al-mahdi/fourth-special-deputy-ali-ibn-muhammad-samari-ra.

44. Ibid.

45. Kohlberg, "Taqiyya in Shi'i Theology," 348.

46. Ibid.

47. Tabatabai, *Shi'ite Islam*, 193.

48. Ibid., 193–94.

49. Ibid., 195.

50. Ibid., 201–2.

51. Ibid., 202–3.

52. Ibid., 204.

53. Ibid., 205

54. Ibid., 20–7.

55. Ibid., 207.

56. Ibid., 208–9.

57. Ibid., 209–10.

58. Allamah Muhammad Baqir al-Majlisi, *Bihar al-Anwar*, 26.6, https://archive.org/stream/BiharAlAnwarVol515253ThePromisedMahdiEnglishTranslation-Part2/Bihar-Al-Anwar-Vol-51-52-53-the-Promised-Mahdi-English-Translation-Part-2_djvu.txt

59. Ibid.

60. Ibid.

61. Ibid.

62. Ibid.

63. Ibid.

64. Ibid.

65. Islam. Nahjul Balagha, Khutba 141, 187, "Muslim Prophecies and the Appearance of Imam Mahdi," Iawwai.com, http://www.iawwai.com/MuslimProphecies.html.

66. "Muslim Prophecies and the Appearance of Imam Mahdi," Iawwai.com, http://www.iawwai.com/MuslimProphecies.html.

67. "Rafsanjani Says Muslims Should Use Nuclear Weapon Against Israel," Iran Press Service, December 14, 2001.

68. Vali Nasr, *The Shia Revival: How Conflicts Within Islam Will Shape the Future* (W.W. Norton, 2007), 220.

69. Reza Kahlili, "Iran Supreme Leader: The Islamic Messiah Is Coming Soon to Kill All Infidels," Daily Caller, June 15, 2014.

70. Ibid.

71. Ibid.

72. Mazyar Mokfi and Charles Recknagel, "Could Ahmadinejad's Mix of Mysticism and Politics Lead To A Power Grab?," Radio Free Europe/Radio Liberty, August 5, 2009.

73. Kahlili, "Iran Supreme Leader."

74. "Rafsanjani Says Muslims Should Use Nuclear Weapon."

75. Golnaz Esfandiari, "Iranian Ex-President Says U.S. Seeks Arrest of Hidden Imam," Radio Free Europe/Radio Liberty, June 22, 2015.

76. Ibid.

77. Ibid.

78. Ibid.

79. Thom Shanker, "Perhaps Thinking of Legacy, Bush Has Rice on the Move," *New York Times*, January 19, 2007.

80. Donna Abu-Nasr, "Saudi Government Cracks Down on Shiite dissidents," Associated Press, April 1, 2009.

81. "Saudi Shiite Cleric Nimr Al-Nimr Rejoices in the Death of Saudi Crown Prince Nayef: 'He Will Be Eaten by Worms and Suffer the Torments of Hell in His Grave,'" Middle East Media Research Institute (MEMRI), June 27, 2012.

82. Ben Hubbard, "Iranian Protesters Ransack Saudi Embassy After Execution of Shiite Cleric," *New York Times*, January 2, 2016.

83. "Saudi Arabia Severs Ties with Iran: Official," Reuters, January 3, 2016.

84. "Iran says Saudi Arabia Will 'Pay a High Price' for Execution of Shiite Cleric Nimr al-Nimr," ABC.net.au, January 2, 2016.

85. Ibid.

86. Ibid.

87. "Hizbullah Secretary-General Nasrallah in Response to Al-Nimr Execution: This Will Spell the End of the Saud Regime and Clan," Middle East Media Research Institute (MEMRI), January 3, 2016.

88. "Saudi Arabia Severs Ties."

89. See chapter eight.

90. "Rita Says No to Million," Sydney Morning Herald, September 13, 1953.

91. Pope Francis, Apostolic Exhortation *Evangelii Gaudium*, November 24, 2013, 253.

92. Amir Taheri, *Holy Terror: Inside the World of Islamic Terrorism* (Adler & Adler, 1987), 241–43.

Chapter Eight: "In Iran, Nothing Is What It Seems": Life inside the Islamic Republic

1. "Journalist Offers Inside Look at Modern Life in Iran," PBS NewsHour, March 24, 2015.

2. Ibid.

3. Simon Worrall, "'To Live in Tehran You Have to Lie': Revealing Hidden Lives in Iran," *National Geographic*, September 7, 2014.

4. Ira Silverman, "An American Terrorist," *New Yorker*, August 5, 2002.

5. Robert Mackey, "Just Another American Hit Man, Actor and Journalist Living in Iran," *New York Times*, September 16, 2009.

6. Hugh Tomlinson, "Ashtiani Freed after 9 Years on death row," The Times, March 19, 2014.

7.   Benjamin Weinthal, "Iran Sentences Woman to Death by Stoning," *Jerusalem Post*, December 10, 2015.

8.   Weinthal, "Iran Sentences Woman."

9.   "Iran Confirms Stoning Sentence against Adulteress: Report," Agence France-Presse, November 29, 2008.

10. Weinthal, "Iran Sentences Woman."

11. "Iran Regime Sentences Man to Have Eyes Gouged Out," National Council of Resistance of Iran (NCRI), August 5, 2015.

12. Ibid.

13. Ibid.

14. Ibid.

15. Bernard Lewis, trans., *Music of a Distant Drum: Classical Arabic, Persian, Turkish, and Hebrew Poems* (Princeton University Press, 2001), 105.

16. Parisa Hafezi, "Getting Drunk in a Muslim Country: Iran's Secret Party Scene Revealed," *Independent*, March 26, 2014.

17. Adam Taylor, "Iran Is Opening 150 Alcoholism Treatment Centers, Even Though Alcohol Is Banned," *Washington Post*, June 9, 2015.

18. Worrall, "'To Live in Tehran You Have to Lie.'"

19. Neil MacFarquhar, "Iran Cracks Down on Dissent," *New York Times*, June 24, 2007.

20. "Iran Bans Western Haircuts, Eyebrow Plucking for Men," Reuters, April 29, 2007.

21. Ibid.

22. Robert Tait, "Western-Style Barbers Get the Chop in Iran," *Guardian*, August 24, 2007.

23. "Iran Police Shut Clothes Shops, Hairdressers," Associated Press, June 16, 2008.

24. Dudi Cohen, "Iran Presents 'Islamic Haircut Catalogue,'" YNet News, July 5, 2010.

25. Ibid.

26. Dudi Cohen, "Iran's New Enemy: Imported Ties," YNet News, May 22, 2008.

27. Ibid.

28. "Not So 'Happy': Iranians Arrested over YouTube Hit," Agence France-Presse, May 21, 2014.

29. Ibid.

30. "Flowers and Beatings for Women Attending Book Fair + Photo," Mohabat News, May 23, 2012.

31. "The Civil Code of the Islamic Republic of Iran," Article 1041, www.alavian-dassociates.com/documents/civilcode.pdf.

32. Ibid., Article 1210 and Article 1041.

33. Amir Taheri, *The Spirit of Allah: Khomeini and the Islamic Revolution* (Hutchinson, 1985), 90–91.

34. Ibid., 34.

35. UN Voices Alarm at Growing Number of Child Marriages in Iran," Agence France-Presse, February 5, 2016.

36. Ibid.

37. Ibid.

38. Farshid Motahari, "Iran Rejects Obligation to Register Temporary Marriages," Deutsche Presse-Agentur, March 6, 2012.

39. Ali Akbar Dareini, "Iranian Official Backs Temporary Marriage," Associated Press, June 3, 2007.

40. Najafi Quchani, *Siyahat-e Sharq*, Tehran, 1984, 399–401, in Baqer Moin, *Khomeini: Life of the Ayatollah* (St. Martin's, 1999), 30.

41. Afshin Valinejad, "The Rules of Love, As Told by an Iranian Cleric," *Christian Science Monitor*, June 29, 2012.

42. Ibid.

43. Farshid Motahari, "Iran Rejects Obligation to Register Temporary Marriages," Deutsche Presse-Agentur, March 6, 2012.

44. Laurence D. Loeb, *Outcaste: Jewish Life in Southern Iran* (Gordon and Breach, 1977), 16.

45. Ibid., 21.

46. Ibid.

47. Farajollah Parvizian, interview with the author, May 9, 2003.

48. Larry Cohler-Esses, "How Iran's Jews Survive in Mullahs' World," *Forward*, August 18, 2015.

49. Jason Rezaian, "Iran's Jewish Community Reflects a Complicated Relationship with Israel," *Washington Post*, October 2, 2013.

50. Ibid.

51. Cohler-Esses, "How Iran's Jews Survive."

52. Steve Inskeep, "Iran's Jews: It's Our Home and We Plan to Stay," NPR, February 19, 2015.

53. Cohler-Esses, "How Iran's Jews Survive."

54. Inskeep, "Iran's Jews."

55. Cohler-Esses, "How Iran's Jews Survive."

56. Ibid.

57. Inskeep, "Iran's Jews."

58. "US Neocons Sabotage Initiatives not in Israel's Favor: Journalist," PressTV, January 18, 2016.

59. Benjamin Weinthal, "Are Iran's Broken Human Rights Promises a Sign of Failure for Nuclear Deal?," *Jerusalem Post*, March 15, 2015.

60. Ibid.

61. "Minority Report: Why Baha'is Face Persecution in Iran," Reuters, November 11, 2013.

62. Ibid.

63. "Situation of Human Rights in the Islamic Republic of Iran," United Nations General Assembly, October 6, 2015.

64. "Minority Report."

65. Jamsheed K. Choksy, "How Iran Persecutes Its Oldest Religion," CNN, November 14, 2011.

66. Ibid.

67. Robert Tait, "Ancient Religions Clash in Modern Iran," *Guardian*, October 4, 2006.

68. Ibid.

69. Fereydoun Rasti, "Muslim Youth Leaving Islam for Zoroastrianism in Iran," YouTube, April 20, 2014.

70. "Iran: Convert Stabbed to Death," Compass Direct, November 28, 2005.

71. Ibid.

72. Weinthal, "Are Iran's Broken Human Rights Promises a Sign?"

73. Stoyan Zaimov, "Iran Sentences 18 Christians to Prison for Their Faith in New Crackdown on Christianity," *Christian Post*, June 3, 2015.

74. Weinthal, "Are Iran's Broken Human Rights Promises a Sign?" *Jerusalem Post*, March 15, 2015.

75. Hermoine Macura, "Iran's President Rouhani Is Under Fire for Cracking Down on Christian Churches," *Christian Post*, August 11, 2015.

76. Ibid.

77. Stoyan Zaimov, "Pastor Saeed Abedini 'Viciously Beaten' in Iranian Prison, Told His Only Way Out Is to Deny Jesus Christ," *Christian Post*, June 11, 2015.

78. Adam Kredo, "Obama Pardons 21 Iranians Convicted of Violating Sanctions," Washington Free Beacon, January 18, 2016.

79. "Iranian Pastor Sentenced to Death: Nadarkhani Refuses to Convert," International Business Times, September 29, 2011.

80. "IRAN: Christians Barred from Holding Easter Celebration in Churches in Northwestern city," National Council of Resistance of Iran (NCRI), April 7, 2015.

81. Stoyan Zaimov, "Iran Sentences 18 Christians to Prison for Their Faith in New Crackdown on Christianity," *Christian Post*, June 3, 2015.

82. "Iran Threatens to Kill Evangelical Christians Unless They 'Repent', Christians Say," BosNewsLife, October 2, 2011.

83. Sultanhussein Tabandeh, *A Muslim Commentary on the Universal Declaration of Human Rights*, trans. F. J. Goulding (London: F. T. Goulding and Co., 1970), 18.

84. Ibid.

85. Adam Kredo, "Iran Executed 1,084 People in 2015," Washington Free Beacon, January 12, 2016.

86. Elaine Sciolino, *Persian Mirrors: The Elusive Face of Iran* (Free Press, 2000), 78, 86.

87. Saeed Kamali Dehghan, "Iranian Media Banned from Mentioning Former President Mohammad Khatami," *Guardian*, February 17, 2015.

88. Ibid.

89. Susannah Cullinane, "Blair: 'Perversion of Islam' behind Middle East Problems," CNN, October 6, 2015.

90. Amir Taheri, *Holy Terror: Inside the World of Islamic Terrorism* (Adler & Adler, 1987), 241–43.

Chapter Nine: "I Will Not Submit to This Dangerous Charade": Iran's Green Revolution

1. "Basij Killed Neda in Tehran," CNN iReport, June 20, 2009.

2. Ali Jahanii, "Neda Agha Soltan, Killed 20.06.2009, Presidential Election Protest, Tehran, IRAN," YouTube, June 22, 2009.

3. "Neda Soltan, Young Woman Hailed as Martyr in Iran, Becomes Face of Protests," Fox News, June 22, 2009.

4. Joan Baez, "We Shall Overcome (2009), YouTube, June 25, 2009; Andrew Himes, "Joan Baez Sings 'We Shall Overcome' to the people of Iran," The Sword of the Lord, n.d..

5. Ryan Mauro, "Bon Jovi Isn't Giving Up on Iran's Green Revolution—and Neither Should You," Angelofiran's blog, n.d.; "Sunday, Bloody, Sunday: U2 Goes Green for Iran," SashaHalima.com, July 2009.

6. Roger Cohen, "The Making of an Iran Policy," *New York Times*, July 30, 2009.

7. Mauro, "Bon Jovi Isn't Giving Up."

8. Robert Fisk, "Battle for the Islamic Republic," *Independent*, June 21, 2009.

9. Laura Secor, "Laura Secor: The Iranian Vote," *New Yorker*, June 13, 2009.

10. Ibid.

11. Ibid.

12. "Iran's Controversial Election Results Raises Questions Over Its Relations to U.S.," Fox News, June 13, 2009.

13. "Ahmadinejad Hails Election as Protests Grow," CNN, June 13, 2009.

14. Borzou Daragahi, "Riots Erupt in Tehran as Iranian President Ahmadinejad Declares Victory," *Los Angeles Times*, June 13, 2009.

15. Secor, "Laura Secor: Tehran Updates," *New Yorker*, June 15, 2009.

16. Secor, "The Iranian Vote," *New Yorker*, June 13, 2009.

17. Michael Axworthy, *Revolutionary Iran: A History of the Islamic Republic* (Oxford University Press, 2013), 403.

18. Secor, "The Iranian Vote," *New Yorker*, June 13, 2009.

19. Daragahi, "Riots Erupt in Tehran."

20. Ian Black, Saeed Kamali Dehghan, and Haroon Siddique, "Iran Elections: Mousavi Lodges Appeal against Ahmadinejad Victory," *Guardian*, June 14, 2009.

21. Colin Freeman, "Iran Elections: Revolt As Crowds Protest at Mahmoud Ahmadinejad's 'Rigged' Victory," *Telegraph*, June 13, 2009; "Neda Soltan, Young Woman Hailed as Martyr."

22. Daragahi, "Riots Erupt in Tehran."

23. Robert F. Worth and Nazila Fathi, "Protests Flare in Tehran as Opposition Disputes Vote," *New York Times*, June 13, 2009.

24. "Former IRGC head Mohsen Rezai Running for Iranian Presidency," Payvand Iran News, March 5, 2013.

25. "Violence Grips Tehran Amid Crackdown," *New York Times*, June 20, 2009.

26. Daragahi, "Riots Erupt in Tehran."

27. Black, Dehghan, and Siddique, "Iran Elections."

28. Colin Freeman and David Blair, "Defeated Iranian reformist Mir-Hossein Mousavi calls for more protest against Mahmoud Ahmadinejad," *Telegraph*, June 14, 2009.

29. Black, Dehghan, and Siddique, "Iran Elections."

30. "Violence Grips Tehran."

31. Daragahi, "Riots Erupt in Tehran."

32. Angela Moscaritolo, "Iran Election Protesters Use Twitter to Recruit Hackers," *SC Magazine*, June 15, 2009.

33. "Drawing the Line: Iran's Supreme Leader Stands Staunchly by Mahmoud Ahmadinejad," Agence France-Presse, June 19, 2009.

34. Ibid.

35. "Former IRGC Head Mohsen Rezai."

36. "Violence Grips Tehran."

37. Black, Dehghan, and Siddique, "Iran Elections."

38. Thomas Erdbrink, "Ahmadinejad Reelected in Iran as Demonstrators Protest Result," *Washington Post*, June 14, 2009.

39. Worth and Fathi, "Protests Flare."

40. "Iranian Leader: Fiery Clashes over Election 'Not Important,'" Associated Press, June 14, 2009.

41. "Ahmadinejad Hails Election."

42. Erdbrink, "Ahmadinejad Reelected."

43. Black, Dehghan, and Siddique, "Iran Elections."

44. Erdbrink, "Ahmadinejad Reelected."

45. "Iran's Election Authority: Partial Recount Shows Election Valid," CNN, June 29, 2009.

46. Black, Dehghan, and Siddique, "Iran Elections."

47. Daragahi, "Riots Erupt in Tehran."

48. "Violence Grips Tehran Amid Crackdown," *New York Times*, June 20, 2009.

49. Ali Akbar Dareini and Jim Heintz "Iran Revolutionary Guard threatens protesters," Associated Press, June 22, 2009.

50. "Violence Grips Tehran."

51. Ali Akbar Dareini and Nasser Karimi, "Witnesses Report Fierce Clashes on Tehran Streets," Associated Press, June 20, 2009.

52. Nazila Fathi and Michael Slackman, "Iran Stepping Up Effort to Quell Election Protest," *New York Times*, June 24, 2009.

53. Ibid.

54. Erdbrink, "Ahmadinejad Reelected."

55. Sabina Amidi, "Obama: Ahmadinejad and Mousavi Not Very Different," *Jerusalem Post*, June 15, 2009.

56. Ibid.

57. "Iran: 'Arab Militias' Attack Pro-Mousavi Protesters," AdnKronos International, June 19, 2009.

58. "Iran Admits 4,000 June Detentions," BBC, August 11, 2009.

59. "Iran Opposition Says 72 Killed in Vote Protests," Agence France-Presse, September 3, 2009; "Iran Official Says 36 Killed in Post-Vote Unrest," Agence France-Presse, September 10, 2009.

60. Jay Solomon, "Nuclear Deal Fuels Iran's Hard-Liners," *Wall Street Journal*, January 8, 2016.

61. Sabina Amidi, "'I Wed Iranian Girls before Execution,'" *Jerusalem Post*, July 19, 2009.

62. Ibid.

63. Ibid.

64. "Iran Cleric: Harsh Punishment for Protest Organizers," Associated Press, June 26, 2009.

65. Ibid.

66. Ibid.

67. Ibid.

68. Michael Slackman, "Iran Council Certifies Ahmadinejad Victory," *New York Times*, June 29, 2009.

69. "Iran Cleric: Harsh Punishment."

70. Black, Dehghan, and Siddique, "Iran Elections."

71. Erdbrink, "Ahmadinejad Reelected."

72. Black, Dehghan, and Siddique, "Iran Elections."

73. Ibid.

74. Erdbrink, "Ahmadinejad Reelected."

75. Thomas Erdbrink, "Iran Leader's Top Aide Warns U.S. on Meddling," *Washington Post*, June 19, 2009.

76. Ibid.

77. Ibid.

78. David Blair, "Iran Election: Barack Obama Refuses to 'Meddle' over Protests," *Telegraph*, June 17, 2009.

79. "Statement from the President on Iran," WhiteHouse.gov, June 20, 2009.

80. Parisa Hafezi and Fredrik Dahl, "Ahmadinejad Compares Obama to Bush," Reuters, June 25, 2009.

81. "Interview With Hillary Clinton," Fareed Zakaria, CNN, August 9, 2009.

82. Hillary Rodham Clinton, Interview with Bahman Kalbasi of BBC Persia, October 26, 2011, http://www.state.gov/secretary/20092013clinton/rm/2011/10/176237.htm.

83. Brad Hoff, "Rise of Islamic State Was 'a Willful Decision': Former DIA Chief Michal [sic] Flynn," *Foreign Policy Journal*, August 7, 2015.

84. Clinton, Interview With Bahman Kalbasi.

85. Charles Krauthammer, "2009: The Year of Living Fecklessly, *Washington Post*, December 25, 2009.

86. "Interview with Hillary Clinton," Fareed Zakaria GPS, CNN, August 9, 2009.

87. Debra Heine, "Hillary Clinton: U.S. Was 'Too Restrained in Our Support' of the 2009 Iranian Green Revolution," PJ Media, September 9, 2015.

88. Jay Solomon, "Nuclear Deal Fuels Iran's Hard-Liners," *Wall Street Journal*, January 8, 2016.

89. Ibid.

90. Ibid.

91. Ibid.

92. Barbara Slavin, "EXCLUSIVE: U.S. Contacted Iran's Ayatollah before Election," *Washington Times*, June 24, 2009.

93. Solomon, "Nuclear Deal."

94. Ibid.

95. Freeman, "Iran Elections."

96. "Iran's Presidential Candidates," BBC, June 12, 2009.

97. Patrick Goodenough, "Iranians' Support for Nuclear Program Cuts across Political Lines, CNS News, February 23, 2010.

98. "Iran Candidate Mousavi Backs Women's Rights," BBC, May 30, 2009.

99. Ibid.

100. Ibid.

101. Black, Dehghan, and Siddique, "Iran Elections."

102. Secor, "The Iranian Vote," *New Yorker*, June 13, 2009.

103. Mohsen Makhmalbaf, "I Speak for Mousavi. And Iran," *Guardian*, June 19, 2009.

104. Blair, "Iran Election."

105. Dareini and Heintz, "Iran Revolutionary Guard Threatens Protesters."

106. Andrew Bostom, "Message to Michael* Ledeen on Mousavi, Montazeri, and the Soylent Green Movement," AndrewBostom.org, January 5, 2015.

107. Ibid.

108. Ibid.

109. Ibid.

110. "'God Is Great' Echoes throughout Tehran," Associated Press, June 19, 2009; "Protesters shout Allah o Akbar & Death to Dictator (1 July)—Iranian Riots & Protests," Videos from the Iranian Riots, July 2, 2009.

111. "Drawing the Line: Iran's Supreme Leader Stands Staunchly by Mahmoud Ahmadinejad," Agence France-Presse, June 19, 2009.

112. "Demanding to Be Counted: An Apparently Rigged Election Is Shaking the Fragile Pillars on Which the Iranian Republic Rests," *Economist*, June 18, 2009.

113. "The Seven-Point Manifesto of the Iranian Resistance," PJ Media, June 16, 2009.

114. Freeman, "Iran Elections."

115. Ibid.

116. Jon Lee Anderson, "After the Crackdown," *New Yorker*, August 16, 2010.

117. Ibid.

118. Ibid.

119. Ibid.

120. Charlie Spiering, "Obama: Islamic State 'Perverted One of the World's Great Religions,'" Breitbart, March 23, 2016.

121. Amir Taheri, *Holy Terror: Inside the World of Islamic Terrorism* (Adler & Adler, 1987), 241–43.

INDEX